Agriculture in India

Agriculture in India

Crisis and Prospects

Edited by

Manu Gautam

RAWAT PUBLICATIONS

Jaipur • New Delhi • Bangalore • Guwahati • Kolkata

ISBN 978-81-316-1225-5

Published by
Prem Rawat for **Rawat Publications**
Satyam Apts, Sector 3, Jawahar Nagar, Jaipur 302 004 (India)
Phones: 0141 265 1748 / 265 7006
E-mail: info@rawatbooks.com
Website: www.rawatbooks.com

New Delhi Office
4858/24, Ansari Road, Daryaganj, New Delhi 110 002
Phone: 011-23263290

Also at *Bangalore, Guwahati* and *Kolkata*

Typeset by Rawat Computers, Jaipur
Printed and bound in India

Contents

Preface

Agriculture is the backbone of Indian economy. It has a wide ranging impact on many sectors of our economy. During 1960's the share of agriculture in Indian GDP was more than 60 per cent and then slowly it started declining and reached 15.4 per cent in 2018. Though, in the last two years it has again bounced back and in the financial year 2020–21 it touched 19.9 per cent. Apart from its sizeable share in GDP, two-third of Indian workforce is engaged in agriculture; thus depending on it for their livelihood. Other sectors of India failed to generate employment similar to that of agriculture. Nearly 60 per cent of the household consumption of food is met through products from agriculture. It also caters to the development of many industries in our country like agro-based cottage industries which receive raw materials from this sector. To add some more, cotton and jute textiles, sugar manufacturing, plantation industries (rubber, coffee, tea, etc.), edible oils etc. also depend to agriculture sector. The value of agriculture in India extends from its commercial significance in terms of exports of agricultural products to earning significant revenue from agriculture and thus proves that it still acts as a backbone of our economy.

Despite all these crucial aspects of our agriculture, it is still one of the most neglected sectors of India which is marred by lack of funds and infrastructure, improper delivery mechanism, environmental factors, less production per hectare as compared to other developed countries, declining income of farmers and labours, inclination towards water guzzling crops creating major water shortage and many other factors. All these conditions have forced many peasants to leave agriculture as their ancestral occupation and shift to other opportunities; though with lesser satisfaction and success. Another important development brewing in Indian agriculture is corporate inclusion. Backed with resources and investment, these gigantic business houses have made a hardcore entry encompassing all segments of agriculture. It goes without saying that such bold and bigger moves have the capacity to destabilise the fine threads of peasant's culture. The question of sustainability, thus, in terms of Indian agriculture has become more significant now than ever before.

The Government of India is trying to revive profit margins in agriculture by launching various schemes and packages for peasants and labours. The Department of Agriculture, Cooperation and Farmers' Welfare has been allocated ₹ 1,34,400 crore in 2020–21, a 32 per cent increase over the revised estimate of 2019–20. In 2020–21, Agricultural Research and Education has been allocated ₹ 8,363 crore, a 7 per cent increase over the revised estimate of 2019–20. During the dry spells of summer when agriculture activity takes a halt; through MGNREGA, government is providing employment at village level to curb out-migration. Seeing the impact of erratic monsoon and dwindling irrigation, government has emphasized to create water conservation structures through MGNREGA. Such steps will be crucial to enhance the agriculture activity by restoring groundwater and thereby increasing irrigation as a whole.

The various complexities mingled with huge potential in Indian agriculture always fascinate researchers and academicians to work deeply and explore solutions that lasts a mile. The present book 'Agriculture in India' deals with several nuances concerned with agriculture as discussed above. It is a compilation of articles presented in two national seminars held at Madhya Pradesh Institute of Social Science Research, Ujjain (an ICSSR Institute) on topics of agriculture. This edited volume includes the papers majorly on thematic areas, viz.: (i) food security and governmental initiatives; (ii) irrigation in dry land areas, watershed management; (iii) change in occupational structure from agriculture to other means of livelihood; (iv) issues related with overall agricultural growth, impact of welfare schemes on employment and livelihood; (v) issues related with marginalized and their dependence on agriculture; (vi) rural poverty, sustainable livelihood and employment opportunities; (vii) migration, employment and its social impact; (viii) changing livelihood, dependence on agriculture and agricultural labour in villages; (ix) welfare schemes to address rural poverty and migration; (x) changing rural–urban migration continuum and future of agriculture sector; and (xi) suggestive framework/mechanism to address rural poverty, migration and agriculture. This volume is an attempt to identify, document and comprehend various policy perspective on agriculture development, irrigation, migration, rainfed areas, livelihood agriculture, rural poverty, and implementation of government policies related with these aspects. The chapters of this volume have deliberated upon the implementation of these schemes on the ground and also made suggestions to make mid-course policy corrections for better outcomes for the overall agriculture development of the country.

In this academic endeavour, I have received unconditional support from our mentors and friends. I would like to express my sincere thanks to Professor Nalini Rewadikar, President and Professor Yatindra Singh Sisodia, Director, MPISSR, for inspiring me to edit this seminar volume. I owe a lot to Professor Y.G. Joshi, Professor Sandeep Joshi, Dr Ashish Bhatt, Dr Sunil Singh Chandel and Dr Tapas Dalapati for their valuable suggestions and inputs during the course of editing of this assignment. I also wish to extend my thanks to Indian Council of

Social Science Research, Ministry of Education, Government of India for sponsoring both the national seminars on which the proceedings of this edited volume is based. I also express my special thanks to all the paper contributors, without their cooperation this volume would have not seen the light of the day. Finally, I would like to express my sincere thanks to Mr Pranit Rawat of Rawat Publications, Jaipur, for showing interest in the manuscript and for bringing out the volume for the academic fraternity.

Manu Gautam

Introduction

The importance of agriculture in India is enmeshed with the culture and lifestyle of peasants, village economy and livelihood of millions of rural workforce. Indian agriculture has seen many ups and downs since Independence in terms of agricultural productivity, irrigation facility, mechanization of agricultural process, shifting from food crops to cash crops and from livelihood agriculture to sustainable agriculture. The productivity in agriculture was also affected by monsoon vagaries. It is feared that due to increasing temperature and change in climatic conditions, the severity of rural poverty will increase which will not only impede economic growth of India but will also jeopardize efforts to achieve the UN's SDGs to eradicate extreme poverty and halve the number of global poor by 2030.[1] Rainfall has decreased in Punjab over the past 30 years by 7 per cent annually. It has substantially affected the yield of rice and wheat. It is estimated that by 2080 the rice yield will be lower by more than eight per cent.[2] The dependence on monsoon is still continuing but prior to 1990's it was much stable. The fluctuation in monsoon rains, post-1990's and also currently, has disrupted the normal agriculture season in terms of timely and adequate irrigation. The aspect of lower productivity in comparison to other economies raises mute questions to be answered. The fall in per capita income of farmers over decades have stripped the future of Indian agriculture. Apart from this, by 2050; as per the estimates of United Nations, over 10 billion people will require food for their sustenance.[3] On the contrary, the land for agriculture is decreasing due to rapid urbanization and other factors. So, how prudent it will be for the governments to decide regarding the optimization of agriculture situation.

Another economic crisis which the agriculture sector is facing is its continuous fall in terms of its percentage in GDP. In 1950–51, 45 per cent of India's GDP was contributed by agriculture, when 70 per cent of its total workforce was employed in this sector. Compared to this, during 2020–21, the GDP portion from agriculture has come down to only 15 per cent with 42 per cent of the workforce still involved in activities related to agriculture. Till such uncertainties lie in this sector, it would be difficult to see agriculture shining.[4]

One of the major outcomes of such uncertainties is the migration of peasants, not for some months but a complete shift to other occupational opportunities. Change in such occupation makes peasants vulnerable due to involved precariousness of new occupation which marks increased poverty and questionable livelihood. Another feature which comes out due to the vulnerability of agricultural condition and poor irrigation facility is the aspect of food insecurity of small and marginal peasants and agricultural labours. It was shown in earlier studies that majority of landless agricultural labour households survived on cereals, and had only one main meal per day, which is a stark indicator of food insecurity.[5] It should be the prime motive of the policy makers to substantially uplift the dwindling conditions of our farmers to at least maintain their adequate daily food requirement.

Status of Rural Poverty and Migration: Impact on Agriculture

Landless agricultural labourers living on subsistence level forms the major portion of rural population. The percentage of peasants without land is substantially higher in the total rural labour force. Due to the forces of poverty and financial obligations this labour force mostly opts for out-migration. A phenomenal portion of this labour force has been moving out from their native areas to nearby cities. They are not only migrating but also changing their occupation from agricultural to other non-agricultural activities.

The most significant reasons for such out-migration are – decreasing profits in terms of income from agriculture and agricultural productivity, substantial reduction in average monsoon resulting in depleting water sources, shortage of markets where they can get appropriate return of their produce and also depleting land holding from generation to generation. The attraction to out-migration also generates in the anticipation of higher wages, living in cities with modern facilities and amenities and a ray of hope for a reasonably secure future of their families and children. The whole idea of out-migration due to poverty and other reasons results in diminishing agriculture from the fabric of our society.

More than two-thirds (69%) of India's population live in rural areas as per the figures of Census 2011. The other side of the coin is rapid urbanization in the nearby places of villages practicing agriculture. A significant source of this growth is rural-to-urban migration, as an increasing number of people do not find sufficient economic opportunities in rural areas and instead move to towns and cities. Census 2011 data show that for the first time, India's urban population has grown faster than its rural population since the last census. 31 per cent of India's population is now classified as urban, up from almost 28 per cent in 2001.[6] In 2007–08, the National Sample Survey Office (NSSO) measured the migration rate (the proportion of migrants in the population) in urban areas at 35 per cent. In addition to migration, natural population increase and the inclusion in census data of newly-defined urban areas also account for some of this urban growth.

Despite India's impressive rates of economic growth over the past three decades, vast numbers of Indians are unable to secure a meaningful livelihood. In 2010, 29.8 per cent of all Indians lived below the national poverty line, while 33.8 per cent of rural Indians lived below the national rural poverty line, according to World Bank data.[7] While wage and education gaps between rural and urban Indians are declining, rural India is still characterised by agrarian distress, a chronic lack of employment, and farmer suicides. Thus, the rural–urban divide has been one of the primary reasons for India's labour mobility.

The high man–land ratio in rural areas is another factor of migration. It aggravates rural poverty and promotes surplus labour. In the situation of unequal distribution of resources; more children, higher dependency ratio, larger family size and surplus manpower are the problems faced by poor who are under greater social pressure of these problems. The increased workforce among them is unable to get absorbed on land that has limited quantity and productivity. The nature of the owner-labour relationship is exploitative. The traditional system of farming yields low income from agricultural work and leads to poor conditions of living. In such a situation surplus labour and high man–land ratio become additional push factors of migration.

The Government of India in recent times have initiated plethora of schemes for rural development to ameliorate situations of poverty and increase income of peasants. It may be constructing their homes through Pradhan Mantri Awas Yojana (PMAY), or reinforcing MGNREGA where the rural poor can get financial support during non-agricultural seasons or by enhancing the support system to elderly population through various social assistance programmes like NSAP, where pension is universally being provided to the octogenarians. These various programmes do provide essential and crucial help to the rural poor and peasants but the moot question remains unanswered that despite all these efforts of government why the pace of migration is increasing and putting pressure on agrarian society.

One of the fallouts of all these schemes is also worth noticing. The implementation of MGNREGA, PMAY, NSAP and other schemes provides a part of financial backing to the peasants. As a result these peasants specifically involved in agriculture labour are not very much interested to work in the agricultural fields. They are of the view that bare minimum help is being provided by the government and the remaining can be earned by moving outside as per day labour wages are higher in the nearby places. The financial backing with these schemes has made these peasants complacent in their behaviour. A casual labour is not very much interested in getting ₹ 300 as the wage in the village but is concerned to earn more than ₹ 500 in the adjoining cities. The concern of the labour in the village reflects that he/she is getting sufficient help from the government schemes and is not enthusiastic enough to spend their time in labour work at village sites. These practices also contribute to widening dearth of casual agriculture at the village

The development of rural non-farm sector also plays an important role in strengthening of the agricultural scenario in its entirety. It has been witnessed repeatedly that non-farm sector has been successful in making inroads in the domain of agriculture.[8] Despite this fact, seasonal and permanent exodus from the villages is a continuous process and it needs to be tackled for a sustainable growth.

The complete web of poverty and migration resulting in leaving agriculture by masses is definitely going to impact the predominant peasant economy. Against this backdrop, this volume will make an effort to discuss various issues, challenges and possibilities faced by rural poor and peasants. An effort will also be made to get some concrete suggestions for not only stabilizing the poverty and out-migration scenarios but also ways to improve the condition of rural poor and agriculture in the country as a whole.

Food Security and Rainfed Agriculture in India: Issues, Challenges and Prospects

The question of adequate food security has always remained a focused area of priority in India over decades. India being an agricultural country and that too on subsistence agriculture, has posed serious questions on sustainability of its peasants. The average land holding size at less than one and half hectares in India is still way below than the average of developed countries. With such miniscule piece of land at stake, the sustenance of peasants completely depends on the agriculture produce for their food secured life. Another dimension which is crucially significant is the availability of water for irrigation. Being a monsoon dependent country, it becomes inevitable for the farmers to wait for good rainfall despite having the availability of other agricultural inputs like fertilizers, seeds, etc. The absence of proper irrigation network along with a weak monsoon results in crucial crisis for food security. It forces them primarily for migration to nearby cities for employment and in other cases taking up non-farm activities. The whole phenomenon completely paralyzes the ethos of agriculture and simultaneously results in shrinking of agricultural activities, unavailability of labour and mounting pressure on the nearby satellite towns. Percentage difference in average rainfall from the previous year and the percentage increase in gross area are responsible for 55 per cent of agricultural growth whereas the remaining factors such as level of agricultural inputs, crop diversification and introduction of new HYV[9] also plays a pivotal role in overall agricultural growth performance.

Less investment on research and development in the field of agriculture poses enormous challenges in its growth. Lack of new technologies and major breakthroughs in agriculture is one of the major barriers to boost farm productivity. While the National Agriculture Research System played a major role in the green revolution, in recent years there has not been any major breakthrough in research. One of the main reasons for this is the lack of financial resources. If we compare the data of the percentage of agricultural GDP spending on research and development in Asia, then the figures revealed that India spent 31 per cent of its agricultural GDP on research and development in 2010, in the same year China spent almost double of that amount. Even our neighbour Bangladesh spent 38 per cent of its agricultural GDP on research and development in that year.[10] As a result of this resource crunch, there has not been diffusion of new agricultural innovations and practices that is critical for enhancing farm productivity. The gap in agricultural yield is significant between India and many developing and developed countries. For example, paddy yield in India is less than the world average. Yields in China are almost double to those of India for paddy. Within India there is a large yield gap between potential and realised yields.[11] Regarding green revolution (GR) based development, it is also debated that it was based on an unbalanced growth pattern within agriculture, where the use of natural resources was more than what is required.[12] Moreover, evidence suggests that India's food and nutritional insecurities today are the aftermath of the green revolution strategy promoted since the 1960's.[13]

Another factor which hampers the growth of agriculture is its overdependence on rainfed areas. Rainfed area currently constitutes 55–60 per cent of the net sown area of the country. Among the cultivated area about 45–50 per cent will continue to remain under rainfed farming.[14] The productivity of rainfed areas is low and unstable with year to year wide fluctuations depending on rainfall behaviour. The percentage of irrigated area under principal crops (2011–12) in India was 35, whereas in case of total food grains, it was 50.5 per cent.[15] Under principal crops, its percentage is 46.90 and under food grains category, it is 49.8. It clearly shows that the area of principal crops is less than half of its total area. Similarly, the national average of net area in irrigation is 40 per cent. The percentage of Net Irrigated Area (NIA) to Net Sown Area (NSA) is 40.53. The difference among various states under NIA to NSA is also wider. In Madhya Pradesh it is 33.87, whereas in the states of Punjab, Haryana and Uttar Pradesh it is well above at 94.48, 81.31 and 72.17 per cent, respectively.[16] The states of Andhra Pradesh and Bihar have also higher averages at 54.39 and 48.74 per cent, respectively. Such inter-state differences pose a huge challenge in meeting the ever rising demands of voluminous agricultural productivity.

One of the main constraints to the growth of agriculture in the states were large turn off and soil erosion in most parts of the state resulting into water congestion due to impeded drainage in early parts of the monsoon season and inadequate moisture in the later part when it is needed the most. Nearly 75 per cent of the cultivated area is subject to rainfed agriculture. Low cropping intensity due to practice of keeping land fallow in *kharif* and taking only one crop on residual/conserved moisture in *rabi* season. Rainfed agriculture has also resulted in large production of cultivable waste land and fallow land. The large tribal population, small and marginal farmers were having low investment capacity for adoption of high technology.

In India, more than 65–70 per cent of peasants are small farmers. Almost 41 per cent of the agricultural production comes from these small farmers. It is ironical that despite such phenomenal agricultural growth these farmers own only one-third of cultivable land which comes to around 33 per cent. Their agricultural production can easily compete with large farmers. Their efforts in producing agricultural crops are very crucial in the development of agriculture. The enormous percentage of small farmers along with their family constitutes the bulk of states' hungry and poor population. It is also known that 85 per cent of India's farmers operate less than five acres of land, half of which in many parts of India may be dry/rainfed and only a part of their income comes from farming activity now with others coming from wages, off-farm and non-farm activities.[17] It is the duty of government to create not only favourable policies for these small farmers but should also increase substantial investment in agricultural research, technology and infrastructure. It would be challenging to determine the status of food security among these small farmers in various pockets of the country.

Similarly, landless labourers also constitute most significant part of food insecure population. These labourers are totally dependent on the work done in agricultural fields. At present the wages of these labourers has increased to a respectable level. Villages having easy access to urban areas face shortage of agriculture labourer as they migrate to cities for getting employment. Increase in labour wages has been more pronounced in urban areas and particularly in construction activities. The importance of public distribution system (PDS) for these landless labourers is very significant. During non-agricultural season, supply of food grains through PDS assures their food security.

In this Volume

This edited volume is an outcome of proceedings of a national seminar on 'Status of Rural Poverty and Migration: Impact on Agriculture' and 'Food Security and Rainfed Areas in India: Issues, Challenges and Prospects' to look into the various facets of rural poverty and migration in the context of agriculture and food security and rainfed agriculture in detail. The themes of these two seminars were: (i) food security and governmental initiatives; (ii) irrigation in dry land areas, watershed management; (iii) change in occupational structure from agriculture to other means of livelihood; (iv) Issues related with overall agricultural growth impact of welfare schemes on employment and livelihood; (v) issues related with marginalized and their dependence on agriculture; (vi) rural poverty, sustainable livelihood and employment opportunities; (vii) Migration, employment and its social impact; (viii) changing livelihood, dependence on agriculture and agricultural labour in villages; (ix) welfare schemes to address rural poverty and migration; (x) changing rural–urban migration continuum and future of agriculture sector; and (xi) suggestive framework/mechanism to address rural poverty, migration and agriculture. In this edited volume 18 papers have been included which comes under the above mentioned themes.

The first paper entitled 'Agrarian Crisis in Rural India: Issues and Challenges' by D.M. Diwakar, is divided in nine sections including introductory contexts about the agricultural crisis in rural India. Section two examines decelerating growth performance of agriculture, section three is on technological breakthrough and crises, four is about institutional crises, land inequality and indebtedness, five is about policy crises, section six is on environmental challenges, seven focuses on crises of governance, eight concentrates on farmers despair and last section consolidates discussion and reflects on possible imperatives in this regard.

The second paper entitled 'Labour Shortage in Indian Agriculture: A Growing Challenge' by Minaketan Behera deals with the present status of labour force employed in agriculture and causes of the labour shortage in Indian agriculture. The paper revealed that there is a scarcity of labour for the agricultural works in India which is affecting consequently the productivity levels of almost all the crops grown in agriculture. The reasons identified for the labour scarcity include rural out-migration of agricultural labour, MGNREGA works and its wage rate, higher wages in other non-farm sector available jobs, seasonal nature of agricultural job and presumption of an agricultural job as a low-esteem one. The paper suggests that the agricultural job has to be made more remunerative by increasing the wages at par with other non-farm jobs available locally.

The third paper, 'Crisis in India's Agriculture Sector: Are Solutions Elusive?' by M. Devendra Babu throws light on the significance of India's agriculture sector since beginning and how it has lost its sheen over the years in spite of number of pro-agriculture schemes and other progress made. As per the author, despite several milestones, the agriculture sector could neither become economically viable nor was able to retain the sustainable source of livelihood for the people who depend on it. This sector is presently passing through a difficult phase for all the stakeholders involved in agriculture than ever before. When unable to counter these risks and uncertainties particularly their indebtedness, some resort to suicides. The new situations and problems have been afflicting this sector on an un-surmountable degree and yearning for lasting solutions like increased irrigation, more capital inflow, systematic cropping pattern and other related significant changes.

The fourth paper entitled, 'How to Accelerate Pulse Production in India?' by Amarnath Tripathi and Udita Mehta talks about reducing protein intake in Indian population as one of the major challenges in India. There is dismal situation of pulse production in India, which is clearly reflected from the recent price rise in pulses. It leads to import a significant amount of pulses from other countries. Most feasible policy option to increase the production is to improve the technical efficiency, as is mirrored from literatures. Against this backdrop, the authors have estimated the technical efficiency in cultivation of four Gram (Chickpea) producing states and three Tur (Pigeon pea) producing states for the period of 1996–97 to 2013–14 in this paper. Stochastic Frontier Analysis for the panel data is used for the estimation of the technical efficiency. In this paper, authors estimated the technical efficiency, and then, regressed the technical efficiency parameters on the climatic factors such as rainfall and temperature to find out if the climatic variables have an impact on the technical efficiency or not. This paper displays an example of the Cobb-Douglas type of production function by imposing the restriction of constant returns to scale. For both the pulses, the rate of decline of technical efficiency was found to be the fastest for Uttar Pradesh signifying an inefficient use of inputs in this state. When regressed upon the climatic factors, results showed that climatic factors have a significant impact on technical efficiency for Tur whereas efficiency of production of Gram is not affected by the climatic factors. Based on these results, the paper by the authors finally comes out with policy implications.

The fifth paper entitled, 'Proprietary Rights, Landlordism, and a Development Discourse: The Past and Present in Madhya Pradesh' by Ajit Kumar discusses about the situation of agriculture in areas where proprietary rights were historically given to landlords. As per the author, in such areas, agricultural investments, agricultural productivity and investments in public goods in the post-Independence period is significantly lower in comparison to areas where these rights were given to cultivators. The differences between landlord and non-landlord areas are not restricted to agriculture alone. Substantial differences are found in human capital investments and outcomes as well. Landlord areas have much lower levels of local infrastructure such as primary schools, high schools and health centers; the availability of village schools is 20 per cent to 60 per cent higher in non-landlord areas. Not surprisingly, they also have lower levels of literacy and higher levels of infant mortality. After Independence and after the formal abolishing of the landlord tenurial system the adverse effects of landlordism persist possibly because the ex-landlords continue to exercise arbitrary power in many of these areas, despite laws to the contrary. This paper examines the nature of the proprietary rights settlement in Madhya Pradesh in the context of the colonial raj and its legacy on the post-Independence agricultural sector.

The sixth paper of the edited volume talks about 'Critical Analysis of Agricultural Finance for Small Farmers' by B.K. Swain. As per the author, small farmers in most developing economies experience considerable difficulties and have to spend significant resources for accessing formal financial markets or micro-finance services. Absence of easy, affordable and reliable access to institutional sources of finance compels most rural poor and low income households to continue to rely on costly informal sources of finance or manage from relatives and friends, neither of which allows them to take full advantage of economic opportunities. Micro-finance service providers are expected to facilitate them by expanding operations into rural areas but have to understand following risks and develop a system to mitigate perceived risks.

The seventh paper entitled, 'Farm Suicides in Cauvery Delta of Tamil Nadu: Sign of Distress' by S. Rajendran and M. Sabarisakthi explores farm suicides in Cauvery delta regions. Unbearable to crop failure, from the past couple of months farm suicides are being regularly reported in the 2,000 year old fertile Cauvery delta, an indication of severe distress emanating from the deficit and scanty rainfall owing to drought and interstate river water dispute between Tamil Nadu and Karnataka. As per media reports, more than 61 farmer suicides have been surfaced. Cauvery delta is known for growing paddy and more than 70 per cent of paddy in Tamil Nadu is produced from this delta alone. Historically water guzzling paddy was grown and now another water intensive – sugarcane – crop. Classical Tamil literature depicts that Cauvery delta – generally referred as Chola Nadu – is famous for producing paddy and had the pride of supplying food to remaining parts of Tamil land. Also they point out that elephants were used to thresh the huge quantum of paddy, grown here. Now the situation is alarming leading to farm suicides manifested from the fragile situation and immediate attention is warranted.

The eighth paper is by Sunita Sangar entitled, 'Redefining the Role of Women for Revitalising the Agrarian Crisis in Rural India'. Agriculture is still a crucial sector in India despite its declining share to GDP over the past decades from 29 per cent (1998–99) to 15.8 per cent (2008–09) to mere 14.1 per cent in 2011–12. Agrarian crisis has witnessed a decline in number of cultivators as rural farmland is put to other uses (Census, 2011). Majority of these farmers are either marginal or small farmers that hold less than one hectare of land. These farms are largely managed by families where women play an important role. Agriculture is no more seen as a profitable and sustainable occupation and increasingly feminized as men migrate to the rural/urban non-farm sector. Women as farmers, agricultural workers and entrepreneurs form the backbone of this shifting agricultural rural economy. Among rural women workers, 65 per cent are employed in agriculture as labourers and cultivators. There are range of challenges that these women face from poor access to agricultural productive resources/technologies/microcredit and capacity building to poor education or R&D for farm women. These constraints have to be converted into opportunities if women have to be participating in the economic development of the country. Recognizing the upcoming need of women in agriculture this paper provides an overview and challenges faced by women in the current agricultural scenario. The objective of the paper is to dwell upon the need for redefining the role of women to address the challenges of gender inequality in the agricultural sector. It will provide specific recommendations for rural women participation that would help counter the obstacles and empower these women in agriculture.

The next paper by Dinesh Kumar Nayak, entitled, 'Production Conditions and Agrarian Change in Rural Odisha' talks about the contemporary crisis arising in agricultural sector, which is known as backbone of a rural economy in developing countries. From the increasing labour shortage, falling supply of manpower, labour migration; few existed drawbacks seen in government schemes of public work provision like MGNREGA, PDS provision of food-security, subsidies allocation and MSP has leading number of farmer suicide; and the case of Odisha is not excluded. In this paper, it is attempted to discuss the agrarian change and production conditions in rural Odisha and India as the changes occurred by different size-classes of land holdings in different time periods. The theories of agrarian change has referred according to Ellis that the interpretations of social and economic change in the rural sector have been discussed. The analysis of the economic change in rural economy such as in the cases of changes in structural growth in the agriculture vis-à-vis other industries; changes in the land ownership and operational landholdings; and the implications of agrarian structure on productivity have been analyzed.

The next paper, which is tenth in the series; by Surendra Singh and Sanatan Nayak is entitled, 'Assessment of Climate and Livelihood Vulnerability in the Bundelkhand Region, India: An Indicator-Based Approach'. This research paper investigates degree of vulnerability among the survey households of two agro-intensive districts of Bundelkhand region of Uttar Pradesh, India viz.,

Jhansi and Jaloun. By using indicator approach, climate and livelihood vulnerability indexes have been developed. Health, education, family structure, perception about climate change, use of technological tools are key indicators have used to develop composite vulnerability index. Study observed that surveyed households are highly vulnerable due to the change in climatic factors, viz., rainfall and temperature. Non-availability of surface water for irrigation is motivated towards groundwater irrigation. However, back-to-back drought years declined groundwater table. Due to this, farmers are changing their cropping as well as livelihood pattern to combat changing climatic conditions. The degree of vulnerability is high in the Jaloun district as compared to Jhansi district.

The eleventh paper entitled, 'State's Initiatives for the Sugarcane Sector Revival: Ground Realities and Problems', is by Abnave Vikas Bajrang. This paper's main objective is to examine the changing role of the state and factors responsible for issues and problems faced by the sugarcane growers and sugar mills in India. This paper is based on the latest available secondary data and existing literature. The result reveals that the state's price policy and failure of regulatory mechanisms are the major factors responsible for the problems of sugarcane sector. Apart from these factors, the falling sugar prices in markets due to fall in global crude oil prices and Brazilian currency may also be factors responsible to some extent, but not as much as claimed by the sugar mills. This paper also found that the short-term measures initiated by the state are inadequate and ineffective to tackle the long-term problems in the sugarcane sector. Finally, this paper suggests the there is need to revise the role of state intervention and the state should take into consideration the need and consequences before giving any kind of assistance and putting regulations to the sugarcane sector. And, the state also has to look at other benefits for the country while imposing any tax or regulation on sugarcane by-produces which help to ensure green development.

Amit Mandal's paper entitled, 'Economic Viability of Marginal Farmers in West Bengal: A District-Level Study' is twelfth in this edited volume. Small scale agriculture is important for agricultural growth, food security, poverty reduction, creation of employment and livelihood of millions of farmers. It is found that 67.09 per cent of marginal holdings cultivated only 22.50 per cent of area at national level while 82.16 per cent of marginal holding operates 52.47 per cent of land in West Bengal in 2010–11. The distribution of land for marginal farmers is relatively more equal in West Bengal. An attempt has been made in this paper to capture the determining factors for the economically viable farmers in the state of West Bengal as many researchers have concentrated their study on agricultural growth, agrarian crisis or stagnation, productivity of crop, etc. This is micro-level field study conducted in three districts of the state using appropriate sampling process. Multiple linear regression model, Probit model and marginal effect have been calculated for the purpose of the study. The paddy productivity, net income from paddy cultivation and annual farm profitability has been analysed and the important determinants for the variation of these across the districts has also been highlighted. It is observed that for the economic viability of the marginal farmers; irrigation cost, hired labour cost and distance from market; squeeze the level of profit across the districts while crop diversification enhanced their level of income.

Thirteenth paper of this volume by Tarujyoti Buragohain, entitled, 'Addressing Food Security and Government Initiatives' talks about measures adopted by government to improve conditions of food security. Government's policy intervention in foodgrain markets has been an integral part of food security. Governments procure foodgrain directly from the farmers at minimum support price (MSP) to meet the various requirements such as for public distribution systems (PDS), Integrated Child Development Scheme (ICDS) and to maintain the buffer stock. Despite declined area under cultivation and number of farmers' households, the production of foodgrain, especially, rice and wheat have been increasing over the years. During eleventh plan the achievement of production of foodgrains is more than the government targeted of production of foodgrain by 4.33 million tonnes. The gap between the government's target of production and actual achievement of production has been reducing. The government procurement of rice and wheat has been increasing over times. The off take of rice from allotment for PDS has increased from 48 per cent in 2004–05 to 96.5 per cent in 2016–17. Similarly, in case of wheat the off take for PDS has increased from 35 per cent to 95 per cent during the same period.

Despite all, as per 'The State of Food Security and Nutrition in the World–2017' report prepared by Food and Agricultural Organization (FAO), International Fund for Agricultural Development (IFAD), United Nations Children Fund's (UNICEF), World Food Programme (WFP) and World Health Organisation (WHO) estimate that, in India, 182.8 million people are severely food insecure for the year 2014–16. About one third – 27.43 per cent – of world's food insecure people live in India.

Fourteenth paper in this volume is by Ankur Jain, whose research paper is entitled, 'Analysis of Growth and Instability in Area, Production, Yield, and Price of Rice in India'. More than 50 per cent of the human population on earth uses rice, especially of the east use rice as the basic diet and as such vast cultivation of rice is common throughout the world. Agricultural growth with stability has been a matter of concern in the strategy of agricultural development in the world especially in developing countries. This paper analyses 41 years data (1970–71 to 2011–12) of rice area, production and yield and calculates the compound annual growth rate and instability across states and national level. The study found that at all India level compound annual growth rate of area, production and yield of rice were positive but it had been declining gradually over the periods. In the recent decade (2000–01 to 2011–12) there is an increase in instability at all India level in area, production and yield of rice. This study also reveals that there is no positive association between growth rate and instability as after reform period growth rate has declined while instability has increased. The possible reasons for increase in instability were low percentage of irrigated area to total cropped area, decline in use of seeds and manure and other inputs necessary for agriculture. After reform period (1990–91 to

2016–17) the instability has increased in case of wholesale price of paddy across various states while instability has declined in case of farm harvest price of paddy during the same period.

Fifteenth paper is by Barun Deb Pal, Parmod Kumar and P.K. Joshi entitled, 'Two-Tier Approach to Prioritise Climate Smart Agriculture in Madhya Pradesh'. This study has followed two-tier approach to prioritize climate smart technologies – first, using the climate smart feasibility index (CSFI) and second, assessing farmers' preference about climate smart technologies for the state Madya Pradesh in India. The CSFI includes – productivity, water, energy and nitrogen use efficiency, and labour intensity. These indicators are aggregated by using their respective weights derived through principal component analysis. Further, farmers' preferences are estimated using stated preference method after providing necessary capacity building to the selected farmers of the state. Results of this assessment reveal that the highly preferred technologies by the farmers are not necessarily highly feasible in terms of CSFI value. Rather farmers prefer the technology which is input saving even if productivity does not increase much as compared to their current practices. This is due to poor accessibility of agriculture machineries and highly dominance of rainfed agriculture in this state. Despite that, farmers are interested to replace their traditional cultivation practices with climate smart practices. In sum, this study fills the gap between scientific knowledge about the agricultural smart technologies, and farmers' preference in adoption of those technologies and it helps investment decision of the policy makers.

Sixteenth paper of this edited volume is by Srikantha Nayaka. The title of his research paper is on 'Agricultural Crops Land Operation: Irrigation Illustration in Mandya district of Karnataka'. In this paper an attempt has been made to analyze the cropping pattern in Mandya district. Agriculture sector remains the largest sector providing means of livelihood. Land and water are the two most important natural resources in the development of agriculture. The cropping pattern of a region is an outcome of a long term agricultural practices, social customs and traditions, physical conditions and historical factors. It also depends on soil, water, climate and biological diversity of that particular region. The integration of agriculture with other aspects of land management and ecosystem conservation is essential in order to promote both environmental sustainability and agricultural production. The farmers of district are being encouraged for traditional agriculture and also to high value commercial agriculture crops. Multiplicity of cropping systems has been one of main features of Indian agriculture and it is attributed to rainfed agriculture and prevailing socio-economic situations of farming community. The agriculture unit of development department are encouraging farmers to take up vegetables along with routine farming. Climate – rainfall, temperature, humidity, different types of soils, size of farms, availability of fertilizer, good quality of seeds, irrigational facilities and price incentives are the factors which effect cropping patterns. Such type of study represents real situation of cropping pattern in Mandya district in Karnataka.

The seventeenth paper talks about 'Migration and Changing Livelihood Profile for Ensuring Food Security Among Tribal Female Youth: Emerging Issues and Challenges in Chhattisgarh' by Vikram Singh and Suman Lakra. This article is based on the preliminary surveys, and secondary sources related to the social citizenship, migration and livelihood. This paper is divided into four parts. First part dealt with the conceptual understanding and different dimensions of social citizenship and its interface in societal structure in rural and urban set-up with reference to modified citizenship which is associated with the phenomenology of migration. Second part is dealing with the changing phenomenon of citizenship and social citizenship in relation to the social/indigenous groups (specifically tribal female youth) who are migrating from rural – semi urban – to urban areas in search of better livelihood and for ensuring food security. It also explains migration as a social process and social change as old as the history of human kind based on positive and negative factors. It also address the decision of an individual/group belong to indigenous group (tribes) to migrate which is often complex and involve a number of push and pull factors because of changed livelihood profile area-wise. The right of the migrants, in forced migration, becomes noticeable in this light. The responsibility on part of the governments to protect the people and devising strategies of protection of those migrant's rights as a right to food then becomes a necessary corollary. Lastly, analysis, suggestions and conclusion has been drawn on the basis of linkages mentioned above in various frameworks.

The last paper of this edited volume is by Animesh Roy, entitled, 'The Question of Development: Land Acquisition, Land Marginalisation, and Proletarianisation of Peasants'. Land dispossession under the neoliberal capitalist development has become a focal point of debate across the Indian states in recent years, particularly in Odisha. Based on the primary data collected through a household-survey conducted among the ESSAR Steel Plant and IFFCO project-affected households in Bhutamundai, a revenue village near Paradeep Port, in 2015, this paper illuminates the maneuver of the expropriation of land by the state and the contestation of peasants with the state. It also attempts to examine the impact of acquisition on the existing livelihood structure of the dispossessed and their social attributes keeping the Marxian 'primitive accumulation' in focus. The study, however, shows that acquisition of agricultural land has substantially reduced the access to cultivable land of the dispossessed farming households. The taken off projects happen to be less labour absorptive. A majority of the dispossessed households that lost their land partially continue the same economic activity (cultivation) on their existing downsized landholdings in the post-acquisition stage while the completely lost households witness a dramatic change in the livelihood structure in the post-acquisition stage. Despite having kept a sizeable proportion of the compensation money in bank and post office as a fixed deposit, the income inequality has surprisingly been higher among the lower quintile of the dispossessed households. This could be attributed to their vulnerable underumployment and unemployment situations under the shock and stress caused by such acquisition.

Agriculture in India, offers a very comprehensive analysis of the situation in both macro and micro perspectives dealing with whole range of issues. It helps to understand various criticisms of agriculture policies and also highlights significant ventures which mark increased productivity, higher returns and ways to make it more sustainable and long lasting. In India, around 51 per cent of geographical area is already under cultivation which is huge. On the contrary, world average is only 11 per cent of the total geographical area.[18] It shows the importance of agriculture in our country. Despite many negative indicators for agriculture being unproductive, it is still one of the major sectors in India which has a huge impact on our economy. Higher budget allocations over the years by various governments have emphasized its importance but there is lot more to be done. For example, the present cropping intensity of 136 per cent has registered an increase of only 25 per cent since Independence which clearly indicates that there is enough scope for improvement. One of the other factors which shows the importance and unprofitability of agriculture simultaneously is that it supports 58 per cent of the population as against 75 per cent at the time of Independence. In the same period, the contribution of agriculture in our GDP has fallen from 61 per cent to 19 per cent only. So it can be said that India's economic security continues to be predicted upon agriculture sector and the situation is not likely to change in the coming foreseeable future.

The changing times in agriculture in terms of irrigation, productivity and profitability is definitely going to raise the bar in the coming years. Payment for Ecosystem Services (PES) can help increase farmer income and sustain ecosystem services by addressing the ecological crisis. PES is a voluntary transaction where a well-defined environmental service is bought from a service provider. Paying farmers to adopt more environment friendly production systems is likely to generate a win-win outcome in terms of poverty alleviation and enhanced ecological benefits.[19] Similarly, implementation of strong agriculture patent regime would strengthen India's agricultural research and development sector. More concerted approaches of state and private players through effective PPPs are required to revitalize the Indian agriculture scenario to a more profit oriented, technology savvy and productive one.[20] Post-harvest management can also raise farmers income substantially. An evaluation study across Bihar, Uttar Pradesh, and Odisha, finds that post-harvest management of crops plays a crucial role in both value generation as well as value distribution along with crop value chains, by mitigating post-harvest losses.[21] On the other hand, hydroponics, a new way of practicing agriculture; where conventional agriculture in vast lands depending on monsoon water and chemical fertilizers is completely shifted to laboratory conditions where the agricultural productivity is not dependent on any climatic conditions. To add on, it gives a complete organic output with very less water and no chemical involvement. Such endeavors will change the whole mindset of practicing conventional agriculture.

Cooperative Federalism, where Central and State governments work together closely to initiate fundamental reforms would be significantly crucial to raise the farmers income in ways that are fiscally and environmentally sustainable.[22] It can be presumed that Indian agriculture scenario will substantially contribute to increase in income and profitability of our peasants in the near future.

Notes

1. Ninan, K.N. (2019), 'Climate Change and Rural Poverty Levels in India', *Economic and Political Weekly*, Volume LIV, No. 2, pp. 36–43.
2. Kumar, Sunny and Baljinder Kaur Sidana (2019), 'Impact of Climate Change on the Productivity of Rice and Wheat Crops in Punjab', *Economic and Political Weekly*, Volume LIV, Issue No. 46, pp. 38–44.
3. http://www.fao.org/fileadmin/templates/wsfs/docs/Issues_papers/HLEF2050_Global_Agriculture.pdf
4. Dhar, Biswajit and Roshan Kishore (2021), 'Indian Agriculture Needs a Holistic Policy Framework, Not Pro-market Reforms', *Economic and Political Weekly*, Volume 56, Issue No. 16-17, pp. 27–35.
5. Rajuladevi, A.K. (2001), 'Food Poverty and Consumption among Landless Labour Households', *Economic and Political Weekly*, Volume 36, Issue No. 28, July.
6. https://censusindia.gov.in/2011-prov-results/paper2/data_files/india/Rural_Urban_2011.pdf
7. https://www.prsindia.org/theprsblog/poverty-estimation-india
8. https://www.nistads.res.in/all-html/Non-Farm%20Occupation%20in%20Rural%20India.html
9. Kumar, M. Dinesh, Arijit Ganguly and M.V.K. Sivamohan (2019), 'What Drives Annual Agricultural Growth Rates in India?', *Economic and Political Weekly*, Volume LIV, No. 1, pp. 33–36.
10. https://thewire.in/agriculture/what-is-the-future-of-agriculture-in-india
11. Dev, S. Mahendra (2020), 'India's National Food Security Strategies and Potential for Regional Cooperation', in Nagesh Kumar and Joseph George (eds), *Regional Cooperation for Sustainable Food Security in South Asia*, Routledge Publications, pp. 160–182.
12. Ghosh, Nilabja and Anita Kumari (2015), 'Sustainability of Indian Agriculture', in Pradeep Agrrawal (ed.), *Reviving Growth in India*, Cambridge University Press, pp. 197–219.
13. Kumar, Richa (2019), 'India's Green Revolution and Beyond', *Economic and Political Weekly*, Volume LIV, No. 34, pp. 41–48.
14. https://www.thehindubusinessline.com/economy/agri-business/rainfed-farmers-are-the-most-neglected/article26272190.ece
15. https://agricoop.nic.in/sites/default/files/State_of_Indian_Agriculture%2C2015-16.pdf
16. https://pib.gov.in/PressReleasePage.aspx?PRID=1688596

17. https://www.downtoearth.org.in/blog/agriculture/future-of-indian-agriculture-and-small-farmers-role-of-policy-regulation-and-farmer-agency-75325
18. https://icar.org.in/files/state-specific/chapter/3.htm
19. Kumar, Lalit, M. Manjula et al. (2019), 'Doubling India's Farm Income', *Economic and Political Weekly*, Volume LIV, No. 23, pp. 43–49.
20. Samuel, P. Manoj, Karim Maredian and R. Kalpana Sastry (2019), 'Road Map for Agricultural Technology Transfer and Commercialisation', *Economic and Political Weekly*, Volume LIV, No. 43, pp. 13–16.
21. Boss, Ruchira and Mamata Pradhan (2020), 'Post-harvest Management and Farm Outcomes: Storage Facilities Matter', *Economic and Political Weekly*, Volume LV, No. 16, pp. 24–27.
22. Gulati, Ashok, Devesh Kapoor and Marshall M. Bouton (2020), 'Reforming Indian Agriculture', *Economic and Political Weekly*, Volume LV, No. 11, pp. 35–42.

1 Agrarian Crises in Rural India

Issues and Challenges

D.M. Diwakar

Introductory Contexts

Once upon a time, agriculture in Indian tradition was much appreciated as a noble profession, next to none, which can be traced out in local wisdom. In academic discourse of social sciences, this sector was categorically advocated by Physiocrates as the primary source of surplus generation. Indian agriculture has grown significantly in terms of area production and productivity. It has been contributing significantly in the gross value added (GVA) of the Indian economy, which is also reflected in the correlation coefficient between GVA of Indian economy as a whole and GVA of agriculture at basic prices between 1951–52 and 2015–16 (Figure 1). It is also revealed in the periodic correlation coefficients that co-variability between GVA of agriculture and GVA of Indian economy after 1990–91 has been weakened, which has been concerns for many

Figure 1

Annual Average Growth Rate of Indian GVA and GVA-Agriculture (1951–52 to 2015–16)

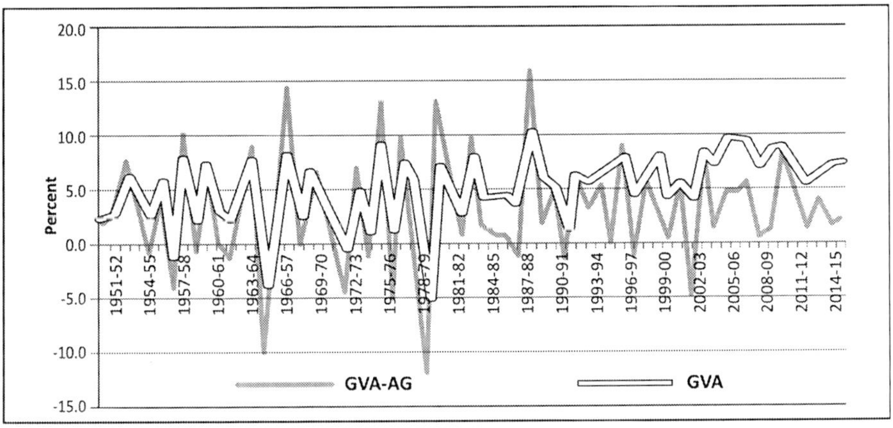

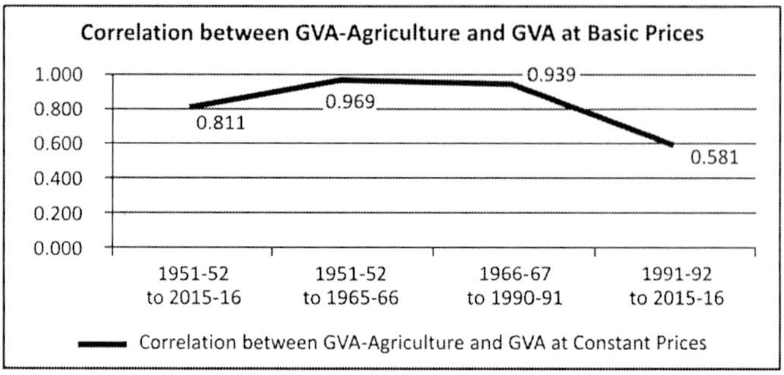

of us. It is precisely because the role of agriculture in transferring income to poor and poverty eradication has been validated earlier and even in recent researches. Demand- and supply-driven interdependence between agriculture and non-agriculture has employment generation potential to address unemployment and poverty. Therefore, development of agriculture is essential not only for agriculture but also for sustainable development of Indian economy.

Needless to mention that rural India constitutes about 69 per cent of population, majority of them depends on agriculture for their subsistence. About 48.9 per cent of the workforce is engaged in agriculture and allied sectors. This sector contributes 17.4 per cent of the gross domestic product (GDP) to the Indian economy (Government of India, 2016: 98–99).

However, various Official Reports brought out by the National Sample Survey Organisation (NSSO) including focused Reports on Situation of Farm Analysis and Situation Assessment Survey of Agricultural Households, Status of Indian Agriculture (Government of India, 2016), besides reports by Official Expert Group (Government of India, 2007a), Report on Accidental Deaths and Suicides in India and plethora of individual scholarly writings through books and journals, a few important among them are of Sainath (2013), Deshpande and Prabhu (2005), Mohanty (2005), Mishra (2006), and many others on agrarian crises. Broadly, two root causes of agrarian crises were underlined – low growth with declining productivity and high dependence of population on lower farm income. Reflecting a little further, stagnation, increasing risk in production and marketing, collapse of the extension system, growing institutional vacuum, and the lack of alternative livelihood opportunities, etc. are inter alia main factors behind agrarian crisis. Credit need has been growing considerably over the time following diversification, commercialisation, and modernisation of agriculture, but timeliness of institutional credit support is yet to be realised to the majority of the holdings in general, marginal and small farmers in particular. Inadequacy of institutional credit-delivery network, poor performance of credit cooperatives, regional rural banks, and commercial banks, to meet their farm-lending targets, and high cost of rural banking, etc. have aggravated further and manifested in tragic suicides. Agrarian crises may be identified through various dimensions such as deceleration in growth performance of agriculture, institutional crises, technological crises, crises of governance, environmental crises, policy crises, and so on, which have been dealt briefly in the following sections.

Decelerating Growth Performance

Agriculture has grown significantly after independence in terms of area, production, and productivity, which is evident from Figure 1. Area of food grains increased from 97.32 million hectares in 1950–51 to 122.07 million hectares in 2014–15, production from 50.82 million tonnes to 252.68 million tonnes, and productivity from 522 kg/ha to 2,070 kg/ha, respectively. In case of pulses area, production and productivity increased from 19.09 to 23.1, 8.41 to 17.19, and 441 to 744, respectively. Area, production, and productivity of oilseeds increased from 10.73 to 25.73, 5.16 to 26.67, and 481 to 1,037, respectively. Cotton grew from 5.88 to 13.8, 5.04 to 35.48, and 88 to 461, sugarcane from 1.71 to 5.14, 57.5 to 359.33, and 33,422 to 69,860, respectively.

The agriculture has increased at an annual average rate of 2.99 per cent during 1951–52 to 2015–16. Before the Green Revolution, agriculture grew by 2.15 per cent and contribution of the Green Revolution is reflected in attainment of higher growth rate during the post-Green Revolution liberalisation era, when agriculture grew at 3.39 per cent. However, this could not be sustained thereafter and agriculture encountered deceleration in the annual average growth rate, which was lower to the tune of 0.30 as growth rate for period in reference was 3.09 per cent between 1991–92 and 2015–16 (Government of India, 2016:

Figure 2

Change in 2014–15 over 1950–51

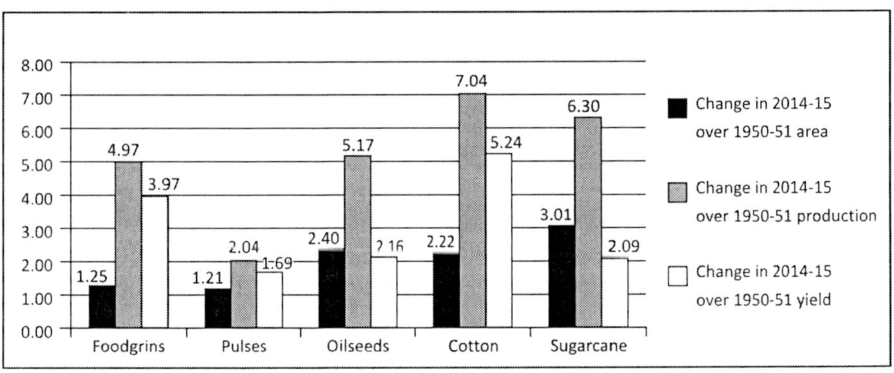

Figure 3

Annual Average Growth Rate of Indian Agriculture (1951–52 to 2015–16)

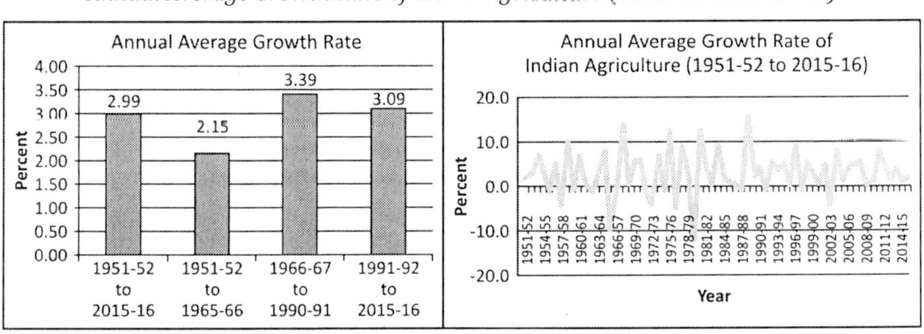

Figure 4

Annual Average Growth Rate of Indian Agriculture (1951–52 to 1965–66; 1966–67 to 1990–91; and 1991–92 to 2015–16) at Basic Prices

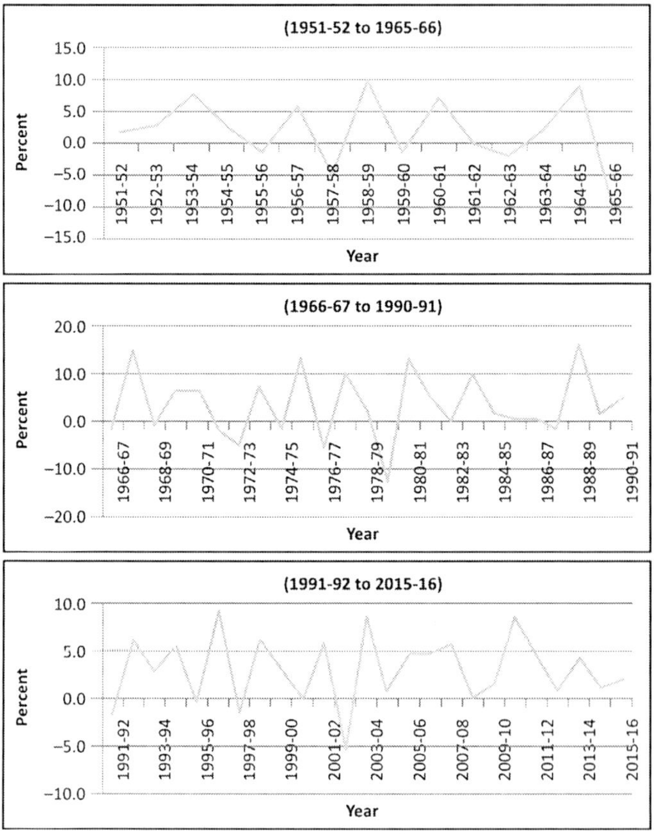

A9–10). With a highly fluctuating growth performance of Indian agriculture (displayed in Figures 3 and 4) amidst uncritical drive of forced commercialisation, modernisation, and diversification, this sector by and large was dependant on vagaries of monsoon and unprotected from the risks of crop failures despite expansion of significant network of irrigation.

Because of highly dependence on vagaries of monsoon, agriculture always remained in uncertainty. Out of 66 years, since 1951–52, Indian agriculture suffered negative growth in 15 years and for 2 years, the growth rate was literally zero, besides this sector also witnessed less than one per cent growth rate in six years. Thus, about one third of the period after independence, agriculture was hit directly by natural calamities and remained almost unprotected. Rising cost of cultivation, embedded with insufficient infrastructure support and slowing down of employment and income, left farmers trapped in the syndrome of indebtedness and despair. Performance of agriculture remained at lower profile with a few exceptions, thanks to unpredictable monsoon and indifference of the government towards this sector.

As a result, contribution of this sector to GDP continued to decline gradually from 59.2 per cent in 1950–51 to 17.4 per cent in 2015–16 (Economic Survey, Government of India, 2016). Crop-wise growth rates of area, production, and yield suggest that overall growth rates of area, production, and yield of all principal crops during 1949–50 to 2006–07 were 0.51, 2.57 and 1.61, for food grains 0.28, 2.35 and 1.75 per cent, and for non-food grains 1.21, 2.91 and 1.38, respectively. Growth rate of area, production, yield for all principal crops during 2007–08 to 2014–15 were 1.2, 1.97 and 0.7, for food grains 0.33, 1.3 and 0.95, and for non-food grains 2.08, 2.64 and 0.48, respectively (Government of India, 2015a).

Other sectors also grew considerably but it was agriculture that still provided livelihood to 48.14 per cent rural households – cultivation (42.92%), livestock farming (1.75%), other self-employed agricultural activities (3.47%), and 32.36 per cent rural agricultural labour households.

If we look at the growth rates of principal crops in pre-Green Revolution period in terms of their area production and yield, that were 1.58, 3.15 and 1.21, for food grains 1.35, 2.82, 1.36 and non-food grains 2.44, 3.74 and 0.89, respectively. Post-Green Revolution, data of growth rates suggest that area and production of all principal crops had lower rate of growth but yield registered higher rate of growth than that of pre-Green Revolution period. So far, non-food grains are concerned, growth rates of area, and production witnessed deceleration. However, productivity registered increasing trend from 0.89 per cent to 1.59 per cent. In case of food grains area declined, production registered lower rate of growth, and yield rate increased. Comparison of 1980s and 1990s suggests that in case of all principal crops, area increased in 1990s but production and productivity registered deceleration. In case of food grains, area declined, production and productivity encountered lower rate of growth than 1980s. So far, non-food grains are concerned area, production, and productivity indicated an increasing trend with deceleration, that is, lower rate of growth than 1980s.

As a result, there was a sign of recovery in area production and productivity of all principal crops. However, in terms of the growth rates of production, it was still lower than the growth rates of the production of 1980s.

Important factors inter alia for such poor performance was continued neglect of agriculture towards structural inequity, prevailing non-development syndrome in infrastructure, lack of adequate budgetary allocation of resources for investment despite the fact that agriculture remains mainstay for majority of workforce and one of the major contributors in the GDP of the Indian economy. Agricultural investment to GDP witnessed declining trend over the years. During 1985–86, it was 2.3 per cent at 1993–94 prices, which declined to 1.6 per cent in 1989–90 and continued to decline further to 1.4 per cent in 1999–2000 and 1.3 per cent in 2003–04. Even at prices of 1999–2000, the level of investment remained at 2.3 per cent only. This clearly indicated a decline in investment real terms. Realisation at the level of the Planning Commission of the Government of India suggests that private investment cannot be sustained without sustained public investment. Thus, syndrome of non-development left this sector under performed.

As a result, employment in rural sector grew at declining rate (Bhalla, 2005). Data from NSS rounds suggest that there was significant decline in employment in primary sector for both males and females (NSSO, 2005, 60: 506). Needless to mention that primary sector covers maximum and negligible portion is covered by secondary and tertiary sectors. However, there was an increasing trend in these sectors, especially for both males and females, and of course, males rate was higher. Another disturbing factor is decelerating real wage rates in agriculture and non-agriculture (Sharma, 2005). However, the question is whether these were substantial to offset the decelerating impacts of primary sector on the income of rural economy. Decelerating growth rate suggests that this sector could not generate sufficient capital and investment even through private sector. Limited benefits of expansion of the post-Green Revolution technology could increase production and productivity but that also could not be sustained. Moreover, the gains could not be transferred significantly to rural poor in particular and farm sector at large in general. The cost of production was increased due to lack of effective infrastructure as well as extension services. The environmental complications of erratic monsoon sytem juxtaposed with confusions arising from use of increased fertilizers and chemicals deteriorated the system in totality. Another factor which was significant for less capital coming to this sector was greater exploitation of poor farmers. This exploitation of farmers was done through usury network of non-institutional credit market in absence of effective institutional credit support.

Cost of cultivation increased significantly with the increasing use of modern technology across the states. Variation in terms of percentage rate of change in cost of cultivation since 1991 at least for a few major commodities suggests that lower range of the cost of cultivation for paddy increased from over 73 per cent in 97–98 to 117 per cent in 2002–03 and about 173 per cent in 2004–05 (Table 1). Upper range of cost increased by over 92 per cent in 97–98 to about 149 per cent in 2002–03 and 124 per cent in 2004–05. Lower range of cost of cultivation of wheat increased by 105 per cent in 1997–98 compared to 1990–91, 132 per cent in 2002–03 and 170 per cent by 2004–05.

Upper range of variation increased from 85 per cent to 106 per cent. Lower range of cost of cultivation for cotton increased by 149 per cent in 97–98 to 184 per cent in 2002–03 and upper range by 235 and 167 per cent, respectively. Cost of cultivation for other crops can be similarly worked out to assess the trend and variation of specific crop across the states. Difference in cost and price structure is another dimension for examination of the viability of the crops. For example, farm harvest price/cost of cultivating cotton ratio in 1997–98 in Haryana was 0.8633 with respect to *Desi* and 0.9656 for American cotton and in Punjab 0.5515 and 0.6914, respectively. In Maharashtra, price–cost ratio was 0.9452. Thus, farmers of these states were not in a position to recover even cost from the returns. In case of paddy Andhra Pradesh, however, was getting ₹ 445 price per quintal against cost of cultivation ₹ 436.77. Escalating cost of production with poor returns from agriculture amidst uncertainty of monsoon, risk of crop failures, absence of effective insurance cover, and almost non-existence of extension services pushed farmers into unprecedented hardships. Terms of trade remained against agriculture even after termination of industrial protection and devaluation of rupee in 1991 (Bhalla, 2005).

Data also suggests that about 40 per cent of the farmers did not like to continue with agriculture (NSSO, 2005, 59th Round). Out of which, 27 per cent were reluctant to continue in this occupation precisely because of non-viability. Interstate variations were even higher than that of all India figures. About 36 per cent of the farmers of Bihar, West Bengal, 34 per cent of Orissa, 30 per cent of Haryana and Jharkhand, 29 per cent of Maharashtra, and even 28 per cent of the farmers of Punjab – agriculturally one of the most developed regions and Kerala, one of the most developed states in terms of social development indicators of the country and Karnataka, and 30 per cent farmers of Haryana did not like agriculture occupation.

Technological Breakthrough and Crises

Agriculture was given priority in the First Five-Year Plan in terms of resource allocation to address the question of food shortage. Advent of Green Revolution was another significant initiative towards securing increased volume of agricultural production at higher productivity. Green Revolution technology comprised irrigation, High Yielding Varieties (HYV) seeds, chemical fertiliser, and pesticides; these combined created a new environment for production and increasing productivity. Irrigation cover has increased significantly from 17.56 per cent in 1950–51 to 47.24 per cent and cropping intensity has increased from 1.11 to 1.39 only. Crop-wise gross irrigation cover has also increased from 18.1 per cent to 51.2 area for food grains, 9.4–18.6 per cent area of pulses, 0.8–28.3 per cent area of oilseeds, 8.2–33.8 per cent area of cotton and 67.3–95.0 per cent area of sugarcane (Government of India, 2015a), but suffered variation of lopsided distribution. Surface and groundwater irrigation captured through public and private investment although contributed significantly in increasing production and productivity in agriculture, its uncritical exploitation has compounded environmental challenges, such as waterlogging, salinisation of soil, depletion of water table, etc. Chemical fertiliser and pesticides combined is another technological input for higher production and productivity which brought a significant return in agriculture. In absence of nutritional mapping of soil (redressal of which still remains a major challenge), generally a thumb rule was applied to use nitrogen, phosphate, and potash (NPK) broadly in proportion of 4:2:1. This ratio was also not a sacrosanct norm, it was 7.4:1.7:1 in 65–66 and still 6.7:2.4:1 in 204–15. It further deteriorated with alarming regional variations causing nutritional imbalances and irreparable damages to soil nutrients. HYV of seeds encouraged farmers for intensive cultivation, which at the end had many positive results. Development of genetically modified seeds, terminator seeds, and composite seeds also contributed towards increasing production and productivity, but fact remains that in absence of effective extension services, these technologies had mix responses in terms of production and productivity, which left Green Revolution much to be desired. However, development in agriculture made this country almost self-reliant on food front along with many complications questioning greenness as such.

Expansion of irrigation network, use of modern technology – HYV seeds, chemical fertiliser, pesticides combined – cropping pattern changed remarkably. Cropping intensity also improved to the level of 139 per cent

(Government of India, 2015a). However, percentage coverage of food grains did not change significantly until 1980–81. Coverage of total cereals hardly changed and remained at the level of about 75 per cent. During 1990–91 to 2000–01, it remained around 65 per cent and in 2012–13, it was 61.9 per cent. Coverage of oil seeds, fruits, and vegetables almost doubled and area under HYV increased from 1.2 per cent of Gross Command Area (GCA) to 41.17 per cent. Paddy coverage of HYV has increased from 0.56 per cent in 1966–67 to 17.34 per cent in 1998–99, wheat from 0.34 to 12.61 per cent, *jowar* from 0.12 to 4.89 per cent, *bajra* from 0.04 to 3.76, and maize 0.13 to 1.89 per cent of GCA. However, unirrigated cover of concealment remained pervasive which affected the cropping intensity, employment, and productivity in agriculture to make the agriculture non-viable. Extension services for technological exposure, soil nutritional mapping and capacity building of farmers were expected, which still remained a distant dream.

Institutional Crises

Institutional crises may be seen in failures of various institutions of backward and forward linkages which were supposed to facilitate agricultural production, productivity and income. These institutions are broadly related to (a) land ownership and operation, (b) credit, and (c) market, extension services, etc.

Land Ownership and Operation

Institutional arrangements have been revisited time and again to address inconsistencies through various forms of property relations ranging from free gift of nature to ownership of community, state, individual, corporate, etc. Institutional reforms basically aimed at unleashing productive forces, technological transformation, and self-reliance towards addressing basic needs through income redistribution, rural employment and increased investment in agriculture (Rudolph and Rudolph, 1987: 314–332).

The programmes and agenda for governance that emerged through freedom struggle were inter alia land to the tillers, irrigation to every field, opportunity to work for everyone who wants to work, etc. Gandhi categorically said that status of landlord would not be different than common people. Landlords would voluntarily depart themselves from the surplus land otherwise peasants would take away forcefully in which violence may take place. Hence, *zamindars* might cooperate by leaving away their land and state would play active role to ensure redistribution of land to the tillers with minimum violence towards distributive justice. He was of the view that the surplus land should be confiscated without any compensation to *zamindars*. Various enactments of tenancy reforms since Bengal Tenancy Act of 1886 till date including abolition of the *Zamindari* System were significant landmarks and land reforms were initiated. However, execution was slow and land reforms agenda remained unfinished which was gradually pushed back. Implementation remained questioned, contrary to the expectations attached with own government of the people of India. Instead of expediting land redistribution, land requisition and

Figure 5

Number and Area of Land Holdings of India by All Class Size (NSSO)

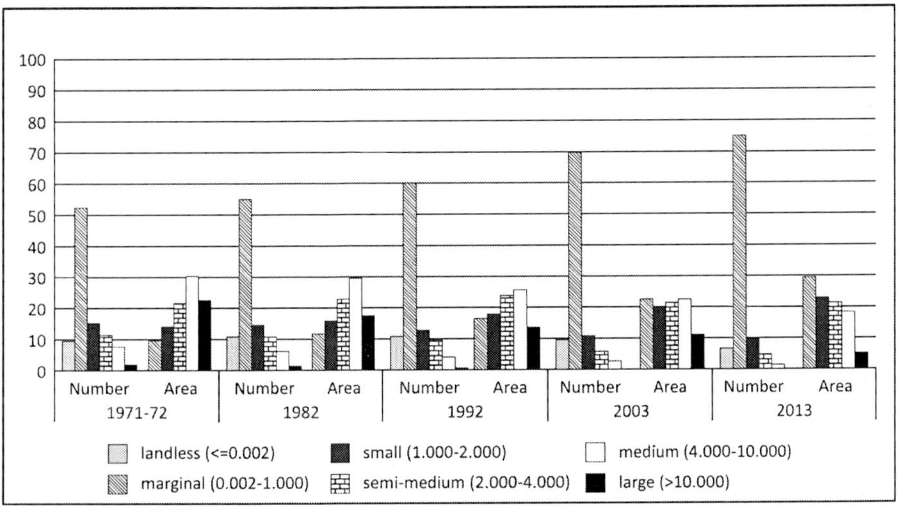

Source: NSSO, 2005, 70th Round.

Special Economic Zone (SEZ) have been brought to the centre stage. Needless to mention here that Indian agriculture is mainly dominated by majority of the marginal and small holdings, with unequal distribution of land as evident from the Figure 5.

Indebtedness, Credit Market, and Institutions

Rural indebtedness is an indication of deficiency of rural income to carry out necessary activities for livelihood support. Even today, languishing agriculture remains the main source of rural income and livelihood support for majority in India. Contribution of agriculture to GDP has been declining not only because the other sectors are growing fast but also because of continued neglect of this sector leading to decline in rural income. Income gap between rural and urban area has been widening. As a result, majority of farmers and agricultural labourers have generally been sustaining their livelihood and cultivation through mobilisation of resources by borrowings. Findings of the Royal Commission (i.e. farmers are born in debt, they live, die in debt, and transfer debt liability to next generation) still hold good, which have been further aggravating peasantry to a syndrome of despair. It is a matter of serious social concern.

Rural credit market has both formal and informal players. Formal players are government, cooperatives, commercial banks, whereas informal credit market is run by and large by moneylenders – often farmer, traders including dealers of inputs, other professionals, friends and relatives, and others who operate as moneylenders. Incidence of indebtedness in farming households is to the tune of 51.9 per cent with an average amount of ₹ 47,000. Out of total indebted agriculture households, landless, marginal, and small farmers constitute about 82 per cent (Government of India, 2015b: 401–05). However, in order to address the deficient need of the farmers, many players (formal and informal) have been operating in the credit market. Key findings of the survey report suggests that incidence of indebtedness was 45.94 per cent of the cultivators' and 28.85 per cent non-cultivators' and over all incidence of indebtedness was 31.44 per cent in the rural households with an average amount of debt of ₹ 70,580, ₹ 25,741, and ₹ 32,522, respectively. About 17.2 per cent incidence of indebtedness was institutional and 19 per cent non-institutional. About 16.9 per cent Scheduled Tribes (ST) households, 30.9 per cent Scheduled Castes (SC), 35.7 per cent Other Backward Caste/Class (OBC), and 31.4 per cent others rural households were indebted with an average amount of ₹ 9,610, ₹ 24,458, ₹ 36,091, and ₹ 44,565, respectively. It was also found that with the increasing assets the amount of indebtedness increased from 19.6 per cent (1st decile asset class) to 41.3 per cent (10th decile asset class). Similar trend was found in incident of institutional indebtedness which has increased ranging from seven per cent (1st decile class of assets to 32.6 per cent, 10th decile asset class); however, in case of non-institutional incidence of indebtedness, no definite trend was revealed. State-wise variations are also alarming.

Market Imperfections

Markets, formal and informal, play significant roles in development of agriculture. Input markets (seeds, fertilisers, water, machine services, etc.) are broadly managed by private players. Public provisions have been too little to serve the purposes. Private players ranges from local market to multinationals (Monsanto, Syngenta, Cargil, etc. seed companies). Moreover, Hariyali, ITC, E-Seva, etc. centres have emerged for single-window solutions. It is not only a costly affair, but it also requires funds liquidity available for the purchase, be it seeds, fertilisers, water, machine services, etc. Majority of marginal and small farmers have been constrained and trapped by the moneylenders at exorbitant rate of interest. It is not only costly but it also is free from accountability, particularly in case of spurious seeds, even if it is not germinated, if germinated not grained. Output markets have been equally sensitive, as minimum support price (MSP) have little coverage. Output price elasticity has been supply sensitive and farmers have been forced to sell their output to middleman at distressed prices to fetch their unmet need.

Policy Crises

Policies in agriculture being an unorganised sector having asymmetric information, agro-climatically and politically sensitive, and strong link with consumer has been very important. India has a rich stock of agricultural policies initiatives (such as Food Grains and Agriculture Policy Initiatives 1943, 1947, 1050, 1957, 1966, 1990, 1999, and 2000) reflected in planning documents, High Power Committee, National Farmer Commission 2004 with a perspective of Central Government and stakeholders perspectives have completely been missing. Thus, regional specification, variations and requirements remained almost unrepresented and hence, summarily non-implementable (Deshpande, 2016).

Although, it has always been claimed that agriculture being mainstay for the survival of the majority, it has been concerns of policy makers. Many policies have been formulated and executed. Institutions and agencies have been put in place to facilitate development of this sector, be it related to backward and forward linkages of production, exchange, distribution and consumption. Fact remains that the agriculture and peasants are yet to get their due place and share in the mainstream development of the economy. Many policies for land and water management, technology, credit and inputs, processing, marketing, prices, storage, distribution and protection against vulnerabilities, etc. have not been sufficient to repose the confidence and safeguard farmers' interest. This sector was accorded priority since the First Five-Year Plan in terms of resource allocation to address the question of food shortage. Green Revolution with Grow More slogan, Credit Cooperative Banks and Societies, Small Farmers Development Agency, Programmes for self and wage employment, million wells scheme, etc. were a few to list them. However, if we look at the budgetary allocation in terms of Revenue Expenditure, it was not commensurate to the promises and declined gradually particularly after liberalisation, as shown in Table 1.

Table 1

Percentage Share of Agriculture and Allied Sectors in Total Revenue Expenditure across the Major States of India

Major States	*1985–86*	*1990–91*	*2000–01*	*2007–08*	*2012–13*
Punjab	5.76	6.04	3.83	2.87	3.21
Haryana	8.47	8.18	4.99	6.13	4.48
Andhra Pradesh	6.35	4.95	3.65	3.84	4.52
Karnataka	7.96	7.11	7.01	12.09	9.72
Tamil Nadu	7.40	9.45	6.13	4.26	6.00
Gujarat	7.92	6.08	3.22	4.41	5.59
Rajasthan	7.10	6.58	3.40	3.25	4.81
Maharashtra	16.47	13.28	7.02	5.36	5.20
Madhya Pradesh+	15.93	14.11	8.37	9.28	9.90
West Bengal	7.96	6.02	4.14	2.98	2.62
Bihar+	7.58	6.74	3.18	4.29	5.35
Uttar Pradesh+	5.36	6.43	4.47	4.38	3.66
All India	9.52	8.73	5.37	5.31	5.30

Source: Reserve Bank of India.

Administered Price Policy for select crops was put in place. Basic objectives of this price have been to maintain floor price so that farmers are protected from distress selling of crops. Government of India announces MSP for 25 crops before respective kharif and rabi seasons. This administered price includes costs of production and permissible margin as well. However, if we look at the MSP of select major crops, it appears highly ineffective and undependable because of weak structure and coverage of crops for procurement.

Thus, remunerative prices to farmers remained always a challenge. Farmers have been compelled to sell their output to middlemen at Farm Harvest

Prices, which have been quite below the costs. Subsidies as a per cent to GDP have been quite low and most of the time declining (Deshpande, 2016: 32). Terms of Trade have mostly been against agriculture. Recent trend between 2004–05 and 2014–15 is also in continuity with a few exceptions (Government of India, 2015a). This trend has created wide gap between peasants and professors (Patnaik, 2015). Crop Insurance is yet to become meaningful for non-viable farmers. Privatisation of insurance has made it further vulnerable.

Aggressive commercialisation and capitalist farming for hunting profit has made farmers more vulnerable after advent of Corporate Farming and Agribusiness. Globalisation and World Trade Organization (WTO) with its implications on agriculture has distanced this sector away from the level playing field. Agriculture and Trade Policies, suffered from 'big but poor' syndrome (Government of India, 2016a. Jandhan Aadhar Mobile and Direct Bank Transfer for transparency in Mahatma Gandhi National Rural Employment Guarantee Act (MGNREGA), which has reduced fund floating, delay payment, and leakages to a certain extent but still remained a major challenge to address to rural unemployment (Government of India, 2016: 55–60).

Environmental Challenges

Surface irrigation and waterlogging, salinity of soil, over exploitation of groundwater, droughts and floods, vagaries of monsoon, climate change, El Nino effects, etc. are a few concerns for the development of agriculture. Average rainfall has been fluctuating and most of the time below normal as evident from the following graph. These have pushed the farmers and agriculture labourers in worst ever conditions. Agro climatic zone and region-wise specific factors causing low productivity as environmental challenges have also been identified by the working group of the Planning Commission (Government of India, 2007b).

Table 2

Region-Specific Factors Causing Low Productivity

Agro-Climatic Region	*States/Parts of States*	*Region-Specific Constraints*
Western Himalayan region-1	J&K, HP, Uttarakhand	Severe soil erosion, degradation due to heavy rainfall/floods and deforestation, low SRRs, poor road, poor input delivery, inadequate communication infrastructure and marketing
Eastern Himalayan region-II	Assam, NE States, Sikkim	Aluminium toxicity and soil acidity, soil erosion and floods, shifting cultivation, low SRRs, non-availability of electricity, poor road, poor input delivery system and communication infrastructure
Lower and middle gangetic plains regions-III and IV	West Bengal, Bihar, Eastern UP	Flood/water logging, improper drainage, salinity/alkalinity, arsenic contamination, low SRRs, non-availability of electricity, high population growth, poor road and communication infrastructure

Cont'd...

...Cont'd

Agro-Climatic Region	*States/Parts of States*	*Region-Specific Constraints*
Upper and trans-gangetic plains region-V and VI	Western UP, Punjab, Haryana	Groundwater depletion, decreasing total factor productivity, micronutrient deficiency, non-availability of electricity, and high population density
Eastern plateau and hills region-VII	Orissa, Jharkhand, Chhattisgarh	Moisture stress, drought, and soil acidity, iron toxicity, low SRRs, non-availability of electricity, high population growth, poor road, poor input delivery and communication infrastructure

Source: Cited in Report of the Working Group of Sub-Committee of National Development Council on Agriculture and Related Issues on Region/Crop Specific Productivity Analysis and Agro-Climatic Zones, Planning Commission, Government of India (February 2007).

Crises of Governance

Governance remained basic issues in the context of development in parliamentary democracy but unfortunately Polantza's hypothesis was validated and governance remained confined to law and order towards serving the interest of ruling class. Loknayak Jaiprakash underlined this very categorically. He said, 'The failure to implement those laws for such a protracted period of time has inevitably led to the growth of the rural violence that we are now witnessing. It is not the so-called naxalites who have fathered this violence but those who have persistently defied and defeated the reform laws for the past so many years – be they politicians, administrators, landowners, or money lenders .... Also responsible are the course of law where the procedures and costs of justice have conspired to deny a fair deal to the weaker section of our society' (Narayan, 1971). Even his own followers proved Kalecki's hypothesis right. Kalecki said, 'Whenever social upheavals did enable representatives of lower middle class and rich peasantry to rise to power, they invariably served the interest of the big

Figure 6

Average Rainfall Trends in India

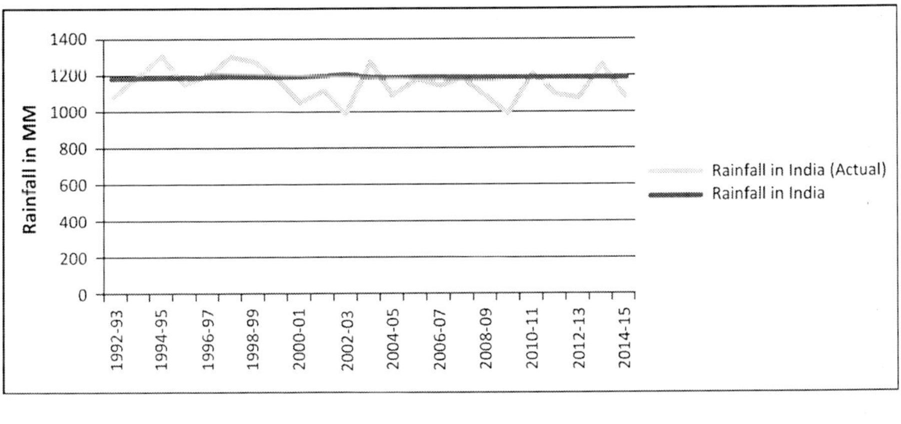

business (often allied with the remnants of the feudal system)' (Kalecki, 1976: 30). Thus, if the Congress did not pursue land reforms, non-Congress governments with exception did not prove substantially different either. As a result, land concealment beyond ceiling continued on many counts. Irrigation coverage languishing at 47 per cent after seven decades of independence is a testimony of political will for agricultural development. Implementation of minimum wages and gender differential of wages are another dimensions of indifference. None implementation of schemes and programmes, lower allocation of resources, input markets instability, decelerating growth, low minimum support prices, weak support system and delivery mechanism, lacking participatory policy perspectives, etc. are to name a few lapses of governance responsible for aggravating agrarian crises.

Farmers in Despair and Suicides

Vagaries of monsoon added with rising costs and uncertainty of access to reliable technology, market, and public credit institutions amidst unprotected risks with non-profitable agriculture aggravated the syndrome of frustration among farmers across the states of India irrespective of level of development of agriculture. Initially in the hope of getting favourable response, farmers invested capital mobilising through public and private institutions and stayed in production for couple of years to make their fortunes. Richer lots of farmers could sustain for couple of years because of their staying power and relatively better access to credit and inputs even if they suffered losses. Unfortunately, many of them, especially from smaller farm size could not sustain growing burden of loans from moneylenders, traders, and dealers of inputs for many years. Because of loss of face before the community consequent upon mounting burden of debts, failures of credit, insurance and procurement delivery mechanisms, and agencies they were forced to commit suicides. In India, one farmer committed suicide every 32 minutes between 1997 and 2005.

Various studies and reports have been conducted on this serious problem. Indira Gandhi Institute of Development Research (IGIDR) has brought a comprehensive study on suicides of farmers (Mishra, 2006: 41) for the Government of Maharashtra. Study found various reasons for suicides. About 86.5 per cent suicides were because of indebtedness, 73.9 per cent for deteriorating economic status, and 40.5 per cent because of crop failures. Loss of face in community because of non-payment of loan, unable to marry their marriageable sisters and daughters, etc. About 91 per cent of suicides were committed by males. As per police record, number of suicides in Maharashtra in 2004 alone was 4,147. Study reported that number of suicides increased from 11,866 to 14,729 between 1995 and 2004. Study suggests that suicides in females registered decline after 1999. Another study (Mohanty, 2005) revealed that cash crop growers and small and marginal farmers of Amaravati and Yavatmal districts were trapped in debt with an expectation to get better returns from cultivation, and committed suicides.

Kisan Sabha estimates that more than 5,000 farmers committed suicide in Andhra Pradesh since 1998, more than 3,000 committed suicide in Maharashtra, about 1,000 farmers committed suicide in Punjab from 1998 to the present, and about 5,000 committed suicide in Karnataka over the same period. 'It was estimated that 488 farmers committed suicide in Wayanad District in Kerala between 2001 and 2005' (People's Democracy, 2006). Another study (Vidyasagar and Sumanchandra, 2004) argued that, 'The central issue of farmers' suicides is the debt trap. Small and marginal farmers, especially those who lease land from others are not eligible for availing institutional credit and crop insurance. Thus, they land at the doorsteps of the usurious moneylenders. This debt trap is tightening because of the drastic shifts in the cropping pattern that is market driven'. Seeds, fertiliser, and pesticide dealers are at the centre of a growing controversy in Andhra Pradesh. They are the new moneylenders to a peasantry strapped for credit. 'The banks have given no loans in the past seven years', says Malla Reddy, general secretary of the Andhra Pradesh Ryuthu Sangham (APRS). 'So many farmers are forced to depend on sources like these for credit. The same man advises them on what to buy and then sets the rates for the purchase'. With the seed dealers tacking on hefty interest rates to their credit sales, the problem gets sharper. Report of Nageswara Rao revealed to a charge of two per cent a month on bills, but says there was no choice. Times were bad (Rao, 2005). Series of Reports from Sainath appeared in *The Hindu* is an eye opener for many of us.

The *Deccan Herald* dated 11 August 2005 reported that movement against State Repression claims that about 40,000 farmers committed suicides in Punjab alone since 1988, whereas state government admitted only 2,116 cases. Rising cost of cultivation, lack of market security, exorbitant rate of interests charged by moneylenders, dishonouring contracts, etc. were inter alia a few important reasons. After 1996, loan amounts increased four times but public institutions' share was merely 20 per cent. Deshpande and Prabhu (2005) found that most of the suicides were debt driven.

Table 3

Farmers' Suicides in India

Year	*MH*	*AP*	*KA*	*MP and CG*	*Yearly Total of Big Five States*	*Yearly Total All India Farm Suicides*	*Big Five Farm States as Per cent of All Farm Suicides*
1995–2002	20,066	12,716	18,070	18,432	69,284	1,21,157	57.19
2003–2011	33,752	20,610	19,083	25,511	98,956	1,51,338	65.39
1995–2011	53,818	33,326	37,153	43,943	1,68,240	2,72,495	61.74

Source: Sainath, 2013.

Table 3 suggests that about 2,72,495 farmers committed suicide during 1995–2011. National Bureau of Crime Report 2015 brought alarming fact that the share of farmers' suicides has been increasing, as given in Table 4.

Table 4

Features of Suicides in Farming Sector During 2013–15 in India

Year	*Suicides in Farming Sector*	*Total Suicides*	*Percentage Share**
2013	11,772	1,34,799	8.7
2014	12,360	1,31,666	9.4
2015	12,602	1,33,623	9.4
Percentage change	2.0	1.5	–

Source: NBCR, Accidental Deaths and Suicides in India, 2015, p. 263.

Delivery mechanism of institutional credit and its defined connivance with local middle men and functionaries often hatches conspiracy to confiscate land of the poor marginal and small farmers, forcing them to commit suicide. Suicide committed by Manasa Ram of Maraucha Ishwari Singh Village of Suratganj Block in Barabanki district of Uttar Pradesh is an example of many such cases. However, efforts of social activists foiled this conspiracy and confiscation got cancelled later.

Barwani and Khangaon districts witnessed indebted farmers' suicide recently. Crop failure drives farmer to end life appeared in *The Hindu* dated 5 January 2017: apparently upset over successive crop failure, for the last three years and his inability to repay loans, a 35-year-old farmer named Dinesh

Figure 7

Percentage Share of Major Causes of Suicides Among Farmers/Cultivators During 2015

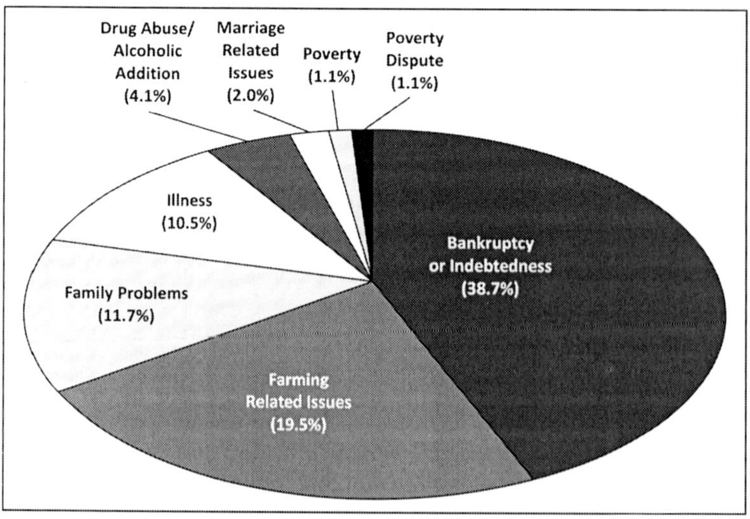

Source: NBCR, Accidental Deaths and Suicides in India, 2015, p. 263.

Figure 8

State/UT-wise Suicides Committed by Farmers/Cultivators During 2015

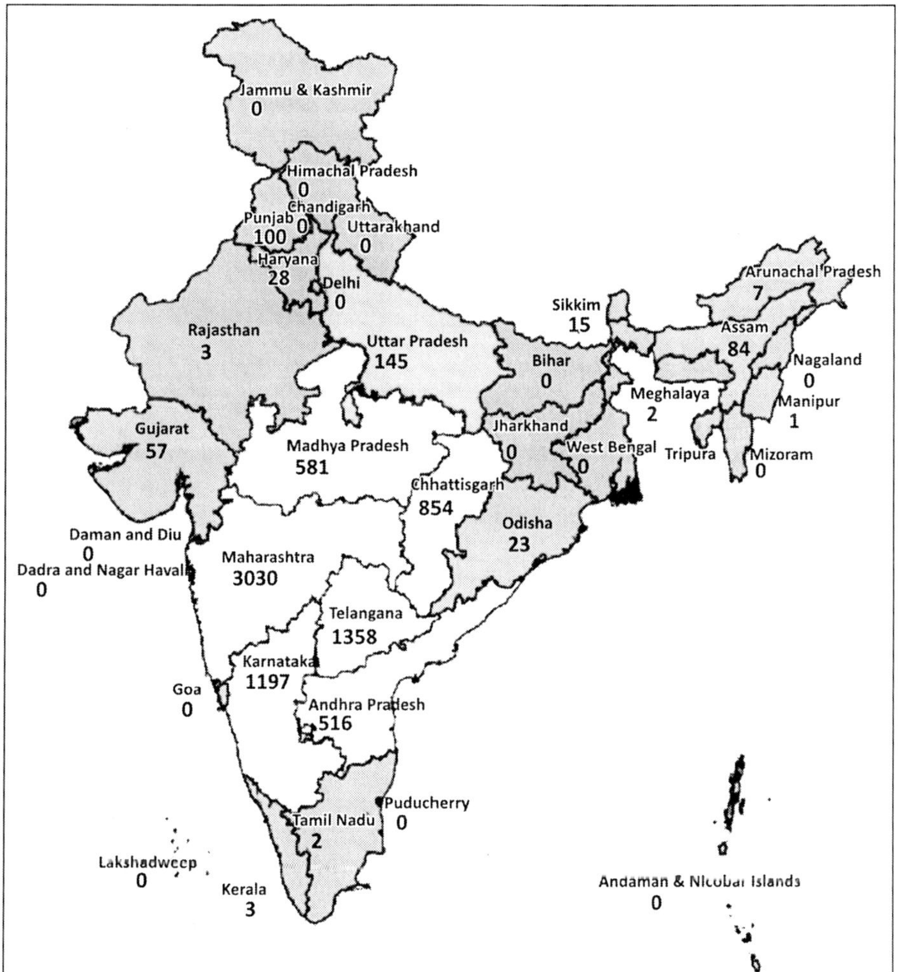

Chandore of village Umarkhali of the Khargone (West Nimar) district of Madhya Pradesh committed suicide after eating poisonous substance. Dinesh Singh reportedly had taken a loan amounting ₹ 14,00,000 for papaya cultivation on his 18 acre land and crop was not fetching even cost price.

Tenant farmers have seldom access to institutional credit in absence of ownership of land as collateral security and, therefore, they are forced to be trapped in usurious exploitative network. They often sell their crops at pre-decided price to the input dealers or at best at farm harvest price to petty traders. Kisan Sabha deliberated upon this serious crisis and noted, 'While every such death is a tragic individual reality for grieving families and loved ones, there are important common features to the farmers' suicides. These farmers invested heavily in inputs – biological inputs, electricity, machinery, and other components of fixed and variable costs. These costs have risen sharply in the period of liberalisation, and are especially onerous when the farmer invests in seeds produced by private companies, particularly multinational corporations. The farmers were often the victims of plain cheating – they were sold spurious seed and other inputs by unscrupulous traders. Since 1991, farmers have had to witness the massive withdrawal of the formal sector of credit from the countryside, and have had to borrow from the informal sector at usurious rates of interest for their production and consumption needs. Finally, when they reaped a harvest, neo liberalism and the new trade regime robbed them of prices that could not even cover their costs, let alone earn them a livelihood. Where the output itself is destroyed by pest, disease or natural disaster, the farmer was un-indemnified by any system of insurance, and inadequately compensated, if at all, by the state. It is the stark reality that, for many in our society and in such a situation, suicide appears as the alternative of last resort' (People's Democracy, 2006).

Market-driven farms diversification, not necessarily designed differently but for the interests of corporate sectors, which exploited farms undermining ecological and fertility balance. Globalisation and new trade regime has made framers condition vulnerable and exposed to uncertainty (Vidyasagar and Sumanchandra, 2004, CSD, NIRD). There is every possibility of worsening condition of poor farmers further with the emphasis on investment through corporate contract farming. Unless means of production is reoriented in favour of producers and meaningful employment, and employability of poor cultivators are ensured through public sector initiatives for infrastructure development as well as input and output markets are regulated in the interest of producers, it will be difficult to rescue farmers from the syndrome of distress and despair leading towards suicides.

Consolidating Reality for Imperatives

The earlier discussion on the dimensions of agrarian crises rooted in the syndrome of decelerating growth of agriculture amidst rising costs and inadequate infrastructure leading to deficient employment and income for the livelihood of rural workers, specially cultivators and agricultural labourers. It emerged from the analysis that decelerating growth with inadequate institutional arrangements forced majority of the peasants in the debt trap. Majority of indebted households were from the poorest lot in terms of size of land possession and monthly per capita consumption expenditure. So far, sources of loan were concerned formal sector – commercial bank remained the major player followed by cooperative societies. Moneylender was yet significantly present in the rural borrowing market and other informal sources, that is, traders, friends and relatives, professionals, and others were not different from moneylenders with a few individual exceptions. Institutional credit remained favourable for increasing size of land possessions but mostly in poor states. Banks remained effective after nationalisation until 1980s but its performance declined significantly in late 1990s. Per hectare credit to agriculture was also declined. Analysis suggests that the genesis of indebtedness were rooted in continued neglect of agriculture resulted in decelerated growth syndrome. Declining investment and inadequate infrastructure acted as a drag on institutional and technological transformation and modernisation with ecological balance. Poor support system for credit, input, insurance, and marketing with dependence on vagaries of monsoon resulted in crop failures and lower returns leading to misery, distress, and despair.

In this syndrome, cultivators were often not in a position to repay the loan. They hardly sustained the loss of face before the community and committed suicides. Thus, most of the unfortunate suicides were debt driven. Consecutive failures of governance in terms of effective policies and their implementation right from the redistribution of land to the tillers to accelerating growth with employment and justice were witnessed. Instead of correcting those lapses, the economy has been moving in a different direction in the interest of the rich and corporate sectors with a faster pace of reforms. Interestingly despite symptoms of all the negative indications against the poor, contradictory policies for reforms have been put in place with a lip service to the poor. Unless poor producers are brought in the mainstream of production, control over the means of production and distribution on sustainable basis this process of marginalisation, distress, and despair, which has emerged out sharply in the era of reforms and globalisation of markets may not be checked. Lowering the rate of interest on institutional loans and Right to Work may have positive effects subject to effective implementation, which is always doubtful. However, Right to Work on ad hoc basis cannot be continued for long. Sustainable employment generation led growth process for poor producers need to be put in place. This needs stronger and active role of state which has been narrowing down during reform process. State has compromised with anti-poor development players. Therefore, pro-poor activism of civil society and effective mobilisation and resistance of peasants and social activists have become necessary to create pressure on state to perform pro-poor role to achieve growth with employment and justice.

References

Bhalla, G.S., (2005): The State of the Indian Farmers, G. Parthasarathi Memorial Lecture in 88th Annual Conference of the Indian Economic Association, 28 December.

Deshpande, R.S., (2016): State, Agriculture and Policy Making, Presidential Address, *Indian Journal of Agriculture Economics*, Vol. 71, No. 1, January–March.

Deshpande, R.S. and Prabhu, N., (2005): Farmers Distress: Proof Beyond Questions, *Economic & Political Weekly*, Vol. 40, Nos. 44 and 45, 4 November.

Government of India, (2007a): Expert Group Report on Agrarian Crisis in India.

——, (2007b): Economic Survey, Ministry of Finance, New Delhi.

——, (2015a): Agricultural Statistics at a Glance, Ministry of Agriculture and Farmers Welfare.

——, (2015b): Accidental Deaths and Suicides in India, NBCR, 2015.

——, (2016): Economic Survey, Ministry of Finance.

——, (2017): Economic Survey, Ministry of Finance.

Kalecki, Michal, (1976): *Essays in Political Economy of Development*, Lok Sabha Starred Question No. 611, dated 9 May 2005.

Mishra, S., (2006): Farmers' Suicide in Maharashtra, *Economic & Political Weekly*, Vol. 41, No. 16, 22–28 April, pp. 1538–45, see also, Suicide Mortality Rates across States of India, in the same issue, p. 1567.

Mohanty, B.B., (2005): We are Like the Living Dead: Farmer Suicides in Maharashtra, Western India, *Journal of Peasant Studies*, Vol. 32, No. 2, April, pp. 243–76.

Narayan, J.P., (1971): *Face to Face*, Sarvaseva Sangh Prakashan, Varanasi.

National Sample Survey Organisation, (2005): Indebtedness of Farmer Households in India, NSS Report No. 498, 59th Round, January–December 2003.

Patnaik, P., (2015): Peasant and Professors, *Telegraph*, 25 May.

Rao, N., (2005): *The Hindu*, 11 September.

Rudolph, L.I. and Rudolph, S.H., (1987): *In Pursuit of Lakshmi: The Political Economy of India State*, Orient Longman, Bombay.

Sainath, P., (2013): Farmers Suicides Rate Soar Above the Rest, *The Hindu*, 8 May.

——, (2006): India Together, various issues, 2006 and see also *The Hindu*, various issues.

——, (1996): *Everybody Loves Drought*, Penguin Books India.

Sharma, H.R., (2005): Recent Trends in Wage Earnings of Agricultural Labourers State Level Analysis for Different Social Groups, *Arth Vijnana*, Vol. XLVII, Nos. 3–4, September–December, pp. 329–44.

Shetty, S.L., (2004): Distributional Issues in Bank Credit, Multi-Pronged Strategy for Correcting Past Neglect, *Economic & Political Weekly*, Vol. xxxix, No. 29, 17 July.

Vidyasagar, R.M. and Sumanchandra, K., (2004): Study on Farmers' Suicides in Andhra Pradesh and Karnataka, CSD, NIRD.

2 Labour Shortage in Indian Agriculture

A Growing Challenge

Minaketan Behera

Introduction

The importance of agriculture in the context of the Indian economy is paramount. Not only it is a pivotal component in achieving several of India's goals – attaining food security, an eight per cent gross domestic product (GDP) growth rate, and enhancing rural income – but it is also the sector with highest share of workers in the country. The average growth rate in the agriculture sector in the last five years has been 4.1 per cent. Labour is the most important input in increasing production in traditional agriculture. Agriculture labour may be defined as labour who works in agriculture or allied activities for the whole or part of the year in return for (in cash or kind or both) for full-time or part-time work. The agriculture labourer has no risk in the cultivation and no right of lease or contract on land but merely works on another person's land for wages. The definition includes workers who are engaged in other agri-based occupation such as dairy farming, horticulture, poultry, etc. It also includes the people who do not work throughout the year but only for a part of the year. Agriculture Labour Enquiry Committee defined agriculture labour household as the household whose main source of income is derived as wages for working on farms of others agricultural labourers are the most-exploited unorganised class of the rural population of the country. From the very beginning, landlords and *zamindars* exploited these labourers for their benefit and converted some of them as slaves or bonded labourers, and forced to continue the system generation after generation. It led to wretched condition and total deprivation of the rural masses. After 72 years of independence, the situation has improved. However, they remain largely unorganised and as a result, their economic exploitation continues. Their level of income, standard of living and the rate of wages have remained abnormally low.

During the last three decades or so, the national and state economies in India have been witnessing pervasive changes in the occupational pattern of workers and labour markets. These are manifested in the movement of labour geographically from the rural to the urban areas, and occupationally, from the agricultural to the non-agricultural sectors and increasing participation of women in paid work. Increasing urbanisation and expansion of urban jobs, diversification of economic activities in the rural areas itself favouring non-farm and informal sectors (petty business, construction works, small transport operations, etc.), and the implementation of the Mahatma Gandhi National Rural Employment Guarantee Act (MGNREGA) and special food security programmes for the below poverty line families have contributed to the observed structural shifts in the work patterns and people's participation in the labour markets. Rural workers, by and large, are exhibiting exemplary dynamism, getting increasingly disinterested in agricultural work and are moving out of agriculture and rural areas. Since agriculture involves highly labour-intensive operations and workers are withdrawing from farm activities, the agricultural sector is facing acute shortage of labour and rising wages and costs – a dual loss indeed. Labourers constitute a vital input in agricultural production, but they are migrating to different parts of the country for earning a better livelihood, adding to the existing imbalance between labour demand and supply of labourers (Deshingkar and Start, 2003). Usually as an economy matures, there is a movement of excess agricultural workers from low-productivity agriculture to higher-productivity sectors like manufacturing and services, and thus from rural to urban areas, and form lower wages to higher wages. The pace of this movement accelerates with higher economic growth which gives rise to greater job opportunities in the non-agricultural sectors. FICCI, 2014 calculated that labour is four times more productive in industry and six times more productive in services compared to agriculture. Higher productivity usually implies higher wages. Thus, the natural movement away from agriculture. Such shifts are also coupled with technological advancement of the primary sector leading to lower labour intensity and higher capital investment in several instances.

Data Sources

The chapter is based on secondary data sources. It includes both published and unpublished reports and articles. It also based on various published and unpublished reports of the National Sample Survey Organisation (NSSO) and Labour Bureau, Government of India, New Delhi. The data on employment were taken from the reports of last NSSO surveys, that is 55th Round (1999–2000), 61st Round (2004–05), 66th Round (2009–10), and the 68th Round (2011–12). It is based on Census data as well.

Distribution of Agricultural Workforce in India

Economic development involves structural change in the overall economy of any country. According to Kaldor, 'One of the best known generalisations in economics is that development involves a continued fall in the share of the "primary" sector in total output and employment and continued rise in the share of the "secondary" and "tertiary" sectors'. In this section, the shares among the three major categories, viz., total agricultural workers (cultivators + agricultural labour) only cultivators and only agricultural labourers were considered for looking distribution of agricultural workforce in India, during period of 1961 to 2011. It can be seen from the Table 1. Table 1 shows that the Indian population is tremendously increasing since the period of 196l–2011. However, the working population engaged in agricultural in 1961 was 72.36 per cent, whereas, in 2011 it was only 54.60 per cent. It shows that dependency of population on agriculture has declined and cultivator's percentage has also declined during the same period. However, the agricultural labourers workforce has increased in during the period of 1961–1991, whereas, in 2001 it had slightly declined. However, the agricultural labourer workforce has increased in 2011. The percentage of cultivators has also declined during the periods of 1961–2011. The proportion of agricultural labourers was estimated at 19.56 per cent, 26.98 per cent, 26.02 per cent, 27.16 per cent, 26.69 per cent and 30.00 per cent in 1961, 1971, 1981, 1991, 2001 and 2011, respectively. From this, it may be concluded that agricultural workforce is shifting from agriculture to other sectors.

Table 1

Distribution of Agricultural Workforce in India During 1961–2011

Year	*Total Population (in millions)*	*Total Agricultural Workers (in %)*	*Total Cultivators (in %)*	*Total Agricultural Labourers (in %)*
1961	439	72.36	52.80	19.56
1971	548	70.12	43.14	26.98
1981	683	68.35	42.33	26.02
1991	844	67.01	39.85	27.16
2001	1,027	58.40	31.71	26.69
2011	1,210	54.60	24.60	30.00

Source: Census of India 1961–2011.

Agricultural Workforce in India as per NSSO

India's agriculture labour market is in a state of flux. Going by the National Sample Survey Office's periodic surveys, 34 million workers left the sector between 2004–05 and 2011–12. NSSO data shows that India's overall employment growth since 2004–05 has been anaemic. At an average, only around two million people were added to the workforce since 2004–05, compared to around 12 million people that were added to the workforce every year as an average between 1999–2000 and 2004–05. However, the addition to non-agricultural employment has actually been around six million people every year since 2004–05, as the workforce employed in agriculture had started declining in absolute numbers and consistently so, since then. The size of the workforce in agriculture declined by around 30.57 million between 2004–05 and 2011–12, although the size of the total workforce increased (Figure 1). This is first such period when a reduction in absolute numbers has been reported in agriculture. It has been observed that over time that as economies progress and

Figure 1

Total Workforce vs. Agricultural Workforce (2011–12)

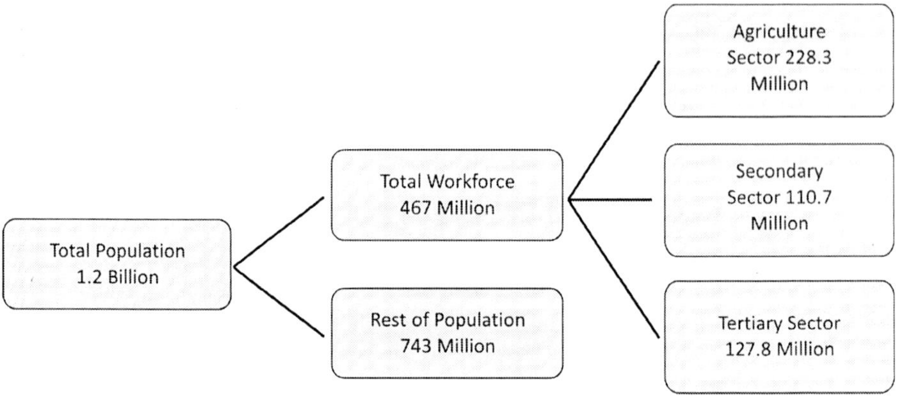

move towards development, workforce tends to move away from primary sectors of the economy. Consistent with this empirical evidence observed worldwide, even in India, the percentage of people employed in agriculture has been consistently declining from around 60 per cent in 1999–00 to 49 per cent in 2011–12 (Table 2).

Table 2

People Employed in Agriculture and Overall Employment

Year	*Total Workforce*	*Agricultural Workforce*	*Percentage*
1999–00	397	238	59.9
2004–05	457	259	56.7
2009–10	460	245	53.3
2011–12	467	228	48.8

India has also been experiencing a similar trend in its workforce movement. However, the trend has not been limited to just declining share of agriculture in total employment but also has led to a significant decline in absolute number of people employed in the agricultural sector. A comparison across two time periods, 2004–05 and 2011–12, indicates that while the size of the total workforce in the country increased by roughly around 10 million, the size of the agricultural workforce reduced by 30.57 million people. In the process, the share of agricultural workforce in total workforce declined from 56.7 per cent to 48.8 per cent in the same period (considering principal and subsidiary activities). It not only indicates that fewer people are being added to the workforce in agriculture but also highlights the net migration to other sectors. Between 2001 and 2011, India added 181.5 million to its population, half of which was in the rural areas. With agriculture being the mainstay in rural areas, what it signified was that enough labour should be available for agriculture. Moreover, agriculture in India has been characterised by a high degree of disguised unemployment. In other words, even if some amount of labour were taken out from agriculture there would be no difference to output and productivity. Both these put together would suggest that labour availability for agriculture should not be a problem. This has been the popular perception.

Moreover, yields, especially for food grains have been increasing in the last several years. As per data from the Ministry of Agriculture, Directorate of Economics and Statistics, the Compound Annual Growth Rate of food grains yield between 1999 and 2004 was 0.1 per cent but increased to 2.5 per cent between 2004 and 2009. Increase in yield could not have been possible if there was a shortage in agricultural labour.

However, in reality, the magnitude and pace of the shift away from agriculture has been substantial as evidenced here. It also has begun to make an impact as the shortage in agricultural labour is currently not being compensated by adequate measures to reduce the overall labour intensity of the sector. As a result, the primary sector in many Indian states is experiencing severe labour shortage and escalation in farm wages, which are adversely impacting the profitability of the farmer.

State-wise Effect of Agriculture Labour Availability

This reduction is a cumulative effect of similar reductions across all major states. Close to 79 per cent of this reduction has been contributed by five states only – Uttar Pradesh, Karnataka, West Bengal, Bihar and Rajasthan while the remaining states constitute the rest 21 per cent (Table 3).

Table 3

Reduction in Labour Availability in Agriculture

State	*Agricultural Labour (Million)*		
	2004–05	*2011–12*	*Reduction (Million)*
Uttar Pradesh	43.30	34.83	8.47
Karnataka	17.60	12.91	4.69
West Bengal	15.50	11.79	3.71
Bihar	21.30	17.67	3.63
Rajasthan	17.40	13.83	3.56
Others	143.83	137.31	6.52
Total	258.93	228.36	30.57

Source: NSSO Reports 61st and 68th Rounds, Census of India.

An analysis across states shows that for Kerala, Uttarakhand, Karnataka, etc. even though the absolute magnitude of reduction is not large, it forms a substantial share of the agricultural workforce these states had in 2004–05. The analysis clearly highlights that between 2004–05 and 2011–12, a large percentage of the agricultural workforce across states moved away from agriculture.

Crop-wise Effect of Agriculture Labour Availability

The impact is more pronounced in case of certain crops which are labour intensive and are also widely grown in the country. A combination of these two factors highlights that paddy, wheat, cotton, sugarcane and groundnut are among the most likely crops to be affected by labour scarcity.

What Caused the Labour Crisis in Indian Agriculture?

Labour shortage is an economic condition in which there are insufficient qualified candidates (employees) to fill the market-place demands for employment at any price. Such a condition is sometimes referred to by economists as 'an insufficiency in the labour force'. The number of agricultural workers in rural India has declined sharply in the recent past, even as their proportion in the total workforce has been declining steadily. This trend is in conformity with the structural transformation the country has witnessed that is characterised by a decline in the share of agriculture in GDP and transfer of workers from farm to non-farm sectors.

There are two critical factors that affect the movement of labour away from the agriculture sector. They are pull and push factor.

Job Opportunities in Non-Agricultural Sector

The first is the 'pull' factor. With accelerated economic growth, job opportunities in non-agricultural sector are created much faster and this leads to a pull on labour away from agriculture to higher productive and higher paying manufacturing or services sector. According to a survey conducted in 2011 to assess the key reasons behind labour scarcity, 'higher wages in other locally available jobs' was ranked 'first' among various reasons identified. The survey reported that this was because higher wage rates prevailing in non-agricultural works like masonry, carpentry, electrical and plumbing which were locally available, attracted agricultural labourers. As the skill set required in agriculture is negligible, labour tend to adapt other skill sets if they get higher wages.

Agricultural Job as a Low-Esteem Job

Agricultural jobs being seasonal, labourers remain unemployed during lean season. This makes them seek a regular/permanent job that could provide them income throughout the year. This reason was ranked 'second'. Working as an agricultural labourer was considered as a low-esteem job in the rural areas and this reason was ranked 'third'. Out-migration due to improvement in educational status, migration to nearby town/city for higher wages, and migration to foreign countries were ranked the fourth, fifth, and sixth, respectively. A report in the *Economist* outlined how agriculture labourers were increasingly seeking jobs as 'security guards' in cities and towns, which besides giving them a higher wage also reduced their drudgery.

However, India's economic growth has lost its momentum signifying a low pull factor on labour away from agriculture. Moreover, in the non-agricultural sector, demand for labour has largely been informal in nature and mainly from small-scale enterprises. The proportion of informal labour and the small scale of employment (firm size) have also meant that productivity is relatively lower in India's non-agricultural sectors. In other words, the pull factor has not been strong. It can be much stronger if India embarks on a period of sustained high growth and reform its labour laws. While the trend of rural to urban migration is visible in India, the pace of migration has been quite slow, signifying slow, and low pull factors at work.

Social Welfare Programmes such as MGNREGA

Social welfare programmes such as MGNREGA (Mahatma Gandhi National Rural Employment Guarantee Act), has in effect been boosting rural incomes and incentives, thereby reducing the 'push' factor of movement away from agriculture. MGNREGA has broken the long stagnation in real wage rates in rural India and is contributing towards the goal of inclusive growth. Employment under this scheme during 2009–10 reached 13 per cent of the total scope for employment under this programme, which corresponds to about three per cent of the total labour supply of rural labour households. The expansion of MGNREGA is bound to cause a reduction in the availability of rural labour for other activities.

According to the rural residents, MGNREGA has two impacts on socio-economic status in rural areas, that is, positive and negative. Former impact of MGNREGA is that it increases bargaining power among the labourers and empowering the women in terms of wage rate (equal to men). The labourers are now not dependent on landlord's work and they do not need to leave the village for subsistence. Later, impact emphasise that it created labour shortage for agriculture and increased high wage rate in the rural areas due to minimum wage rate of ₹ 120–150 (depending on region/state).

Increased Literacy

Increased literacy among both males and females has been the other reason for workers quitting farming. The literacy rate for rural males has increased by eight percentage points and for females by 11 percentage points between 2004–05 and 2011–12. Literate youths normally prefer moving to non-farm sectors that pay higher wages.

Conclusion

In India, agriculture is the main sector, which has employed a major portion of its total workforce since a long time ago. However, the structural changes in the national and state economies, large-scale migration of labour from agriculture and operation of the rural development and poverty alleviation programmes have systematically reduced the relative importance of agriculture in labour allocation decisions of rural households. Consequently, there has been considerable reduction in labour supply to agriculture. Between 2004–05 and 2011–12 was the first instance of workforce reduction in agriculture declined by around 30.57 million in spite of the total size of workforce continued to increase.

Higher remuneration and growth of opportunities in alternate sectors is leading to the migration of workforce away from agriculture. This has resulted in labour shortage, increase in wages, and consequent escalation of cost of cultivation. Government schemes like MGNREGA are affecting labour adversely and need immediate policy interventions. Mechanisation in agriculture is the best alternative for labour shortage but it has some limitation such as costly, small land-holding, high maintenance charges, etc. Agriculture R&D has to play a vital role in terms of offering a substitute for labour in farm operations and in terms of offsetting cost-push inflation resulting from the structural shift in labour employment and rise in wages.

References

Census of India, (2011): Primary Census Abstracts, Registrar General of India, Ministry of Home Affairs, New Delhi.

Deshingkar, P. and Start, D., (2003): Seasonal Migration for Livelihoods, Coping, Accumulation and Exclusion. Working Paper No. 220, Overseas Development Institute, London.

FICCI, (2014): Labour in Indian Agriculture: A Growing Challenge, Report, http://ficci.in/spdocument/20550/FICCI-agri-Report%2009-03-2015.pdf

Gulati, A., Jain, S. and Satija, N., (2013): Rising Farm Wages in India: The 'Pull' and 'Push' Factors, Discussion Paper No. 5, Commission for Agricultural Costs and Prices, Department of Agriculture and Cooperation, Ministry of Agriculture, Government of India, New Delhi.

Hirway, I., (2012): Missing Labour Force: An Explanation, *Economic & Political Weekly*, Vol. 47, No. 37, pp. 67–72.

Kannan, K.P. and Raveendran, G., (2012): Counting and Profiling the Missing Labour Force, *Economic & Political Weekly*, Vol. 47, No. 6, pp. 77–80.

National Sample Survey Organisation (NSSO), (2013): Key Indicators of Employment and Unemployment in India, 2011-12, NSSO 68th Round, Ministry of Statistics and Programme Implementation, Government of India, New Delhi.

Rangarajan, C., Iyer, P. and Kaul, S., (2011): Where is the Missing Labour Force?, *Economic & Political Weekly*, Vol. 47, No. 39, pp. 68–72.

3 Crisis in India's Agriculture Sector

Are Solutions Elusive?

M. Devendra Babu

Introduction

India lives in villages and is predominantly an agrarian economy. Agriculture is the main source of livelihood for a vast majority of population even today. Employment in the agriculture sector in the total workers is more than 50 per cent. This sector is an important source of raw materials for industries. The major problems afflicting agriculture sector in India at the time of independence were: chronic food crisis, marginal and small farms, traditional farming system, low irrigation facilities, low productivity, lack of go-downs/storage facilities, marketing problems, lack of formal credit, and low rate of growth. Droughts and famines have been a way of life of people in many parts of our country. According to an estimate, 19 per cent of the total area of the country accounting for 12 per cent of the population is chronically subjected to drought (Planning Commission, 1973). Drought causes miseries to both human and animal population. The low and unstable agricultural productivity in drought areas is a major factor leading to regional imbalances. It is also a source of strain on the financial resources of the nation as the governments have to spend huge sums of money to provide relief to the affected population and animals.

The central and state governments have evolved a number of schemes and programmes since 1960s for the development of agriculture sector. All the Five-Year Plans have given top priority to this sector. These include providing infrastructure, inputs, credit, and minimum support price for the select produce. Over the years, it made tremendous progress benefiting not only those involved in the sector but also the country as a whole. In spite of a number of pro-agriculture schemes and progress made, it could not become economically viable and a sustainable source of livelihood for the people who depend on it.

This sector is presently passing through a difficult phase than ever before. It is facing multifarious problems and threatening the very foundations of the economy. The cultivators who were into this activity are showing a kind of negligence and gradually withdrawing from this occupation. The rural youths have been abandoning cultivation and set their eyes on jobs in towns and cities. The old generation who are still attached to agriculture are constantly encountering unprecedented risks and uncertainties. When unable to counter (and cannot) these risks and uncertainties, they resort to suicides. The new situations and problems have been afflicting this sector on an un-surmountable degree and yearning for lasting solutions.

Objective and Design of the Study

In the aforementioned background, this chapter broadly makes an attempt to critically review the situation of agriculture sector in India from independence time to present day. The specific objectives are as follows:

- To review the status, schemes and programmes adopted for development of agriculture in India in the post-independence period;
- to critically review the present challenges the agriculture sector is facing; and
- to make policy suggestions for a vibrant and sustainable agriculture sector.

The analysis is based on quantitative information. This again is based on secondary sources of information gathered from various published reports, particularly the government documents and reports. It is both descriptive and analytical study. The study is organised into four sections – after this section, the second section deals with the status and programmes evolved for the development of agriculture in India since independence; the third section evaluates the impact of various schemes and policies on the development of agriculture; and the last section brings out the challenges and measures needed to overcome the present problems in agriculture sector in India.

Status and Programmes for Agriculture Development

At the time of independence, India's agriculture sector was backward and primitive in nature. Droughts and famines were the common features. The infrastructure this sector needed was completely absent (Singh, 1975). It was largely dependent on monsoon rainfall. The credit facilities were very limited. The basic food-grain crops, such as cereals and pulses, were largely grown. Overall, the quantity of food grains produced was insufficient to meet the domestic requirement.

A report entitled 'India's Food Crisis and Steps to Meet It' (The Agricultural Production Team, 1959) had the following conclusions/recommendations:

- Population of 480 million by the end of 1966. Need to feed them. Food-grain production must be raised from 70 to 110 million tonnes by that time;
- from the effective combination of land, capital, and trained manpower resources will increase the food supply which India needs;
- output would be increased if scarce capital and trained manpower is concentrated in most-productive areas;

- an emergency programme is required; and
- an experimental intensified programme in each state to determine realistic food-production potentials.

As a response to the aforementioned, Government of India invited three American agricultural experts in the year 1959 for suggesting plan for increased food production in India. The experts suggested a 10-point pilot programme. The 10-point pilot programme was popularly known as 'Package Programme'. These 10-points of the programme were as follows:

- Price stabilisation – a guaranteed minimum price for grains should be established and published in advance;
- land reforms and food production;
- public works programme – land levelling, minor irrigation, etc. through Community Development Programme;
- cooperatives – the stranglehold of money lenders and traders must be broken, provide credit, marketing facilities, and supply inputs;
- extension work improvement through Community Development;
- soil and water conservation – hundreds of lakhs of good but unused land should be brought into production (total land area is 800 million acres of which 350 million is cropped). Irrigated land, now 51 million acres, could eventually be increased to 150 million acres;
- chemical fertilisers – procurement and production of fertilisers should be given high priority;
- improvement of cereal production;
- multiplication and distribution of improved seeds – only 15–20 per cent of cropped land is planted to improved varieties, thus vigorous seed production and distribution programme should be put into effect; and
- livestock development and food production – the better management of livestock.

To overcome the chronic food shortage and backwardness of agriculture and based on the aforementioned experts suggestions, the governments at the centre and states launched special schemes and programmes since 1960s. The immediate need then in front of India was to increase the food-grain production. The important programme launched in this direction was Intensive Agricultural Development Programme (IADP).

Intensive Agricultural Development Programme

Government of India accepted in general the recommendations of the team of American experts. A programme IADP was launched in 1960–61. The main objectives of IADP were as follows:

- To demonstrate, in pilot districts, the most effective ways of expanding national food production by cooperative effort between the centre, the state, the district, the block, the village, and the individual cultivators. Mainly a package of services to IADP districts (new inputs, credit, price assurance, fertiliser, improved seeds, plant protection programme, etc.) was proposed;

- to increase the income of the cultivator and his family;
- selection of favourable areas, maximum irrigation facilities and minimum natural hazards, providing adequate supply of fertilisers, credit, etc.;
- integrated and intensified approach to the problem of agricultural production;
- immediate goal of the programme sought to achieve rapid increase in the level of agriculture production through a package of services;
- provision for village planning for public works such as godowns, local roads, and minor irrigation (under CDP); and
- need for coordination by village, block, district, state, and centre for the use of all available resources was stressed (Sherman, 1968).

Small Farmers Development Agency

In 1969, the Reserve Bank of India had appointed a committee called the 'All India Rural Credit Review Committee' (Chairman: B Venkatappaiah). This committee recommended establishment of Small Farmers Development Agency (SFDA).

Marginal Farmers and Agricultural Labourers Development Agency was also established with SFDA to assist the marginal farmers and agricultural labourers in maximum productive use of their small holdings and skills by undertaking animal husbandry, horticulture, etc.

Drought Prone Area Programme was launched during fifth Five-Year Plan (1973–74). A special focus was given for the areas that were prone to frequent droughts. The schemes implemented under this scheme range from soil and water conservation, land levelling, and contour bunds. This scheme is still in vogue, of course with new nomenclature called Integrated Watershed Management Programme (Parikh, 1997).

Rastriya Krishi Vikas Yojana

Confronted with unstable food-grain production and an overall deceleration in the agriculture sector's growth, the then central government introduced a massive scheme called Rastriya Krishi Vikas Yojana (RKVY) in the years 2007–08 for a period of five years co-terminus with 11th Five-Year Plan. The major objective of this programme is to achieve a four per cent annual growth in the agricultural sector during 11th Five-Year Plan period by ensuring a holistic development of agriculture and allied sectors. This scheme is extended till the end of 12th Five-Year Plan period, that is, 2016–17 with an allocation of ₹ 63,246 crore. Under this scheme, the centre provides additional grants to states over and above the existing central schemes and funds. The states have to draw up integrated long-term plan along with vision document for agriculture and allied sectors. Keeping the objective of the scheme, the states prepared decentralised plans at the district level called Comprehensive District Agriculture Plan for agriculture and allied sectors for the 11th Five-Year Plan period 2007–08 to 2011–12. An increase in the agriculture sector's growth rate to 3.7 per cent during 11th Five-Year Plan compared to 2.4 per cent during 10th Five-Year Plan is attributed to the RKVY programme.

The other schemes such as subsidies on fertilisers, seeds and other inputs, and price support for select agriculture produce are all continuing. Efforts are being made to streamline the subsidies so that the real benefits reach the farmers than the intermediaries such as fertiliser companies.

Impact of Programmes and Policies on Agriculture Sector

As a result of implementation of various programmes, there were some improvements in the sector but many basic problems continued to exist. The areas where the sector had seen improvements and where the problems still persists are presented in the succeeding text.

The important variables such as net sown area, irrigated area, production, and yield of food grains over the years unfold the extent of progress made. In the total area, the net sown area was 118.75 million hectares (41.76%) during 1950–51, 143 million hectares (46.91%) in 1990–91, and in 2011–12 it stands at 140.8 million hectares (46.04%). With regard to irrigated area, there has been an increase from 20.85 million hectares in 1950–51 to 65.26 million hectares in 2011–12. In percentage terms, the share of net irrigated area to net sown area has increased from 17.56 per cent in 1950–51 to 33.58 per cent in 1990–91 and to 46.35 during 2011–12 (Table 1).

Table 1

Land Utilisation Pattern in India (in Million Hectares)

Classification of Land	*1950–51*	*1990–91*	*2011–12*
Geographical area	328.73	328.73	328.73
Reporting area for land utilisation	284.32	304.86	305.81
Forest	40.48	67.81	70.02
Not available for cultivation (area under non-agricultural uses + barren and un-cultivable land)	47.52	40.48	43.52
Other uncultivated land excluding fallow land (permanent pasture and other grazing land+ cultivable waste land + miscellaneous land)	49.45	30.22	26.10
Fallow lands	28.12	23.37	25.38
Net area sown	118.75	143.00	140.80
Total cropped area (gross cropped area)	131.89	185.74	195.25
Area sown more than once	13.15	42.74	54.44
Cropping intensity	111.07	129.89	138.67
Net irrigated area	20.85	48.02	65.26
Gross irrigated area	22.56	63.20	91.53

Source: Department of Agriculture and Co-operation, Directorate of Economics and Statistics, Ministry of Agriculture, Government of India (Agricultural Statistics at a Glance, 2014–15), pp. 300–03.

The information on area, production, and yield of food grains is given in Table 2. It can be seen from the table that the area under food grains during 1966–67 was 115 million hectares and the same has increased to 125 million hectares in 2011–12. Similarly, the production has also been increased from 95 million tonnes to 259 million tonnes in the aforementioned periods. The index of agricultural production (food grains), which is a measure of growth rate, reveals an upward movement over the years. The growth rate of food grains, which was 105.4 in the year 2007–08, went up to 123.3 in 2013–14 (Government of India, 2016–17). With respect to yield also, the same upward trend is observed. In the individual crops also, there has been expansion in the area, production, and yield. However, the area under cultivation was highest during 1990–91 (140 million hectares) and a decline to the extent of 15 million hectares is observed in the later years.

A positive development in the Indian agriculture is that the country with insufficient food grains in 1960s and depending on imports especially from the United States under PL 480 Act, thanks to the Green Revolution, now the country has adequate production to take care of all people.

Table 2

Area, Production, and Yield of Major Crops in India;
Area ('000 hectares); Production ('000 tonnes); Yield (kgs/hect.)

Crops	*Item*	*1966–67*	*1970–71*	*1980–81*	*1990–91*	*2000–01*	*2011–12*
Rice	Area	35,250.8	37,586.7	40,171.5	42,686.6	44,712.0	44,006.3
	Production	30,437.9	42,225.2	53,631.4	74,291.4	84,976.6	105,310.9
	Yield	863.5	1,123.4	1,335.1	1,740.4	1,900.5	2,393.1
Wheat	Area	12,837.6	18,240.5	22,278.8	24,167.1	25,730.5	29,864.8
	Production	11,392.8	23,832.5	36,312.6	55,134.5	69,680.8	94,882.1
	Yield	887.5	1,306.6	1,629.9	2,281.4	2,708.1	3,177.1
Total food grains	Area	115,299.9	124,310.7	126,674.5	140,427.5	121,048.0	124,754.9
	Production	95,019.4	108,421.0	129,585.7	182,493.1	196,813.8	259,323.2
	Yield	643.8	872.2	1,023.0	1,299.6	1,625.9	2,078.7
Total oilseeds	Area	15,945.6	16,494.4	17,602.5	24,147.5	22,769.9	26,308.2
	Production	6,575.4	9,540.2	9,373.1	18,608.7	18,439.9	29,798.7
	Yield	412.4	578.4	532.5	770.6	809.8	1,132.7
Sugarcane	Area	2,301.3	2,615.1	2,666.6	3,686.0	4,315.7	5,037.7
	Production	92,826.1	126,368.0	154,248.0	241,045.5	295,960.0	361,036.6
	Yield	40,336.4	48,322.4	57,844.4	65,394.9	68,577.5	71,667.6

Source: Directorate of Economics and Statistics (DES), Ministry of Agriculture, Government of India.

Relative Position

Let us see where India stands in regard to yield of food grains *vis-a-vis* other countries. Table 3 provides information on yield of certain food grains in different countries. Of the countries in the table, the yield of rice, wheat, and oilseeds per hectare were lower than the world average in 1980–81 and

2010–11. Of the various countries, India stands one above Africa from below. The yield of rice, wheat, and oilseeds per hectare in China was almost double to that in India in both the years. In this respect, India also badly compares with America and Europe.

Table 3

Yield Comparison among Countries/Regions: Rice, Wheat, and Oilseeds (quintals per hectare)

Countries/ Regions	*Rice*		*Wheat*		*Oilseeds*	
	1980–81	*2010–11*	*1980–81*	*2010–11*	*1980–81*	*2010–11*
China	41.4	65.5	18.9	47.5	11.0	21.2
India	20.0	32.6	14.4	28.3	4.9	10.0
Philippines	22.1	36.2	NA	NA	8.6	9.3
Africa	18.3	25.2	11.0	23.2	6.3	8.3
America	24.2	50.9	19.8	31.0	16.1	27.3
Asia	27.9	44.5	16.1	28.8	7.9	14.5
Europe	42.9	61.9	21.9	36.0	11.5	18.1
Oceania	49.9	93.4	9.8	16.7	8.2	12.7
World	27.5	43.7	18.6	30.0	11.9	20.4

Source: Kumar, 2013.

Another important indicator that is used to measure the status of food availability is per capita. Table 4 reveals the per capita food-grain availability in India over the years. The per capita food-grain availability in the year 1951 was 1,441.4 kg per year and it increased to 1,465.1 kg per year in 2013. A glance at the net availability of cereals reveals that over the years it almost remained stagnant. In fact, lesser per capita is witnessed since 2001 onwards. Similar pattern is observed in the case of pulses. Its lower per capita is observed since 1981 compared to previous years. The decline in the per capita food-grain availability is discernible since 2001 onwards. The decline in the net availability of cereals and pulses will have repercussion on food security aspect.

Table 4

Per Capita Net Availability of Cereals and Pulses in India (kg per year)

Year	*Cereals*	*Pulses*	*Food Grains*
1951	1,219.8	221.5	1,441.4
1961	1,458.9	251.8	1,710.7
1971	1,524.2	186.8	1,711.1
1981	1,523.1	136.8	1,660.0
1991	1,710.0	151.8	1,861.8
2001	1,409.6	109.5	1,519.1
2011	1,498.6	156.9	1,655.6
2013	1,307.0	158.0	1,465.1

Source: Department of Agriculture and Cooperation, Directorate of Economics and Statistics, Government of India.

There are ups and downs in the agriculture sector's growth over the years. In certain years, it witnessed negative growth. Overall, the growth of agriculture sector as compared to other sectors is very low. However, the growth rate of this sector picked up during XI plan period and the same uptrend is projected during 12th Five-Year Plan period. Any retard in the growth will have negative impact on the people and the economy (Table 5).

Table 5

Plan-wise Sectoral Growth Rates, 1997–2012 (in %)

Sector	*IX Plan (1997–2002)*	*X Plan (2002–2007)*	*XI Plan (2007–2012)*	*XII Plan (Projected)*
Agriculture, Forestry and Fishing	2.5	2.3	3.0	4.0
Mining and Quarrying	4.0	6.0	5.2	5.7
Industry	4.3	9.4	7.9	7.6
Services	7.9	9.3	10.1	9.0
Total GDP	5.5	7.8	8.2	8.0

Source: (1) Rural Development Statistics, Ministry of Rural Development, Government of India; (2) Planning Commission, 2013, 12th FYP-2012–17 (Vol. 2), Government of India.

Sectoral Contribution to GDP

The strength of the sector lies in its level of contribution to the total income of the country. In this respect, Table 6 provides information on sectoral contribution to gross domestic product (GDP). It can be seen from the table that the contribution of agriculture and allied activities to the GDP was very high compared to other two sectors till 1970–71. However, in the later years its contribution had declined drastically that is to 13.95 per cent in 2012–13 from the high of 35.69 per cent in 1980–81. Its share now is less than one-third of the share of 1951–52.

Table 6

Sector-wise Share to Total GDP (at 2004–05 prices)

Year	*Share to Total GDP*				*GDP Annual Growth Rate (in %)*			
	Agri-culture and Allied Activities	*Industry*	*Mining and Quarrying*	*Services*	*Agri-culture and Allied Activities*	*Industry*	*Mining and Quarrying*	*Services*
1951–52	51.45	16.69	2.02	29.63	1.49	5.50	12.33	2.67
1960–61	47.65	20.09	2.16	30.19	6.74	11.25	14.97	5.66
1970–71	40.85	24.62	2.48	33.28	6.43	7.46	4.94	5.16
1980–81	35.69	25.66	2.62	37.65	12.89	5.24	12.19	4.62
1990–91	29.53	27.63	3.48	42.55	4.02	7.33	10.46	5.19
2012–13	13.95	27.27	1.98	58.79	1.42	0.96	–2.16	6.96

Source: Planning Commission, Government of India.

Capital Formation in Agriculture Sector

Again, the growth of any sector depends on the quantum of investment made. In other words, the question is how much capital formation is taking place in the agricultural sector in India? Table 7 presents the gross capital formation in agriculture sector over the years. The table reveals that a drastic decline in the total capital formation (at constant prices) from a peak of 20.69 of GDP in 1993–94 to a low of 4.83 in 2010–11. The fall is seen in both public and private sectors. This would have negative impact on the growth of the sector.

Table 7

Gross Capital Formation in Agriculture and Allied Sectors as per cent of GDP

Year	*At Constant (2004–05) Prices*			*At Current Prices*		
	Public	*Private*	*Total*	*Public*	*Private*	*Total*
1993–94	10.96	27.99	20.69	6.15	12.34	9.77
2000–01	5.21	15.22	12.17	5.60	12.81	10.69
2005–06	6.80	7.16	7.07	7.64	8.15	8.03
2010–11	3.29	5.31	4.83	5.70	8.51	7.82

Source: Central Statistics Office (CSO), Government of India.

Employment in Agriculture Sector

Coming to the number of people engaged in agriculture sector in India, Table 8 unfolds that of the total workers (main + marginal) nearly 70 per cent (cultivators and agricultural labourers) were engaged in this sector during 1961. The same declined to 55 per cent in 2011. It brings out the fact that this sector still provides employment more than the other two sectors.

Table 8

Share of Workers in Agriculture Sector in India – 1961 and 2011

Category of Workers	*1961*		*2011*	
	Number	*%*	*Number*	*%*
Cultivators and agriculture labourers	13,09,92,268	69.52	26,30,22,473	54.60
Other workers	5,74,25,184	30.48	21,87,20,838	45.40
Total workers	18,84,17,452	100.00	48,17,43,311	100.00

Source: Census of India, 1961 and 2011.

Another relevant issue with regard to development of agriculture sector is land holdings and area owned across different classes. The information on this is presented in Table 9. It can be seen from the table that the number of land holdings are high at marginal and small category, and the trend has been increasing except in small category during 2010–11. On the other hand, the area owned by these two categories is very negligible even during 2010–11. A small number under large category owns large area.

Table 9

Number of Land Holdings and Average Size of Holdings in India

Size Groups	Number of Holdings (in '000)				Average (in Ha.)			
	1970–71	1990–91	2000–01*	2010–11	1970–71	1990–91	2000–01*	2010–11
Marginal	36,200	63,389	75,408	92,826	0.40	0.39	0.40	0.39
	(50.98)	(59.44)	(62.88)	(67.10)				
Small	13,432	20,092	22,695	24,779	1.44	1.43	1.42	1.42
	(18.92)	(18.84)	(18.92)	(17.91)				
Semi-medium	10,681	13,923	14,021	13,896	2.81	2.76	2.72	2.71
	(15.04)	(13.06)	(11.69)	(10.04)				
Medium	7,932	7,580	6,577	5,875	6.08	5.9	5.81	5.76
	(11.17)	(7.11)	(5.48)	(4.25)				
Large	2,766	1,654	1,230	973	18.1	17.33	17.12	17.38
	(3.90)	(1.55)	(1.03)	(0.70)				

Notes: 1. * Excluding Jharkhand state; 2. The figures in parentheses are percentages; 3. Marginal (less than 1 hectare), small (1–2 hectares), semi-medium (2–4 hectares), medium (4–10 hectares), and large (10 hectare and above).

Source: Department of Agriculture and Cooperation, Agricultural Census Report, 2010–11, Government of India.

Challenges and Solutions

The agricultural sector with a pathetic situation at the time of independence – famines and droughts, scarcity of food grains, starvation, and hunger moved a long way in erasing these stigmas. The remarkable performance made over the years, however, could not mitigate the inherent problems of the sector. With all the improvements in infrastructure facilities, and overall development in agriculture sector, the life of the farmer could not be made happy. This means the challenges that persist in the sector continue to be unresolved. The problems that existed at the time of independence at least some of them still persist. The schemes and programmes evolved then have been continued with more vigour and with different nomenclatures even today. The agricultural growth rate has been volatile over the years and in certain years, it was very negligible. Again, on the one hand, the total food-grain production has been increasing, and on the other, the net availability has been declining. The contribution of this sector to GDP in recent decades has been very low and, on the other hand, the proportion of people engaged in this sector is very high. This sector over the years is not getting due importance in terms of investment both from public and private as compared to manufacturing and service sectors.

India has grown tremendously in the areas of knowledge, science and technology, financial resources, planning, management, and institutions. With all these strategic strengths, is it not possible to overcome the present crisis manifesting the agriculture sector in India? Certainly, it is possible to overcome the present difficulties of the agriculture sector. In this direction, the following measures need to be considered and earnestly implemented on a priority basis.

India needs food security. It has to maintain higher food-grain production. However, there are signs of declining net sown area. Chand (2014) maintains that there is a need to study whether this is perennial and going to be aggravated or casual in certain years. It would be disaster if measures were not taken earnestly to arrest decline in the net sown area. Here comes the question of impact of various schemes such as wasteland development on the expansion of area under cultivation, watershed programme on conserving water, and to cope with droughts and famines. A thorough review is required on the efficacy of these programmes. If no substantive outcomes forthcoming from these, then it is time to evolve appropriate schemes and programmes.

Even after planned development of more than 65 years, 54 per cent of agricultural area is rainfed. The monsoon rains are erratic and it is difficult for the farmers to cope with the failure of rain. The need is to go for permanent irrigation facilities for dry land areas. In the late 1970s, there was a discussion on linking rivers of northern India with that of south Indian rivers (Ganga to Cauvery) and it was also called 'Garland Canal'. The project could not take concrete shape because of two main reasons – one, the unfavourable topography and two, requirement of huge financial resources. With the advancement of science and technology, it would be possible to overcome the hurdles of topographical problems. Furthermore, the fiscal resources of both centre and states have increased tremendously in recent years. With these major advantages, the governments at the centre and states should think seriously of linking rivers from north to south and thus bring more and more dry land area under assured irrigation.

Connected to the aforementioned issue is that the water use practices in India is very poor and inefficient. Water is wasted grossly. A few crops such as paddy and sugarcane consume most of the available water leaving little to other crops thus perpetuating inequity in the water availability. Priority should be given to optimise water use through drip and sprinkler systems on a large scale. Besides, the traditional water bodies, such as ponds, tanks, streams, and the canals, need to be rejuvenated not only to impound water but also for the purpose of percolation along the water routes.

The majority of land holdings are marginal and small. The average size of land is 1–2 acres and from this, there is no guarantee of providing required number of days of employment and income for the family. It is also a problem to make interventions to enhance productivity in such small size holdings. Thus there is need to arrest further sub-division of holdings on the one hand and on the other, a system of cooperative farming in the villages have to be encouraged.

Cropping pattern is another problem. There is no scientific cropping pattern followed in India. There is no proper information dissemination to farmers with regard to demand – supply of agriculture items, international requirements, etc. The cultivation of same crop over the years led to deterioration of soil health leading to low yield. As seen earlier, the yield of certain crops is far below that of China, America, and other European countries. The need is to enhance the productivity. So many interventions are required in this aspect. By effective use of information communication and technology, it is possible to manage the cropping pattern, production levels, etc. This has to be streamlined and strengthened to overcome fluctuations in the production levels and the resultant volatility in the prices.

Among many problems of agriculture sector, the most important in recent times is volatility in prices of the produce. The policy of support prices for certain agricultural commodities is not at all helping the farmers. What is needed is to integrate post-harvest processing with the production process, so that there will be value enhancement, which benefits everyone in the chain link. If a portion of the people engaged in agriculture is absorbed and used in the post-harvest production process would relieve the labour force from this sector thus enhancing the incomes of the farmers. Furthermore, expansion and sustainability of non-farm activities in both rural and urban areas is also merits immediate consideration.

Indebtedness of farmers is another cause of concern which, of late, pushing them to suicides. As per National Crime Registration Bureau between 1995 and 2010 about 256,913 farmers committed suicides in the country (Rao, 2012). In spite of widespread presence of banking and financial institutions in the country, access to institutional credit by cultivators is abysmally low at around 12.33 per cent in the year 2011.

In most of the states after decentralisation of governance, most of the state functions including agricultural activities have been transferred to local governments. The development plans that the local governments prepare at present leave much to be desired. They hardly prepare a perspective and integrated plan. There is no vision document. These local governments allocate the scarce funds on a large number of schemes/projects whose utility is short term. The only once where a medium-term plan was prepared by the local governments was for the 11th Five-Year Plan period. This was not continued for the 12th Five-Year Plan. This means falling back on bureaucratic system rather than placing primacy on local institutions and people. Hence, importance has to be given for bottom-up participatory planning. Furthermore, knowledge is very important. However, knowledge building at the grassroot level is not given priority so far in India. The governments especially the panchayats have to take up knowledge/capacity building on a massive scale among the farmers and youths in the villages. For this, the forums such as *grama sabha*, self-help groups, cooperatives, and agricultural universities have to be engaged.

References

Chand, R., (2014): Agricultural Growth, Farmers' Income and Nutrition Security: Linkages and Challenges, Professor L.S. Venkataramanan Memorial Lecture-12, Institute for Social and Economic Change, Bengaluru.

Government of India, (2014–15): Economic Survey - 2014–15, New Delhi.

——, (2016–17): Economic Survey - 2016–17, New Delhi.

Kumar, P., (2013): *Demand and Supply of Agricultural Commodities in India*, Macmillan India, New Delhi.

Parikh, K.S., (1997): *India Development Report, 1997*, Oxford University Press, New Delhi.

Planning Commission, (1973): Task Force on Integrated Rural Development, Government of India, New Delhi.

Rao, P.S.M., (2012): Rural Credit Not Reached the Poor (in Kannada), Vijaya Karnataka, Bengaluru.

Sherman, E.J., (1968): The IADP Path to Intensive Agricultural Development, The Ford Foundation, New Delhi.

Singh, S.K., (1975): *The Indian Famine 1967: A Study in Crisis and Change*, People's Publishing, New Delhi.

The Agricultural Production Team, (1959): Report on India's Food Crisis and Steps to Meet It, The Ford Foundation (Chairman: Sherman E. Johnson).

4 How to Accelerate Pulse Production in India?

Amarnath Tripathi and Udita Mehta

Introduction

There is a plethora of literature suggesting adverse impact of climate change on agriculture (Gupta et al., 2014; Jha and Tripathi, 2011; Rosenzweig and Parry, 1994; Mendelsohn et al., 1994). Almost each aspect of impact of climate change on agriculture, for example, agriculture as a whole, different crops, different sub-sectors of agriculture like livestock, fisheries, etc. as well as differential impact across regions, mitigation, and adaptation to climate change, etc. has been studied. In the case of pulses, most of the studies talk about its role in adapting agriculture to climate change because pulses do not require nitrogen, which reduces demand for nitrogen fertiliser and reduced demand helps to reduce production of nitrogen fertiliser which, in turn, decreases emissions of greenhouse gases and consumption of energy (FAO, 2016). Likewise, pulses fix nitrogen in the soil which, in turn, increases soil fertility and shrinks demand for nitrogen fertiliser generated from other crops (FAO, 2016; Gan et al., 2011) estimated that durum wheat preceded by a biological nitrogen-fixing crop, such as chickpeas or lentils, lowered its carbon footprint by 17 per cent compared with durum preceded by a cereal crop. The impact was even found stronger in a pulse-pulse wheat system, with the carbon footprint of the durum wheat down by 34 per cent compared to a traditional cereal-cereal – durum rotation.

Nevertheless, assessing impact of climate change on pulses particularly focusing on India where pulses are considered a good source of proteins for humans because of vegetarian dietary pattern of the majority of the population in the country. It is even more interesting to be noted that protein deficiency in Indians has rising trend (Tripathi and Srivastava, 2011). Hence, there is an enormous pressure on increasing pulse production in India from both health and food consumption perspectives.

Figure 1

Pulse Acreage in India Since 1950

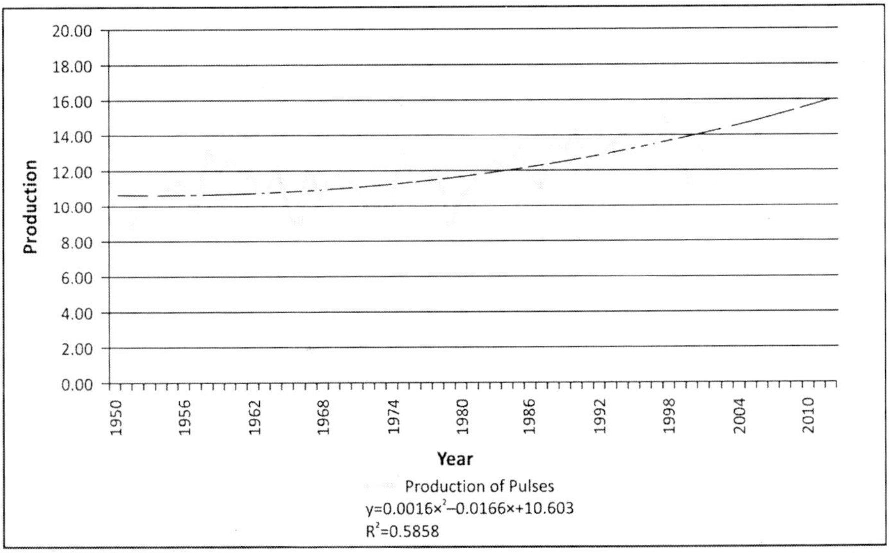

For last two decades, both pulse acreage and production in India have not increased substantially. Starting from the year 1950, the area under pulse seems to have increased but the rate of this increase is falling steadily, as is reflected from Figure 1. Cultivated area under pulses was about 19 million hectare in 1950 and it increased to 26 million hectare in 2011. It indicates a marginal increase in pulse acreage, which is result of the Green Revolution and its biasedness towards wheat and rice. In the mid 1960s, the new High Yielding Variety (HYV) seed for wheat was introduced in India, which led to the expansion of the area sown under wheat. In economic analysis, land is a fixed factor of production, hence if area under a particular crop increases, it would lead to a fall in the area of some other crop. In case of wheat, a large part of this expansion came at the expense of pulses and a very small extent at the expense of winter rice and Barley (Ryan and Asokan, 1977). Similarly, the production of pulses has been increasing but at a decreasing rate (Figure 2). From 1997 onwards, the rate of increase has a significant decline, which again lends evidence to the fact that Green Revolution has had an adverse effect on the growth of pulses. The HYV variety of seeds of wheat acted somehow as a direct disincentive for the farmers to undertake the production of any other crop than cereals.

Stagnancy in cultivated area under pulses could be understood as land is limited resource and cannot be increased beyond a limit. Therefore, yield becomes important factor to be considered to escalate pulse production. Nevertheless, yield of pulses in India is lower than the most of countries like China, Brazil, Nigeria, Thailand, Myanmar, etc. (Government of India, 2016). Within the country, yield of both rice and wheat has increased by more than double during the period from 1970–71 to 2013–14, while average yield of pulses has

Figure 2

Pulse Production in India Since 1950

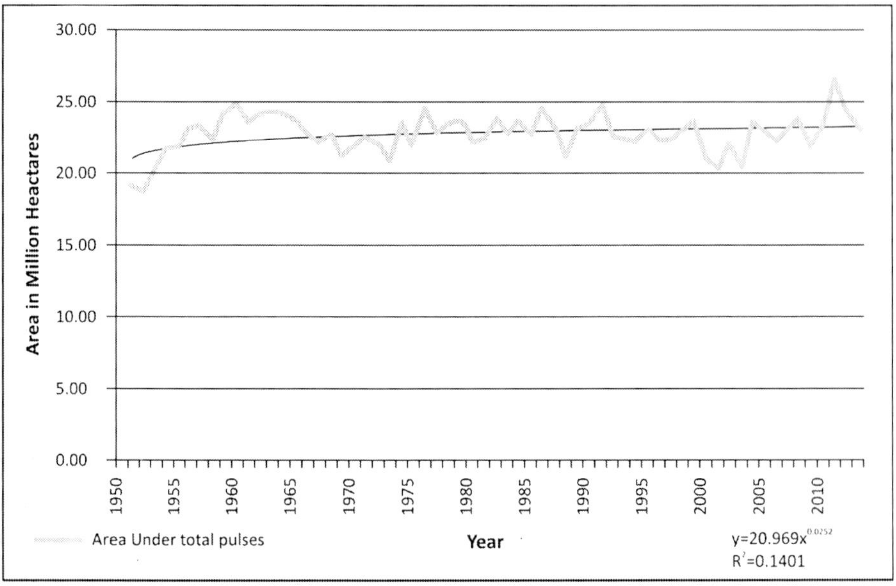

increased by 46 per cent only during the aforementioned period (Government of India, 2016). Low yield in pulses is mainly attributed by the fact that pulses are largely grown in unirrigated and dry-land areas. Economic theories suggest that yield could be increased either through technological progress or using inputs efficiently or both. Technological progress depends on innovations and technological transmission; those themselves depend on certain factors and conditions such as investment in agriculture research and development, etc. Henceforth, simplest and the most feasible policy option to increase production is to improve technological efficiency.

Technical efficiency in production of pulses particularly in India is likely to depend on changes in climatic factors because these are largely grown in unirrigated conditions in the country. It is interesting to note that irrigated area under cereals increased from about 16 million ha in 1950–51 to around 60 million ha in year 2011–12, while in the same period, irrigated area under pulses has increased to about 4 million ha from around 2 million ha (Figure 3).

Pressure on increasing production of pulses and their high dependency on rainfall motivates to study production efficiency of pulses in view of climate change. Such study will provide policy inputs to increase pulse production and to make its production resilient to climate change as well. In this backdrop, the present study makes an attempt to estimate technical efficiency in cultivation of two major Indian pulses, namely, Tur (Pigeon Pea) and Gram (Chickpea) separately, using stochastic frontier approach. The stochastic frontier function is estimated twice for each crop – first without climatic factors and then considering climatic factors (rainfall and temperature) as input in stochastic function.

Figure 3

Irrigated Area of Different Crop Groups in India Since 1950

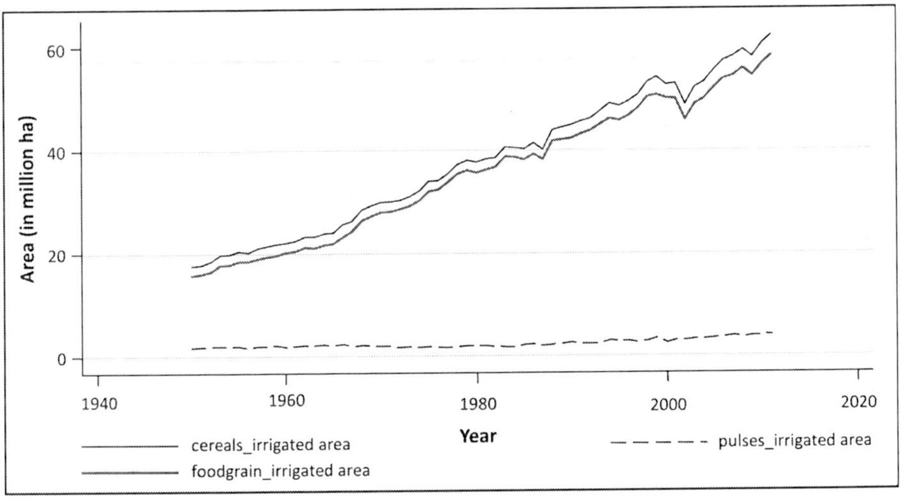

Source: Authors' calculation based on data collected from government publication entitled *Agricultural Statistics at a Glance* published by the Directorate of Economics and Statistics, Ministry of Agriculture and Farmers' Welfare, GoI, India.

Technical efficiencies estimated from both the situations are compared for each crop to see if climate factors contribute to production inefficiency significantly. This chapter adopts time-varying inefficiency model proposed by Battese and Coelli (1995). Panel data covering four Indian states (Bihar, Madhya Pradesh, Rajasthan, and Uttar Pradesh) for gram and three states (Gujarat, Madhya Pradesh, and Uttar Pradesh) for tur for the periods between 1996–97 and 2013–14 are used for estimation of technical efficiency. Crops, states, and period of the study are chosen based on criterion of data availability.

The rest of the parts of the chapter are divided into three sections that are discussed as: Section II presents theoretical model, methods, specification of variables, data, and sources of data. Section III describes results and gives arguments in favour of the results in order to validate key findings based on observations collected from preliminary interactions with farmers and previous literatures as well. Section IV concludes whole study and discusses policy implications based on the findings

Methods and Data

Two-stage framework is applied in this chapter – first, technical efficiency is calculated using the stochastic frontier function with and without climatic factors and then, estimated technical inefficiencies are compared. The chapter uses panel data approach and follows Battese and Coelli (1995) in order to estimate stochastic frontier production function. Cobb-Douglas production function is considered for estimation of stochastic frontier function because of its simplicity other well-known properties (see Handerson and Quandt, 1971, for its properties). Information on all variables is available in ratio, for example, output is available in terms of quantity of output produced in single unit of land. Similarly, inputs are also available in terms of quantity of inputs consumed in single unit of land. Land being a constant factor brings in the short run condition of law of variable proportions, which makes the variables insignificant after a certain point of time. To overcome this problem, one can suggest the use of information on acreage and multiply it with all variables. However, it would not be the best solution as existing information on acreage is collected based on census while information on variables used in this chapter area collected-based sample. Hence, to find the best solution of the aforementioned problem, we impose the restriction of constant returns to scale in estimation of production function.

Source of Data and Period of the Study

This study is based on two sets of data – the first set of data includes output of two pulses (tur and gram) and inputs used in production of these pulses, and the second set of data comprises of climatic factors (rainfall and temperatures). The first set of data were collected from Cost of Cultivation of Principal Crops in India (CCI) published by the Directorate of Economics and Statistics (DES), Ministry of Agriculture and Farmers' Welfare, Government of India; however, the second set of data were composed from data archives provided by Indian Institute of Tropical Meteorology, Pune. The DES compiles cost data for principal crops collected from the Commission of Agriculture Cost and Prices (CACP) for certain period of time in CCI and publishes this volume with some time interval. The first volume was brought out in 1991 and since then total four volumes have been published. The first volume provides information for the period from 1970–71 to 1990–91. The second volume provides information for years after 1991–92 and up to year. The third volume provides information up to year 1996–97. The fourth volume contains information for the period 1996–97 to 2003–04. Information after 2003–04 gathered in this study are collected from Price Policy Report published by the CACP.

In order to assess production efficiency in pulses, two major pulses (tur and gram) cultivated in India were chosen. For gram, a panel of four states, namely, Bihar, Madhya Pradesh, Rajasthan, and Uttar Pradesh was chosen, while a group of three states, namely, Gujarat, MP, and UP was selected for tur crop. Time period for the empirical analysis is decided from 1996–97 to 2013–14. All the aforementioned selections are based on criterion of data availability. We select those crops and states for which required data are available constantly for the study period. Year 1996–97 is chosen as beginning year of the study period because all required data are consistently available since this year and these are available till year 2013–14, hence it is chosen as end year of the study period. Years before 1996–97, required information are missing in the publication entitled 'Cost of Cultivation of Principal Crops in India' for some years for each selected state.

Results and Discussions

Descriptive Analyses

Among four selected states, gram yield is the highest in Uttar Pradesh, but it has been more stable in Madhya Pradesh compared to other states for the study period from 1995–96 to 2013–14 (Table 1). The table illustrates that input use is also the maximum in Uttar Pradesh in all inputs except for fertiliser, animal labour, and irrigation. These are found the highest use in Madhya Pradesh. Input use is the lowest in Rajasthan in all inputs except for irrigation. It could be because of arid and semi-arid climate of Rajasthan. In the case of tur, Uttar Pradesh again stood first in tur yield, while it is found lowest in Madhya Pradesh among selected states (Table 1). More inputs are used in Gujarat compared to other selected states; however, tur yield in the state is marginally lower than that in Uttar Pradesh. It suggests soil characteristics like fertility, etc. are better in Uttar Pradesh than Madhya Pradesh. Yield of other foodgains like rice, wheat, etc. is also higher in Uttar Pradesh. High crop yield in the state is attributed to soil fertility and availability of irrigation facility. About 77 per cent of total cultivated area is irrigated in Uttar Pradesh, this figure is about 67 per cent, 48 per cent, 36.5 per cent, and 36.3 per cent in Bihar, Gujarat, Madhya Pradesh, and Rajasthan, respectively (Government of India, 2016).

Table 1

Average Yield and Average of Inputs Used in Gram and Tur Production in Selected Indian States for the Period 1995–96 to 2013–14

Variable	*Bihar*	*Madhya Pradesh*	*Rajasthan*	*Uttar Pradesh*	*Gujarat*	*Madhya Pradesh*	*Uttar Pradesh*
	Gram				*Tur*		
Yield (kg/ha)	9.32	10.00	7.35	10.39	8.66	7.30	9.00
	(2.46)	(0.99)	(1.62)	(1.86)	(1.82)	(1.48)	(1.63)
Seed (kg)	72.75	87.16	57.16	91.25	12.00	20.22	62.11
	(7.52)	(3.49)	(4.09)	(6.03)	(1.78)	(2.06)	(194.12)
Fertiliser (kg)	34.50	34.60	11.49	24.68	71.03	18.85	6.36
	(11.45)	(4.58)	(6.06)	(11.93)	(20.92)	(11.15)	(9.81)
Manure (kg)	4.33	17.61	5.78	79.28	2,310.22	536.06	81.50
	(15.25)	(30.87)	(15.00)	(90.18)	(1,696.50)	(518.50)	(97.39)
Human labour (h)	290.69	260.62	248.35	369.18	682.82	415.24	550.78
	(54.24)	(22.44)	(43.06)	(45.44)	(102.88)	(54.85)	(65.61)
Animal labour (min)	1,096.80	1,741.17	940.90	1,608.33	4,309.97	3,310.90	1,390.87
	(1,143.69)	(960.64)	(631.76)	(1,170.90)	(1,268.33)	(1,524.35)	(689.71)
Irrigation	2.47	6.08	7.97	4.45	3.70	0.47	1.90
	(3.68)	(2.08)	(4.88)	(1.91)	(2.28)	(0.43)	(1.57)
Machine	15.46	14.87	11.86	15.39	10.57	7.28	10.69
	(6.74)	(2.68)	(1.96)	(6.21)	(4.00)	(3.91)	(1.48)

Econometric Analyses

The time trend variable accounts for Hicksian neutral technological change. The value of its coefficient in both the cases is very small and statistically insignificant, indicating poor technological progress over the 18-year period in the case of pulses in India. Since technical progress is very slow, significant growth in output per hectare is mainly accounted by growth in inputs. However, most of the inputs are not found statistically significant, affecting to output per hectare in both the pulses as coefficients of most of inputs are statistically insignificant. Only parameter of seed, animal labour, and irrigation is found statistically significant in the case of Chickpea, while coefficient of human labour and machine is statistically significant in the case of Pigeon Pea. The signs of the coefficients of the aforementioned inputs are as expected, with the exception of the negative estimate of the animal labour in the case of Chickpea.

In stochastic frontier function estimated for both Chickpea and Pigeon Pea separately, the value of η is found negative in both the cases. It infers that the degree of inefficiency increases over time in both pulses in India. The magnitude of η is found much higher in the case of Chickpea compared to Pigeon Pea. It means inefficiency in production of Chickpea is increasing over time with faster rate than that in Pigeon Pea. In addition, the estimate of η is found statistically significant in the case of Chickpea, implies that the inefficiency effects are significant in determining level and variability of output of Chickpea per hectare. Trend of technical efficiency presented in Figures 2 and 3 for Chickpea and Pigeon Pea, respectively, collaborates the estimates of in η both the cases. Both figures illustrate that technical efficiency of production of both Chickpea and Pigeon Pea has been declining for the period from 1995–96 to 2013–14. Declining trend in technical efficiency is consistently observed for both pulses and each select state in India.

Climate change could be a possible reason behind the aforementioned decrease in technical efficiency in pulses as these crops highly depend on rainfall. We noted earlier that very small chunk of irrigated area is devoted to pulses, while sensitivity of crop productivity to precipitation depends on irrigation (Mondel et al., 2015). A significant increasing trend in annual mean, maximum, and minimum temperatures has been observed in recent years across the country and increasing trend found more widespread in the country during recent years compared to previous years (Kothawale et al., 2010). Similarly, rainfall variability, both temporally and spatially, increases over time in India. Importance of rainfall for pulse cultivation could be observed from recent statistics on cultivated area provided by the Ministry of Agriculture and Farmer's Welfare, Government of India – it says that pulse acreage during monsoon season of 2016 has increased to 142 million hectare from 102 million hectare during the same season in 2015. Almost 40 per cent increase in pulse acreage in India is largely determined by the rainfall as India has received good monsoon rainfall during the current year.

Keeping the aforementioned views in mind, the present chapter attempts to examine if changing climatic factors contributes to technical inefficiency significantly in pulses in India. To accomplish this, technical efficiency is estimated again by controlling impact of climatic factors in stochastic production frontier. New estimates of stochastic production function presented in third and fifth columns of Table 2 indicate adverse impact of climatic factors on output of both pulses. The results show that rainfall has positive and statistically significant impact on production of Pigeon Pea. It is grown in monsoon season in India and hence good rain during monsoon season has good chance to increase its production. Negative and statistically significant impact of maximum temperature was found in case of both the pulses. However, it is observed that minimum temperature has positive impact on production of both the pulses.

Table 2

Estimates of Stochastic Production Frontiers

Variables	*Tur*		*Gram*	
	Without Climatic Factors	*With Climatic Factors*	*Without Climatic Factors*	*With Climatic Factors*
Intercept	-1.60	-0.14	**-1.85**	**-1.62**
Lnseed	-0.03	-0.01	**0.99**	**1.21**
Lnfertiliser	0.01	-0.004	-0.03	-0.05
Lnhumanlabour	**0.42**	**0.41**	0.11	0.03
Lnanimallabour	0.08	0.05	**-0.07**	**-0.06**
Lnmanure	-0.01	-0.01	0.01	0.01
Lnirrigation	-0.05	-0.02	**0.02**	**0.03**
Lnmachine	**0.21**	**0.21**	-0.07	-0.04
Time trend	0.01	0.01	0.002	-0.01
State dummy	0.09	0.03	-0.02	-0.01
Rainfall	-	**0.22**	-	-0.03
Minimum temperature	-	3.73	-	**0.48**
Maximum temperature	-	**-4.24**	-	**-0.55**
μ	0.05	0.21	-117.51	-127.71
η	-0.41	-0.31	**-1.41**	**-1.64**
Ln (σ_S^2)	**-3.09**	**-3.07**	3.67	3.66
Inverse logit of γ	-1.09	**-0.46**	**7.88**	**8.01**
$\sigma_S^2 = \sigma_u^2 + \sigma_v^2$	0.05	0.05	39.18	38.96
$\gamma = \dfrac{\sigma_u^2}{\sigma_S^2}$	0.25	0.39	1.00	1.00
σ_u^2	0.01	0.02	39.17	38.95
σ_v^2	0.03	0.03	0.01	0.01
Observations	54.00	54	72.00	72
Wald chi^2 (9)	**22.50**	**34.47**	**174.90**	**214.96**
Log likelihood	14.12	18.42	44.52	49.47

Figure 4

Trend of Technical Efficiency for Chickpea

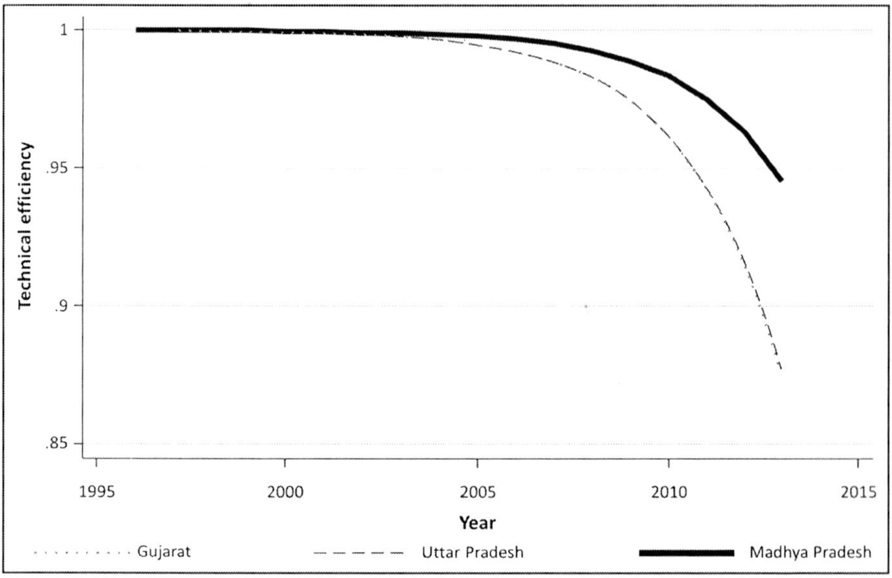

Figure 5

Trend of Technical Efficiency for Pigeon Pea

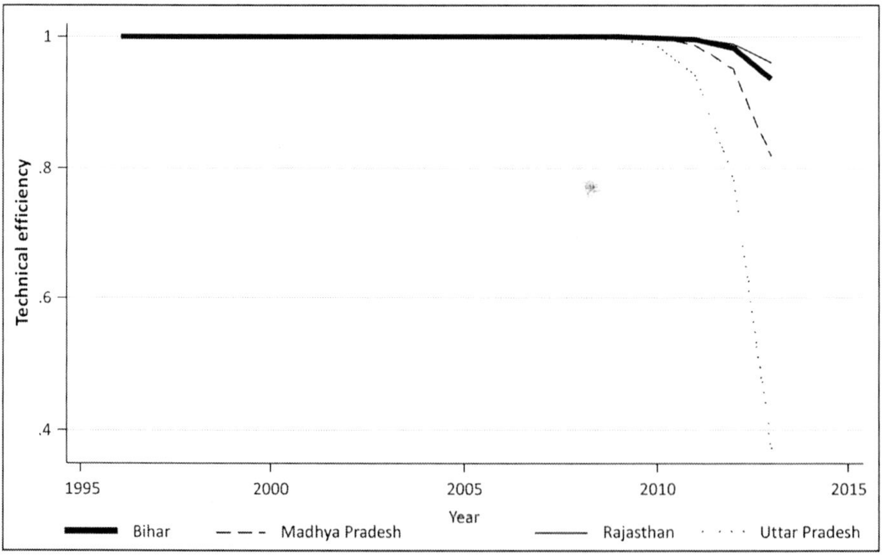

Conclusions

In this chapter, we have done two types of analyses. First, we have estimated the technical efficiency for gram and tur separately using the stochastic frontier analysis. Second, we have regressed this estimated technical efficiency on the climatic variables such as climate and rainfall. We found out that the state with the highest input use has the highest yield in case of Gram. Uttar Pradesh is the highest yielding state for Gram. However, the yield is more stable for Madhya Pradesh because of abundance of inputs like fertiliser, animal labour, and irrigation, irrigation being the most important one. Rajasthan has the lowest yield of gram. The reason for this can be attributed to climatic and soil conditions prevailing in the state. Uttar Pradesh also dominated tur yield even the input use was better in Gujarat because of better irrigation practices in Uttar Pradesh.

Pulses on the whole have shown poor technological progress. This signifies a lack of research and innovation in case of pulses leading to a poor yield. This result holds true for both the pulses. It was also observed that not all the inputs are significant in the pulse yield. Only seed, animal labour, and irrigation is found statistically significant in the case of Gram and human labour and machine is statistically significant in the case of tur.

The efficiency in production of both the crops has been falling significantly in the selected period but the efficiency of gram has been falling at a faster rate than the efficiency of tur. It must be noted that our results suggest a strong significance of technical efficiency. Lastly, we have tried to estimate the impact of climate change on technical efficiency. It can be said that climate is one of the major reason for the falling technical efficiency. The increasing temperatures have a significant impact on the rainfall patterns. Pulses, as we know are a rainfed crop and any changes in the climatic patterns would be directly reflected in the yield of the crop.

Not only this, the current scenario calls for better irrigation technology, soil conservation, and better agricultural practices as they seem to be directly effecting the crop productivity. Farmers need to be made aware of the role of climatic and environmental factors in increasing or decreasing the crop yield in any period of time. In a country with huge dependence on agriculture sector, a falling technical efficiency is for sure a signal of future problems to be encountered.

References

Battese, G.E. and Coelli, T.J., (1995): A Model for Technical Inefficiency Effects in a Stochastic Frontier Production Function for Panel Data, *Empirical Economics*, Vol. 20, pp. 325–332.

FAO, (2016): Pulses are Praised for Their Health, Environmental and Economic Benefits. How Can Their Full Potential be Tapped?, Proceedings, www.fao.org/fsnforum/sites/default/files/files/128_pulses/PROCEEDINGS.

Ford, J.E. and Hewitt, D. (1979): Protein Quality in Cereals and Pulses, *British Journal of Nutrition*, Vol. 42, No. 2, p. 325.

Gan, Y., Liang, C., Wang, X. and McConkey, B., (2011): Lowering Carbon Footprint of Durum Wheat by Diversifying Cropping Systems, *Field Crops Research*, Vol. 122, No. 3, pp. 199–206.

Government of India, (2016): Agricultural Statistics at a Glance 2015, Ministry of Agriculture and Farmers' Welfare, GoI, New Delhi.

Gupta, S., Sen, P. and Srinivasan, S., (2014): Impact of Climate Change on the Indian Economy: Evidence from Food Grain Yields, *Climate Change Economics*, Vol. 5, No. 2.

Handerson, J.M. and Quandt, R.E., (1971): *Microeconomic Theory: A Mathematical Approach* (2nd Ed.), McGraw Hill Company Limited, New York, USA.

Jha, B. and Tripathi, A., (2011): Isn't Climate Change Affecting Wheat Productivity in India. *Indian J. Agric. Econ.* 66 (3), 353-364.

Kothawale, D.R., Munot, A.A. and Krishna Kumar, K., (2010): Surface Air Temperature Variability Over India During 1901-2007, and Its Association with ENSO, *Climate Research*, Vol. 42, pp. 89-104.

Mendelsohn, R., Nordhaus, W.D. and Shaw, D., (1994): The Impact of Global Warming on Agriculture: A Ricardian Analysis, *The American Economic Review*, Vol. 84, No. 4, pp. 753-771.

Mondal, M.M.A., Fakir, M.S.A., Nurul Islam, M. and Samad, M.A., (2011): Physiology of Seed Yield in Mungbean: Growth and Dry Matter Production. *Bangladesh Journal of Botany*, Vol. 40, pp. 133-138.

Rosenzweig, C. and Parry, M.L., (1994): Potential Impact of Climate Change on World Food Supply, *Nature*, Vol. 367, No. 6459, pp. 133-138.

Ryan, J.G. and Asokan, M., (1977): Effect of Green Revolution in Wheat on Production of Pulses and Nutrients in India. *Indian Journal of Agricultural Economics*, 32 (3). pp. 8-15.

Tripathi, Amarnath and Srivastava, Shraddha (2011): Inter-state Migration and Changing Food Preferences in India, *Ecology of Food and Nutrition* Vol. 50, Issue 5, pp. 410-428.

5 Proprietary Rights, Landlordism, and a Development Discourse

The Past and Present in Madhya Pradesh

Ajit Kumar*

Agricultural Growth and Tenurial Forms

The trends in agricultural growth in India have diverged depending upon the tenurial forms of regions. Growth has been impressive in regions where peasants were dominant in the agrarian structure. In contrast, in regions where landlordism was dominant growth has not been impressive. This difference is a legacy, which Republican India inherited from the Colonial Raj whose establishment chose to institute either a ryotwari settlement or a proprietal rights settlement in different regions. Landlords were the core element in the proprietal rights settlement, which covered large swathes of territory in India and in popular usage, they are referred to as the *zamindari* settlement. In Central Provinces, this settlement was known as the *malguzari* settlement. The name *malguzari* comes from the pre colonial period when the Marathas had subjugated large parts of central India and in course of settling land revenue used the word *malguzar* to refer to revenue-farmers who were assigned the responsibility of collecting land revenue from the peasant in the village.

Landlordism and Policy Outcomes

Areas in which proprietary rights in land were 'historically given to landlords have significantly lower agricultural investments, agricultural productivity and investments in public goods in the post-independence period than areas in

* In 2015 under the auspices of the 'Centre for Panchayati Raj', National Institute of Rural Development & Panchayati Raj, Hyderabad, I began the case study of Singhana Gram Panchayat. This was a part of a larger documentation project initiated by the Ministry of Rural Development (MoRD) Government of India. The objective of this project was to document the work of effective gram panchayats from backward districts listed by MoRD. Dhar was one such district and their local administration identified Singhana (Manawar block) as one of their effective gram panchayats. The field data were collected in the first week of May 2015.

which these rights were given to cultivators'. The differences between 'landlord and non-landlord areas are not restricted to agriculture alone: we find substantial differences in human capital investments and outcomes as well. Landlord areas have much lower levels of local infrastructure such as primary schools, high schools and health centres; the availability of village schools is 20 per cent to 60 per cent higher in non-landlord areas. Not surprisingly, they also have lower levels of literacy and higher levels of infant mortality...'. After independence and after the formal abolishing of the landlord tenurial system the adverse effects of landlordism persist possibly because the 'ex-landlords continue to exercise arbitrary power in many of these areas, despite laws to the contrary' (Banerjee and Iyer, 2002: 1, 4, 5, 11, and 12).

Objectives of the Chapter

This chapter examines the nature of the proprietary rights settlement in the 'Central Provinces' region of Madhya Pradesh. Furthermore, the chapter also presents some elements of the emerging discourse, which empirically shows that agricultural growth has taken place in regions in spite of barriers posed by landlord tenures. This development discourse has been discussed with reference to inclusive growth.

The proprietary rights settlement in the 'Central Provinces' region of Madhya Pradesh has been examined with reference to the formation of the Central Provinces (CPs) and the nature of the *malguzari* settlement in CP, both of these aspects are legacies of the Colonial Raj. This chapter focuses on Madhya Pradesh and its 'Central Province' region but excluding Chhattisgarh. This region refers to the Hindi-speaking territory of Saugor and Narmada comprising the following districts: Sagar, Damoh, Jabalpur, Mandla, Seoni, Narsinghpur, Hushangabad, Betul, Chhindwara, Balaghat, and the Nimar district between the Narmada and the Tapti Rivers.

The Past

The Evolution of Central Provinces

'The Colonial Raj united the diverse tracts of central India into the Central Provinces in 1861 and enlarged it in 1903 by attaching Berar to it. Lord Canning, the Viceroy of India merged the Hindi territory of Saugor and Nerbudda (till then a part of the North-Western Provinces) with the Hindi and Marathi state of Nagpur (escheated to the government in 1854) and constituted this amalgam into a bilingual province with Nagpur as its capital in 1861' (Baker, 1969: 2). Narmada valley, the heartland of Madhya Pradesh, 'was acquired by the East India Company (EIC) in 1818 from the Bhonsales of Nagpur' (Raghavan, 1985: 169).

This province comprised two linguistic regions. The 'Hindi region covered the northern and eastern parts of the province and consisted of 14 districts grouped into the three administrative divisions of Narmada, Jabalpur and Chhattisgarh: while the Marathi region occupied the southern part of the province and consisted of four districts grouped into the division of Nagpur.

Four additional Marathi districts lay adjacent to the division of Nagpur on its western side and comprised the division of Berar' (Baker, 1969: xiv, 1, 2).

From Mr Fraser acting Chief Commissioner of CP, we learn that the economy of CP and Berar was stagnant because it was a landlocked place and that 'until the opening up of the country by the railway it was a landlocked place', where 'prices were low', 'population sparse' and 'surplus grain could not find a market' (LRPIG, 1902: 70). The 'stimulation given to wheat and exports following the opening of rail communication through the Nerbudda valley in 1870' was clearly evident (Harnetty, 1977: 367, 342). Rail links by improving agricultural growth and increase in exports succeeded in making the agricultural sector of Central Provinces economically a viable proposition, which in turn brought 'market' forces into play in the region.

Malguzari Settlement and the Mistakes of the Colonial Raj

Malguzari settlement is the name by which the grant of proprietary rights to erstwhile revenue farmers of Central Provinces came to be known. The proprietary right was created by 'consolidating the position of the revenue-farmer whom we found managing the village and paying the Government revenue' (Baden-Powell, 1988: 464). The Marathas were ruling over central India before being defeated by the Raj. Under the Marathas, the revenue-farmers had some undefined privileges but nothing resembling the law-bound absolute proprietal rights granted to them almost as a gift by the Raj.

Under this settlement, the government 'settled the land on the *malguzars*, who were revenue farmers for entire *mahals* or estates and not for individual holdings. This was as a consequence of decisions taken by the Government of the North-Western provinces for the territories of Saugor-Nerbudda in 1854, and by the GoI for the territory of Nagpur in 1860'. As a result, the settlement proceeded on a common basis throughout the province from 1863. Under the terms of this settlement, the *malguzars* were responsible for paying the revenue, which was assessed at 50 per cent of the assets of the *mahal*, and the settlement was to be in force for 20–30 years. The settlement also included the holders of 116 ancient *jagirdaris* and *zamindaris* who were required to pay a small quit revenue or *Takoli* (Baker, 1979: 10). Under this settlement, the *malguzars* were granted the following two kinds of rights:

- The right to transfer, mortgage, or partition the village. Partitioning the village would lead to two separate entities known as *mahals*.
- The home farm rights of the *malguzar* were of two types: *Sir* and *Khudkasht*. The home farm right was a 'corollary of the proprietary right in the *mahal* or village. If the latter right was given up then the former, i.e. his right in land only was recorded as Malik-Makbuza' (Nanekar, 1968: 4). Malik- Makbuza referred to plot-proprietors.

In the Central Provinces as a whole, *malguzari* rights 'were vested at this time in 27,427 persons in possession of 19,897 estates' and all castes were represented in the landlords class. The settlement of land revenue conferring proprietary rights on the *malguzars* of the central provinces was completed in all districts by 1870.

Baden-Powell repeatedly says that the 'grant of these proprietary rights was admittedly a mistake in many forms: and in Nimar and in Chanda the grantees were considered to have so little right to treat the cultivators in any degree as their "tenants" that serious proposals were made to modify the Settlements'. In the Central Provinces, 'grant of the proprietorship to *malguzars* is now – regarding it as a measure of uniform applicability-almost universally admitted to have been a mistake'. There was a general recognition 'that it was a mistake to find proprietors at all'. In 'writing of the conferment of proprietary right in Chanda and Nimar, the Secretary of State went so far as to observe "... a grievous mistake had been made in applying to these districts a system of revenue-administration unsuitable to their conditions"'. Since it was decided 'not to withdraw the gift once made; but the terms of it enabled the Government' to secure the *raiyats* by granting occupancy-rights to all village-tenants of Chanda (Baden-Powell, 1988, Volume II: 386, 388, 456, 463, and 437).

Why was the conferral of property rights a mistake? It was a mistake because in relative terms, free peasants became bound-tenants and got enmeshed into a usurious loan-debt trap leading to a low productivity crop cultivation. Raghavan citing Harnetty says that the grant of proprietary rights to *malguzars* at one stroke 'converted the *malguzar* from a revenue farmer into a landlord with almost undisputed authority over his tenants whose customary rights were correspondingly reduced'. The consequence was a steady erosion of peasant rights (Raghavan, 1985: 171). How did the peasants lose their rights? This happened over time and as a process in which the *malguzari* settlement and the emerging market forces were the key elements. These elements in turn led to commercial men becoming *malguzars*. With a change in the composition of the *malguzar* body local customs weakened. Before the conferral of proprietal rights, the peasants were protected by traditions and customs.

Mr A.H.L. Fraser, Officiating Chief Commissioner of the Central Provinces, pointed out that while in principle the revenue-farmer 'could in a few of the most fertile tracts force up rents by competition, but his demands were limited by the fact that it was more difficult to secure ryots than land'. The 'tradition in favour of the ryots only began to weaken when the conferral of proprietary rights' accompanied 'by a long-termed settlement with the village farmer' and 'the growing demand for land caused by the greater security ensured by British rule' enabled 'the newly-created landlords to increase rents without fear of the revenue's Officers demands upon them being increased' (LRPIG, 1902: 67, 68).

The *malguzars* as a category was not a homogeneous group. KBA Hussein, a settlement official, identified two groups keen on acquiring land but with different motives. The commercial men always aimed at getting the tenants under their control by making them indebted and taking over their produce. The landlords were keen on expanding their home farms by dispossessing tenants of their lands (Harnetty, 1987: 16). With the advent of commercial men, growing market forces and the weakening of local customs, the scope for accumulation increased for which land was essential. *'Sir'* is the word used to describe the home farms of the Malguzar. Could the Malguzar actually expand his *sir* holdings? Did they do it?

In parts of the provinces, 'the struggle to make the raiyati land sir land has already begun. It has been ascertained that in 56 villages of Hoshangabad district the landlords now hold 28,697 acres against 13,718 acres held by them at the last settlement, whereas the raiyats hold only 44,483 acres against 55,506 acres at the last Settlement. The cultivated area of these villages has increased by under 10 per cent, while the portion of it held by the landlords has more than doubled. The contest in this respect between the landlord and tenant is strongest where the proprietary right in the land has passed to the money-lending classes, who are not restrained by old customs and the kindly relations which existed between the old land-holding families and their tenants. In conferring proprietary rights in the Central Provinces it was never the intention of the Government to destroy the rights of the tenants and in order to preserve these rights a limit must be placed on the conversion of raiyati lands into sir land' (Baden-Powell, 1988: 491).

By the time the country became independent, a thin stratum of landlords with proprietal rights and protected tenants had emerged in Central Provinces below whom were a vast mass of impoverished peasantry. Soon after independence, India took steps to reform its agrarian structure but with very limited success.

The Present – After Independence

Land Reforms in India

Daniel and Alice Thorner's writing in 1960 had pointed out that the unprecedented wave of land reforms should have made the large holders reorganise and intensify 'production on their land'. Not only would this modernisation have 'yielded the owners abundant returns' but also it might have 'given India a great increase in output, so essential for the development of the country and the success of the Five Year Plans'. However, this did not happen. Instead, 'in vast areas of the country the larger holders find it simpler and more lucrative to give out much of their land on rent to petty tenants and weak cropsharers'. In addition, 'to taking rent, the larger holders often lend money at usurious rates of interest to their petty tenants and cropsharers'. Furthermore, 'the larger holders may act as traders in agricultural commodities. They take over the produce of the smaller people of their village, often paying them less than the going market prices'.

High rents, 'high rates of interest and low prices leave the mass of petty peasant producers with very little to invest in the development of the land; and keep them at the mercy of the more powerful people in the village'. Thus, 'on the one hand, the grip of the larger holders serves to prevent the lesser folk from developing the land; and on the other hand, the larger holders do far less than they might to modernise production on that part of their land that they farm directly with hired labourers' (Thorner and Thorner, 2005: 17).

Those who had the resources did not have the will to improve the productivity potential of their land while the impoverished peasantry had the will but not the resources. This neglect of the last five decades has foreclosed the one option India had in providing work to the rural underemployed.

Profiling Madhya Pradesh: Land Relations and Agricultural Productivity

The 'Report on land Reforms in Madhya Pradesh' says that in respect of ceiling, tenancy, and distribution of government and community land 'the implementation of the programme has been far from satisfactory' (Land Reforms Unit, 2002: 140). Shah and Vijay Shankar go on to say that even if the 'full potential of the land ceiling legislation were to be realised, the resultant size of holdings distributed to the landless would not be economically viable. This would only add to the ongoing proliferation of marginal and small holdings, resulting from a stagnation in the growth of cropped area and heightened demographic pressure. The low levels of productivity of these farms have already forced a massive entry into the labour market of even "landed" households. The existing pattern of agricultural development in MP has not been successful in checking this trend towards the pauperisation of the peasantry'. They further say that the number of extremely large operational holdings (10 ha plus) 'has come down over time, the distribution of land holdings in MP remains highly skewed, with a substantial share of cultivated area being operated by a few, relatively larger holdings' (Shah and Vijay Shankar, 2002: 371–373).

The Madhya Pradesh Abolition of Proprietary Rights (Estates, Mahals, alienated lands) act, 1950 came into force and at one stroke did away with landlordism. The coming into force of the 'Madhya Pradesh Land Revenue Code, 1954' gave some protection to one category of tenants (Nagpur District Gazetteer, 1966: 282–283). Writing about the impact of land reforms on Vidarbha (The Marathi part of Central Provinces) Professor Nanekar pointed out that the abolition of intermediary interests did away with the 'legal superstructure of feudalism. But it had nothing to do with the concentration of land'. There has been a spurt in land partitions and 'of absentee landlordism' (Nanekar, 1968: 217, 219, and 221).

Till the early 1980s, the state of Madhya Pradesh 'recorded some of the lowest growth rates of growth of land and labour productivity in the country'. During the 1980s, 'largely due to the spread of Green Revolution technology aided by increasingly unsustainable groundwater extraction, there has been an increase in the rate of growth of crop yield. Even then, the overall level of crop yield in the state continued to remain at about two-thirds of the national average in 1992–95, which implies the existence of substantial productivity gap. A comparison of the average productivity levels of the state with the national average shows that such a gap continues to exist for almost all the major crops and crop groups' (Shah and Vijay Shankar, 2002: 383 and 384).

While MP was one of the worst performer in agricultural growth between 1960 and 1980 with the net state domestic product from agriculture growing at 'an annual rate of around one per cent in this period, which was nearly half of the national average' but from 1980 'the overall of agriculture went up to 4.6 per cent during the 1980s and continued to grow, although at a slower rate, through the 1990s' (Vijay Shankar, 2005: 5015). This growth has been because of the 'application of the green revolution package (in the form of the soya-wheat monoculture cycle)' (Shah, 2005: 5010).

To sum up, two trends are evident in Madhya Pradesh. One, land relations are skewed in Madhya Pradesh. Two, there has been a significant increase in agricultural productivity but whether this increase can be sustained in the long run is uncertain.

Improving Irrigation Facilities in Madhya Pradesh

Madhya Pradesh has considerably improved its irrigation facilities. Till the 'early 1970s, only seven per cent of the gross cropped area was irrigated in MP' but by 2000–03 'the ratio of gross irrigated area to gross cropped area reached 24 per cent' (Vijay Shankar, 2005: 5016). Shah et al. say that MP has multiplied 'the state's irrigated area quickly, at small incremental cost, delivering double-digit agricultural growth'. Madhya Pradesh 'tripled irrigated area in canal commands (from all sources) from 0.808 mha in 2006 to 2.5 mha in 2012–13'. Madhya Pradesh achieved this 'miraculous expansion in canal irrigated area' by going in for a performance-linked demands and performance-linked support strategy which involved six components (Shah et al., 2016: 19, 21, and 22).

The Development Discourse

Given the fact that ryotwari areas have shown greater dynamism in agricultural growth what are the prospects for regions carrying the burden of landlord tenures? Will the provision of irrigated water overcome this burden? This seems to be a key question which needs to be examined and in today's context where the primary sector has been marginalised.

Shah et al. have in another published work shown how Saurashtra in spite of a tenurial system more complex and fragmented than that of the *malguzari* system of Vidarbha could still outperform Vidarbha in crop productivity. While in 1990–93, the gross value of output of agriculture (GVOA) 'per hectare of net sown area for Saurashtra and Vidarbha was nearly equal' by 2005–08, the GVOA of Saurashtra 'was more than three times that of Vidarbh's'. The authors have attributed this success to three factors: recharging of groundwater, providing eight hour of uninterrupted power supply of full voltage every day and the sowing of hybrid Bt cotton seeds. To sum up, Saurashtra successfully converted 'rainfed cotton to irrigated cotton' (Lerche, 2014: 88, 89–91).

The success of Saurashtra and to an extent of Madhya Pradesh in improving agricultural productivity proves that it is not necessary to alter land relations to induce growth. However, will this growth be inclusive? Without inclusive growth can the 'demand' impulses of the local economy be strengthened? Let me illustrate my point by citing a case study. Singhana gram panchayat[1] in Dhar district in Madhya Pradesh has done exemplary work in recharging groundwater through Mahatma Gandhi National Rural Employment Guarantee Act (MGNREGA) water percolation works and at one time was disbursing more than one lakh rupees daily as wages. During the last two years, MGNREGA funds have dried up and surprisingly this was questioned by the shopkeepers of Singhana who went in a delegation to meet the block authorities. Their interest in MGNREGA works stemmed from the fact that a good portion of the daily wage disbursal came to them when the labouring people of Singhana would buy their daily necessities from the local shopkeepers. This impulse of 'local' demand emerging out of the increasing purchasing power of the labouring class is what inclusive growth is all about. It is this type of growth, which will strengthen both the local economy and the village community by deepening the linkages between the two.

References

Baden-Powell, B.H., (1988): *The Land: Systems of British India*, Vol. II, Book I: General, Crown Publications, New Delhi (Reprint).

Baker, D.E.U., (1969): Politics in a Bilingual Province: The Central Provinces and Berar 1919–1939, PhD Thesis.

——, (1979): *Changing Political Leadership in an Indian Province: The Central Provinces and Berar 1919–1939*, Oxford University Press, New Delhi.

Banerjee, A. and Iyer, L., (2002): History, Institutions and Economic Performance: The Legacy of Colonial Land Tenure Systems in India, *The American Economic Review*, Vol. 95, No. 4 (September 2005), pp. 1190–1213.

Harnetty, P., (1977): Crop Trends in the Central Provinces, 1861–1921, *Modern Asian Studies*, Vol. 11, No. 3, July 1977, Published Online: 28 November 2008.

——, (1987): The Landlords and the Raj: The Malguzars of the Central Provinces, *Studies in History*, Sage Publication, New Delhi/Newbury Park/London.

Kumar, A., (2015): Policy Insights for Vidarbha's Economy, *Economic & Political Weekly*, Vol. L, No. 6, 7 February, pp. 73–74.

——, (2015): A Case-Study of Singhana Gram Panchayat: Effectiveness in Local Governance (Manawar Block, Dhar District, Madhya Pradesh), Submitted to Centre for Panchayati Raj, National Institute of Rural Development and Panchayati Raj, Hyderabad (Unpublished).

Land Reforms Unit, (2002): A Report on Land Reforms in Madhya Pradesh, in Praveen K. Jha (ed.) *Land Reforms in India: Issues of Equity in Rural Madhya Pradesh*, Vol. 7, Sage Publications, New Delhi.

Lerche, J., (2014): Agricultural Labourers, the State and Agrarian Transition in Uttar Pradesh, *Economic & Political Weekly*, Vol. 33, No. 13, pp. A29–A35.

LRPIG, (1902): Land Revenue Policy of the Indian Government, Published by Order of the Governor General of India in Council, Office of The Superintendent, Government Printing, Calcutta.

Mishra, D.P., (1956): The History of Freedom Movement in Madhya Pradesh, Government of Madhya Pradesh, Nagpur Government Printer, Madhya Pradesh.

Nagpur District Gazetteer, (1966): Maharashtra State Gazetteers, Nagpur District, (Revised Edition), Gazetteers Department, Government of Maharashtra, Mumbai.

Nanekar, K.R., (1968): *Land Reforms in Vidarbha: An Enquiry into the Implementation of Land Reforms in the Vidarbha Region*, Oxford & IBH Publishing Co, New Delhi.

Raghavan, T.C.A., (1985): Malguzars and Peasants: The Narmada Valley, 1860–1920, *Studies in History*, Vols. 1 and 2, Sage Publications, New Delhi/Beverly Hills/London.

Shah, M., (2005): Ecology, Exclusion and Reform in Madhya Pradesh, *Economic & Political Weekly*, Vol. XL, No. 48, 26 November, pp. 5009–5013.

Shah, M. and Vijay Shankar, P.S., (2002): Land Reforms in Madhya Pradesh: Redefining the Agenda, in Praveen K. Jha (ed.), *Land Reforms in India: Issues of Equity in Rural Madhya Pradesh*, Vol. 7, Sage Publications, New Delhi.

Shah, T., Mehta, Y., Kher, V. and Palrecha, A., (2014): Generating Agrarian Dynamism: Saurashtra's Lesson for Vidarbha, *Economic & Political Weekly*, Vol. XLIX, Nos. 26 and 27, Supplement, 28 June–5 July, pp. 86–94.

Shah, T., Mishra, G., Kela, P. and Chinnasamy, P., (2016); Har Khet Ko Pani? Madhya Pradesh's Irrigation Reform as a Model, *Economic & Political Weekly*, Vol. 51, No. 6, 28 June–5 July, pp. 19–24.

Stokes, E., (1982): Agrarian Relations: Northern and Central India in Dharma Kumar (ed.), *The Cambridge Economic History of India*, Orient Longman, Hyderabad.

Thorner, D. and Thorner, Alice, (2005): *Land and Labour in India*, Chronicle Books, New Delhi.

Vijay Shankar, P.S., (2005): Four Decades of Agricultural Development in MP: An Agro-Ecological Sub-Region Approach, *Economic & Political Weekly*, Vol. XL, No. 48, 26 November, pp. 5014–24.

6 Critical Analysis of Agricultural Finance for Small Farmers

Bijoy Kumar Swain

Introduction

Small farmers in most developing economies experience considerable difficulties and have to spend significant resources for accessing formal financial markets or micro-finance services. Absence of easy, affordable, and reliable access to institutional sources of finance compels most rural poor and low-income households to continue to rely on costly informal sources of finance or manage from relatives and friends, neither of which allows them to take full advantage of economic opportunities. Micro-finance service providers are expected to facilitate them by expanding operations into rural areas but have to understand following risks and develop a system to mitigate perceived risks.

Agricultural Risk

Financing potential small farmers necessitates careful appraisal of the profile of small farmer, his business profile and business cycle, and cash flows of rural households in order to properly estimate the repayment capacity of small farmer and his/her willingness to repay the credit with interest on time. Since many of the small farmers do not keep proper business and financial records, this calls for developing a method to collect reliable critical data and information through various means, which is time consuming and expensive. While financing small farmers for raising crops of economic importance, it is absolutely essential and desirable to have a thorough understanding of the agricultural risks that small farmers face. Agricultural risk, which includes following types of risks, namely climate risk, production risks, and price and market risks in particular, is extremely difficult for them to manage since they do not have adequate technical and managerial skills and financial support.

Climate Risks

Climatic parameters like temperature, humidity, rainfall, sunshine, wind, etc. during critical phases, namely crop planting, its growth period, flowering, and harvesting significantly influences crop productivity and quality of farm products. Sometimes, abrupt and unforeseen climatic changes result into outbreak of pests and diseases, leave alone drought, floods, cyclones, etc. causing unbearable crop loss.

Production Capacity Risks

Farmer's capacity to innovate and share knowledge among resourceful farmers is very crucial for the agriculture production. Their access to institutions engaged in researching and disseminating proven and demonstrated production technology including better methods of crop harvesting as well as easy access to inputs of crop production such as seeds, fertilisers, pesticides, water of standard quality and reasonably priced, and farm equipment play a significant role in ensuring expected level of productivity. However, in most developing countries, small farmers in particular are mostly deprived of all these facilities and services or some of them as a result of which their farm output is less in terms of quantity and quality.

Market Risks

Small farmers often face herculean or harrowing problems during post-harvest stage in terms of processing, packaging, transport, handling, storage, and marketing. Since these facilities and services are not available on time and at reasonable rates at one place, they have to move from pillar to post and ultimately sell the produce at a very low price. In most cases, their return on the investment and other resources is quite low, making crop farming an unviable proposition. Market risk is such an unpredictable that sometimes it is common for a farmer to harvest fairly good crop yields by adopting efficient crop-management practices (production, harvest, and storage) only to face a drop in price at the time of sale due to excess supply in the market. In saturated markets, farmers are forced to sell at low prices, often below the cost of production. Some countries have experimented and introduced 'crop insurance' as one of the instruments to protect farmers from weather-induced agricultural risks.

The main objectives of the scheme are as follows:

1. To provide insurance coverage and financial support to the farmers in the event of failure of any of the notified crops and losses suffered on account of natural calamities such as drought, flood, hailstorm, cyclone, pests, and diseases,
2. to encourage the farmers to adopt scientific farming practices and use high value inputs, and
3. to help stabilise farm incomes, particularly in disaster years. Few countries have also been experimenting on a weather-based insurance, mostly aberrations in the rainfall having impact on crop output in a specified geographical area during a particular period of the crop season.

In some countries, for example India can increase wheat production by 30 million tons or around 40 per cent and double paddy production at current levels of technology. This can be achieved by bridging the existing gap between the actual crop yields at field level and the potential yields. Various studies based on the data recorded in 2013–14 and 2014–15 on yields realised with improved agronomic practices and the existing actual average yields in different states have recommended exploiting this potential. In this case, for achieving the expected level of productivity of wheat and paddy per unit of area and resources and realising optimum rate of return on investment as indicated above particularly at the level of small farmers, it is necessary that farmers need technical and financial guidance, based on analysis of farm soil and water, on cropping system, adoption of scientific techniques, and judicious use of seeds, fertilisers, pesticides, water, labour, and credit. The technology of integrated nutrient supply, water, and pest management needs wider dissemination among farmers through mass scale field demonstrations in coordination with bank staff.

The Farm Inputs and Equipment Regulatory and Development Authority needs to be established to ensure that the inputs including farm equipment and machinery being supplied are of standard quality, reasonably priced, and timely delivered. The crop farming must necessarily be combined with livestock and or fish farming, poultry, dairy, sheep, pig farming to mitigate production, income, and financial risk. While the first Green Revolution had its genesis in the 'seed-fertiliser-irrigation' technology, the second Green Revolution should originate from 'radiation-induced mutation technique and biotechnology' along with integrated nutrient, pest, and water management technology. The International Atomic Energy Agency has called for increased investments in radiation-induced mutation techniques that help in producing crop varieties with high yields and disease resistance, and can grow in stressful conditions such as drought, flood, and salinity. This technique has been in use since 1920s and more than 3,000 varieties of 170 different plant species have been released for cultivation. Similarly, biotechnology in recent years has created unprecedented opportunities and revolutionised research activities in the area of agriculture viz, plant tissue culture and genetic engineering leading to transgenic plants carrying desirable traits like insect and herbicide resistance; tolerance to salinity, drought, and major pests; enhancing nitrogen-fixing ability, improving storage, proteins, and crops.

Agricultural finance for small farmers helps them not only for crop production but also for food processing and thereby addressing problems related to malnutrition, poverty, and hunger worldwide. India should, therefore, concentrate on inventing new seeds and planting material of various field crops through application of new technology. As about 800 million persons are sought to be covered under Food Security Act, not only food productivity and output has to be substantially stepped up but also government would have to procure, store, and distribute around 57 million to 67 million tons of food grains, that may need additional transport, processing, and storage facilities.

Transactional Costs

In most developing countries, there are number of villages with low population density and grossly inadequate basic necessities and infrastructure. Also, more importantly small farmers are often scattered across large geographical regions comprising relatively socio-economically backward, hilly, tribal, drought-prone, and desert areas, which make lending costly since it presents logistic challenges, such as marketing effort, identification and selection of borrowers, pre-sanction and post-disbursement supervision, follow-up for recovery of loans and dealing with loan delinquencies, etc. This, therefore, certainly increases transactional cost and causes inconvenience to borrowers for visiting bank branches when needed. It is acknowledged that lending without tangible collateral presupposes supervision and follow-up on a continuing basis. Rural Financial Institutions (RFIs) have to undertake need-based research and design procedure for lending and distribution channels that are cost effective and convenient for both clients and RFIs. Effective coordination with local level institutions of repute and resourceful persons, development of flexible and easily replicable structures for marketing, credit delivering and monitoring loans, and technology application are critical requirements to increase clientele outreach and make RFIs financially sustainable in due course of time.

Key Steps to Expanding into Rural Markets

Financing small farmers means RFIs need to visit hard-to-reach locations and therefore they need to open branches at strategic potential business centres in rural areas, which is capital intensive and work with rural households, which is difficult and cumbersome. In order to optimise the return on the capital invested for opening the rural branch in due course RFIs should meticulously survey the potential business area through collecting most reliable required statistics and information and properly analyse them for taking the decision. For offering sustainable financial services in a group of manageable number of villages around the branch, RFIs need to develop a comprehensive business plan (perspective plan for five years and annual action plan) for each rural branch and implement with an integrated and result-oriented strategy, which should, inter alia, include the design of effective risk-assessment methodologies, the development of strategic collaborations with value chain participants to mitigate perceived agricultural risks, and create cost-effective distribution channels.

Selection of Branch Location

The selection of a centre for opening rural branch is critical to initiating business in the first year and then gradually and significantly developing business to achieve financial sustainability in a reasonable period, say five years. The selection of the centre should, therefore, not only be based on business potential and its growth in subsequent years but should also focus on the extent of perceived agricultural risks. For this purpose, following, among others, are the key variables, which need to be properly evaluated before opening rural branch.

Business Potential

Determining the existing level of business as well as future business potential of the region comprising a group of a manageable number of villages, say 15–20 villages, is necessary, for which statistics and information need to be collected and analysed, namely total number of households in the region, number of farmer households and Bank Credit to Agriculture in India households, and types of business activities being pursued by households in three sectors of rural economy. These are as follows:

1. Agriculture (crop farming, horticulture and plantation, livestock farming, fish farming, forestry, etc.),
2. manufacturing and processing (rural, cottage, tiny, artisan-based industries, processing, storage, preservation, etc.), and
3. business and service sector (self-employed, professional, traders, transport and service providers, micro- and small business enterprises, etc.), composition of farmers based on land holding (small farmers and others), types of crops cultivated, their planting and harvesting month, types, quantity and value of inputs (seeds, fertilisers, pesticides, fuel, electricity, diesel) used, quantity and value of farm and livestock products, types and value of non-farm products (manufactured), and goods and services delivered by service providers.

Support Services and Infrastructure

Borrower Profile

RFIs are expected to design loan products to match the credit needs of borrowers for which they should familiarise with the farmers and other rural households and collect required information about them that can help RFIs understand profile of household and economic activities they pursue, cash flow that they generate, and the nature and extent of agricultural risks they present. Collection of this information and its analysis on a continuing basis helps RFIs design a number of loan products including savings, insurance, and non-farm credit products tailored to the needs of new clients. It will also help the institutions launch its rural expansion with clients that represent the lowest risk for the institution. Massive effort would be required to collect comprehensive details about small farmers by developing a structured schedule, pre-testing it, and then finally administering to a representative group of farmers, sharply focusing on their current and emerging debts, sources of income, and all forms of expenditures including social and religious ceremonies, gaps between income and expenses, ways and means being adopted to bridge the gap from time to time, and the quality of assets including land, livestock, farm tools, irrigation facilities, etc. that generate income, their current and future plans for investment in farm and non-farm activities, etc. Additionally, the objective of this exercise is to understand the characteristics, potential, and credit risk associated with different types of farmers of the region. RFIs can use this information to determine which type of farmers offer a lower or more balanced risk profile. Farmers can broadly be classified into three categories on the basis of risks associated with the frequency and regularity of their cash flows.

Low-Risk Farmers

This includes farmers having easy access to irrigation facilities, raising multiple crops, and also possessing some livestock, which facilitate them to generate regular income, preferably monthly.

Medium-Risk Farmers

This includes farmers growing more than one crop and having some livestock, which help them earn regular income and pay at least the interest on a monthly basis and the principal in lump sums two to three installments in one year.

High-Risk Farmers

Farmers raising only one crop in a year with no other source of assured income and cannot pay interest or principal on a monthly or quarterly basis but can only pay both in lump sums at the end of the crop cycle.

Client-Targeting and Product Design

RFIs need to appreciate the fact that the branch in a defined geographical area of its operation may target the clients comprising most households of integrity who can demonstrate their willingness as also capacity to repay loan with interest on time. Initially only those households presenting no or low risk can be considered for financing. Loan portfolio may have to be balanced with different categories of households from farm and non-farm sector in order to minimise credit risk and make RFI operationally viable. Of course, priority should be given to more number of small farmers, say maximum 30 per cent in terms of loan portfolio. By thorough analysing the profiles of different economic activities and households as mentioned earlier, loan officers should design appropriate loan products for different economic activities under farm and non-farm sector. Loan products must focus loan amounts, rate of interest and mode of payment, loan-term in months, grace period, schedule of loan repayment indicating number, and frequency of installments in particular. RFIs may need to appreciate that loan products should not be of the type that 'one-fits-all' since they may differ in the light of agro-ecological regions of the country.

There can be several loan products for farmers for raising crops, such as loan products for short-duration vegetable crops and other crops (whet, rice, corn, soybean, oilseeds, pulses, etc.). Crop production loan includes all items of cost that is incurred to raise the crop, such as:

1. Purchase of inputs of crop production (seeds, fertilisers, pesticides, fuel, etc.),
2. meeting expenses of labour for land preparation, planting, other cultural operations during crop growth, harvesting and post-harvesting operations, etc. and

3. charges for irrigation and other contractual services, say farm equipment/ machinery, etc. are disbursed before land preparation and planting of the crop cycle and are intended to finance part of the production costs, agricultural inputs, land preparation, crop maintenance, and harvest. In general, these loans have a longer term and one or more disbursements. The loan repayment schedule should match the crop cycle; traditionally there is a grace period between initiation of crop and the sale of the production. The loan term and frequency of installments are closely related to the cost structure of the crop and harvest and selling period. Production loans can be classified by type of crop primarily produced by the farmer.

Factoring

Immediately after the crop is harvested the market receives overwhelming supply of crop produce, which results into sharp drop in prices and that remains during a particular period of time. Under such circumstances, if farmers have to sell their crop products, since they need cash to meet their family expenses and repay not only borrowed money for crop cultivation but also to repay money borrowed for family expenses during the season of crop growth, they receive very depressed prices. They need to store their product for some time after which the prices start rising. If they receive credit to tide over the immediate problem of liquidity during this period, they can store their product and wait for better prices. This loan is known as 'factoring' loan, which is a key mechanism to help farmers with short-term liquidity needs. Factoring is a transaction whereby the RFIs/banks purchases farmers' crop against the security of 'warehousing receipts' that provides immediate liquidity to the farmer. The RFIs/banks later receive payment when the purchaser of the crop settles the account. Farmers often have difficulty managing cash flows prior to harvest, and factoring allows access to liquidity during vulnerable periods throughout the year.

Tips to Minimise Risks

Experience suggests that RFIs can minimise the risks of financing small farmers by targeting low-risk activities, viz.,

1. Initially RFIs can finance only those crops that small farmers widely cultivate and they have full knowledge of costs, income, production, marketing, etc. and RFIs gain adequate field experience.
2. Finance short-cycle products (vegetables and legumes) that have monthly cash flows and after gaining experience consider financing crops with longer cycles and seasonal incomes from other sources. Bank Credit to Agriculture in India.
3. Collect data and information of the prospective borrower's household and analyse them to understand all sources of income and avenues of expenses that can help to determine effective credit needs and repayment capacity and not restricting to the borrower's economic activity to be financed. What is required is to have a total view or integrated approach and not piecemeal or isolated.

4. RFIs should identify local sources of financing for small farmers and endeavour to complement the unmet financial requirements to raise crops. This approach prevents the institution from assuming all financial risks.
5. Endeavour to finance those crops with established demand in the existing markets with which farmers are well linked.
6. In case of perennial plantation crops and fruit trees (coffee, tea, rubber, guava, mango, oranges, apples, etc.) provide short-term/working capital finance to meet seasonal expenses such as maintenance, harvest, and post-harvest requirements for crops that are already in the production phase.

Constraints to Rural Women's Access to Credit

Women in rural areas contribute significantly to agricultural production through their hard labour in carrying out practically all farm operations, namely planting, weeding, applying fertiliser, pesticides, and water, harvesting, and post-harvest operations including transporting and marketing. It is estimated that women in developing countries are engaged to produce between 60 per cent and 80 per cent of the food and are responsible for half of the world's food production. In case of activities allied to agriculture that include dairy, poultry, sheep, goat and pig rearing, sericulture, bee-keeping fisheries, forestry, etc. their contribution is almost 100 per cent. Often men tend to borrow to raise high-value cash crops whereas women mostly care for producing food that has first-priority family consumption and balance selling in local markets. Since much of their food crop production is consumed within the home, women farmers supplement their income by working as part time labourers on other farms and engaging themselves in activities allied to agriculture as also non-farm activities that generate regular cash income. The difference in the profile of male and female farmers has real implications for their distinguishing ability to access credit in terms of loan amounts, loan term, and access to alternative credit sources. However, women as the primary small-scale agricultural producers have to face far more difficulties than men for accessing credit from formal institutions. This has been largely due to women's inability to possess title to land and house and participate in the decision-making process as also to access to resources, such as farm inputs, extension services, etc.

Micro-Finance Institutions and commercial banks, more importantly in India and Bangladesh appreciating the role and responsibilities of men and women rural households have designed products and delivery mechanisms that best meet those savings and credit needs. The key differences between the profiles of male and female farmer households in rural areas can facilitate Micro-Finance Institutions to design products and delivery mechanism for extensively expanding their MF operations into rural areas. Women engaged in farm and non-farm activities also find it difficult to access credit as it involves travelling to the nearest branch for completion of loan appraisal formalities, loan disbursement, and repayments. In order to reach a larger number of women in rural areas, the institution may need to adapt its product design and service delivery model to address the mobility constraints of rural women. The adaptations include completion of loan appraisal formalities, loan disbursement, and repayments through visit to women clients in a village or a specified locality by the staff, preferably female staff, in a planned way that can substantially increase the business and reduce cost. The formation and nurturing of Self-Help-Groups by RFIs/MFIs and subsequently linking them with bank's branch in India and other countries is one of several innovative approaches to serve women client. This kind of adjustments can result in significant shifts in the gender balance of clients in rural areas.

Selection of Staff

RFIs need to have adequate number of staff having specialised knowledge and skill to systematically promote, develop, accelerate, and manage the growth of rural finance. The ideal staff for rural finance should have an educational background and expertise in agricultural and animal husbandry, preferably better understanding of rural economy and ability to adjust with rural environment. The candidate should have through knowledge of the agricultural sector that includes, among others, techniques and economics of crop production, use of yield-maximising inputs, and marketing intelligence. Experience suggests that traditional urban-oriented loan officers neither have these required skills/expertise/neither experience nor they adjust with rural environment. Besides, knowledge to collect and analyse field data on crop yields, production costs, and income at borrower's level, they should be able to understand the economics and dynamics of non-farm sector as it is an integral part of rural economy and finance. This has significant implications from the angle of optimum utilisation of staff services in rural area as agriculture is a seasonal activity, minimising risks and improving the operational viability of RFI and achieving inclusive growth of rural areas. The criteria for rural loan officer can be of 21–35 years of age, a degree in agriculture with subjects of agronomy, agricultural extension, farm management, agricultural economics, etc. and has at least two years of work experience. After joining RFI, he should be thoroughly trained in and exposed to credit appraisal system and procedure. He should possess good communication skill, farmer-friendly approach towards small farmers and women clients and willing to work in the field at least 60 per cent of the time and travel daily by motorbike. Gradually, he should be able to finance non-farm sector activities thereby covering progressively all rural households in the village. To motivate and retain him/her, his/her remuneration, bonus, promotion, and other non-financial incentives should be linked with his/her performance to achieve RFI's mission and business goals, which should be reviewed each year.

Key Success Factors for Rural Expansion

Diversify Portfolio Composition

Agricultural financing has been well acknowledged as carrying an element of significant risks on one hand and RFIs have to be not only operationally viable but also to be financially sustainable in the long term if they have to continue to finance agriculture on the other. Thus, RFIs in order to minimise the incidence of risks as much as possible and attain operational viability in the initial years of operation and gradually financial sustainability may need to diversify their loan portfolio rather than concentrating only on farm sector in rural areas. RFIs should, therefore, diversify loan portfolio composition offering loan products to most clients pursuing different types of economic activities under the farm and non-farm sectors in their geographical area of operation, such as farmers engaged in crop farming and activities allied to agriculture, rural households engaged in rural and cottage industries, small grocery shops in the villages, service providers and manufacturers, etc. Ideally, the agricultural portfolio should not be larger than 30 per cent of the total portfolio. Limiting the share of agricultural portfolio enables a more efficient use and allocation of loan officers' time due to the seasonality of agricultural demand, which requires processing most loan applications in specific months of the year. This seasonality creates operational bottlenecks in some months and under-utilisation of Bank Credit to Agriculture in India by having a diversified portfolio an institution can smooth the seasonal demand throughout the year.

Increase Risk Exposure Gradually

As mentioned earlier, institution should begin by financing low-risk farmers in low-risk regions, then expand financing to longer-term and more seasonal crops once further market information is gathered and the institution has increased experience in the region. Low-risk farmers are generally those with monthly cash flows who have substantial experience and access to god commercialisation channels.

Understand Local Financing System Used by Small Farmers

Over a period of time resource, poor small farmers have themselves evolved their system of cultivating crops on their small and sometimes fragmented pieces of land. As for example, they take help from other farmers to hire farm equipment and machinery, such as tractors, power tillers, harvesters, and pump-sets for conducting important farm operations on time and speedily, such as transporting inputs and farm products, preparing land, planting crops and harvesting operations, irrigating growing crops, etc. Similarly, they purchase production inputs, more importantly fertilisers and pesticides from input dealers/suppliers/traders and use them for increasing output and saving crop losses from infestation of insects and pests. They purchase from grocery shops their daily requirements of food and from merchants other requirements during the entire period of crop growth. All these suppliers are paid after the harvest and sale of farm produce. In the meantime, they also borrow from village moneylenders to meet expenses towards children education, medicines, social and religious ceremonies, etc.

While suppliers of all these services do exploit small farmers, they get their work done through this system and make a living out of it. Understanding of this system, therefore, provides a good insight to RFIs and MFIs in order to facilitate them to design loan products to match their requirements. These important local and in some cases informal financing sources share part of farmers' risks. RFIs and MFIs may, therefore, not try to fully replace the system or compete with all of them initially but rather offer financial support to farmers to complement their cash requirements or to replace expensive or inconvenient sources of financing. After gaining significant field experience and winning farmers' confidence, RFIs and MFIs may gradually endeavour to replace the traditional exploitative system.

Create Flexible Distribution Channels to Reduce Transactional Costs

To reach remote locations, institutions generally implement flexible systems like mobile banking or build low-cost networks of points of service using existing clients with storefront businesses to offer a transaction system close to the clients. Mobile banking requires the creation of working routes in the region, servicing different villages throughout the week. Loan officers are assigned to two or three routes per week. During the route visits, loan officer market the product, visit clients to assess their businesses and farms, and collect loan payments when necessary. The working routes usually vary in length from 20 to 60 km and have small villages as end points. Loan officers offer services to all businesses along the route and in the end village or town. This strategy helps cover vast areas with limited infrastructure while keeping operational costs low. Points of service networks increase the services to clients in rural areas, but pose other challenges in building relationships with the points of sale and controlling cash flows. Here technology becomes an important component to connect the points of sale with the organisation. A simpler option could be the forming of strategic alliances with banks or postal services to enable clients to make loan payments at these locations. This option does not require the acquisition of new technologies or maintaining and controlling a point of sale network.

Foster Strategic Collaboration with Value Chain Players

Market and price risk could jeopardise a successful crop, and a drop in crop prices or lack of demand could reduce dramatically a farmer's capacity to pay back a loan. One way to ensure greater stability of prices and demand is to identify potential local alliances between agro-industries or retailers with farmers associations. Harvest contractors are powerful instruments to reduce price and demand volatility. Value chain players could also be valuable partners to mitigate market risks. The organisation will need to assign a staff responsible to foster and manage those strategic alliances with other players.

Conclusion

The approach to serving the rural poor has evolved in the last 40 years. The 1970s were marked by the prevalence of highly subsidised, centrally planned, and bank-run credit programmes. The landscape has shifted dramatically in some regions, producing a dynamic marketplace where a broader range of factors including innovative MF provider, value chain players, and insurance companies are combining efforts to mitigate agricultural risks and finance products with strong demand and secure markets. Today demand, supply, and prices define the priority crops that financial institutions will finance. Traditional loan analysis, focusing on a fixed set of production costs for selected crops, has been replaced by an integrated analysis of the financial needs of farm-household production units. No longer is the repayment capacity of farmers estimated by evaluating only the main crop, rather risk analysis today is focused on the combined activities and cash flows of the farm-household unit.

Financial institutions no longer try to replace all sources of finance by one mega loan; rather institutions today seek to provide a complementary source of liquidity for small farmers. Sharing credit risks with local players has proven a more prudent strategy for banks. Although this new approach has enabled some financial institutions to successfully provide financial services in many regions, though there is still a huge unmet demand in rural areas. MF providers should better understand the rural context and agricultural risks and adopt integrated strategies to enter rural financial markets in a sustainable and prudent manner. The collaboration with different value chain players will help share and mitigate the multiple risks faced in rural areas. Finally, collaboration and new technologies to improve distribution channels will be key components to expand financial services to the new frontier.

References

Basu, P., (September 2005): A Financial System for India's Poor, *Economic & Political Weekly*, Vol. 40, No. 37, pp. 10–16.

Chavan, P. and Ramkumar, R., (May 2002): Micro Credit & Rural Poverty: An Analysis of Empirical Evidence, *Economic & Political Weekly*, Vol. 37, No. 10, pp. 955–965.

Kumar, M. and Bohra, N., (January 2010): Microfinance as an anti-poverty Vaccine for Rural India, *International Review of Business & Finance*, Vol. 2, No. 1, pp. 29–35.

Mishra, A., (January 2001): Coordination Failure in the Rural Credit Markets, *Journal of Microfinance*, Vol. 3, No. 1, pp. 96–114.

Patel, A., (December 2010): Agricultural Credit by Commercial Banks in India: Need for Creating Enabling Environment, *Bank Quest*, https://www.microfinancegateway.org/sites/default/files/mfg-en-paper-agricultural-credit-by-commercial-banks-in-india-need-for-creating-enabling-environment-dec-2010.pdf.

Ramachandran, V. and Swaminathan, M., (December 2014): *Financial Liberalization & Rural Banking in India*, Published by Indian Statistical Institute, http://library.isical.ac.in:8080/jspui/bitstream/10263/3152/1/Binder1.pdf.

Sahasraraman, A. and George, D., (April 2013): *Cost of Delivering Rural Credit in India*, Published by IFMR Finance Foundation.

Vetrivel, S. and Kumarmangalam, S., (2010): Role of Microfinance Institutions in Rural Development, *International Journal of Information Technology and Knowledge Management*, Vol. 2, No. 2, pp. 435–441.

7 Farm Suicides in Cauvery Delta of Tamil Nadu

Sign of Distress

Shanmugam Rajendran and
Manickam Sabarisakthi

Introduction

Suicides are complex in nature to pinpoint a factor, which led a person to commit suicide. However, the circumstantial evidence may be inferred from the spot for ascertaining a suicide case. Studies on farm suicides generally attribute the indebtedness as a key factor for committing suicide. Here in the case of delta region, many factors including debt, crop withering, and quarrel over debt among family members and so on are cited as reasons for suicides. While some farmers collapsed in their fields due to crop withering, a few farmers with unbearable cope up with the crop failure committed suicide by consuming pesticide. Many of such suicides are surfaced from eastern parts of the old delta. Sadly, a farmer from upland in Trichy district attempted suicide over the loan obtained for crop cultivation. All these culminated from the severe distress, crop withering, and non-availability of water.

Farm Suicides

The all India survey (Times News Network, 2016) on farmers' suicides was commissioned by the Government of India to the Bangalore's Institute for Social and Economic Change and the findings are unnerving. According to the preliminary report of this study, in Karnataka 46 per cent of victims' household revealed that crop failure was a major cause for suicide. It also suggests that as crop failure is the root cause, individual farmers should be brought under the ambit of crop insurance.

More than 9.18 lakh ha of land is cultivated in this delta in normal years. Over the years, due to non-availability of sufficient water, area under cultivation has been consistently declining and now paddy is grown in less than eight lakh ha due to paucity of water. The patterns of irrigation source are also changing faster. Earlier assured sources of canal water were the major sources for paddy crop. Due to non-availability of assured irrigation source regularly, farmers went in for digging bore wells and are irrigating around 30 per cent of total cropped area. Fragile rural economy has been witnessing stress and as Sen (2016) explains agrarian distress is partly due to recurrence of below-normal rainfall.

In the delta zone, a 70-year-old experienced farmer – S. Govindaraj – of Ragunathapuram in Thiruthuraipoondi taluk of Thriuvarur district after much persuasion broadcasted paddy seeds as samba crop in his five-acre field, which did not germinate for want of sufficient moisture. Unbearable to the futile exercise, he was missing since 31 October and his body was found lying on the southern banks of Maraikka Korayaru River on 3 November in the year 2016. It is revealed by the family members that the deceased spent ₹ 50,000 and unbearable to the loss-consumed poison. D. Rajeshkanna, a middle-aged farmer with three children from Keezhathirupanthuruthi village near Cauvery River 13 km from Thanjavur, raised through direct sowing method on his 2.5 acre land and no rain was in sight and water from the river either. Upset with this, he had giddiness, had severe heart attack, and died while uprooting paddy seedlings as farm worker in his village on 4 November 2016.

Another farmer, Vellaian from Thirupattur in Thiruthuraipoondi taluk in Thiruvarur district committed suicide as he could not control the agony of paddy crop failure in his farms. It was a depressing movement for another small farmer Rathinavel from Andarkadu village in Thiruvarur who also committed suicide over the failure of crop germination from the direct-sowing method.

Yet another but young farmer, T. Azhagesan, 36 year old from Athichghapuram village 29 km from Thiruvarur district in Mannargudi taluk of Kottur block, depressed over poor germination of paddy seeds even after two months of sowing. He was upset for a couple of days, and when he visited the fields on 5 November, he died due to heart failure on the field itself. Passer-by noticed his body and informed the Kottur police station. It was found that not even 50 per cent of the seeds sprouted from his fields. Another farmer, K. Lekan, a 50 year old of Thayanur village in delta's Trichy district, quarrelled with his wife over the repayment of loan for cultivation of paddy. Unbearable to this, he attempted suicide by hanging himself on the night of 5 November 2016 in his house. Timely intervention by his neighbours had him rescued by releasing the noose and the got admitted to district headquarters hospital.

In a tragic incident of yet another farm suicide, 59-year-old Navaneetham of Keezhakavalakkudi near Keelvelur taluk of Thiruvarur died of sudden heart failure. He raised paddy seedlings for his two-acre plot and arranged to lift the seedlings to his filed on 7 November 2017. He planned to pump the water by diesel motor from Pichai branch channel flowing near the field, but the channel had also dried up. Upset with this, he died of cardiac arrest on the same night. in his house. All these depict an important point that the Cauvery delta is under distress and the rural economy is in fragile condition. Once a lush-green area covered with green blankets across the historic delta region, now perched fields and wilted crops welcome the visitors.

The state government realising the drought like situation targeted to raise paddy during samba season in about 8.85 lakh acres in delta districts of Thanjavur, Thiruvarur, and Nagapattinam. Even this could not be taken up as only 4.45 lakhs acres are under direct sowing and by transplanting, 3.97 acres have been cultivated. Even the limited area under cultivation is withering for want of water. Consequently, both farmers and agricultural labourers are hard hit.

Monsoon Failure

The Cauvery delta[1] receives a maximum rainfall to the tune of 75 per cent from north-east monsoon during the months of October to December with an average of around 1,000 mm. It is benefitted, though to a limited scale from south-west monsoon as well. During the south-west monsoon, water flows to the river Cauvery, which originates from neighbouring Karnataka and water is normally released from the Mettur dam during the second week of June every year for cultivation in Delta region. This year truant rainfall during south-west monsoon resulted in low storage and consequently there was a political and legal fight between the upper riparian and lower riparian states of Karnataka and Tamil Nadu, respectively, during the months of September and October 2016 (Janakarajan, 2016). Agitators rampaged the property and caused huge damage to both private and public properties. Road transportation is completely halted thereby causing a whooping loss of more than ₹ 25,000 crores to the state exchequer. People were put to misery and a huge amount of property was lost during arson by antisocial elements.

Due to stress and laxity of the state, farmers have no option but to end their precious lives. Now there has been a new trend among farmers to call for halting the cultivation of crops whenever there is distress. In other words, farmers boycott crop husbandry by announcing crop holidays. This is quite possible in agriculturally prosperous regions unlike resource poor areas, where traditionally farmers are rich and have enough stock of food grains for their sustenance. Nevertheless, such trend is a serious warning to food security of the country.

The 'kuruvai'[2] paddy crop could not be raised in the delta for the past five years. There were a couple of showers this year and farmers were advised to go in for direct sowing of paddy.[3] Indeed those who have filter points raised nurseries and went in for transplanting the seedlings during kuruvai season on about 4.5 lakh acres in the delta. Those who do not have such assured irrigation source expecting rains sowed[4] the seeds through broadcasting method as 'samba' crop. Though it is not common practice in this delta, some experienced farmers whenever water was not released from Mettur dam and failure of south-west monsoon, followed this method and got decent harvest, if not maximum yield and production. In fact, under direct sowing method, many crops like ragi, *jowar*, and *bajra* are grown as mixed; thereby risk of crop failure is reduced as some returns are assured and fodder is a major source of return. Here, farmers give equal importance for getting fodder to protect their livestock.

Direct sowing of paddy is an ideal technique in dry-land agriculture system. Here in dry regions it is easy for inter-culture, which is paving way for more shoots in a clamp. However, weed growth would be more under direct sowing, which ultimately leads to more labour for weeding out. At the same time, though resource use efficiency is low in transplanting method, it is efficient in dry-land system of paddy cultivation.

The south-west monsoon was poor and erratic in the neighbouring states including Kerala and Karnataka thereby putting more pressure on sharing of river waters. It is pity that the entire state of Kerala has been declared as drought hit and state machinery is gearing to take stock of the situation to mitigate any disaster. This state received 34 per cent of rainfall during south-west monsoon and 69 per cent deficit rainfall is expected during north-east monsoon (Ann, 2016). Another neighbour, Karnataka is no way better. The state has declared 111 taluks of 176 total taluk as drought hit. It was blessing in disguise that the northern Karnataka[5] received sufficient rainfall and only southern part including the catchment area for the river Cauvery is under severe stress. This state has been pleading the union government to support the drought mitigation measures and requested ₹ 3,375.79 crores as immediate assistance. A rough estimate as revealed by the agriculture minister, cropped area of 25.57 lakh hectare has been affected. Already a central team has made a three-day survey. As south Karnataka in Cauvery catchment and ayacut area is under distress, water may not be released any more to Tamil Nadu.

Paddy is the single-largest crop grown on around 63 per cent of gross cropped area in the delta. Canal is irrigating to a lion share of 58 per cent followed by wells (30%). Around 23 lakh tonnes of paddy is produced in the Cauvery delta districts. Due to erratic rainfall and irregular release of water from Mettur dam this year, the production will be affected to a greater extent.

Here in the state of Tamil Nadu, anticipating excessive rainfall now, official machinery is discussing about the flood threat of north-east monsoon. So far, no official meeting or discussion either at local or at state level on drought mitigation has been convened. First time, the Tamil Manila Congress leader and former union minister, G.K. Vasan, a popular leader who has strong support with local farmers, called for declaring the state as drought affected. The Tamil Nadu Farers' Association in its meeting on 8 November urged that Tamil Nadu should be declared as drought-hit state. It is reported that all these ill-fated farmers used direct-sowing method of paddy seeds in anticipation of normal north-east monsoon. Non-availability of quality seeds is another handicap for the local farmers. Unlike earlier days, now farmers do not keep[6] home-grown paddy seeds for next season and completely depend on market.

Low Storage and Crop Loss

Anticipating copious inflow[7] into Mettur and good north-east monsoon, water was released from the dam on 20 September 2016. Now due to low inflow and poor storage, the discharge has been reduced to mere 1,500 cusecs. As on 7 July 2016, the storage is stood at 13.803 tmc against its maximum capacity of 93.47 tmc. Poor storage in the water spread area of Mettur dam evokes the neighbouring villagers to raise crops under '*muzhuvadai*' farming. Farmers fear that similar to south-west monsoon, north-east monsoon will be failed. The end result is that water has not touched the tail-end delta region covering Thiruvarur and Nagapattinam districts. This has resulted in conflicts and fights among farmers over getting water and creating yet another law and order nuisance.

Left with no choice, pinning hopes on the north-east monsoon, farmers went in for direct sowing of paddy. Now the rain god is deceiving the farmers and the crop is withering not only leading to stress and farm suicides. It is feared that not only the investment made would go in vain but also rural economy will come in severe distress. All these farmers died due to stress and pesticide poisoning. It is feared that the situation will become worse if the trend continues as feared by farmers' associations.

Due to poor rainfall during south-west monsoon water storage in many dams has been reduced considerably across the subcontinent. In the country, 91 larger dams show a dismal storage level. Dams in states like Tamil Nadu, Kerala, Himachal Pradesh, and Tripura show low storage of water in dams continuously for two years.

According to a report (Watwani, 2016), 51 districts in six states, which comprise the Western Ghats, have received deficit rainfall between 1 June and 10 September 2016. Here a maximum of 34 per cent deficit in Kerala followed by Karnataka (21.4%) and Tamil Nadu (9.4%). This trend may invite trouble in the domain of law and order. During summer 2016, severe drought in prosperous Maharashtra made the authorities to invoke 144 to control the mob, who assembled for collecting water. For fulfilling the quest of locals in Latur, water was transported by containers through rail lines from Gujarat. It was pointed out that encouraging water guzzling sugarcane crop resulted in shortage of water as this crop alone uses for almost 90 per cent of total water available for irrigation (Jamwal, 2016).

This year rainfall during October in Tamil Nadu was one of the lowest in the past few decades with a deficit rainfall of 63 per cent. This state recorded 66.2 mm of rainfall against the average of 181 mm (Lakshmi, 2016). People are praying to get good showers, though belated. According to a comprehensive coverage on drought in India, this is a second consecutive deficit monsoon with 254 districts and 2.55 lakh villages being affected. This report further states that 2016 drought is the third worst drought since 1991 (Mahapatra, 2016).

Not only direct-sowing crop but also transplanted crop is withering at large scale. Hoping that water released from Mettur will be supplemented by north-east monsoon farmers who have raised nurseries with the help of bore well water and transplanted short duration ADT36 variety after spending more than ₹ 30,000 per acre investment. Now 45-day-old crop is withering and farmers allow cattle to graze the paddy fields on 5,000 acres in Kasavalanadu villages (an ayacut region of Grand Anicut Canal) close to Thanjavur town.

Employment Hit

Failure of monsoon and crop failure also affect the farm workers and bring unbearable miseries. People from neighbouring but backward districts like

Pudukottai and Ramanathapuram migrate to Thanjavur delta and temporarily settle down for undertaking farm operations (Rajendran, 1993). Sometimes they flock their cattle and ovine for tending them on the fields, which brings a sizeable source of additional income. Now it has been changing as employment is not assured. Local farm workers also hit. Even farm labourers who eke out their livelihood by employing draught animals also affected a lot. These are due to two reasons. Firstly, water is not released on time due to erratic rainfall and secondly mushrooming of farm machineries.[8] This trend is common in other dry-land areas as well.

Crop Loan and Safety Net

Non-availability of credit facilities on time adds further woes to already-stressed farmers. Though crop loans from primary agriculture credit cooperative societies (PACCS) has been earmarked for ₹ 3,840 crores during 2016–17 in Tamil Nadu, less than 25 per cent alone has been disbursed owing to a number of hurdles. Farmers revealed that the local officials insist that the loan amount waived last year by the state is to be deposited in PACCS for availing fresh crop loan. Although each district is allotted with ₹ 120 crores a small amount ranging from ₹ 20 crores to ₹ 50 crores alone has been disbursed. Crop loans by formal sources need to be pushed in the interest of affected farmers. Officials should be considerate on sanctioning crop loans to farmers in the fragile areas.

Due to lack of awareness farmers including in delta region do not opt for safety net like crop insurance. For instance, registration for crop insurance for borrowers and non-borrowers was fixed as 30 November 2016. The Thanjvaur district administration set a target of bringing under crop insurance is earmarked as 85,000 farmers. Unfortunately, so far only 13,000 farmers joined in this. This is due to a combination of factors like delay in issuing *sitta* and *adangal* documents by the village administrative officer, cumbersome format and non-cooperation of cooperative credit societies' employees (Ragavan, 2016).

Nature is not showing any mercy to the delta farmers. In Nagapttinam district, crop varieties like ADT46, ADT39, CR1009, and BPT5204 are two month old on 1.2 lakh hectares and rats damage the crop. To control rodents, ₹ 400 is paid to a labour as wage. Demonetisation is another curse and cash crunch is severely affecting the farm sector. Farmers are unable to pay wages to labourers for want of small denominations of ₹ 100 and ₹ 50. Some farmers postpone carrying out farm operations to avoid irk of farm workers. This would certainly affect the crop production. Similarly, whatever farmers sell in the market, traders are unable to make payments daily. On the one hand, vegetable prices have fallen from 10 to 15 per cent and business has been declined by 75 per cent in Trichy vegetable market.

Conclusion

Farmers' suicides in the Cauvery delta show a serious distress situation and that an immediate intervention from policy circle is required. Safety net measures like crop insurance and allowances may be provided as immediate relief. Intensive counselling at household level is another intervention, which may reduce the suicides immediately. Local educational institutions and their community service wings may be utilised for educating and counselling the distress farmers. Long-term measures like identification and propagation of drought resistant and high-yielding varieties of seeds to be distributed. Alternative livelihood strategies like fish rearing, cattle rearing, and farm forestry may be taken up in the delta.

The authorities should thoroughly investigate the farm deaths case by case and based on the reports, adequate compensation would be given. There is electioneering in Thanjavur legislative constituency and hence political overtones may creep in and the administrators shall look this issue on humanitarian ground and provide compensation. Already the BJP leaders started blaming the state government for its inaction to extend the new crop insurance policy to all farmers. The state BJP president remarked as '... with the state failing to implement the new crop insurance scheme, farmers were not getting the real benefit of crop insurance. This had a direct bearing on the difficulties of delta farmers and now there have been deaths of grief stricken farmers due to crop failure' Ann, 2016.

Sensing drought and crop failure, the state government covers 14 lakh farmers with an annual budget of ₹ 457 crores. Three agencies including ICICI, New India Insurance, and Agriculture Insurance Corporation are assigned the task of covering the farmers under crop insurance. A farmer has to pay ₹ 325 as premium per acre and both centre and state governments share remaining. Task has to be taken up on war footing to save precious lives of farmers.

Notes

1. Cauvery delta districts include Ariyalur, Trichy, Pudukottai, Thanjavur, Thruvarur, Nagapattinam, and Thiruvarur. However, the last three districts form a major area under the deltaic zone.
2. *Kuruvai* a short-duration crop season during June to July; *samba* a long-duration grown during August to September; and *thaladi* a short-duration crop season grown during October to November.
3. Direct sowing of paddy has been abandoned as the flood irrigation is practiced here for long time.
4. The State Department of Agriculture and experienced farm scientists and Farmers' Association leaders called for direct-sowing method.
5. Northern Karnataka generally receives poor rainfall and hence is always subjected to crop failure and agrarian distress and contrary to this, this year many parts received excessive rains thereby putting hardships to agriculture and people.
6. In earlier days, healthy seeds were carefully collected, processed, and stored for next season. Now paddy is threshed with harvest combiners and hence germination quality of these seeds is less. Hence, farmers have no option but to buy seeds from the open market at high rate.

7. Due to Supreme Court's orders, the Karnataka government released water into the river Cauvery though is insufficient.
8. Although some machineries like pump sets augment the demand for labour, the net result would be labour displacing.

References

Ann, (2016): Kerala Declares Statewide Drought, *The Hindu*, Madurai, 1 November, p. 6.

Jamwal, N., (2016): Marathwada's Dry Story, *Down to Earth*, Vol. 24, No. 24, pp. 8–13.

Janakarajan, S., (2016): The Cauvery Water Dispute, *Economic & Political Weekly*, Vol. 51, No. 41, 8 October, pp. 10–15.

Lakshmi, K., (2016): South TN, Interior Parts to Get Moderate to Heavy Rains, *The Hindu*, Madurai, 1 November, p. 4.

Mahapatra, R., (2016): It is Not a Drought: But a Cumulative Outcome of Decades of Policy Sins, *Down to Earth*, Vol. 24, No. 24, pp. 18–23.

Ragavan, V.N., (2016): Practical Difficulties Hinders Farmers to Insure Their Crops, *Dinamani*, 28 October, Trichy, p. 20.

Rajendran, S., (1993): Changing Patterns of Farm Power Use in Agriculture: A Study of Tamil Nadu Villages, *Ph.D. Thesis* submitted to the Bangalore University Through the Institute for Social and Economic Change, Bangalore (unpublished).

Sen, A., (2016): Some Reflections on Agrarian Prospects, *Economic & Political Weekly*, Vol. LI, No. 8, pp. 12–15.

Times News Network, (2016): Hounded by Creditors, Let Down by Crop, Farmers Chose to End Lives, *Times of India*, Bangalore, 21 October, p. 16.

Watwani, J., (2016): Is This a Sign? *Down to Earth*, Vol. 25, No. 11, pp. 14–16.

8 Redefining the Role of Women for Revitalising the Agrarian Crisis in Rural India

Sunita Sangar

Introduction

Agriculture is still a major occupation and forms the basis to the livelihood and food security for poor farmers in India. The deceleration in agricultural growth is a cause for concern. Agriculture is still a crucial sector in India despite its declining share to GDP over the past decades from 29 per cent (1998–99) to 15.8 per cent (2008–09) to mere 14.1 per cent in 2011–12. Agrarian crisis has witnessed a decline in number of cultivators as rural farmland is put to other uses (Census, 2011). Majority of these farmers are either marginal or small farmers that hold less than One hectare of land. These farms are largely managed by families where women play an important role. Agriculture sector employs 80 per cent of all economically active women as they comprise 33 per cent of the agricultural labour force and 48 per cent of self-employed farmers. With increased feminisation of agriculture in the country, it is very significant to recognise women's role in agriculture if overall agenda of inclusive growth has to be achieved. While, agriculture is no more seen as a profitable and sustainable occupation, women increasingly been taking up responsibilities in agriculture.

Women as farmers, agricultural workers, and entrepreneurs form the backbone of the agricultural rural economy. They play a significant role in agriculture labour force and in agricultural activities to a varying degree, and their contribution to agricultural productivity and growth is extremely significant. Women, however, are faced with a range of constraints depending on the sociocultural and agro-ecological contexts. These constraints have to be addressed if women have to be participating and contribution to the economic development of the country. *Recognising the upcoming need of women in agriculture, this chapter provides an overview of major challenges faced by women in the current agricultural scenario.* The objective of the chapter is to dwell upon the need for redefining the role of women to address the challenges of gender inequality in the agricultural sector. It will provide specific recommendations for rural women's participation that would help counter the obstacles and empower these women in agriculture.

Challenges Faced by Women in Agriculture: An Overview

Women comprise the majority of agricultural labourers in India. Among rural women workers, 65 per cent are employed in agriculture as labourers and cultivators (Census, 2011). An estimated 20 per cent of rural households are *de facto* female headed, due to widowhood, desertion, or male out-migration (Planning Commission, 2007). Gender divisions in agriculture are stark with all activities involving manual labour assigned to women while all operations involving machinery are generally performed by men (NCW, 2004). Women work for longer hours and participate in most of the field work related to crop production and have a significantly higher involvement in livestock production, forest resource production, and fishery. In rural areas, the incidence of poverty is high with largest fraction of the poor belonging to agricultural labour followed by 'self-employed in agriculture' category. Generally, poorer the family, the greater is the involvement of women in agricultural activities. With large number of women left to handle agriculture, their importance both as workers and as managers of farms has been growing, as an increasing number of men move to non-farm jobs.

Women have extensive workloads with dual responsibility for many of the farm operations and household management (fetching water, cooking, and taking care of children). At farms, women are involved in farm-related activities in production of major grains and millets that range from their involvement in the land preparation, seed selection and seedling production, sowing, applying manure, fertiliser and pesticide, weeding, transplanting, threshing, winnowing, and harvesting; in livestock production, fish processing, collection of non-timber forest produce (NTFP), and more. Besides women play important role in animal husbandry, with multiple roles ranging from animal care, grazing, fodder collection, and cleaning of animal sheds to processing of milk and livestock products. Keeping mulch animals, small ruminants, and backyard poultry is an important source of income for poor farm families and agricultural labourers. Besides, there are landless women who work as either agricultural labourers or lease in land for cultivation. Largely women are involved in the collection of NTFP, particularly tribal women. Women's role in agriculture necessitates special inputs from our policies and programmes. With agriculture continuing to remain a very important source of livelihood for women special schemes/programmes along with enabling policies targeted women in agriculture in India (Sulaiman et al., 2003).

The nature and extent of women's involvement in agriculture varies greatly from region to region and sometimes within the region. Their involvement varies widely among different ecological sub-zones, farming systems, castes, classes, and stages in the family cycle. Regardless of these variations, there is hardly any activity done without involvement of women in agricultural production, except ploughing in which women are not actively involved. With mechanisation, their involvement in several activities has further reduced and they are involved in drudgery-oriented practices. Studies on women in agriculture conducted in India and other developing and under-developed countries all point to the conclusion that women contribute far more to agricultural production than has generally been acknowledged.

Key Challenges

Despite women's significant role in agricultural development, they have virtually no access to agricultural information, services, or production assets, and have very limited control over their earnings. Training and extension programmes are often designed primarily for men. Expansion of women participation in agriculture production is hampered by poor access to input supplies, extension advice, credit, and the most important agricultural resource-land. Key challenges faced by women include the following:

Poor Access to Agricultural Productive Resources

Lack of entitlement to land (and other assets such as house, livestock, and so on) is a severe impediment to efficiency in agriculture for women cultivators since in the absence of title women cannot get credit or be entitled to irrigation and other inputs, especially technology (Saxena, 2012). Women constitute two-third of the agricultural workforce but only 12.78 per cent women have operational land-holding (Agriculture Census, 2010–11).[1] In addition, disaggregated data on women's land ownership and operational access to different kinds of land – homestead land (rural–urban) and tenurial land – is still not presented in our national statistics.

Women land rights are little recognised in the revenue records as well. Without titles to land, women are not even recognised, by the state as eligible for getting a credit for doing agriculture, as client for extension services or as candidate for membership in institutes such as co-operative sectors. Most of the women are small and marginal farmers or landless; lack of opportunities in the non-farm activities and little linkages to the market further makes their efforts economically unsustainable. An overview of the key publications/schemes/policy papers/reports related to women and land rights reveals that reasons for the decline in the land ownership by women are both cultural and legal that need to be addressed.

Lack of Data on Government Land Distribution Programmes

From the mid-90s, government land distribution in most states mandated that land allocated by the government shall be jointly owned by husband and wife. However, there is no reliable data to capture if women indeed received land in joint titles with their husbands. Micro studies reveal that often this norm has not been adhered to during implementation. Lack of sex-disaggregated data limits the scope of policy making and social action in several ways. It limits the scope of women-targeted welfare and development programmes because women continue to be hidden under the household as targets with no information on agriculture-related interventions – bank loans, *kisan* credit cards (KCCs), technology assistance, and extension services remain focused on men.

Lack of Linkage Between Micro-credit and Capacity Building

Country has large number of micro-finance projects that concentrate on women, as women are more unlikely to misuse the money and also share the benefits with the entire household. However, these projects had little impact on gender balance in property ownership and control. Micro-finance did lead to her economic independence but no control over resources because of their being semi-literate or not having enough skills-based training/capacity building to move towards the next step of successful entrepreneurs (Kumar, 2013). This is also leading the poor growth of agri enterprises in the country.

Poor Participation in the Decision-Making Process

Women participate in all type of farm activities and do more work as compared to male workers but their participation in decision-making related to farm and income-generating activities is low. Men dominated in a majority of the farm decisions in farm families. Decisions related to buying and selling of land, machines, and other agricultural implements; improvements of harvest and livestock management were mainly taken by head of the family or husbands (Sharma et al., 2013). They are not even consulted at the time of purchase of animals and change of crops.

No Recognition as Farmers

Indian agriculture sector employs 80 per cent of all economically active women and comprises 33 per cent of the farm labour force and 48 per cent of self-employed farmers. With 60 per cent of India's population neither engaged in farming, women contribute to almost 70–80 per cent of activities but neither legally nor socially recognised as farmers. According to recent NSSO, about 18 per cent of farm families in India are headed by women, but face problems of access to *pattas* or titles to land. Women are only *de facto* heads of the farms and are often without any transfer of legal titles. Lack of recognition of their rights hampers Indian women's possibilities not only to become more successful and productive farmers but more importantly gain self-sufficiency and decision-making power that can improve the livelihoods of their families and the whole community.

Poor Access to Agricultural Technologies

Women perform all unmechanised agricultural tasks and are mostly involved in backbreaking and drudgery-associated activities, access to latest agricultural technologies is poor. The studies carried out so far in the field of agriculture indicate that despite the key role of women in crop husbandry, animal husbandry, fisheries, forestry, and post-harvest technology, those in charge of formulating packages of technologies, services, and public policies for rural areas have often tended to neglect the productive role of women. There is inadequate development with respect to technologies specifically tailored to women.

Besides, involvement of women in technology development and transfer has also received poor attention from both scientific and administrative departments of government. Poor ownership of assets, which is already mentioned, further hampers agriculture extension not geared to serve women.

Poor Education

Women workers in agriculture suffer from high illiteracy rate among them and drop-out of schools. Women do not know their legal rights, which hamper their social and political empowerment as well. Illiteracy also impedes their access to skill up-gradation and capacity-building programmes, access to credit, access to subsidies on inputs by government programmes, and access to technologies and related training modules offered by the agriculture extension system.

Inadequate Research and Development for Farm-Women

A large part of our National Agricultural R&D system is not yet gender sensitised. At present, it is not mandatory for scientists to explicitly mention the gender-based outcomes or utilities of their research in the proposal, while at international level, for example with CGIAR Centres, there is already a strong gender component included in the research programmes. Even curriculum on agricultural research, training, and extension is not women oriented.[2]

Lack of Opportunities for Linking Farm and Off-Farm Activities

With agriculture becoming a non-profitable proposition for economic sustenance of rural households, importance of non-farm activities for income-generation activities is growing. Women are rarely involved in the backward and forward production linkages with agriculture. Poor linkages between the non-farm activities and farm activities further hampers opportunities for value addition and market linkages for economic empowerment/livelihoods promotion of women.

Lack of Convergence Between Various Government Programmes

Substantial public investments have been made for strengthening of the rural economy and the livelihood base of women. There are number of programmes/schemes/incentives by various government departments/ministries for farm-women. Due to lack of adequate convergence among the various schemes implemented by various ministries, particularly, Ministry of Agriculture, Ministry of Rural Development, and Ministry of Women and Child Development, economic empowerment of women in agriculture, at best, remains scattered and isolated. Lack of convergence among these government programmes/schemes not only impedes entitlements to reach the needy women but also impedes optimisation of efforts and resources.

Recommendations

Efforts have been initiated in the recent past both by governmental and non-governmental organisations to incorporate gender perspective into the development agenda to ensure women's full and equitable participation in agricultural development programmes. Statistics, however, still indicate that these efforts have not been sufficient enough to bridge gender inequalities. Some of the recommendations that could pave a way forward for women in agriculture may include the following.

Access to Land Rights

Focus on endowing women with land is an important instrument for their empowerment. There is a need to strengthen women's land rights. Despite various efforts to facilitate ownership of land for women by the government, women make a very meagre proportion of it. There is a need for collecting gender-disaggregated data on land ownership and put in place mechanisms for it. This is, however, only possible through a good synergy between the centre and the states/UTs. Government-led allocations should concentrate on women, especially vulnerable and marginalised women. Mostly women are denied both government land allocations as well as family inheritance. Access to land and other productive resources can enable access to public services, new agricultural technologies (seed/irrigation/fertilisers and other inputs), extension and credit, and other subsidies of the government. There is a need for women to have effective and independent rights in land. Effective rights means rights not only in law but also in practice, and independent rights being rights that women enjoy in their own capacity. Effective and independent land rights for women are important to achieve welfare, efficiency, equality, and empowerment. Gender-disaggregated land-ownership database at all levels starting from the revenue village upwards, as well as farmers involved in urban and peri-urban farming need to be collected, analysed, and maintained for more focused interventions for women farmers.

Linking Women Collectives, Micro-Credit, and Capacity Building

There have been successful cases of collectives from states such as Gujarat and AP which are small sized, voluntary, socio-economically homogenous, and participate in decision-making experiences (Agarwal, 2010). There are several successful examples where in the absence of land women have been able to successfully manage enterprises in rural areas through the various forms of women collectives. Women as part of the UNDP–IKEA project in Uttar Pradesh (UP) were encouraged to form self-help groups (SHGs) and provide better access to credit for setting up enterprises, Women-led federations in the dairy and craft industry were set up and large number of SHGs have availed loans without collateral. Women collectives such as women's cooperatives, producer women's groups, and other forms of group efforts should be promoted to overcome the constraints of small and uneconomic land-holdings to disseminate agricultural technology and other inputs, and for marketing of produce (Agarwal, 2010). Further, these collectives would also serve as an institutional base for provision of credit- and capacity-building initiatives such as skill upgradation through training and capacity building for the proper use of these technologies to these women. Directed interventions to benefit farm-women in a substantial manner would be appropriate. Women should get economic opportunities and reap market benefits without dependence on middleman. Successful projects under, Mahila Kisan Sashaktikaran Pariyojana (MKSP) project under National Rural Livelihoods Mission (NRLM) may be expanded to other states for the benefit of women farmers.

Participation in Decision-Making

Since women's contribution to economic development is vital, there is a need of proportionate increase in her involvement in decision-making process because the success and progress of any production depends upon the plans made and decisions taken. Women should be given experience in decision-making process, including participatory personnel management and budget management. The patriarchal forms of decision-making have to undergo a change before women are able to fully enjoy the autonomy as an individual. Education and improvement in their economic independence will help in increasing women's involvement in decision-making in family (Singh et al., 2012).

Recognition as Women Farmers

Gender equity is an important concern for sustainable agricultural development. Women involved in agriculture and allied sectors and related value chain development should be recognised as farmers in their own right. Women farmers should include landowners and women working on others lands, tenant farmers, livestock-rearing women farmers, fisherwomen, and women dependent on forests with a special focus on the most marginalised, according to National Policy for Farmers, 2007.

Majority of women farmers are small and subsistence workers with limited land rights Efforts will be made to support women farmers in their land ownership, livelihoods, their visibility and identity, entitlements over agricultural services, social protection cover, and equal participation in user associations and decision-making bodies. Recognition of women in agriculture as farmers would help women farmers gain the access to land, water, insurance, and markets. It will also help women farmers get water rights, seed rights, and land rights that will ensure the country's food security. Certification of women farmers will give them legally the same entitlements as male farmers including entitlement to KCCs, a programme providing affordable credit for farmers without complicated screening process, while women farmers have very little access to it. Recognition of women farmers would not only help improve their livelihoods but also help achieve goal of food and nutritional security in the country (please refer to Section VI). This will be an important step to enable women empowerment and meet inclusive development goal of the country since it will also take forward the recommended measures with respect to women in agriculture given by the National Commission on Farmers along with the National Policy for Farmers, 2007.

Empowering Women Farmers Through Convergence Approach

Substantial public investments have been made for strengthening of the rural economy and the livelihood base of women. To effectively address the issue of poverty alleviation and economic empowerment of women, there is a need to optimise efforts through inter-sectoral approaches. Convergence among different government programmes could benefit women farmers benefit. There is enough evidence to understand that implementation of special programmes had improved farm-women's access to information on agricultural technology, led to increased adoption of technology and realisation of economic benefits (Sulaiman et al., 2003). It will be crucial to forge effective functional linkages with various departments, agencies, and institutions including NGOs and farm-women groups to document and disseminate lessons and experiences from on-going initiatives. Schemes such as, Rashtriya Krishi Vikas Yojana (RKVY), NRLM, and National Food Security Mission (NFSM) are targeting women. There are other schemes such as National Literacy Mission, which can facilitate women farmers access to government subsidies, loans (KCC), recognition of their entitlements, etc. Convergence with National Rural Health Mission (NRHM) would not only help women's access to health facilities but also utilise health facilities for their children while they are at work.

Improving women's work participation and their role in agriculture need to be encouraged within the pretext of general agrarian crisis in the country. Strengthening and expansion of MKSP, under NRLM in this context will be useful for the empowerment of women farmers. Concerted efforts will be made to ensure that women have access to the benefits of general schemes for farmers rather than targeted schemes for women especially in the context of high proportion of women managing homestead and cultivation on account of migration of men. Focus will be on the schemes/programmes on soil conservation, social forestry, dairy development, horticulture, organic farming, livestock including small animal husbandry, poultry, fisheries, etc. where women are dominant workers, are expanded to benefit, and are empowered with input support and universal availability of extension services offered by different line departments. Women farmers' skills and capacities will be utilised to ensure that at least half of the extension workers are women. Successful women farmers will be identified and especially equipped to work as last mile extension workers and trainers.

Women as Custodians of Traditional Sustainable Agricultural Practices

Ill effects of Green Revolution that lead to exploitation of natural resources – soil and water biodiversity – are already visible resulting in fatigue in agricultural productivity. The loss of biodiversity in India and specifically food crops is a serious concern of food security and sustainability of the agricultural sector in India. The agriculture system is looking for sustainable solutions and practices. Women can play a crucial role in this context. Women have been traditionally known to conserve genetic diversity (seed banks, selection, and preservation) and champion good agricultural practices, including practices that help in building resilience to climate uncertainties. Traditional agricultural methods utilised by subsistence women farmers such as seed preservation, soil health management, bio-fertilisers, integrated pest management, integrated nutrient management organic farming, crop-rotation techniques, and other environment friendly agricultural practices may be promoted on a large scale. Women organised into collectives can further exchange knowledge; seeds too pursue sustainable agricultural practices.

Priority in Government Programmes

Efforts are needed to prioritise women in all government land redistribution, land purchase, land lease schemes, and rural housing programmes to enable women to own and control land through issue of individual or joint land *pattas*. In the case of private land, joint registration of land with spouses or registration solely in the name of women should be encouraged along with measures such as concessions in registration fee and stamp duty etc. to incentivise land transfers to women. Women's rights over common property resources (CPRs) should be recognised and secured through appropriate policy interventions as envisaged under Biodiversity Act, 2002, and through appropriate state-level policy interventions including lease of common land and/or forest land to secure their livelihoods. Panchayats have to play an important role in prioritising women SHGs for CPRs. Women should be empowered to become informed members and decision makers in key agriculture programmes like Agriculture Technology Management Agency (ATMA) and in forest-based, livestock-based, and poultry- and fisheries-based livelihoods programmes.

Technological Empowerment and Drudgery Reduction

Rural women make significant contributions to household production, economy, and food security. They play a major role as labour in agriculture and are employed mostly in drudgery prone activities. They work long hours and are unable to attend formal training courses leaving their domestic responsibilities leading to obstruction of livelihoods opportunities. Along with drudgery, they also face problems related to health and energy efficiency with use of tradition technologies (cook stoves and *chulhas*) at the household level. Since women have different ergonomical characteristics than men, it is necessary to develop technologies to suit them and reduce their burden and drudgery especially for small holders and marginal women farmers. Modifying available equipment to suit the ergonomic needs of women, testing them in different locations, producing them in bulk, is urgently required.

Women especially need women-friendly implements/tools, which can reduce drudgery, save time and enhance output, and can be handled comfortably. Steps are required to involve women farmers in on-farm participatory research for agricultural technology and development of women-friendly implements/tools. Database of women-friendly technologies/equipments available for all stages in the agriculture value chain for bulk purchase with list of manufacturers should be developed. There should be a focus on reducing farm-based drudgery, entrepreneurship, and promotion of science and technology for women farmers (including horticulture, livestock management, fisheries, and gathering and processing forest-based minor products and peri-urban agriculture). Providing women with the skill, and training them in the use of equipment is the most-important need of the hour. The consequences of new technologies on women-specific occupations and the constraints responsible for their transfer have to be separately studied in detail so that technological packages can be gender friendly, socially sound, and can be coupled with appropriate packages of services and government policies. Given the demographic dividend, the younger generations of women farmers will be equipped to access and use scientific knowledge, climate information, and farm technology to reduce labour, adapt to climate vagaries, and increase production.

Promoting Rural Enterprises for Women

Development of farm and non-farm enterprises in rural areas continue to be the key factor in reducing poverty. However, more than 90 per cent of rural women in India are unskilled that restricts them to low-paid occupations. Poor control over land and other production assets, which restricts their access to institutional credit and renders them dependent on high-cost informal sources of credit. Women entrepreneurship in rural areas through capacity building in the key areas such as finance, literacy skills, marketing, production and managerial skills, etc. would play a crucial role. Encouraging women entrepreneurship for women involved in agriculture and allied activities can create opportunities for income generation in rural areas.

Report on condition of work and promotion of livelihoods in the unorganised sector (2007) revealed large disparity in work participation across rural and urban areas among women, while half of the adult women participation in workforce, only little more than one-fifth of urban women participate in the workforce. Higher work participation rate per se among women in rural areas is because women in rural areas are mostly engaged in agriculture and allied activities with restricted other work opportunities and thus does not mean that the economic condition is better than their counterparts in urban areas. Enterprises focusing to bring linkages between farm and non-farm activities would be useful for rural development. This was also one of the key strategy for poverty alleviation in rural India since 10th Five Year Plan.

Women collectives like SHGs, cooperatives, and farming enterprises will be encouraged and incentivised in sustainable agriculture practices by providing support for post-harvest storage, processing, and marketing facilities. This will be done by leasing in land and facilitating changes in tenancy laws. Institutional and funding support for the formation of women producers associations and existing women's federations/cooperatives to process, store, transport, and market farm produce, milk, fish, crops, etc. will be provided.

Research and Development for the Relevance of Farm-Women

Adding gender perspective during the research process would enhance applicability of knowledge, methodologies, and technologies in terms of their adoptability and acceptability by and for women. Successful integration of gender component in agricultural R&D requires a sound research structure/framework, strong partnerships, capacity building, and advocacy. It is important to include women perspective as an in-built component in research projects and identify certain gender-based monitoring and evaluation indicators to assess the output and outcomes. Developing gender-desegregated data would be the key for further planning. As a matter of policy, this can begin with addition of a separate module on gender for Agricultural Research Services (ARS) trainees during the foundation courses. Research studies that would identify the needs, requirements, potential, and constraints faced by women in agriculture sector especially in the areas of technological development, access to inputs, credit, and other productive resources, marketing intervention would be very useful. Promotion of 'action research' on critical issues including women's access to land, water, CPRs, impact of macro-economic changes on women farmer, and implications of legal and regulatory framework on vulnerable groups such as landless farmers, tribal farm-women, and those affected by natural calamities would further help in understanding and solving the issues of women in agriculture.

Value Addition and Market Linkages for Livelihoods Promotion of Women

Livelihoods promotion through value chain development and marketing linkages would help break the gender stereotypes that prevail in traditional agriculture and have been keeping poor and uneducated women in low paid, less skilled, and more insure work. Ensuring gender equality throughout the value chain would prevent traditional pattern of gender discrimination from being repeated. Women producers most often have participation restrains and face additional challenges such as cultural and legal discrimination, which prevents them from accessing productive assets, finance, education, and technology. They are still often concentrated in the less-profitable stages of the value chain and struggle to engage in the value chains more lucrative activities. Value addition has to be converted into an opportunity and not a threat for women's employment with appropriate market linkages. This increasing recognition of the role of women in agriculture would further reiterate National Policy for Farmers, 2007 of the government of India that envisaged several measures aimed at empowerment of women farmers with better access to inputs and services, technologies, credit, and support services.

Recognising the Importance of Women's Role in Climate Change

Climate change is a reality now, and is among the factor, which has already begun to have an influence of agricultural production. India's agricultural sector depends greatly on the variations in climate. Women are affected differently, and often more severely by climate change and its associated natural disasters such as floods, droughts, cyclones, and storms. The effect of climate change can drive women into dangerous situations/risks and vulnerabilities. This is largely because men and women are bound by distinct socio-economic roles and responsibilities that give rise to differences in vulnerability and ability to cope with these climate-change consequences. Women's role in issues related to climate change has long been overlooked; however, it will be important for the local grassroots initiatives to place the empowerment of women and girls at the heart of debate and action on climate change. To facilitate women's involvement in the climate change, state government should ensure inclusion of women in their adaptation plans. Linkages with the State Climate Change Action Plan, which has been developed by every state in order to adhere to the requirements of the laudable National Action Plan on Climate Change in 2008 by the Ministry of Environment & Forests must also be ensured. Women can play an important role to earn carbon credits as compensation for doing well to the environment.

Conclusion

Women have been categorised as disadvantaged farmers due to various challenges faced by them. They are only de facto heads of the farms and are often without any transfer of legal titles. They are not even recognised as farmers. As a result, they remain excluded from many government opportunities such as access to insurance, markets, credits, etc. Lack of recognition of their rights hampers Indian women's possibilities not only to become more successful and productive farmers but more importantly gain self-sufficiency and decision-making power that can improve the livelihoods of their families and the whole community. Studies show that if women had the same access to those resources as men they would produce 20–30 per cent more food and their families would have access to better health, nutrition, and education (FAO, 2011). Since gender relations in general are socially, culturally and historically constrained and reconstructed (Agarwal, 1994). They are to be continuously redefined with the changing context.

Women have to play a larger role in agriculture with goal of agriculture shifting from only food security to food and nutritional security. Efforts are required to mainstream gender concerns in all agricultural development programmes. However, engendering agriculture may not be restricted to women's inclusion in the list of beneficiaries or training programmes. Majority of women farmers are small and subsistence workers with limited land rights. Efforts are needed to support women farmers in their land ownership, livelihoods, their visibility and identity, entitlements over agricultural services, social protection cover, and equal participation in user associations and decision-making bodies. Various ministries/departments are working towards the goal but have often tended to function in compartmentalised manner. These fragmented efforts are not sufficient to bring about the desirable impact. There is a need to prepare a plan of action to address the issues and challenges affecting women in agriculture.

Women can also play an important role in bringing the linkages between agriculture and nutrition. Campaign may be launched in selected districts where nutrition indicators are poor in popularising cultivation of nutritional crops, horticulture products, and traditional varieties. Procurement of such crops may be prioritised here so that the same can be used in Anganwadis, for supplementary nutrition, and in school mid-day meals.

First Global Conference on Women in Agriculture, 2012, which was organised in India, concluded that investment in women has much greater benefits in terms of social and economic development (GCWA, 2012). The conference deliberated at length and came out with some key elements through which women can empower themselves, for example by forming SHGs and having access to resources, policy support, and linking themselves to market for needed socio-economic benefits. The women also need support in terms of gender-oriented research, capacity building through vocational training for required entrepreneurship and knowledge using modern communication. This will also ensure household food and nutrition security. As the country has embraced the SDGs, the importance of women farmers cannot be ignored as it finds mention in 3 of the 17 SDG targets. While the progress in India on the legislative front has been significant, time has come to specifically remove barriers in law and implementation. Legal provisions will have to be made effective to ensure there are no barriers to equal participation of farm-women in primary societies dealing with agriculture, water use, fisheries, and forest products. Exploitation that arises out of land ownership by women such as witch hunting should also be addressed through state-level actions.

Redefining women's roles in the current agrarian crisis would also require opportunities for women beyond agriculture production, for example their role in reducing post-harvest loses, increasing efficiencies in value chain, linking up on-farm and off-farm practices, promoting rural enterprises through skill development and capacity-building/credit support for livelihoods opportunities and technologies for drudgery reduction to ease the time constraints faced by women. It is very significant to recognise and redefine women's role in the changing agricultural scenario if overall development goal of inclusive growth or attainment of SDGs have to be achieved.

Notes

Recommendations given in the National Commission of Farmers, 2006 and National Policy of Farmers that reiterated on giving recognition to women involved in agriculture. To give it a legal acceptance 'Women Farmers' Entitlement Bill, 2011' that was introduced as a private bill in the Rajya Sabha by Prof. M.S. Swaminathan, MP, Rajya Sabha and renowned agricultural Scientist on 11 May 2012. There is a need for its examination and approval by the government through focused stakeholders consultations.

1. Agricultural Census 2010–11, provides female operational holdings and does not capture land ownership.
2. Recommendations of National Consultation on Gender Perspective in Agriculture held on 8–9 August 2011.

References

Agarwal, B., (1986): Women, Poverty and Agricultural Growth in India, *Journal of Peasant Studies*, Vol. 13, No. 4, pp. 165–220.

——, (1994): *A Field of One's Own: Gender and Land Rights in South Asia*. Cambridge: Cambridge University Press.

——, (2003): Gender and Land Rights Revisited: Exploring New Prospects via the State, Family and Market, *Journal of Agrarian Change*, Vol. 3, Nos. 1 and 2, pp. 184–224.

——, (2010): Rethinking Agricultural Production Collectivities, *Economic & Political Weekly*, Vol. 45, No. 9, pp. 64–78.

Agriculture Census, (2011): Office of the Registrar General and Census Commissioner, Census data, 2011, Ministry of Home Affairs, Government of India, New Delhi.

FAO, (2011): The State of Food and Agriculture (Women in Agriculture: Closing the gender gap for development), Food and Agriculture Organization of the United States, Rome.

Galab, S. and Rao, N.C., (2003): Women's Self Help Groups, Poverty Alleviation & Empowerment, *Economic & Political Weekly*, Vol. 38, No. 12, pp. 1274–1283.

GCWA, (2012): Global Conference on Women in Agriculture, Organized from 13–15 March 2012, at NASC Complex, New Delhi. Synthesis Report of the Conference available at http://www.apaari.org/wp-content/uploads/downloads/2012/06/Synthesis-Report-GCWA.pdf

GoI, (2018): Report of the Working Group on Agricultural Extension for Agriculture and Allied Sectors for the Twelvth Five Year Plan (2012–17), Ministry of Agriculture.

Hirway, I., (2006): Where is Gender in the Eleventh Plan Approach Paper?, *Economic & Political Weekly*, Vol. 41, No. 32, pp. 3464–3466, 12 August. Available at https://www.google.co.in/webhp?source=search_app&gws_rd=cr#

ICAR, (2011): Recommendations of National Consultation on Gender Perspective in Agriculture held on 8–9 August 2011. A National Consultation on Gender Perspective in Agriculture was organized at NASC Complex, Pusa, New Delhi on 8–9 August 2011.

Innovative Finance and Micro Finance in Agriculture for the Eleventh Five Year Plan (2007–2012), Planning Commission, January 2007.

Kumar, Lakshmi, (2013): Illusion of Women Empowerment in Microfinance: A Case Study, *Economic & Political Weekly*, Vol. 48, Issue 15, pp. 70–76.

Lal, R., and Khurana, A., (2011): Gender Issues: The Role of Women in Agriculture Sector, *Zenith International Journal of Business Economics & Management Research*, Vol. 1, No. 1, October. Available at http://zenithresearch.org.in/

MORD, (2010): Guidelines for Mahila Kisan Sashaktikaran Pariyojana (MKSP), National Rural Livelihoods Mission (NRLM), Ministry of Rural Development, New Delhi: Government of India, New Delhi.

MWCD, (2007). Report of the Working Group on Empowerment of Women for the XI Plan, Ministry of Women & Child Development, Government of India, New Delhi.

National Policy for Farmers, (2007): Department of Agriculture & Cooperation, Ministry of Agriculture, Government of India, New Delhi.

National Policy on Skill Development & Entrepreneurship, (2015): Skill Development & Entrepreneurship, Government of India, New Delhi.

NCW, (2004): Report of the National Task Force on Technological Empowerment of Women in Agriculture, National Commission for Women, New Delhi.

NIPCCD, (2010): Statistics on Women in India, (2010). National Institute of Public Cooperation & Child Development, New Delhi.

NSSO, (2010): National Sample Survey Organisation: *Employment and Unemployment Situation in India 2007-08 – NSS 64th Round (July 2007-June 2008)*, New Delhi. National Sample Survey Office, Ministry of Statistics & Programme Implementation, Government of India, New Delhi.

Planning Commission, (2007): Report of Sub-group on Gender and Agriculture, Submitted to: Working Group on Gender Issues, Panchayat Raj Institutions, Public Private Partnership.

——, (2011): Final Report, Twelfth Plan Working Group on Disadvantaged Farmers Including Women, Chairperson by Bina Agarwal, submitted to the Planning Commission, Government of India, Yojna Bhavan, New Delhi.

Rao, N., (2005): Women's Rights to Land and Assets: Experience of Mainstreaming Gender in Development Projects. *Economic & Political Weekly*, Vol. 44, Nos. 44–45, pp. 4701–4708.

Saxena, N.C., (2012): Women, Land and Agriculture in Rural India, Supported by UN Women, United Nations Entity for Gender Equality and the Empowerment of Women (UNWOMEN), New Delhi.

——, (2013): Land, Livestock and Rights of Women in Rural India, In G. Kelkar, and M. Krishnaraj (eds), *Women, Land and Power in Asia*. New Delhi: Routledge.

Sharma, S., Rao, P.K. and Sharma, R., (2013): Role of Women in Decision-Making Related to Farm: A Study of Jammu District of J&K State, *International Journal of Scientific and Research Publications*, Vol. 3, No. 1, pp. 1–4.

Singh, A.K., Baliyan, Kavita and Baliyan, Sandeep Kumar, (2012): Status and Decision Making Power of Agricultural Farm Woman: A Study in West U.P., In K. Nagaraj Rao, H. Singh, and A. Sukhwal (eds), *Rural Management in Post-Reform Era,* published by Society for Advancement of Villagers Education and Rural Assistance (SAVERA), India, New Delhi: Bookwell Publication, pp. 84–104.

Sulaiman, R., Jafry, T. and Ashok, M.S. (2003): Cafeteria for Women in Agriculture, NCAP Working Paper 4, 74 pages, National Centre for Agricultural Economics and Policy Research, New Delhi.

Twelfth Five-Year Plan, (2012–17): Department of Agriculture and Cooperation Ministry of Agriculture, Government of India, New Delhi.

9 Production Conditions and Agrarian Change in Rural Odisha

Dinesh Kumar Nayak

Introduction

In today's context, the term 'rural' should be seen as a symbol for describing the marginalised and excluded rather than as a geographical space (IRDR, 2013), as the boundaries between rural and urban are merging and there is much greater interaction between the two. In terms of geographical space, however, India remains nearly 70 per cent rural with the pace of urbanisation having slowed down in recent times. The chances that nearly 60 per cent or more of the population will remain geographically rural (Unni, 2014). In the similar way, nowadays agriculture sector has been synonymised with the 'rural' due to its role of backbone for any rural economy in developing countries as far the dependency of household/individual is concerned.

Agriculture is the source of most vital requirements such as food, clothing, and raw materials. Not only it meets such requirements for a population now increasing at a fast pace but it must also strive to meet them adequately. This calls for a better public understanding of the different problems with which our agriculture is faced in expanding and developing economy. Again, agriculture has a record of about more than 12,000 years during these period which it has been experiencing a series of spatio-temporal changes.

The understanding of the contribution of agriculture is of special significance for setting up of goals of agricultural development for a region. Agricultural development helps the process of economic growth in various ways. Agricultural development means higher level of production of food and other agricultural products, higher income, and better standard of living for farmers. Agricultural development holds out benefit not only to farmers alone when agricultural sector grows, but its impact is also felt in other sectors of economy and it accelerates the overall economy of a region. In the development[1] discourse though it has been encouraged and discussed for the transforming agricultural economy into industrialised and then service sector, contrast to the case of Indian economy of change that has been observed more like from agriculture to service as per structural share of gross domestic product (GDP) is concern. The contribution of agriculture to GDP is decreasing over the years, but this sector plays a vital role in the Indian economy as it continues to provide employment and livelihood to the large proportion of population. Due to this importance of agricultural sector, it reflects in the government's various schemes and policies such as to improve the productivity of land, enhancing farm income and livelihood security of the dependent large mass of population.

For the developing countries like India, where a majority of families, in both the farm and non-farm sectors, derive their livelihoods from agriculture, sustainability of agriculture cannot be discussed or even defined in isolation of the issue of livelihoods. Livelihood is defined as adequate stock and flow of food and cash with an individual or a family to meet its basic needs. Livelihood security then means secured ownership of, or access to, resources and income-earning activities, including reserves and assets to offset risks, ease shocks and meet contingencies.

There are four principal ways of acquiring livelihoods by the rural households explained by Acharya (2006) such as production-based, labour-based, exchange- or market-based, and transfer-based livelihood. A large proportion of the small and marginal farmers gain livelihoods through production on small pieces of land. For these households, availability or access to inputs and improved methods of production are quite critical for their livelihoods. Second is the labour-based livelihood. Most of the small landholders and landless rural households derive livelihoods by selling their labour. For their livelihoods, demand for labour, wage rates, and prices of food are the critical factors. Third is the exchange- or market-based livelihood. Those rural households, which produce surplus food and non-food agricultural products or non-farm goods, earn their livelihoods by selling these surpluses in the market. The marketing system for these products and relative prices of what they sell and what they buy, affect their livelihoods. The fourth set of livelihoods is transfer-based entitlements. The households without any income-earning asset or able-bodied person to work depend for their livelihoods on transfers from the government or other social organisations, government's social security, and food assistance programmes.

Outlining the aforementioned things on agriculture and livelihoods of the dependents, the agrarian change has analysed in the following sections on land distribution in Odisha.

Changes in the Agrarian Land-Holdings Structure

To study the agrarian structure, the data sources for distribution of 'ownership[2] holding' of land is provided by National Sample Survey Office NSSO while 'number of operational holdings' and 'area operated' both are taken from the NSSO and *Agricultural Census*. Data on ownership and operational holdings have been collected regularly by the NSSO since its eighth round (1954–55). So far, seven land-holding surveys including the 70th round survey have been conducted and in case of Odisha Agricultural Census, there are eight rounds have been reported quinquennially since 1970–71 under the Government in

Revenue and Excise Department. For the sake of better comparable between the various years' data up to the available publications of the period from 1981–82 to 2012–13 (NSSO) and 1980–81 to 2010–11 (Agricultural Census of Odisha) has been exercised.

Any significant change in agrarian structure should have some impact on the size distribution of land-holdings. In this section, various aspects of this distribution are examined to see whether any such structural change is indicated. There are 13 size classes of disaggregated land distribution, which are merged to form 5 broad size classes along the lines adopted in the *Agricultural Census of India* and displayed as classes called categories such as: marginal (1 hectare or less), small (1.001–2.000 hectares), semi-medium (2.001–4.000 hectares), medium (4.001–10.000 hectares), and large (larger than 10.000 hectares). Here, for the sake of better comparison of Odisha's land-holding are categorised as the four groups of farmers based on their land area holdings are: marginal (up to 2.50 acre), small (2.51–5.00 acres), medium (5.01–10.00 acres), and large (10.01 acres and above).

Distribution of land-holding structure also relates to the categories of household and its changes. Three categories of households are such as: (a) households not operating land, (b) owning but not operating, and (c) neither owning nor operating. It may be seen that during the 80s, the proportion of households not operating land decreased at the all-India level while in Odisha this figure had partially stable. However, during 90s, the proportion of such households rose hugely in Odisha and all-India as well. It may also be seen from the table that changes of such households not operating land was largely contributed by those who owning but did not operating. There was significant appearance of increase in the proportion of households who neither owned nor operated any land.

The average land owned area has decreased to 0.59 hectares (all India) and 0.38 hectares (Odisha) in 2012–13, which was 0.73 hectares (all India) and 0.48 hectares (Odisha) in 2002–03, given the population increase in the same decade (Table 1). This falling size of land-holding has serious implication on the livelihoods of farmers' household community. It impulses them to look for other subsidiary sources to support their livelihood.

Apart from the observed decline in average size of holdings, the nature and extent of temporal variations in the size distribution of ownership holdings has observed. It is seen that the highly skewed nature of size distribution of ownership holdings has by and large, remained unchanged over time, notwithstanding the progressively downwards shift in the distribution. The size distribution of ownership holdings in India is characterised by predominance of landless households and marginal holders. During 2003, the marginal holdings and the landless (below 0.002 hectare) constituted about 80 per cent of the rural households but owned only 23 per cent of total area. The medium and large holders accounted for only 3.6 per cent of the households but had a combined share of about 35 per cent in the total land owned in 2003. Gini's coefficient of concentration of ownership of land-holdings, computed on the basis of data for the size classes came to 0.71, 0.71, and 0.74 in 1982, 1992, and 2003, respectively.

The proportion of marginal holders has risen from 67 per cent in 1982 to 80 per cent in 2003. This rise in the proportion of marginal holders has been accompanied by a steady decline in the proportion of small, medium, and large holders.

Table 1

Changing Proportion of Average Area Owned and Landless Households in Rural Areas, 1992–2013

State	*Year*	*Average Area (ha.) Owned per Household*	*Percentage of Landless Households*	*Average Area (ha.) Owned per Household Excluding Landless Households*
Odisha	1992	0.74	13.80	0.86
	2003	0.48	9.56	0.53
	2013	0.38	5.39	0.40
All-India	1992	1.01	11.30	1.14
	2003	0.73	10.04	0.81
	2013	0.59	7.41	0.64

Source: NSSO Report Number 399, 492, and 571.

Note: Land-holdings 'less than or equal to 0.002 hectares' is classified under 'landless' category.

Landlessness

Data generated in NSSO for all-India, it reveals no significant change in the percentage of landless households since 1961–62, that it was 11.3 per cent in 1982, same in 1992 and slightly lower 10 per cent as well as in 2003. With the progressive increase in the number of rural households, decline in average area owned is inevitable. The increasing pressure of rural population on the limited land base is reflected in the steady decline in the average area owned per household over the years. In 1982, the average area owned per household was 1.28 hectares. Gradually and steadily, it came down to 1.01 and 0.73 hectares in 1992 and 2003 respectively. Excluding the landless households, the average area owned was estimated to be 0.81 hectare in 2003, which is nearly 56 per cent of the estimate (1.44 hectares), obtained in 1982.

Percentage of landless households in rural areas of Odisha and all-India is shown in Table 1. The figures of landlessness for Odisha and India as well have seen as declined in the last decade during 2003–13. However, this NSSO's landlessness figures are criticised as underestimation (Rawal, 2014). In addition, the definition of landless who are owning less than 0.002 hectares of land is doubtful to capture the actual situation. Against this, Basole and Basu (2011) have remarked that a more realistic definition must consider all households owning less than one acre (0.40 hectares) as effectively landless. According to the effective landless margin, there were 60.1 per cent of households in 2002–03 (Basole and Basu, 2011) and later it rose to 66.1 per cent during 2012–13. It implies that some section of rural population becomes deprived of direct dependency from land and their livelihood. It again forces them to move out from agriculture and look other alternative options to live their households.

Land Ownership Across Size-Class

There is viability crisis due to intergenerational sub-division, fragmentation, and marginalisation of land; people need to cultivate tiny pieces of land. Table 2 shows the proportion of marginal holdings increased to 91 per cent in case of Odisha and 83 per cent in case of all-India in 2013 from 86 per cent (Odisha), 80 per cent (all-India) in 2003. Similarly, the area under marginal holdings increased by 14 percentage (Odisha) and six percentage (all-India) points in this period. The proportion of households in all other categories of holdings small, medium, and large has witnessed a decline. It is also observed that percentage of area owned by large holdings declined both in case of Odisha and all-India.

Table 2

Percentage Distribution of Households and Area Owned for Different Size Category of Ownership Holdings, 1992–2013

State	Year	Percentage of Households				Percentage of Area Owned			
		Marginal	Small	Medium	Large	Marginal	Small	Medium	Large
Odisha	2013	90.87	6.83	1.97	0.33	56.15	24.83	14.23	4.79
	2003	85.50	9.70	3.70	1.00	41.52	27.06	19.72	11.76
	1992	75.15	14.42	7.34	2.52	26.37	27.16	25.99	20.48
All-India	2013	82.83	10.00	5.01	2.17	29.76	23.54	22.07	24.64
	2003	79.60	10.80	6.00	3.60	23.05	20.38	21.98	34.63
	1992	71.88	13.42	9.28	5.42	16.93	18.59	24.58	39.90

Source: NSSO Report Number 492 and 571.

Note: Till 2002–03, the 'marginal' category of land-holding included 'landless' category also. Land-holdings 'less than or equal to 0.002 hectares' is classified under 'landless' category in 2013.

Ownership Holdings of Odisha with Comparison to Other States

For the states, the average area owned per household varied over a wide range, with Kerala showing the lowest value (0.23 hectare) and Rajasthan reporting the highest (2.08 hectares). Besides Kerala, Tripura (0.26 hectare), West Bengal (0.30 hectare), Tamil Nadu (0.34 hectare), Uttaranchal (0.37 hectare), Bihar (0.38 hectare), Sikkim (0.45 hectare), and Odisha (0.48 hectare) were the states that reported an average area less than 0.50 hectare. The national average was 0.73 hectare. In addition to Rajasthan, six more states reported average holding size exceeding one hectare. They were Madhya Pradesh (1.31 hectares), Arunachal Pradesh (1.17 hectares), Mizoram (1.11 hectares), Chhattisgarh (1.06 hectares), and Maharashtra and Gujarat (both 1.02 hectares). As per NSS Report No. 491, the all-India proportion of landless households was 10.0 per cent. The proportion was much larger in the Group of UTs (40%) and Sikkim (31%). Apart from these, landlessness was high in Arunachal Pradesh (22%), Maharashtra (18%), Tamil Nadu (17%), and Himachal Pradesh (15%) while Odisha's place is closer to country's average (10%).

Considering the country as a whole, the large and medium holdings, at the top 10 per cent bracket, owned 48 per cent of the total land in 1981–82 their share declining to 35 per cent in 2002–03. At the bottom, the proportion of marginal holdings increased from 60 per cent in 1982 to 80 per cent in 2002–03, while the proportion of area under marginal holdings rose from about 12 per cent in 1981–82 to 23 per cent in 2002–03. In fact, the proportion of marginal holdings to total number of holdings increased in Odisha during the last decades. An increasing trend in the percentage of area owned by marginal households is also observed in Odisha. The decline in the shares of the top three classes, both in number and area of ownership holdings is noticeable both in Odisha and as well in all-India.

The general feature that emerges from this distributions is that there is a rise in the percentage of households in the lowest category for both holdings and area owned, and a decline in the percentage of households in the categories of semi-medium and upwards. Only in respect of the small and semi-medium holders there was some amount of variation, both in magnitude and direction of change has observed. There is no doubt in the declining trend of the proportion of small holders in Odisha. The proportion of area under small holdings reveals much more varying trends across the states. Assam, Bihar, Gujarat, Haryana, Himachal Pradesh, Karnataka, Punjab, Maharashtra, Rajasthan, and Uttar Pradesh reported perceptible rise in proportion of area under small holdings during these periods, which is the reason reflected in all-India's figure. This was in contrast to the trend observed in the proportion of small holdings. The results presented in NSSO Report No. 491, 59th round reveal that the percentage of landless households as estimated increased by 2 per cent that is 2002–03 survey (9.6%) from the estimated proportion for 1982, in Odisha.

Land Operated Area and Holdings

The distribution of operational land-holdings and area operated over the years from 1981 to 2013 (Table 3) both in case of Odisha and India seen that there is little reduction in land inequality (see Figure 1) among bottom around 70 per cent of households who belongs to marginal and small holders. While on the other hand the less than 20 per cent of large size-group households owned around 45 per cent of land operated area.

Table 3

Changes in the Percentage Distribution of Operational Holdings and Area Operated for Different Size, 1992–2013

State	*Year*	*Household Operational Holdings*				*Area Operated of Household Operational Holdings*			
		Marginal	*Small*	*Medium*	*Large*	*Marginal*	*Small*	*Medium*	*Large*
Odisha	2013	86.25	10.28	2.92	0.54	55.88	24.98	13.87	5.27
	2003	78.40	15.20	5.20	1.20	43.00	28.70	18.80	9.50
	1992	60.00	24.30	12.00	3.70	22.10	30.20	27.90	19.90
All India	2013	73.20	15.30	8.10	3.41	27.71	23.44	23.50	25.35
	2003	69.80	16.20	9.00	5.00	22.60	20.90	22.50	34.00
	1992	62.80	17.80	12.00	7.40	15.60	18.70	24.10	41.60

Source: NSSO Report No. 492 and 571.

Figure 1

Lorenz Curves for the Distributions of Operational Land-Holdings

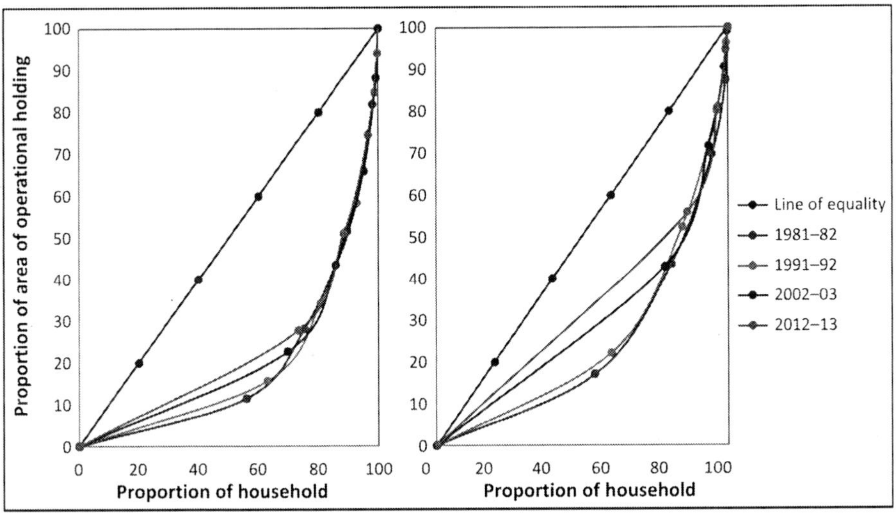

Source: Operational holdings data from NSSO Report No. 492 and 571.

Operational Holdings in Odisha vis-à-vis All-India

The number of operational holdings increased rapidly from 71 million in 1981–82 to 101 million in 2002–03, which is understandable considering the growth of population. However, the rate of growth of operational holdings, which accelerated over the decade from 1981–82 to 1991–92, appears to have slowed down[3] in the decade prior to 2002–03. If we assume that the 96:100 ratios of kharif holdings to agricultural-year holdings obtained for 1991–92 is maintained, then the number of operational holdings in 2002–03 with the agricultural year as reference period would be about 106 million. The virtual disappearance of joint holdings also has made some contribution to the rise in the number of operational holdings, though mostly during the first 10 years of the period under consideration. There were 0.62 per cent joint holdings, that is holdings operated jointly by members of two or more households, in 1981–82. By 2002–03, the proportion of joint holdings had come down to a tiny fraction (0.4%). According to Agricultural Census, data of Odisha also shows there was 22 per cent increase in operational holdings from 1980–81 to 2000–01; it was 19 per cent in the decade of 80s and dramatically reduced to three per cent increase in 90s. Hence, the trend in number of operational holdings both in NSSO and Agricultural Census for India and Odisha respectively is same rising and slowed down, in the studied period.

Changes in Operational Land-Holdings in India

In a land-scarce country with a significant section of the rural population below the poverty line, the case for ensuring that everyone has access to some minimum amount of land seems compelling for economic arguments in favour

Figure 2

Percentage of Operational Holdings in India, by Size-Class 1970–71 to 2010–11

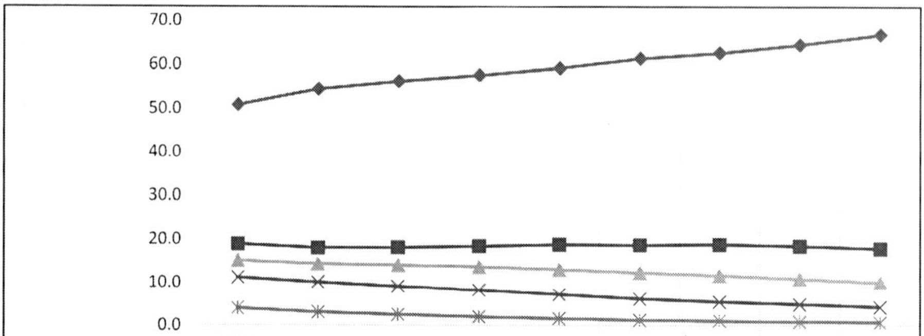

	1970-71	1976-77	1980-81	1985-86	1990-91	1995-96	2000-01	2005-06	2010-11
Marginal	50.98	54.58	56.39	57.79	59.44	61.58	62.88	64.77	67.10
Small	18.92	18.06	18.08	18.45	18.84	18.73	18.92	18.52	17.91
Semi-Medium	15.04	14.30	14.01	13.64	13.06	12.34	11.69	10.93	10.04
Medium	11.17	10.07	9.08	8.15	7.11	6.14	5.48	4.93	4.25
Large	3.90	2.99	2.44	1.97	1.55	1.21	1.03	0.85	0.70

Source: Number of operational holdings data taken from Agricultural Census, 2010–11

of land-holdings reshuffle view (Basu, 2010). Basu edited two points from various scholars' documents that in inverse farm-size relationship the small farms tend to be more productive than large farms, it suggests land-holding reshuffle could raise productivity by breaking large farms into several more small farms.

In Figure 2, it has shown that the trend in the percentage share of operational land-holdings by size-class from 1970–71 to 2010–11 in India. For all over the period, it has observed that there has been increasing trend in the marginalisation of land-holding as the number of marginal class of land-holdings are consistently has been increasing at a significant level from 1970–71 to 2010–11, at the decreasing share of all of the rest size-classes of land-holdings.

Similarly Figure 3 explains the percentage of area operated by operational holdings in India by different size-classes from 1970–71 to 2010–11, while the distributional share in these period shows changes among two groups, that is which have gained (marginal, small, and semi-medium) in their operated land area share and on the other hand the second group consists of large holders and medium holders have decreased in the share of operated area in recent years and decades. However, to analyse the actual holdings one has to observe the average operated area per holder among different size-classes to see the actual picture of this land-holdings and operation-based agrarian structure.

The average area operated (in hectares) by per holder among different size-classes from 1970–71 to 2010–11 are shown in Table 4, and it is clearly visible that there is no such significant change in India as per se to size-classes operational land for agricultural purpose. Because none of the size-classes have

Figure 3

Percentage of Area Operated by Operational Holdings in India, by Size-Class 1970–71 to 2010–11

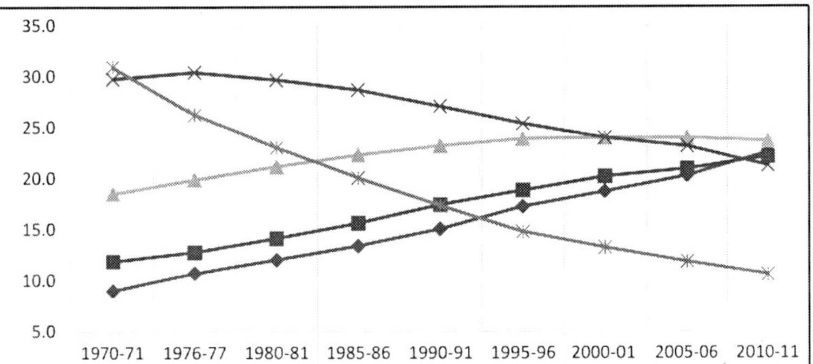

	1970-71	1976-77	1980-81	1985-86	1990-91	1995-96	2000-01	2005-06	2010-11
Marginal	9.00	10.72	12.05	13.39	15.04	17.21	18.70	20.23	22.50
Small	11.89	12.80	14.14	15.62	17.42	18.81	20.16	20.91	22.08
Semi-Medium	18.50	19.85	21.15	22.28	23.19	23.85	23.96	23.94	23.63
Medium	29.74	30.38	29.64	28.65	27.04	25.34	23.97	23.11	21.20
Large	30.87	26.25	23.02	20.05	17.32	14.79	13.22	11.82	10.59

Source: Number of operational holdings data taken from Agricultural Census, 2010–11

gained in their average area operated over these periods and the pattern of size-class shows the case of Indian farmers can be categorised in the small and marginal size groups though there is larger inequality in the agricultural land-distribution has been observed among these size-groups. There is consistent decrease in average area operated in India since 1970–71.

Table 4

Average Area Operated (in Hectares) of Operational Holdings in India, by Size-Class 1970–71 to 2010–11

Size Groups	*1970–71*	*1976–77*	*1980–81*	*1985–86*	*1990–91*	*1995–96*	*2000–01**	*2005–06**	*2010–11*
Marginal	0.40	0.39	0.39	0.39	0.39	0.40	0.40	0.38	0.39
Small	1.44	1.42	1.44	1.43	1.43	1.42	1.42	1.38	1.42
Semi-medium	2.81	2.78	2.78	2.77	2.76	2.73	2.72	2.68	2.71
Medium	6.08	6.04	6.02	5.96	5.90	5.84	5.81	5.74	5.76
Large	18.1	17.57	17.41	17.21	17.33	17.20	17.12	17.08	17.38
All Sizes	2.28	2.00	1.84	1.69	1.55	1.41	1.33	1.23	1.15

Source: Number of operational holdings data taken from Agricultural Census, 2010–11.

Note: *Excluding Jharkhand.

Changes and Regional Variations in Land-Holdings

Apart from the observed decline in average size of holdings, the nature and extent of temporal variations in the size distribution of ownership holdings has observed in India. It is seen that the highly skewed nature of size distribution of ownership holdings has by and large, remained unchanged over time, notwithstanding the progressively downwards shift in the distribution. The size distribution of ownership holdings in India is characterised by predominance of landless households and marginal holders. During 2003, the marginal holdings and the landless (below 0.002 hectare) constituted about 80 per cent of the rural households but owned only 23 per cent of total area. The medium and large holders accounted for only 3.6 per cent of the households but had a combined share of about 35 per cent in the total land owned in 2003. Gini's coefficient of concentration of ownership of land-holdings, computed on the basis of data for the size classes came to 0.71, 0.71, and 0.74 in 1982, 1992, and 2003, respectively.[4] The proportion of marginal holders has risen from 67 per cent in 1982 to 80 per cent in 2003. This rise in the proportion of marginal holders has been accompanied by a steady decline in the proportion of small, medium, and large holders. The number of operational holdings increased rapidly from 71 million in 1981–82 to 101 million in 2002–03, which is understandable considering the growth of population. However, the rate of growth of operational holdings, which accelerated over the decade from 1981–82 to 1991–92, appears to have slowed down[5] in the decade prior to 2002–03. If we assume that the 96:100 ratios of kharif holdings to agricultural-year holdings obtained for 1991–92 is maintained, then the number of operational holdings in 2002–03 with the agricultural year as reference period would be about 106 million. The virtual disappearance of joint holdings also has made some contribution to the rise in the number of operational holdings, though mostly during the first 10 years of the period under consideration.

In Table 5, it has shown that the states/region-wise percentage share of operational holdings in India and its variations in changes from 2005–06 to 2010–11. During 2010–11 the share of North India (26.17%) in the percentage share of number of operational land-holdings is top followed by South India (25.99%), then east, west, central, north-east, and at bottom Union Territories; and the same proportional share in the number of operational land-holdings was seen for the 2005–06 in India. The per cent variation from the year 2005–06 to 2010–11 at regional level in India for the number of operational land-holdings, it is seen that all the regions in India except Union Territories (–1.98%) has increased with the Central India has maximum variation of 10.99 per cent followed by east, north, south, west, and north-east; while it is a matter of concern that the agricultural area of land-holdings has been decreasing for all regions of India including India total.

Among the States in India, Uttar Pradesh has maximum share followed by Bihar and then Maharashtra in the number of operational holdings. However, the case is not same while it has observed for the area operational land-holdings, it is Rajasthan that has maximum share though its marginal number of land-holdings as compare to the top in row States. In the proportional share of area of operational holdings, the rest top order after Rajasthan are Maharashtra, Uttar Pradesh, Andhra Pradesh, and Gujarat. As per regional variations in number and area of operational holdings, the many states are seen that while there is increase in the number of holdings at the same time the area of land-holdings has been getting decreased from the 2005–06 to 2010–11.

Table 5

Region-wise Per cent Share of Number and Area of Operational Holdings

S. No.	States/UTs	2010–11 (in %)		2005–06 (in %)		Variation (in %)	
		Number	Area	Number	Area	Number	Area
1	Haryana	1.17	2.28	1.24	2.26	0.87	1.76
2	Himachal Pradesh	0.69	0.60	0.72	0.61	3.00	-1.34
3	Jammu & Kashmir	1.05	0.56	1.07	0.58	5.15	-3.03
4	Punjab	0.76	2.49	0.78	2.50	4.88	0.10
5	Rajasthan	4.98	13.24	4.79	13.23	11.35	0.94
6	Uttar Pradesh	16.86	11.04	17.38	11.31	3.86	-1.59
7	Uttarakhand	0.66	0.51	0.71	0.53	-0.98	-3.66
A	North India	26.17	30.73	26.69	31.03	4.99	-0.19
1	Goa	0.06	0.06	0.04	0.04	47.17	45.90
2	Gujarat	3.53	6.20	3.61	6.49	4.83	-3.61
3	Maharashtra	9.90	12.39	10.61	12.64	-0.12	-1.19
B	West India	13.49	18.64	14.26	19.16	1.26	-1.92
1	Andhra Pradesh	9.52	8.96	9.32	9.15	9.39	-1.35
2	Karnataka	5.66	7.62	5.87	7.82	3.31	-1.81
3	Kerala	4.94	0.95	5.34	0.98	-1.06	-2.83
4	Tamil Nadu	5.87	4.07	6.34	4.31	-0.92	-4.92
C	South India	25.99	21.59	26.87	22.27	3.55	-2.27
1	Bihar	11.70	4.00	11.34	3.95	10.47	2.19
2	Jharkhand	1.96	1.98	0.00	0.00	NA	NA
3	Odisha	3.37	3.04	3.37	3.17	7.14	-3.33
4	West Bengal	5.15	3.45	5.41	3.49	1.87	-0.29
D	East India	22.18	12.48	20.12	10.61	7.60	-0.27
1	Chhattisgarh	2.71	3.19	2.68	3.29	8.23	-2.42
2	Madhya Pradesh	6.41	9.92	6.12	10.10	12.19	-0.99
E	Central India	9.12	13.11	8.80	13.39	10.99	-1.34
1	Arunachal Pradesh	0.08	0.24	0.08	0.23	0.00	6.37
2	Assam	1.97	1.88	2.13	1.93	-1.09	-1.64
3	Manipur	0.11	0.11	0.12	0.11	0.67	0.00
4	Meghalaya	0.15	0.18	0.16	0.15	3.45	19.09
5	Mizoram	0.07	0.07	0.07	0.07	2.22	-4.55
6	Nagaland	0.13	0.67	0.13	0.74	5.33	-8.44
7	Sikkim	0.05	0.07	0.06	0.07	2.74	-1.83
8	Tripura	0.42	0.18	0.44	0.18	2.30	1.79
F	North-east India	2.97	3.39	3.18	3.47	0.10	-1.49
1	A&N Islands	0.01	0.01	0.01	0.01	0.00	0.00

Cont'd...

...Cont'd

S. No.	States/UTs	2010–11 (in %)		2005–06 (in %)		Variation (in %)	
		Number	Area	Number	Area	Number	Area
2	Chandigarh	0.00	0.00	0.00	0.00	0.00	0.00
3	D&N Haveli	0.01	0.01	0.01	0.01	7.14	-4.76
4	Daman & Diu	0.01	0.00	0.01	0.00	0.00	-25.00
5	Delhi	0.01	0.02	0.02	0.02	-20.00	-21.05
6	Lakshadweep	0.01	0.00	0.01	0.00	0.00	0.00
7	Puducherry	0.02	0.01	0.02	0.02	6.45	-8.33
G	Union Territories	0.07	0.06	0.08	0.07	-1.98	-10.62
	India Total	100	100	100	100	4.97	-1.20

Source: Number and area of operational holdings data taken from Agricultural Census, 2010–11

In the case of Odisha, the share of percentage number of operational holdings has 3.37 per cent (comprise around 45 lakhs) of number of operational holdings out of India total for both the time periods 2005–06 and 2010–11, and are more than all north-east region states of India. The per cent variations in the number of operational land-holdings in Odisha have been increased at 7.14 per cent; while the area of operational holdings has been decreased at -3.33 level per cent.

For all size classes of land-holdings such as marginal, small, semi-medium, medium and large, Tables 6–10, respectively, are shown by regional level for the changes in per cent of number and area of operational holdings in India and variations from 2005–06 to 2010–11. In the case of marginal size class east, south, and north regions have maximum per cent share in number of operational land-holdings while the west, central, and north-east regions have minimum share. States like Bihar, Odisha, Jharkhand, and West Bengal comprise the central region in India, which has maximum per cent variations in both number and area of operational land-holdings.

Table 6

Region-wise Per cent Share of Number and Area of Operational Holdings in India, Marginal Size-Class

S. No.	Regions	2010–11 (in %)		2005–06 (in %)		Variation (in %)	
		Number	Area	Number	Area	Number	Area
1	North	26.43	27.45	27.36	29.17	7.15	5.50
2	West	9.25	11.42	9.26	11.26	10.83	13.70
3	South	27.06	24.38	28.56	25.35	5.10	7.83
4	East	27.81	25.75	25.58	23.27	11.93	13.79
5	Central	6.54	7.99	6.12	7.58	18.68	18.17
6	North-East	2.83	2.95	3.05	3.29	3.02	0.76
	India Total	100	100	100	100	10.91	12.12

Source: Number and area of operational holdings data taken from Agricultural Census, 2010–11.

In Table 7, it has revealed that the changes and variations in per cent of number and area of land-holdings among different regions in India for the small size-class group. Here, East region, which is maximum share of marginal size-class has placed below in the per cent share of number and area operational land-holdings than north, west, and south. Central and north-east regions are at bottom place. Though the West region has significant share in number and area of operational holdings, it has observed that there is marginal decreased in the number of operational land-holdings from 2005–06 to 2010–11, and the similar case has been found in case of north-east region. In remaining all regions other than west and north-east included India total, there has been increase in the number and area of operational holdings in these period.

Table 7

Region-wise Per cent Share of Number and Area of Operational Holdings in India, Small Size-Class

S. No.	*Regions*	*2010–11 (in %)*		*2005–06 (in %)*		*Variation (in %)*	
		Number	*Area*	*Number*	*Area*	*Number*	*Area*
1	North	22.42	22.25	22.67	23.11	2.38	2.50
2	West	22.16	22.22	22.99	21.79	–0.18	8.57
3	South	25.90	25.72	25.50	26.02	5.18	5.27
4	East	13.22	13.71	13.12	13.31	4.33	9.64
5	Central	13.24	13.18	12.15	12.55	12.79	11.82
6	Northeast	3.01	2.87	3.49	3.14	–10.78	–2.88
	India Total	100	100	100	100	3.55	6.47

Source: Number and area of operational holdings data taken from Agricultural Census, 2010–11.

Table 8

Region-wise Per cent Share of Number and Area of Operational Holdings in India, Semi-Medium Size-Class

S. No.	*Regions*	*2010–11 (in %)*		*2005–06 (in %)*		*Variation (in %)*	
		Number	*Area*	*Number*	*Area*	*Number*	*Area*
1	North	25.13	25.59	24.72	25.50	0.00	–0.16
2	West	23.35	23.26	25.03	24.12	–8.23	–4.05
3	South	23.21	22.79	23.60	23.62	–3.27	–3.99
4	East	9.18	9.28	8.44	8.33	–16.76	–13.77
5	Central	15.53	15.54	14.74	15.04	3.60	2.77
6	North-East	3.54	3.47	3.39	3.32	2.71	4.13
	India Total	100	100	100	100	–1.64	–0.51

Source: Number and area of operational holdings data taken from Agricultural Census, 2010–11.

In the case of semi-medium size-class (Table 8) in region-wise per cent share of number and area of operational holdings, the remarkable change has been observed for the east region where both the percentage share of number and the area of operational holdings has fall down to fifth place, that is after north, west, south, and central regions. It shows that the number and area operational holdings in medium size-classes in the states Odisha, Bihar, Jharkhand, and West Bengal are fewer than the regions north, west, south, and central India.

In Tables 9 and 10, it has revealed that the kind of more similar trend as in case of semi-medium size-class changes in the percentage share of number and area operational holdings has been found in the case of medium and large size-class group also. There are fewer per cent of number and area of operational holdings of medium and large size-class present in east region of India. In addition, their variation from 2005–06 to 2010–11 is the highest among all regions, that is the per cent of number and the area of operational holdings has been decreased in this period.

Table 9

Region-wise Per cent Share of Number and Area of Operational Holdings in India, Medium Size-Class

S. No.	Regions	2010–11 (in %)		2005–06 (in %)		Variation (in %)	
		Number	Area	Number	Area	Number	Area
1	North	35.30	36.44	32.74	33.93	-0.62	-0.68
2	West	20.87	20.50	23.65	22.61	-18.70	-16.16
3	South	18.23	17.81	19.23	19.14	-12.64	-13.94
4	East	5.06	4.82	3.86	3.56	-31.71	-30.36
5	Central	16.87	16.84	17.24	17.53	-9.83	-11.16
6	North-East	3.63	3.51	3.18	3.15	4.93	2.95
	India Total	100	100	100	100	-7.84	-7.53

Source: Number and area of operational holdings data taken from Agricultural Census, 2010–11.

Table 10

Region-wise Per cent Share of Number and Area of Operational Holdings in India, Large Size-Class

S. No.	States/UTs	2010-11 (in %)		2005-06 (in %)		Variation (in %)	
		Number	Area	Number	Area	Number	Area
1	North	56.53	55.39	53.19	53.76	-5.66	-6.93
2	West	12.13	12.53	12.59	11.23	-14.49	0.76
3	South	12.64	11.92	14.32	13.73	-21.66	-21.56
4	East	3.08	4.20	1.46	2.54	-37.50	-16.18
5	Central	12.02	10.95	14.69	13.40	-27.33	-26.20
6	North-East	3.80	4.98	3.65	5.29	-7.50	-14.95
	India Total	100	100	100	100	-11.22	-9.66

Source: Number and area of operational holdings data taken from Agricultural Census, 2010–11.

Operational Holdings, Area, and Tenancy Status

The key characteristics of agrarian structure in Odisha (see Table 11) reveals that the number of operational holdings in Odisha has increased for all over the periods from 1980–81 to 2010–11, but it has rapidly increased during the 80s, and similar revival case seen during 2000–10 (14.76%) after a slow increment of the 90s. On the other hand, total area operated in Odisha has reduced both in number of hectare and percentage change in decadal year except only there was a marginal increase during 1990–91.

Table 11

Estimates of Certain Key Characteristics of Agrarian Structure in Odisha: 1980–81 to 2010–11

Characteristics	*1980–81*	*1990–91*	*2000–01*	*2010–11*
Number of operational holdings (thousand)	3,328	3,948	4,067	4,667
Percentage increase (%)	–	18.62	3.02	14.76
Total area operated (thousand hectare)	5,278	5,296	5,081	4,852
Percentage increase (%)	–	0.35	-4.06	-4.51
Average area operated (hectare) per holding	1.59	1.34	1.25	1.04
In total area operated, percentage share of:				
(a) Area wholly owned and self-operated	91.84	92.48	77.37	80.64
(b) Area wholly leased in	0.32	0.19	2.09	3.29
(c) Area wholly otherwise possessed	0.59	0.46	0.71	0.85
(d) Area differently combination of partly owned, partly leased in and partly otherwise operated	0.21	7.22	16.12	8.01
Area leased-in to total operated area (%)	1.27	0.45	7.52	8.05
Percentage increase of area leased-in (%)				2.29
Percentage distributions of leased-in area by terms of lease:				
(a) Fixed money	6.94	15.51	5.37	13.23
(b) Fixed produce	16.96	11.09	19.8	19.87
(c) Share of produce	71.58	61.24	68.94	65.30
(d) Others	4.52	12.16	5.88	1.60

Source: Report on Agricultural Censuses of Odisha, different rounds.

Corresponding increase in number of operational holdings and decrease in its respective area operated for all periods brought out the significant declined in average area operated per holding, respectively. The maximum percentage share has been covered by area wholly owned and self-operated for all over the periods, but changes in the magnitudes, it has differed. The area wholly leased-in and wholly otherwise possessed have similar trends in their percentage change of magnitude, area wholly owned, and self-operated varied oppositely. The percentage change of area leased-in to total operated area has increased significantly for all over the years except 1990–91.

Changes in Agricultural Growth

The Indian economy has undergone structural changes over time with the anticipated decline in the share of agriculture in the GDP (see Table 12) and the same trend has been observed for Odisha, though the marginal higher figure to average India total over the all-time periods. Despite a fall in its share from 55.1 per cent in 1950–51 to 12.27 per cent in 2012–13, the importance of agriculture has not diminished for two major reasons. First, the country achieved self-sufficiency in food production at the macro level, despite challenges of high prevalence of malnourished children and high incidence of rural poverty (Kannan and Sundaram, 2011). Second, the dependence of the rural workforce on agriculture for employment has not declined in proportion to the sectoral contribution to GDP. This has resulted in widening the income disparity between the agricultural and non-agricultural sectors (Chand and Chauhan, 1999). The experiences of developed countries show that transfer of labour force from agriculture to non-agriculture, in particular the manufacturing sector took place. This had brought enhanced productivity growth in agriculture and hence higher income (Gollin et al., 2002). However, India's manufacturing sector witnessed volatile growth and its share in GDP has almost remained constant at around 20 per cent for the last decades since 1980–81. Further, given the fact that the current economic growth pattern is driven by the service sector, labour absorption outside agriculture will be slow until rural education improves dramatically in the near future.

Table 13 depicts the changes in sectoral share composition of Net State Domestic Product (NSDP) by industry in Odisha and India from 80s, 90s, 2000s, and during post-reform and since 1980s to 2012–13 that only the tertiary sector in India and Odisha has consistently increased its share of NSDP composition and the agriculture/primary sector has been significantly at an increasing manner decreased its compositional contribution.

The growth rate of agriculture including different industries primary (forestry and logging, fishing, and mining and quarrying), secondary and tertiary sector during the time period 1980–2013 has shown in Table 14. The growth rate of primary sector is very marginal as comparison to secondary and tertiary sector for all the time periods 1980–81 to 1989–90, 1990–91 to 1999–2000, 2000–01 to 2009–10 and even since 1980–81, 1990–91, and 2000–01 to 2012–13.

Implications of Agrarian Structure on Productivity

Profit derived by per household in agricultural occupation in all size class across different farmer types was less than profit per hectare in Odisha during the year 2002–03. Owner cultivators across all the land size-classes have incurred maximum profit followed by the mix tenants. Although there was no clear pattern observed in individual land size profit per household and per hectare in case of pure tenant and others, at an aggregate per hectare and per household profit of pure tenants was more than the other farmers.

Table 12

Sectoral Composition of NSDP in Odisha and India from 1980–81 to 2012–13

	1980–81		*1990–91*		*2000–01*		*2010–11*		*2012–13*	
	Odisha	*India*	*Odisha*	*India*	*Odisha*	*India*	*Odisha*	*India*	*Odisha*	*India*
Agriculture	43.27	29.87	31.58	25.37	21.99	19.41	17.05	12.81	16.63	12.27
Forestry and logging	13.14	6.38	7.27	4.00	5.01	2.74	2.67	1.60	2.44	1.52
Fishing	0.74	1.08	1.35	1.13	1.65	1.07	1.12	0.69	1.19	0.70
Mining and quarrying	1.30	2.59	2.49	3.37	5.17	2.78	5.51	1.89	2.56	1.57
Primary sector	58.46	39.93	42.70	33.87	33.83	26.00	26.35	16.98	22.82	16.06
Secondary sector	23.85	22.54	34.55	23.34	26.14	22.19	18.61	22.85	20.50	22.24
Tertiary sector	27.43	37.53	35.41	42.79	44.30	51.81	55.04	60.16	56.68	61.70
Total	100	100	100	100	100	100	100	100	100	100

Source: Calculated from the time series data provided by *EPW* Research Foundation on National Account Statistics and Domestic Products of India.

Table 13

Changes in Sectoral Share Composition of NSDP by Industry in Odisha and India from 1980–81 to 2012–13

	1980–81 to 1989–90		*1990–91 to 1999–2000*		*2000–01 to 2009–10*		*2000–01 to 2012–13*		*1990–91 to 2012–13*		*1980–81 to 2012–13*	
	Odisha	*India*	*Odisha*	*India*	*Odisha*	*India*	*Odisha*	*India*	*Odisha*	*India*	*Odisha*	*India*
Agriculture	-3.95	-4.32	-7.93	-5.07	-4.15	-6.64	-5.36	-7.13	-16.22	-12.21	-26.64	-17.60
Forestry and logging	-5.71	-2.13	-2.51	-1.25	-2.08	-1.04	-2.57	-1.22	-2.97	-2.00	-10.70	-4.86
Fishing	0.34	0.05	0.38	-0.06	-0.52	-0.36	-0.46	-0.38	-0.50	-0.58	0.45	-0.39
Mining and quarrying	0.50	0.63	2.19	-0.55	1.47	-0.90	-2.61	-1.20	-0.43	-1.56	1.26	-1.02
Primary sector	-8.82	-5.78	-7.87	-6.94	-5.28	-8.95	-11.01	-9.94	-20.11	-16.35	-35.63	-23.87
Secondary sector	-0.85	0.52	-6.54	-1.52	-7.69	1.12	-5.64	0.06	-7.78	-0.06	-3.35	-0.30
Tertiary sector	2.85	5.26	6.33	8.46	8.69	7.83	12.38	9.88	21.51	16.40	29.25	24.17

Source: Calculated from the time series data provided by *EPW* Research Foundation on National Account Statistics and Domestic Products of India.

Table 14

Growth Rate of Industries in Odisha and India, 1980–2013

	1980–81 to 1989–90		1990–91 to 1999–2000		2000–01 to 2009–10		2000–01 to 2012–13		1990–91 to 2012–13		1980–81 to 2012–13	
	Odisha	India	Odisha	India	Odisha	India	Odisha	India	Odisha	India	Odisha	India
Agriculture	3.08	2.95	1 27	3.02	4.46	2.72	3.98	3.14	1.84	2.60	0.83	2.75
Forestry and logging	–2.72	–0.29	–0.28	0.88	1.10	0.84	0.65	1.38	1.50	1.84	–0.68	1.23
Fishing	9.08	5.56	8.35	4.99	2.83	2.47	2.99	2.94	2.43	2.71	5.90	4.27
Mining and quarrying	8.72	6.84	13.63	3.47	11.31	2.77	3.32	2.39	8.00	3.04	10.81	4.19
Primary sector	2.19	2.87	2.34	2.90	5.24	2.51	3.46	2.86	2.69	2.57	1.60	2.75
Secondary sector	5.00	5.10	1.12	5.34	6.90	8.46	5.40	7.98	3.92	6.71	3.82	5.80
Tertiary sector	6.33	6.24	6.18	7.44	9.88	9.02	9.67	9.05	8.37	8.45	6.91	7.48
Net domestic product at factor cost	4.79	4.88	4.03	5.56	8.25	7.45	7.24	7.50	5.88	6.64	4.49	5.77
Per capita NDP at factor cost	2.92	2.66	2.39	3.50	6.93	5.83	5.89	5.94	4.53	4.91	2.91	3.83

Source: Calculated from the time series data provided by *EPW* Research Foundation on National Account Statistics and Domestic Products of India.

NSSO made survey on farmers' situation assessment where the expenses for cultivation are on purchasing seeds, pesticides/insecticides, fertiliser/ manure, irrigation, minor repair and maintenance of machinery and equipment, interest repayment for borrowed amount, lease rent for land, wage payment made to regular and casual labour, and other expenses. Total receipts a tenant or cultivator's household earned from the quantity of output production and by-products in this process in terms of its money value. During the kharif season, almost all of tenants and cultivators cultivated, while during the rabi season due to scarcity of irrigation facility and its shortage as our country is monsoon dependent, less number of households engaged them in cultivation.

Due to less profitability to the small and marginal size peasants, it certainly impacted on their investment attitude on productive assets and the inputs on agricultural technology, along with the leasing-in and leasing out of land; that is leasing-in land has increased in all size-class households. Farmers acquires information of modern agricultural technology from participating in various training programme, from Krishi Vigyan Kendra, extension worker, television, radio, newspaper, village fair, government demonstration, input dealer, from other progressive farmers, attending farmers study tours, para technician, private agency, NGOs, primary cooperative society, output buyers, food processors, credit agency, and others.

Changes in Cropping Pattern

Cropping pattern has shown a changing trend in recent years (see Table 15). The area under rice has increased from 48.1 per cent of the gross cropped area of the state in 1980–85 to 51.35 per cent during 2005–10. There is a marginal increase in the area under cash crops.

The temporal changes in cropping pattern in Odisha reveal crop diversification in the state. During the period 1980–2010, the area under some cereals (wheat, ragi, jowar, bajra, and small millets); rabi pulses; oilseeds (castor, linseed, and safflower); and cash crops (jute, mesta, and tobacco) declined by varying degrees, and increased under selected cereals (rice and maize); oilseed crop sunflower; cash crop cotton; and condiment and spice crop ginger. The vegetable crops like potato, sweet potato, and onion have not revealed any clear pattern of changes during the period studied. Based on a similar periodical trend change, the cropping pattern across the selected 30 crops revealed three major groups. One, where area under crops increased from 50 per cent to around 60 per cent; two, crops in which area decreased from around 25 per cent to 16 per cent; and three: crops group sharing between 12 and 15 per cent area did not reveal any clear trend of increasing or decreasing area.

Hence, it has observed here that even if there is a process of diversification through the periodical changes in the cropping pattern of around 10 crops (wheat, ragi, jowar, bajra, small millets, castor, linseed, safflower, jute, mesta, and tobacco), it is outweighed by the specialised and concentrated crops. Although the number of such crops is small (viz. rice, maize, sunflower, cotton, and ginger) but total the share of area under these crops is high. Among

Table 15

Charges in Cropping Pattern in Odisha: 1980–2010

Crops		*Share in Total Cropped Area (%)*					
		1980–85	*1985–90*	*1990–95*	*1995–2000*	*2000–05*	*2005–10*
Cereals	Rice	48.12	48.06	47.31	53.97	55.58	51.35
	Wheat	0.83	0.50	0.27	0.21	0.21	0.21
	Ragi	3.55	2.91	2.51	2.41	2.39	2.16
	Maize	1.81	1.83	2.02	1.91	2.21	2.44
	Jowar	0.39	0.36	0.22	0.19	0.14	0.11
	Bajra	0.11	0.09	0.07	0.05	0.04	0.03
	Small millets	2.42	1.24	0.72	0.58	0.41	0.23
	Total cereals	57.25	54.98	53.13	59.32	61.00	56.53
Pulses	Kharif pulses	5.92	6.96	7.24	6.64	6.89	8.34
	Rabi pulses	15.19	15.13	14.91	13.49	12.41	14.57
	Total pulses	21.11	22.09	22.15	20.13	19.30	22.90
Total food grains		78.36	77.07	75.28	79.45	80.30	79.43
Vegetables/	Potato	0.10	0.11	0.11	0.11	0.10	0.11
horticulture	Sweet potato	0.63	0.63	0.54	0.60	0.54	0.56
crops	Onion	0.46	0.49	0.48	0.59	0.29	0.34
	Total vegetable	8.09	7.72	9.01	6.16	7.08	7.71
Cash crops: jute	Jute	0.54	0.39	0.35	0.22	0.15	0.13
Mesta	Mesta	0.48	0.43	0.34	0.36	0.32	0.24
Sunhemp	Sunhemp	0.13	0.15	0.14	0.14	0.13	0.14
Cotton	Cotton	0.04	0.05	0.06	0.30	0.53	0.63

Cont'd...

...Cont'd

Crops		*Share in Total Cropped Area (%)*					
		1980–85	*1985–90*	*1990–95*	*1995–2000*	*2000–05*	*2005–10*
Sugarcane	Sugarcane	0.57	0.51	0.44	0.53	0.29	0.44
Condiments and spices (C&S)	Chillies	0.95	0.98	1.01	1.01	0.92	0.87
	Coriander	0.19	0.21	0.23	0.26	0.21	0.22
	Garlic	0.19	0.23	0.20	0.19	0.13	0.13
	Ginger	0.07	0.08	0.11	0.15	0.18	0.19
	Turmeric	0.28	0.27	0.26	0.30	0.31	0.29
	Total C&S	1.67	1.78	1.81	1.91	1.74	1.69
Tobacco	Tobacco	0.21	0.17	0.13	0.10	0.06	0.04
Oilseeds	Groundnuts	2.79	4.02	3.59	3.34	2.73	2.79
	Til	2.74	3.29	4.35	3.42	3.09	3.53
	Castor	0.51	0.39	0.29	0.29	0.21	0.20
	Mustard	1.45	1.54	1.72	1.49	1.32	1.28
	Linseed	0.39	0.36	0.34	0.35	0.25	0.29
	Niger	1.97	2.05	2.08	1.83	1.70	1.26
	Sun flower	0.01	0.04	0.05	0.07	0.07	0.18
	Safflower	0.05	0.04	0.03	0.03	0.02	0.01
	Total oilseeds	9.92	11.72	12.44	10.82	9.40	9.54
Total cash crops		13.56	15.20	15.72	14.39	12.62	12.86

Source: Calculated from area data obtained from published sources of Directorate of Agriculture and Food Production, Government of Odisha.

Note: List of crops taken here covers 96 to 98 per cent of GCA in the districts of Odisha.

individual crops, rice has the highest share in area, and which has increased over time in the two and half decades under consideration. An important implication of this result is that contrary to the association of crop diversification with agricultural development, in the case of Odisha, specialisation is associated with higher commercialisation and agricultural development.

Conclusion

In this paper, agrarian change and production conditions in rural Odisha and India as the changes occurred by different size-classes of land-holdings in different time periods, the theories of agrarian change has referred according to Ellis that the interpretations of social and economic change in the rural sector have been discussed. The analysis of the economic change in rural economy such as in the cases of changes in structural growth in the agriculture vis-a-vis other industries; changes in the land ownership and operational land-holdings; and the implications of agrarian structure on productivity have been discussed.

Theories of agricultural development seek to describe the evolving role of the agricultural sector and in the different phases of time by different groups of scholar by different approach of development the role of agrarian change has been observed. Earlier dual economy approach (Lewis, 1954; Fei and Ranis, 1964), so-called traditional agriculture was known for its role that it supplies resources to the modern sector of the economy, which has seen changes in later models by the industrialised countries experiences that agriculture would decline in its share of GDP as development proceeds; and in this study, it has observed that in case of Odisha and India the structural change of the economy since 1980–81 till 2012–13 revealed that the sectoral composition of NSDP in Odisha and India has been diversifying from the agriculture/primary sector led-economy towards the tertiary sector led economy. As, this process of diversification is in macro term for the economy as whole, the people-centric and households based diversification more specifically livelihood diversification and its different aspects in the rural sector is crucial to analyse in more details on employment and poverty in rural Odisha; livelihoods diversification and its extent, pattern and determinants; seasonal migration and spatial diversification in rural labour market; implications of livelihood diversification on poverty and inequality.

Notes

1. Economic development where economic growth structural changes in favour of non-agricultural activities, which implies that the share of agriculture in GDP should decline and the share of industrial sector and services should increase.
2. The data on land ownership are being collected by NSSO since its eighth round, due to some definitional changes for the coverage of owner-like possession, the coverage of the term 'ownership' has remained unaltered since the 26th round and the definition of ownership of land remaining the same for the surveys of 1961–62, 1971–72, and 1982, there is no apparent reason for the decrease in area owned

except that some rural land might have been merged in urban land due to urbanization over the years.

3. Estimates of NSS 59th round survey in Report No. 492, Table 3.2.
4. Gini's coefficient of concentration of ownership of land holdings has shown in Statement 3 of 'NSS report number 491'.
5. Estimates of NSS 59th round survey in Report No. 492, Table 3.2.

References

Acharya, S.S., (2006): Sustainable Agriculture and Rural Livelihoods, *Agricultural Economics Research Review,* Vol. 19, No. 2, pp. 205–217.

Basole, A., and Basu, D., (2011): Relations of Production and Modes of Surplus Extraction in India: Part I - Agriculture, *Economic & Political Weekly,* Vol. 46, No. 14, pp. 41–58.

Basu, Kaushik, (2010): *The Oxford Companion to Economics in India,* OUP, India.

Chand, R. and Chauhan, S., (1999): Are Disparities in Indian Agriculture Growing? Policy Brief No. 8. New Delhi: National Centre for Agricultural Economics and Policy Research.

Fei, J.C.H. and Ranis, G., (1964): *Development of the Labor Surplus Economy?: Theory and Policy.* Economic Growth Center, Yale University.

Gollin, D., Parente, S. and Rogerson, R., (2002): Role of Agriculture in Development, *The American Economic Review,* Vol. 92, No. 2, pp. 160–164.

IRDR, (2013): India Rural Development Report 2012/13, Ministry of Rural Development (MoRD), New Delhi: Government of India.

Kannan, E. and Sundaram, S., (2011): Analysis of Trends in India's Agricultural Growth, Working Paper 276, Bangalore: The Institute for Social and Economic Change.

Lewis, A., (1954): Development with Unlimited Supplies of Labour, *The Manchester School,* May 1954. Available at https://la.utexas.edu/users/hcleaver/368/368lewistable.pdf

Rawal, V., (2014): Changes in the Distribution of Operational Landholdings in Rural India: A Study of National Sample Survey Data, *Review of Agrarian Studies,* Vol. 3, No. 2, pp. 73–104.

Unni, J., (2014): Rural Livelihoods in Transition: Whither Labour?, *The Indian Journal of Labour Economics,* Vol. 57, No. 1, pp. 35–51.

10 Assessment of Climate and Livelihood Vulnerability in the Bundelkhand Region, India

An Indicator-Based Approach

Surendra Singh and Sanatan Nayak

Introduction

Intergovernmental Panel on Climate Chagne (IPCC) assessment report re-confirmed that climate change is probably the most complex and challenging environmental problem faced by the world today and increasingly recognised as a potent threat to agriculture in general and to food security in particular (IPCC, 2013). In majority, anthropogenic activities are changing the earth's climate, and this is having an impact on all ecosystems (Ojwang et al., 2010 and Rama Rao et al., 2016). The expected changes in climate will alter regional agricultural systems, with consequences for food production (Kavi Kumar et al., 2007). Globally, climate change is seen as a failure of market mechanisms, wherein, polluters have not had to pay for the negative externalities (Stern, 2007).

For agriculture specific, climate of South Asia is dominated by the monsoon, which returns with remarkable regularity each summer and provides the rainfall needed to sustain over 60 per cent of the world's population (Krishna Kumar et al., 2011). More than 75 per cent of the annual rainfall in India is received during four monsoon months, June through September (IMD, 2016). Climate change can therefore has a profound impact on agriculture through its influence on the monsoon-dominant climate over India (Krishna Kumar et al., 2010; Krishna Kumar et al., 2011). Hence, there is a widely felt need for understanding the nature of climate change over this part of the globe. Climate change projections made for India indicate an overall increase in temperature by 1–4°C (Krishna Kumar et al., 2011). The summer monsoon precipitation over India is expected to be 9–16 per cent more in 2080s compared to the baseline (1970s, i.e. 1961–90) under global warming conditions (Krishna Kumar et al., 2011). In addition, the rainy days are projected to be less frequent and more intense (Goswami et al., 2006; Krishna Kumar et al., 2011). However, different regions are expected to experience differential change in the amount of rainfall in the coming decades (Venkateswarlu and

Rama Rao, 2010). All these expected changes will have adverse impacts on climate-sensitive sectors such as agriculture, forest, coastal ecosystems, availability of water for different sectors, and human health. There are three major approaches of climate change impact assessment, viz., potential impact approach, sensitivity (vulnerability) approach, and adaptive capability approach. Potential impact assessment broadly consists quantitative or time series or long-term climate change impact on agricultural productivity, viz., general circulation method, Ricardian method, and panel data method. However, it does not include qualitative information or social features of the society like caste, religion, farmers' perception about climate change, etc. Therefore, assessment of the potential impacts of climate change in different parts of the world using vulnerability often as a framing device has increased over the past two decades (Malone and Engle, 2011).

Vulnerability is defined as 'the degree to which a system is susceptible or unable to cope with adverse effects of climate change, including climate variability and extremes, and vulnerability is a function of the character, magnitude and rate of climate variation to which a system is exposed, its sensitivity, and its adaptive capacity' (McCarthy et al., 2001). Mathematically vulnerability is expressed as:

$$f(E_i, S_i, A_i)$$

Where, E_j is exposure (the nature and degree to which a system is exposed to significant climatic variations, S_j is sensitivity (the degree to which a system is affected either adversely or beneficially, by climate-related stimuli), and A_j is adaptive capacity (the ability of a system to adjust to climate change, including climate variability and extremes to moderate potential damages, to take advantage of opportunities or to cope with consequences. (IPCC, 2001)

Climate Change and Vulnerability in Agriculture

It is argued that India is particularly vulnerable to predicted climate change impact because of its high population density and high dependency on agriculture (around 53 per cent population directly rely on agriculture for livelihoods), low adaptive capacity, several unique and valuable ecosystems (coral reef, large deltaic regions with rich biodiversity, desert, Himalayan, and coastal), and vast low-altitude agriculture activities (Roy, 2007). Further, India is home to the largest number of hunger and deprived people in the world (360 million undernourished and 300 million poor people). The growth rate of food-grain production is slow, rather decreased during 1996–2008. It increased by just 1.2 per cent annum: from 199 to 230 million tons, as against an annual rate of growth of 3.5 per cent achieved during the 1980 (GoI, 2014; Sridevi et al., 2014). Rising temperatures, changes in rainfall patterns, and an increased frequency of floods and droughts are likely to have serious effects on rural populations in the absence of policies that actively help these households adjust to their changing geography (Somanathan and Somanathan, 2009). Ashalatha et al. (2012) observed that the climatic variation as incidence of drought have significant impact on the production of rainfed crops. The small and medium farmers were more vulnerable to climate change and to a larger extent, adopted coping mechanisms for climate change as is growing day by day, it should be addressed through policy viewpoint at the earliest to avoid short-term effects such as yield and income loss and long-term effects such as suspend agricultural profession by the rainfed farmers. Swain and Swain (2011), in their study in Odisha, examine the nature and determinants of drought risk and vulnerability experienced by selected blocks of drought-prone Bolangir district in western Odisha. They observed that three most-influential biophysical factors of drought vulnerability are rainfall variability, drought intensity, and shortage of available holding capacity of soil and the three most-influential socio-economic factors are low irrigation development, poor crop insurance coverage, and smaller forest area. Moreover, Paltasingh et al. (2012) examined the impact of weather on rice yield in Odisha since rice is the staple food and covers about 70 per cent of cultivated area in this state. Rainfall and temperature are two important weather factors that affect crop yield due to their direct and indirect influences on agricultural practices.

In addition, the studies on vulnerability to climate change in India can be grouped into three categories. The first set of studies is based on climate modelling and deals with the impacts of climate change on different crops and vulnerability of different regions and sectors to climate change (Sinha and Swaminathan, 1991; Lal et al., 1998; Lal et al., 1999; Kavi Kumar and Parikh, 2001a). This category of studies deals with the impacts of climate change on different crops, their productivity, and yield under different climate change on scenarios for different regions. The available evidence suggests significant drop in the yield of important cereal crops like paddy and wheat under the impact of climate change. However, studies on the biophysical impacts of climate change important commercial crops like sugarcane, cotton, and sunflower in the Indian context are scarce. Moreover, in India, mix impact of climate variability has been observed in the studies (Aggarwal, 2009; Sinha and Swaminathan, 1991; Aggarwal and Mall, 2002; Kavi Kumar and Parikh, 2001b; Rathore et al., 2001). Above studies show that agriculture will be affected both negatively and positively by different levels of temperature change depending on the crop varieties and geographic location. For example, many studies have noted that doubling of CO_2 in the atmosphere from the present level will have positive impacts on the yields of rice, wheat, and soybean. However, a temperature rise beyond 3°C of the pre-industrial level will wipe out the positive impact of climate change on these crops (Aggarwal, 2009).

Second set of studies have examined vulnerability of different geographical units such as districts and states to the impacts of climate change either using secondary or using both climate modelling and secondary data (Aggarwal and Mall, 2002; Sanghi and Mendelsohn, 2008; Jacoby et al., 2010; Mathew et al., 2012). These studies have focused on the vulnerability to climate change at different spatial scales in India using secondary data and some studies combining secondary data with climate projections. State-level results indicate a wide range of vulnerabilities for India and reiterate the need to formulate differentiated strategies to reduce vulnerability and build resilience. Individual states show a wide range of sensitivities to food security. For example, the states of Kerala and Sikkim are more sensitive than Punjab. However, Punjab has the highest ecosystem sensitivity, mainly because of the pollution caused by the use of chemical fertilisers. Further, Ravindranath et al. (2011) developed vulnerability profile for the agricultural water and forest sectors for the north-east region of India for current and projected future vulnerabilities to climate change. Outcome of the study indicates that majority of the districts in north-east India are subject to climate-induced vulnerability currently and in the near future.

The third category of studies has examined vulnerability and adaptation to climate change in India at the community and household level (Pandey and Jha, 2011; Aulong et al., 2012; Chaliha et al., 2012; Haldar et al., 2012). This set of studies has addressed questions such as who are the most vulnerable and what are the important features of their vulnerability. These studies have focused on identifying and ranking both the households that are vulnerable and households that have the highest adaptive capacity to climate change. The households living away from the district headquarters are highly vulnerable to the impacts of climate change in comparison to households lining near to the district headquarter (Pandey and Jha, 2011). Further, the distance from the district headquarters and the geographic positioning are important in determining vulnerability of the households or communities (Aulong et al., 2012). Similarly, the bio-physical features have the greatest impact on vulnerability of the communities to climate change (Chaliha et al., 2012). It is evident from the above discussion that many studies have tried to assess vulnerability and adaptive capacity to climate change at various spatial scales, but very few attempted to consider how farming households are adapting to the impacts of climate change at the farm level.

Development of Approaches for Vulnerability Assessment

There has been continuous development in approaches since 1970s for assessing vulnerability. There are numerous ways to organise the approaches for assessing vulnerability, that is structural versus spatial. Each approach was developed systematically after another due to the limitations of the former. In 1970s, researchers predominantly working in the developing world, called for a rethinking of disasters from a political-economic perspective, based on the high correlation between disaster proneness, chronic malnutrition, low income, and famine potential, leading to the conclusion that the root causes of disasters lame more in society than in nature (Hewitt, 1983). Vulnerability, soon generally called social vulnerability, refers to those characteristics of a society that render its member subject to harm and loss in a disaster. Social vulnerability, therefore, is one of the constitutive feature of disaster risk, defined as the latent probability of future loss and damage associated with the occurrence of a physical event and the exposure of social elements to its impacts. Eakin and Luers (2006) have discussed three approaches of vulnerability, viz., (a) risk-hazard, (b) political economy, and (c) ecological resilience. First, risk-hazard, using bio-physical risk threat as the point of departure, risk-hazard researchers have essentially set out to describe a very broad scale on (a) what are we vulnerable to, (b) what are the expected consequences, and (c) when and where those impacts might occur. Risk-hazard approaches tend to consider negative outcomes as function of both bio-physical risk factors and potential loss of a specified exposed population (Brooks, 2003). However, this approach suffers from the predicting degree of vulnerability on the individual or community specific. For example, a community with a fire hall located on a floodplain is more vulnerable than a similar community with a fire hall built outside the floodplain area due to the possibility that the fire hall will be out of commission as a consequence of flooding. Further, risk-hazard is not able to capture socio-economic features of the community or society, which is now the most important factor of vulnerability assessment. Second, political economy approach to vulnerability, which evolved from, and often in response to risk-hazard assessment of climate impacts (Blaikie et al., 1994). The political economy approach emphasises on social-political, cultural, and economic factors together explain differential exposure to hazards, differential impacts, and most importantly differential capabilities to recuperate from the past impacts and cope or adapt to future threats. This model emphasises the underlying causes of disasters and how it creates risk for the society, and has been used widely in emergency management. However, political economy approach is not able to absorb system shock. For example, political economy approach assumes that if any shock occurs in the economy either political or economic pressure, an entire community will face negative consequences. However, it is not true for high-income group community. They have savings, which gets utilised in the recession period. Third, ecological resilience approach and vulnerability is viewed as a dynamic property of a system in which human are interacting constantly with their surrounding biophysical environment (Holling, 1973). Holling (1973) defined ecological resilience as the 'ability of a system to absorb shock and disturbance but still maintain the same relationship with the system that controls the system's behaviour'. Resilience approach tend to give more importance to implications for social and economic changes across the broader geographic space, considering human activities as just one of driving forces and humans themselves as one of the affected species.

Agricultural Vulnerability in Bundelkhand Region

Bundelkhand region is a part of two major cereal-producing states of India, viz., Uttar Pradesh and Madhya Pradesh. However, as far as agro-climatic conditions are concerned, these two states are highly diverse. Soil quality, land size, net investment in agro sector, cropping pattern, and land-use pattern are different in Bundelkhand region compared with other parts of these states. Bundelkhand region consists 13 districts of these two states, viz., Jhansi, Jaloun, Hamirpur, Banda, Datia, Mahoba, Chitrakoot, Tikamgarn, Lalitpur, Panna, Damoh, Sagarand, and Chhatrapur. These 13 districts are highly vulnerable; first, majority of population only depends on agriculture. It means that in this region agriculture is the sole source of employment. Second, due to poor soil quality

Figure 1

Map of Bundelkhand Region

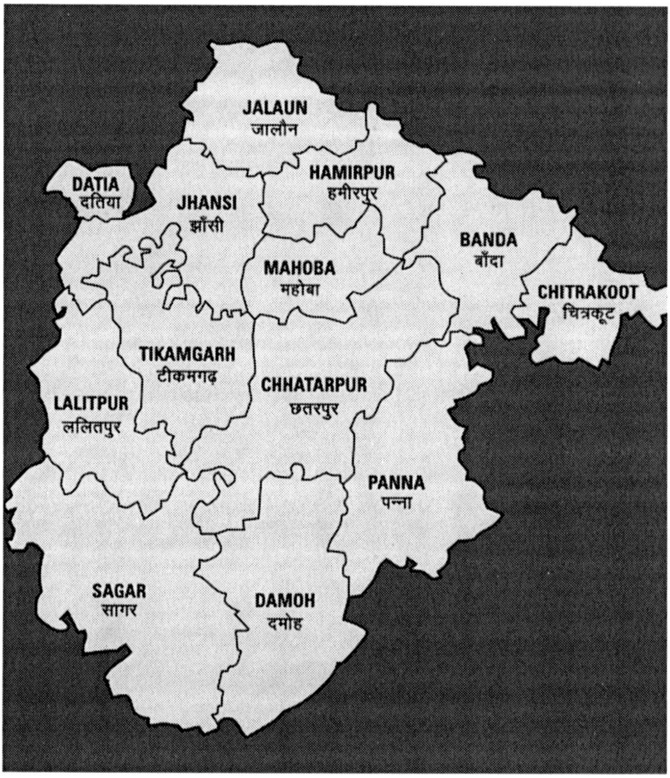

Source: Google Map.

agricultural productivity is lower and not yet suitable for cereals production. However, cereals are main food item in the daily diet. Third, this region has the largest canal irrigation channel but due to back-to-back drought episodes, majority of surface water resources became drier. It means that water is not available for irrigation as well as domestic consumption also. Therefore, farmers are moving towards groundwater irrigation without any environmental impact assessment. Due to this, water scarcity has been observed in the recent years for both agriculture and domestic use. Fourth, Bundelkhand region comes under semi-arid region. Semi-arid areas are particularly exposed to the impacts of climate change on fresh water. In semi-arid area, climate change may extend the dry season of no or very low flows, which particularly affects water users unable to rely on reservoirs or deep groundwater wells (Giertz et al., 2006). Fifth, in Bundelkhand region, farmers also have to contend with other extreme natural resource challenges and constraints such as poor soil fertility, pests-crop disease, and a lack of access to improved seeds. These challenges are usually aggravated by periods of prolonged droughts/floods and are often particularly severe during El Nino events.

Estimation Method

There are numbers of methods available in the literature called, participatory methods, simulation model based, and indicator based. Therefore, quantification of the method before applying on the data must be clear. Some other methods like vulnerability resilience indicator prototype has used national level proxies on sensitivity and adaptive capacity were scaled against global data to get the overall national baseline of vulnerability and resilience for each of the countries (Brenkert and Malone, 2005). Dynamic international vulnerability assessment integrated global model for coastal system that assesses biophysical and socio-economic development (Hinkel and Klein, 2009). Multi-criteria decision analysis (MCDA) interested with adaptive capacity and sensitivity through the analytic hierarchy process and combines a livelihoods framework with MCDA to weigh household attributes according to their relative importance in driving household vulnerability (Eakin et al., 2006; Aulong et al., 2012). Moreover, econometric approaches use household level socio-economic survey data to analyse the vulnerability levels of different social groups (Hoddinott and Quisumbing, 2003). However, among these deferent methods, one of the widely methods for vulnerability assessment is the indicator-based approach. Research continues on the development of quantitative indicators of climate variability and adaptation to climate-related hazards at multiple-scale analysis (Hahn et al., 2009). Further, indicator-based approach is valuable for monitoring trends and exploring conceptual frameworks. Further, composite indices capture the multi-dimensionality of vulnerability in a comprehensible form. However, the major limitation of the indicator-based approach is its inability to capture the complex temporal and social dynamics of the various systems being measured (Luers et al., 2003). On the other hand, the current study used field survey data. Field survey was conducted in May 2015. Further, Data of farmer's perception on copping and adaptation strategies against climate vulnerability has been collected from two districts (Jhansi and Jaloun) of Bundelkhand region by using purposive sampling method. Furthermore, 200 samples have been collected from the ten blocks of both districts. The indicator based approach uses a specific set or combination of indicators (proxy indicators) and measure vulnerability by computing indices, average, or weighted averages for those selected variables or indicators. This approach can be applied any scale such as household, district, and at country level. Indicator-based approach consists three core elements, viz. exposure, sensitivity, and adaptive capacity (Hahn et al., 2009). Exposure is defined as 'the nature and degree to which a system is exposed to significant climatic variations'. Thus, exposure related to climate stress upon a particular unit of analysis. Further, sensitivity is defined as 'the degree to which a system is affected, either adversely or beneficially, by climate-related stimuli'. It is determined by demographic and environmental conditions of the region concerned. Adaptive capacity is 'the ability of a system to adjust to climate change including climate variability and extremes to moderate potential damages, to take advantage of opportunities, or to cope with the consequences'. It is considered to be 'a function of wealth, technology, education, information about climate change, skills, infrastructure, and access to resources, stability, and management capabilities'. In addition, combining three main indicators, composite climate vulnerability and livelihood vulnerability indexes (LVI) have been estimated. The major components and sub-components shown in Tables 1 and 2.

Table 1

Major and Sub-Components for the Climate Vulnerability Index

Major Components	*Sub-Components*
Exposure	Percentage of households feeling that rainfall has declined over the last five years
	Percentage of households perceiving that summer days have become hotter
	Percentage of households perceiving that frequencies of drought over the last five years have increased
	Percentage of households perceiving that water level has declined over the last five years
Sensitivity	Percentage of households perceiving high impact of drought on the farming system
	Percentage of households perceiving that heat waves have become more frequent
	Percentage of households perceiving that temperature has been increasing over the last five years
	Percentage of survey population reporting agriculture as the only source of income
	Average crop diversity index (range: 0–1)[1]
	Percentage of households belonging to BPL category
	Average number of dependents on head of household (unemployed)
Adaptive capacity	Percentage of farmers having crop insurance
	Percentage of households changing their cropping patterns
	Percentage of households switching to non-farm activities
	Percentage of households using improved irrigational facilities
	Percentage of households planting trees around the field
	Percentage of households using early maturing varieties
	Percentage of head of households belonging to illiterate education level (we take illiteracy as a base)
	Percentage of households calling Kisan Call Centre

Note: 1. The inverse of (the number of crops grown by a household +1), e.g. a household that grows rice, cotton will have a crop diversity index = 1/(2+1) = 0.33.

Source: Estimated from Field Survey Data.

The climate vulnerability index (CVI) and LVI used in this study is based on the IPCC vulnerability framework. Exposure index in the current study is measured based on the perception of the respondents on decline rainfall in the monsoon period. Increase in temperature and frequency of drought have been experienced over the last 10 years. Further, due to lack of climate data at village/block level, the indicator-based method on the perception of the people to represent sensitivity at household level. Further, agricultural and socio-economic sensitivity indicators are indexed. Subsequently, adaptive capacity on climate risks has been described as a function of indicator-based method like access of information technology, wealth, finance, and institutional resources (Smith and Wandel, 2006). For this purpose, indicators of particular adaptation actions by farming households to deal with climate risks such as changing crops and planting dates, use of climatic information, access to crop insurance, and educational level of the head of household are included in the adaptive capacity index.

In addition, adaptive capacity is largely consistent with socio-economic approach, while sensitivity with biophysical approach and both are internal dimension. The component of adaptive capacity is viewed as an external dimension. Higher exposure and sensitivity mean higher vulnerability. Adaptive capacity moderated vulnerability and hence is inversely related to vulnerability. Although, lack of standard methods for combining the biophysical and socio-economic indicators is a limitation to this approach.

Table 2

Major and Sub-Components for the Livelihood Security Index

Major Component	*Sub-Components*
Exposure	Percentage of households feeling that rainfall has declined over the last five years
	Percentage of households perceiving that summer days have become hotter
	Percentage of households perceiving that frequencies of drought over the last five years has increased
	Percentage of households perceiving that water level has declined over the last five years
Sensitivity (natural Capital, water, health, and food)	Natural capital - percentage of households using only forest-based energy for cooking purposes
	Water - percentage of households using hand pump water for drinking
	Food - average crop diversity index
	Percentage of households depends on government sources for irrigation
	Percentage of households depends on head of household
	Health - percentage of households using 108 free medical facility
	Percentage of households not having toilet facilities
	Percentage of households not having pucca house
	Percentage of households belonging to BPL category
Adaptive capacity (socio-demographic profile, livelihood strategies)	Percentage of female-headed households
	Percentage of head of household not attaining school
	Percentage of households solely depending on agriculture as source of income
	Average number of households having burden of loan
	Percentage of households changing their cropping pattern
	Percentage of households calling Kisan Call Centre
	Percentage of households living as a Joint family

Source: Estimated from Field Survey Data & Adopted from Hahn et al., 2009.

CVI and LVI use a balanced weighted averages approach based (Sullivan et al., 2002), where each sub-component contributes equally to the overall index score and equal weights are applied to all the three major components. Because each component was measured on a different scale, it was necessary to standardise each a separate index. The same procedure is used in Iyenger and Sudharsan (1982), which is as follows:

$$K_f = \frac{K_a - K_{\min}}{K_{\max} - K_{\min}} \tag{1}$$

Here K_f is the original sub-component for block f and $K_{\max} - K_{\min}$ is the minimum and maximum values, respectively. For each sub-component determined using data from all the 10 blocks. For variables that represents frequencies such as percentage of farmers who have changed their crops, the minimum value was set at 0 and maximum value at 100.

After each component was standardised, the mean of each sub-components is estimated by using the following equation to calculate the value of each major component.

$$K_h = \frac{\sum_{i=1}^{n} index\, K^i_f}{n} \tag{2}$$

Where k_h is one of the three components of the block h, exposure (EXP), sensitivity (SENS), and adaptive capacity (ADP), index K^i_f represents the sub-components indexed by i, that make up for each major component, and n is the number of sub-components in each major component. Once the values for the exposure, sensitivity, and adaptive capacity for a block level were calculated, the three contributing factors were combined using the following equation form Hahn et al. (2009) to obtain the block level vulnerability index (CVI).

$$CVI_d = (E_d - A_d) * S_d \tag{3}$$

Where, CVI_d is the climate vulnerability index scores for the block d (obtained using the IPCC vulnerability framework), E is the calculated exposure score for the block d, A is the adaptive capacity score for the block d, and S is the sensitivity score for the block d. We scaled the CVI based on the results obtained from vulnerability index score, that is 0 (least vulnerable) to 1 (most vulnerable).

Result and Discussion

CVI by using equation three is estimated (Eq. 3). Blocks associated with Jaloun district show highest climatic vulnerability index scores. The overall index (combined all three major indexes viz., exposure, sensitivity, and adaptive capacity) reflects higher climate vulnerability (0.336) for Jaloun district compared with Jhansi district (0.263). At block level, Jaloun block (0.382) has the highest vulnerability and Kalpi (0.253) has the lowest vulnerability scores in the Jaloun district (Table 3). Subsequently, in Jhansi, Mauranipur block has the highest vulnerability index value (0.332). On the other hand, Moth has lower score (0.193) (Table 3). The reason behind lower vulnerability index score for

Moth block is that it is well connected with canal irrigation especially minor irrigation. Whereas, Mauranipur block is less connected with the canal channel.

In addition, high exposure and sensitivity as well as low adaptive capacity increased the climatic vulnerability. In Jaloun district, Jaloun block has the highest climatic vulnerability scores because it has high exposure and sensitivity scores, viz. 0.963 and 0.566. Similarly, in the Jhansi district, Mauranipur block has the highest vulnerability score (0.332) because it has the highest exposure and sensitivity scores also, viz. 0.888 and 0.560 (Table 3). Further, Table 3 clearly reveals that climatic factors in the Bundelkhand region adversely affect agricultural practices. Apart from climatic factors, demographic, social, and economic factors also increased the degree of vulnerability at household level. Therefore, composite LVI is estimated by using field survey data. LVI scores provide more comprehensive information about livelihoods of surveyed farmers. Nature of household, head of household (male or female), dependency on head of household, natural Capital, water, health, and food variables are included as indicators for estimation of LVI (Tables 1 and 2).

Table 3

Climate Vulnerability Index

Districts	*Blocks*	*Major Components*			
		Exposure	*Sensitivity*	*Adaptive Capacity*	*Climate Vulnerability Index*
Jaloun	Orai	0.888	0.617	0.350	0.672
	Konch	0.925	0.597	0.288	0.735
	Jaloun	0.963	0.566	0.288	0.800
	Madhavgarh	0.850	0.605	0.300	0.669
	Kalpi	0.750	0.613	0.338	0.543
Jhansi	Badagaon	0.900	0.624	0.381	0.662
	Mauranipur	0.888	0.560	0.294	0.723
	Moth	0.814	0.478	0.409	0.618
	Garotha	0.808	0.503	0.388	0.613
	Tahroli	0.900	0.483	0.369	0.722
	Jaloun	0.875	0.600	0.313	0.687
	Jhansi	0.862	0.530	0.368	0.667

Source: Estimated by Authors from Field Survey Data.

The LVI score reveals that Madhavgarh block in Jaloun district (0.350) and Tehroli block in Jhansi district (0.310) are the most vulnerable, while other two blocks namely, Kalpi block (0.250) in Jaloun district and Moth block in Jhansi (0.210) are the least vulnerable, respectively (Table 4). Koch block is highly exposed and sensitive and at the same time, low adaptive capacity to deal with climate change and variability became more vulnerable. In totality, higher vulnerability score indicates that households have higher dependency on head of household, female headed, low educational level, belongs to BPL category, etc.

Table 4

Livelihood Vulnerability Index

Districts	*Block*	*Exposure Index*	*Sensitivity Index*	*Adaptive Capacity*	*Livelihood Vulnerability Index*
Jaloun	Orai	0.888	0.517	0.262	0.735
	Konch	0.925	0.428	0.279	0.806
	Jaloun	0.963	0.424	0.216	0.871
	Madhavgarh	0.850	0.518	0.162	0.766
	Kalpi	0.750	0.506	0.240	0.629
Jhansi	Badagaon	0.900	0.376	0.248	0.807
	Mauranipur	0.888	0.395	0.195	0.811
	Moth	0.814	0.499	0.382	0.623
	Garotha	0.808	0.531	0.330	0.633
	Tahroli	0.900	0.470	0.225	0.794
	Jaloun	0.875	0.478	0.247	0.757
	Jhansi	0.862	0.454	0.308	0.722

Source: Estimated by Authors from Field Survey Data.

Conclusion

The study related with climate change/variability follows a systematic framework to assess climate change impact. Therefore, present chapter estimated the magnitude of vulnerability in the two broad indexes, namely CVI and LVI by using indicator-based approach. Further, indicator-based approach follows IPCC framework estimation to covered major three components, viz. exposure, sensitivity, and adaptive capacity. Furthermore, exposure, sensitivity, and adaptive indexes separately estimated from field survey data to avoid errors in secondary level and limitations of mission values. Moreover, household's perception and copping strategies also covered in the vulnerability estimation. Study estimates block level CVI and LVI, respectively. The results shown that blocks have the highest exposure and sensitivity with climatic factors in one hand and on the other hand, have less adaptive capacity and are highly vulnerable.

Policy Suggestions

Study found that less adaptive capacity is increase magnitude of vulnerability. Therefore, adaptation techniques should be improved in the study area. Further, during field survey, responses were collected in terms of weather station establishment nearby farms because climatic factors have been increasing degree of exposure and sensitivity. The following points need the policy intervention in the study area:

1. Combat policy for the climatic variable will keep in centre small and marginal farmers. The study found the degree of CVI and LVI higher in small and marginal farmers.

2. The role of information technology now unforgotten. Therefore, appropriate information at a time should be provided like sowing, germination, and harvesting period.
3. In the Bundelkhand region, findings shows that increase temperature and decline rainfall adversely affecting to the major crops. Therefore, new genetically modified seeds and fertilisers should be introduced by examine local climatic conditions.
4. The role of awareness about exposure and sensitivity related factors should be spread at community level.
5. The climatic conditions are not suitable for rice and major food-grain crops. Therefore, study suggests that farmer's shows grow Kharif pulses to reduce exposure from increases temperature and less water availability.
6. The present study confirms that the degree of vulnerability varies from region to region and community to community. This suggests that households with less sensitivity to climate risks are unlikely to invest in risk-reduction strategies, while households with relatively high sensitivity are more likely to respond to these sensitivities through options that are available for them. Although, Madhavgarh block stands the highest in the adaptive capacity index. Yet its high vulnerability suggests that policy intervention to reduce sensitivity and exposure of the households to deal with risks of climate variability and change is highly warranted.

References

Aggarwal, P.K., (2009): Global Climate Change and Indian Agriculture: Case Studies from ICAR Network Project, Indian Council of Agricultural Research, New Delhi.

Aggarwal, P.K. and Mall, R.K., (2002): Climate Change and Rice Yield in Diverse Agro-Environments of India. II. Effects of Uncertainties in Scenarios and Crop Models on Impact Assessment, *Climate Change*, Vol. 52, No. 3, pp. 331–343.

Ashalatha, K.V., Munisamy, G. and Bhat, A.R.S., (2012): Impact of Climate Change on Rainfed Agriculture in India: A Case Study of Dharwad, *International Journal of Environmental Science and Development*, Vol. 3, No. 4, pp. 368–371.

Aulong, S. et al., (2012): Are South Indian Farmers Adaptable to Global Change? A Case in an Andhra Pradesh Catchment Basin, *Regional Environmental Change*, Vol. 12, issue 3, pp. 423–436.

Blaikie, P. et al., (1994): *At Risk: Natural Hazards, People's Vulnerability and Disasters*, Routledge, London.

Brenkert, L. and Malone, E., (2005): Modelling Vulnerability and Resilience to Climate Change: A Case Study of India and Indian States, *Climate Change*, Vol. 72, No. 1–2, pp. 57–102.

Brooks, N., (2003): Vulnerability, Risk and Adaptation: A Conceptual Framework, Tyndall Centre Working Paper 38, Tyndall Centre for Climate Change Research, Norwich.

Chaliha, S. et al., (2012): Climate Variability and Farmer's Vulnerability in a Flood-prone District of Assam, *International Journal of Climate Change Strategies and Management*, Vol. 4, No. 2, pp. 179–200.

Eakin, H. and Luers, A.L., (2006): Assessing the Vulnerability of Social-Environmental Systems, *Annual Review of Environmental and Resources*, Vol. 31, No. 2, pp. 365–394.

Gbetibouo, G. and Ringer, C., (2009): Mapping South African Farming Sector Vulnerability to Climate Change and Variability: A Sub-National Assessment, IFPRI Discussion Paper 00885, Environment and Production Technology Divison, August.

Giertz, S. et al., (2006): An Interdisciplinary Scenario Analysis to Assess the Water Availability and Water Consumption in the Upper Oueme Catchment in Benin, *Advances in Geosciences*, Vol. 9, No. 1, pp. 3–13.

GoI, (2014): Agriculture at Glance, Ministry of Agriculture, Government of India, New Delhi.

Goswami, B.N., Venugopal, V., Sengumpta, D. et al., (2006): Increasing Trend of Extreme Rain Events Over India in a Warming Environment, *Science*, Vol. 314, No. 5804, pp. 1442–1445.

Hahn, M.B., Riederer, A.M. and Foster, S.O., (2009): The Livelihood Vulnerability Index: A Pragmatic Approach to Assessing Risks from Climate Variability and Change: A Case Study in Mozambique, *Global Environmental Change*, Vol. 19, No. 2, pp. 74–88.

Haldar, P., et al., (2012): Local Perceptions and Responses to Climate Change: Experiences from the Natural Resource-dependent Communities in India, *Regional Environmental Change*, Vol. 12, No. 4, pp. 665–673.

Hewitt, K. (ed.), (1983): *Interpretations of Calamity from the Viewpoint of Human Ecology*, Allen & Unwin, London.

Hinkel, J. and Klein, R.J.T., (2009): Integrating Knowledge to Assess Coastal Vulnerability to Sea-Level Rise: The Development of the DIVA Tool, *Global Environmental Change*, Vol. 19, No. 3, pp. 384–395.

Hoddinott, J. and Quisumbing, A., (2003): Methods for Micro Econometric Risk and Vulnerability Assessment, Social Protection Discussion Paper Series No. 0324, Social Protection Unit, Human Development Network, Washington D.C., World Bank.

Holling, C.S., (1973): Resilience and Stability of Ecological Systems, *Annual Review of Ecology and Systematics*, Vol. 4, pp. 1–23.

IMD, (2016): Annual Report, Indian Meteorological Department of India.

IPCC, (2001): Climate Change: The Scientific Basis, Contribution of the Working Group I to the Third Assessment Report of the Intergovernmental Panel on Climate Change, Cambridge University Press, UK.

——, (2013): Summary for Policymakers, In Stocker, T.F. et al. (eds), *Climate Change 2013: The Physical Science Basis*, Contribution of Working Group I to the Fifth Assessment Report of the Intergovernmental Panel on Climate Change, Cambridge University Press, UK.

Iyengar, N.S. and Sudarshan, P., (1982): A Method of Classifying Regions from Multivariate Data, *Economic & Political Weekly*, Vol. 17, No. 51, pp. 2048–2052.

Jacoby, H., Babassa, M. and Skoufias, E., (2010): Distributional Implications of Climate Change in India, World Bank Policy Research Working Paper 5623, Washington D.C., World Bank.

Kavi Kumar, K.S. and Parikh, J., (2001a). Indian Agriculture and Climate Sensitivity, *Global Environmental Change*, Vol. 11, No. 3, pp. 147–154.

Kavi Kumar, K.S. and Parikh, J., (2001b): Socio-Economic Impacts of Climate Change on Indian Agriculture, *International Review for Environmental Strategies*, 2(2).

Kavi Kumar, K.S. et al., (2007): Vulnerability to Poverty and Vulnerability to Climate Change: Conceptual Framework, *Measurement and Synergies in Policy*, Working Paper 19/2007, Madras School of Economics, Chennai.

Krishna Kumar, K. et al., (2010): The Once and Future Pulse of Indian Monsoonal Climate, *Climate Dynamics*, Vol. 36, No. 11, pp. 2159–2170.

Krishna Kumar, K. et al., (2011): Simulated Projections for Summer Monsoon Climate over India by a High-Resolution Regional Climate Model (PRECIS), *Current Science*, Vol. 101, No. 3, pp. 312–326.

Lal, M. et al., (1998): Vulnerability of Rice and Wheat Yields in NW, India to Future Change in Climate, *Agriculture and Forest Meteorology*, Vol. 89, No. 2, pp. 101–114.

Lal, M. et al., (1999): Growth and Yield Response of Soybean in Madhya Pradesh, India to Climate Variability and Change, *Agriculture and Forest Meteorology*, Vol. 93, No. 1, pp. 53–70.

Luers, Amy L. et al., (2003) A Method for Quantifying Vulnerability Applied to the Yaqui Valley, Mexico, *Global Environmental Change*, Vol. 13, pp. 255–267.

Malone, L.E. and Engle, L.N., (2011): Evaluating Regional Vulnerability to Climate Change: Purposes and Methods, *Climate Change*, Vol. 2, Issue 3, pp. 462–474.

Mathew, S., Truck, Stefan and Henderson-Sellers, Ann, (2012): Kochi, India Case Study of Climate Adaptations to Floods: Ranking Local Government Investment Options Related, *Global Environmental Change*, Vol. 22, No. 1, pp. 308–319.

McCarthy, J.J., Canziani, O.F., Leary, Neil, Dokken, D.J. and White, K.S., (2001): *Climate Change 2001: Impacts, Adaptation, and Vulnerability*. Contribution of Working Group II to the Third Assessment Report of the Intergovernmental Panel on Climate Change (IPCC). Cambridge University Press, Cambridge, pp. 87-88.

Ojwang, G.O., Agatsiva, J. and Situma, C., (2010): Analysis of Climate Change and Variability Risks in the Smallholder Sector: Case Studies of the Laikipia and Narok Districts Representing Major Agro-ecological Zones in Kenya, Food and Agricultural Organization, Rome.

Paltasingh, K.R., Phanindra, G. and Mishra, R.K., (2012): Measuring Weather Impact on Crop Yield Using Aridity Index: Evikdence from Odisha, *Agricultural Economics Research Review*, Vol. 25, No. 2, pp. 205–216.

Pandey, R. and Jha, S., (2012): Climate Vulnerability Index: Measure of Climate Change Vulnerability to Communities: A Case of Rural Lower Himalayas, India, *Mitigation and Adaptation Strategies Global Change*, Vol. 17, No. 5, pp. 487–506.

Rama Rao, C.A. et al., (2016): A District Level Assessment of Vulnerability of Indian Agriculture to Climate Change, *Current Science*, Vol. 110, No. 10, pp. 1939–1946.

Rathore, L.S. et al., (2001): Modelling the Impact of Climate Change on Rice Production in India, *Mausam*, Vol. 52, No. 1, pp. 263–274.

Ravindranath, N.H. et al., (2011): Climate Change Vulnerability Profiles for North East India, *Current Science*, Vol. 101, No. 3, pp. 384–394.

Roy, J., (2007): Climate Change in the South Asian Context with a Special Focus on India: A Review, *AEI Newsletter*, April, Issue. 3, pp. 9–21.

Sanghi, A. and Mendelsohn, R., (2008): The Impacts of Global Warming on Farmers in Brazil and India, *Global Environmental Change-Human and Policy Dimensions*, Vol. 18, No. 4, pp. 655–665.

Sinha, S.K. and Swaminathan, M.S., (1991): Deforestation Climate Change and Sustainable Nutrition Security: A Case Study of India, *Climate Change*, Vol. 19, No. 1–2, pp. 201–209.

Smit, B. and Wandel, J., (2006): Adaptation, Adaptive Capacity and Vulnerability, *Global Environmental Change*, Vol. 16, No. 3, pp. 282–292.

Somanathan, E. and Somanathan, R., (2009). Climate Change: Challenges Facing India's Poor, *Economic & Political Weekly*, Vol. 44, No. 31, pp. 51–58.

Sridevi, G. et al., (2014): Climate Change Vulnerability in Agriculture Sector: Indexing and Mapping of Four Southern Indian States, Quarterly Working Paper, Department of Economic Sciences, University of Bologna, Italy.

Stern, N., (2007): *The Economics of Climate Change: The Stern Review*, Cambridge University Press, Cambridge.

Sullivan, C.A., Meigh, J.R. and O'Regan, D.P., (2002): *Evaluating Your Water: A Management Primer for the Water Poverty Index.* Wallingford, UK: CEH.

Sullivan, C., (2006): *Global Change Impacts: Assessing Human Vulnerability at the Sub-national Scale*, Presented at the International River Symposium, Brisbane.

Swain, M. and Swain, M., (2011): Vulnerability to Agricultural Drought in Western Orissa: A Case Study of Representative Blocks, *Agricultural Economics Research Review*, Vol. 24, No. 1, pp. 47–56.

Venkateswarlu, B. and Rama Rao, C.A., (2010): Rainfed Agriculture: Challenges of Climate Change, *Agriculture Today Year Book*, pp. 43–45.

11 State's Initiatives for the Sugarcane Sector Revival

Ground Realities and Problems

Abnave Vikas Bajrang

Introduction and Motivation

State intervention plays a crucial role in India's sugarcane sector, and therefore no discussion would be complete without considering the role of the state in sugarcane sector. The vital intervention of the state can take a number of forms such as the Sugar Industry (Protection) Act (1932), Essential Commodity Act (1955), Sugar Control Order (1966), State Advisory Prices (SAPs) (1970), Jute Packing Materials Act (1987), Delicensing Sugar Sector (1998), Ethanol-Blending Programme (2012), Scheme for Extending Financial Assistance to Sugar Undertaking (2014), etc. The state intervention is essential in sugarcane sector to get the right market prices for sugar and sugarcane through regulations and controls. In addition, it is also inevitable in the sugarcane sector since the price elasticity of both sugar and sugarcane remains less comparatively as the industrial product prices are hedged to a maximum limit, whereas, agricultural products prices are hedged to minimum limit (Jugale, 2000). Along with this, the risks of yield and price unpredictability, changes in inputs cost, diseases, and also seasonal variations due to water shortage as well as changes in weather are other important factors leading to state intervention in sugarcane sector.

In India, the state's intervention in sugarcane sector is a complex trap of contradictory policies, particularly in the sugarcane production and price policies. Despite many efforts by the state, India's sugarcane sector is reeling under contradictory situations. While on the one hand, the farmers are agitating for better prices and timely payment for their sugarcane produce; on the other hand, the sugar mills constantly oppose this demand. While the sugarcane growers and their organisations demand better sugarcane prices on the ground that the cost of inputs and price of sugarcane has not increased proportionately, the sugar mills argue that they are unable to pay the arrears due to falling international sugar prices and economic policies of the central and state governments. With this background, this paper makes an attempt to look into some of the issues related to state's regulations and controls on sugarcane sector with the critical review of state's policies and programmes.

Objective

To examine the changing role of the state and factors responsible for issues and problems faced by the sugarcane growers and sugar mills in India.

Data

The present analysis is based on the review of existing literature and secondary data which was collected from the Directorate of Economics and Statistics (DES), Department of Agriculture and Co-operation, Ministry of Agriculture, Department of Food and Public Distribution, Ministry of Consumer Affairs, Ministry of Finance, Government of India, and reports of different committees. This paper is organised into four sections. The first section briefly discusses how the state's role in sugarcane sector has changed over the year. The second section deals with critically view on sugarcane price policy and its methodological issues. Third section discusses the consequences of different state's regulations and feasibility of efforts taken by the government for sugarcane sector. In addition, the final section summarises and concludes the paper.

Discussions

State Efforts for India's Sugarcane Sector: A Brief Overview

During the British period, Sugar Industry (Protection) Act, 1932 and Sugarcane Act, 1934 were introduced by the central government to protect the interest of both sugar mills and sugarcane grower. Under the Sugar Factory Control Act (1938), it was mandatory for the mills to purchase sugarcane through co-operative societies, instead of purchasing sugarcane through middlemen. Due to the dominance of co-operative sugar mills, no middleman exists presently between sugar mill and sugarcane growers except officials of the sugar mills. Before independence, various state governments set sugarcane prices, which led to regional variations. As per the Sugarcane (Control) Order 1950, the central government started to fix uniform minimum prices. Under the Industries (Development and Regulation) Act 1951, Government of India took over the regulation of the sugar sector from the states in 1952. Sugarcane and Sugar falls under the Essential Commodities Act (1955). Under this Act, the government was permitted to impose a levy quota at lower prices than the market rates. The rest of the sugar (free sale) quota was controlled by the state under Sugar (Control) Order (1966) as 'monthly release mechanism'. Till the mid-1960s, the sugar sector was fully controlled by the central government. Due to low Statutory Minimum Prices (SMPs) for sugarcane, it was diverted to the Gur and Khandasari units. Therefore, the state adopted partial decontrol policy. Consequently from 1970, the SAPs came into existence.

Sugarcane Development Fund (1982) was set up for research and development and to achieve overall development of sugar sector. Under the Sugar Cess Act (1982), a cess of ₹ 24 per quintal was collected from March 2008 on all sugar produced and sold by the sugar mills. To promote Jute industry, it was made mandatory that sugar be packed in only jute bags under the Jute Packing Materials Act (1987). A major decision of delicensing sugar sector was taken in 1998 when licensing requirement for new sugar mills was removed. The state has made an arrangement for Sugar Stabilisation Fund to stabilise sugar prices and pay better sugarcane prices to the sugarcane growers when sugar prices in the market are low. Apart from these, the central government started to fix Fair and Remunerative Price (FRP) from 2009 to 2010, which is fix on cost of sugarcane production, inter-crop price parity, recovery, sugar prices, availability of sugar and margin, to provide reasonable margins to sugarcane growers on account of risk and profits. To get better prices from sugarcane by-products and reduce pollution, the Ethanol-Blending Programme was started in 2012. The central government partially adopted Rangarajan Committee recommendation on April 2013 and announced partial decontrol of sugar sector. In order to facilitate clearance of sugarcane arrears and timely settlement of sugarcane prices, the central government introduced new soft/interest-free loan scheme (Scheme for Extending Financial Assistance to Sugar Undertaking) to sugar mills in January 2014. In February 2014, the state also notified a Scheme for Marketing and Promotion of Raw Sugar Production and announced subsidies to promote sugar export and raise domestic sugar prices from Sugar Development Fund. The Table 1 presents the summary of efforts taken by the state.

Table 1

Summary of Efforts Taken by the State

Government Effort	*Year*	*Year of Modification*	*Objective*	*Outcome(s)*
Sugar Industry (Protection) Act	1932	–	To protect interest of sugar mills.	–
Sugarcane Act	1934	–	To protect interest of sugarcane growers.	–
Sugar Factory Control Act	1938	–	To abolish middlemen.	No middlemen exist between sugar mill and sugarcane growers except sugar mills' officials.
Sugarcane (Control) Order	1950	2009–10	To fix uniform minimum prices.	Every year the central government fixes FRP before sugar season start.
Industries (Development and Regulation) Act	1951	–	To regulate the sugar sector by the Government of India	–

Cont'd...

...Cont'd

Government Effort	*Year*	*Year of Modification*	*Objective*	*Outcome(s)*
Essential Commodities Act	1955	1991; 1996; 2013	To impose a levy quota at lower prices than the market price	Central government has abolished levy on sugar produce after 1 October 2012. Procurement for PDS operation is being made from the open market by the states/UTs and government is providing a fixed subsidy at ₹ 18.50 per kg.
Sugar (Control) order	1966	2004-05; 2013	To control free sale sugar.	–
State Advisory Prices (SAPs)	1970	–	To divert sugarcane from *Gur* and khandasari units to sugar industry.	State Advisory Price is always higher than FRP.
Sugarcane Development Fund	1982	–	To establish research and development and to achieve over all development of sugar sector.	During the period from 1982-83 to 2015-16 (up to 30.11.2015), a net cess of ₹ 8,785.75 crore was collected.
Jute Packing Materials Act	1987	2012	To promote Jute industry.	The compulsory packaging of sugar in jute bags has been relaxed further. In addition, only 20 per cent of the production is to be mandatorily packed in jute bags.
Delicensing Sugar Sector	1998	–	To solve problem of surplus sugarcane production.	Major change in the sugar sector with the increase in installed capacity of sugar mills.
Fair and Remunerative Price	2009–10	–	To provide reasonable margins to the sugarcane growers.	So far only Karnataka and Maharashtra have passed state acts to implement this recommendation.
Ethanol-Blendin g Programme	2012	2014	To get better prices from sugarcane by-products and reduce pollution and dependency of imports.	The state governments have already been requested to reconsider the regulatory controls on movement of molasses which can be used for producing ethanol.

Cont'd...

...Cont'd

Government Effort	*Year*	*Year of Modification*	*Objective*	*Outcome(s)*
Scheme for Extending Financial Assistance to Sugar Undertaking	2014	–	To facilitate clearance of sugarcane arrears and timely settlement of sugarcane prices.	The central government announced ₹ 6,000 crore interest-free loan for the sugar mills.
Scheme for Marketing and Promotion of Raw Sugar Production	2014	–	To utilise incentive provided under the scheme by the sugar mills for making payment to the sugarcane growers.	About ₹ 183.87 crore was disbursed to sugar mills during Financial Year 2014-15 and about ₹ 99.67 crore was released during 2015-16 sugar season up to 31.12.2015.

Source: Author's compilation from various reports and literature.

As observed above, India's sugar sector is highly controlled by the state regulations and controls which are different from the other countries. As per the Mahajan Committee Report (1998), in other countries like Australia and Brazil, which are largest producer of sugarcane and sugar, no license is required for new mill or to expand the installed capacity. In Australia, sugar sector receives no direct assistance or support from the state. In China, the government follows the policy of self-sufficiency by providing various incentives to the sugarcane growers and controlling government sugar stock. Thailand, a low-cost sugar producer, became one of the major sugar exporters in the world market due to tax incentives, high domestic sugar prices, and subsidised credit to sugar industry and sugar growers by the government. In case of Brazil, the sugarcane area reservation for each sugar mill is not legally determined and there is no state control on sugar prices. No part of sugar production is mandatory acquired for public distribution by the state. Ethanol-blending proportion is also high at around 40–50 per cent in Brazil compared to India where only 10 per cent ethanol blending is targeted by the Indian government, which has not even achieved five per cent.

Impact of State's Policies/Programmes on Sugarcane Production

There is no doubt that the area and production of sugarcane has increased (area effect), but the productivity (yield effect) has not increased significantly especially in Maharashtra. The state's support prices, subsidies on fertilisers and electricity, and assured demand are encouraging sugarcane production relative to other crops. Therefore, the farmers are going for sugarcane area expansion. Moreover, the movement of sugarcane production shifted from sub-tropical region to tropical region in India (see Appendix 1). Sugarcane was grown largely in sub-tropical states like Uttar Pradesh, Punjab, and Bihar. Until the early 1950s, these states had 80 per cent of area under sugarcane and accounted for 70 per cent of sugarcane production. This structural change is an outcome of state's policies and regulations in the tropical region like the fixing minimum prices for sugarcane was not mandatory and did not levy cess on purchase of sugarcane by the sugar mills (Sen Committee Report, 1965). Apart from these factors, the market in tropical region was large, facilitating entry of new sugar mills, emergence of co-operative movement and also the fact that tropical region is best suited for sugarcane cultivation, aided the growth of the sector.

Sugarcane pricing policy is also contributing to a shift from other crops to sugarcane. There are institutional factors including subsidy, which drive area expansion of a particular crop as farmers read the market signal as well as incentives to shift. A lot of sugarcane cultivation is made possible due to the better support price and other support mechanism to the sugarcane farmers where the soil and climatic conditions does not support sugarcane cultivation. For example, out of total sugar mills in Maharashtra state, 40 per cent mills are in drought-prone districts that are more suited to growing oilseeds and pulses. The shift from other crops to sugarcane is mostly because sugarcane farmers enjoy much more subsidised inputs like fertilisers, electricity, and water, especially in Maharashtra. The average fertiliser consumption for all crops is 136 kg/ha, whereas it is 208.4 kg/ha for sugarcane (Fertilizer Statistics, 2010–11). The 13th Finance Commission noticed environmental degradation due to price policies, subsidies, or incentives provided by the state in terms of free electricity and fertilisers, which led to low productivity in India (Government of India, 2009).

Till 1998, the state's licensing policy also favoured establishment new sugar mills or to expand existing capacity of mills only in co-operative sector. Apart from licensing bias, the co-operative sugar mills get large support from the state governments, than the private mills, which dominate Uttar Pradesh. These state policies led to a rapid expansion of sugar mills in Maharashtra, encouraged sugarcane production along with water exploitation in the state. The results of state intervention through policies in the sugar sector have seriously distorted regional production and cropping patterns, and misallocation of resources (World Bank, 1997; World Bank and Government of India, 1998).

For solving water scarcity, Commission for Agricultural Costs and Prices (CACP) recommended bringing Maharashtra's sugarcane cultivation under drip irrigation. It is very difficult to differentiate the irrigation expenditure incurred by the government only for sugarcane. However, sugarcane is a large water-consuming crop, which means sugarcane consumes a large proportion of state subsidies for providing water. As per the Economic Survey of Maharashtra (2013–14), the expenditure incurred for sprinkler and drip irrigation was around ₹ 197 crore in 2008–09 and ₹ 574 crore in 2012–13. However, there is no so much impact of area under the drip irrigation on water situation and not much sugarcane under drip in the Maharashtra (Thakkar, 2013).

Key Constraints of Indian Sugarcane Sector

Dual Sugarcane Price Policy and Its Methodological Issues

The fixation of sugarcane price mechanism varied from country to country and state to state. In all the major sugarcane and sugar-producing countries in the world like Australia, Brazil, Fiji, Mexico, South Africa, and Thailand, there is a direct link between sugarcane and its by-products prices. Thailand and Fiji's sugarcane growers received more than 70 per cent share in the total sugar mills' revenue from sugar and its by-products as sugarcane price, whereas, farmers received around 65–61 per cent in Brazil and 62–63 per cent in South Africa (CACP, 2012). Therefore, the Rangarajan Committee identified a need to change existing price-fixing mechanism in India.

The Sugar and Gur Control Order (1950) was enacted by the central government due to the variations in sugarcane prices. In India, the growers get sugarcane prices based on tonnage of the sugarcane, which is given to the sugar mill rather than recovery of sugarcane. This price fixation mechanism gives more importance to quantity rather than quality of sugarcane. It is not viable for the sugar mills because the poor quality of sugarcane can lead to low output. Though the quantity-oriented pricing arrangement makes profit for short term, it is not sustainable. Unfortunately, even after the introduction of the 1950s Sugar and *Gur* Control Order, the variations till exist in sugarcane prices. Inter-regional and inter-mill variation in sugarcane prices exists due non-linking of recovery properly with sugarcane weight. Baru (1990) identified some problems of linking sugarcane price with quality. First, the sugarcane growers are not adequately rewarded or penalised for the quality of sugarcane supplied to the mills, because the estimation procedures of sugarcane quality is highly aggregative and do not distinguish among the different growers of sugarcane. Second, the sucrose content is totally dependent on mill's extraction efficiency. If the sugar mill's extraction capacity were inefficient, then even if the sugarcane quality is good the recovery level would be lower.

Table 2

Extra Amount Paid by Sugar Mills to Sugarcane Growers

State	*Year*	*Production of Sugarcane (Million Tonne)*	*Difference between FRP and SAP (₹/Qtl)*	*Extra Amount Paid by Sugar Mills to Sugarcane Growers (₹ in Thousand Crore)*
Maharashtra	2010–11	81.89	55	4.50
	2011–12	86.73	35	3.03
	2012–13	69.64	20	1.39
	2013–14	76.90	37	2.84
Karnataka	2010–11	39.65	29	1.14
	2011–12	38.80	30	1.16
	2012–13	35.73	30	1.07
	2013–14	37.90	30	1.13
Uttar Pradesh	2010–11	120.54	60	7.23
	2011–12	128.81	70	9.01
	2012–13	132.42	70	9.26
	2013–14	134.68	60	8.08

Note: SAP, State Advisory Price; FRP, Fair and Remunerative Price.

Source: Calculated based on Directorate of Economics and Statistics, GoI; Indian Sugar Mills Association; and Agriwatch database.

The Essential Commodities Act (1955) is the main step towards sugar sector regulatory framework. According to the provisions of the Act, India follows the central government fixed price (FRPs) of sugarcane based on recommendations of the CACP and after consultations with the state governments and other stakeholders SAP came into existence in the early 1970s. After announcement of FRP, every state government has the autonomy to fix the SAP, which is always higher than FRP. The higher SAP by some state governments compared to the central government fixed FRP has led to increasing sugarcane arrears (CACP, 2014). The huge sugarcane arrears would become unsustainable and ultimately destroy sugarcane cultivation and sugar mills (CACP, 2013). An attempt is made in Table 2 to compare state-wise difference between FRP and SAPs of sugarcane for Karnataka, Maharashtra, and Uttar Pradesh states. It is observed that the difference between SAP and FRP has declined over the years due to the replacement of SMP into FRP especially after 2009. The extra amount (calculated subsidy) paid by sugar mills to sugarcane growers in Uttar Pradesh is almost higher than Maharashtra and Karnataka due to high State Advised Prices (SAPs) announced by the state government. There are also other determining factors. The absorption capacity of the mills in the respective states and state's own production would indicate the shortfall and excess supply of sugarcane. It is also observed that with the decline in sugarcane production, the price difference is reduced.

There are also some methodological issues involved in price fixation in sugar sector system. First, the price for sugar takes ₹ 3,100–3,200 per quintal while fixing prices for sugarcane as base price. The problem with this mechanism is that actual or current sugar price is not directly linked to the fluctuations in sugar prices while fixing prices for sugarcane. There is no guarantee that the sugar price would be same in future or throughout the year. Apart from sugar price fluctuations, the sugarcane price is fixed by state based on average cost of cultivation, recovery, and variety with higher sugar content. The cost of production is one of the major determinants of the price of sugarcane. However, there is no current cost of cultivation data available. Basically, the cost of cultivation survey data received by the CACP comes with a time lag of two-three year. These data used to project the cost of sugarcane cultivation in major sugarcane growing states of Maharashtra, Andhra Pradesh, Maharashtra, Karnataka, Haryana, Tamil Nadu, and Uttar Pradesh, which may not provide the correct picture of sugarcane cultivation costs. Beside these methodological issues, the SAP is generally fixed on the basis of sugarcane prices paid by the nearby mills, especially in Maharashtra. This mechanism of SAP fixation forces mills to pay a certain price to the sugarcane growers, whether the mills can afford it or not. For instance, Karnataka government ordered all co-operative sugar mills to pay farmers ₹ 120 for a quintal of sugarcane in 2007. The central government's SMP was fixed at ₹ 81.18 per quintal. The difference between the two prices was around ₹ 38–39 for a quintal. Most sugar mills paid only between ₹ 60 and 80 for a quintal, except two or three mills. Thus, this dual pricing mechanism of price fixation is leads to uncertainty sugarcane prices.

The major incentive for state to intervene in sugar prices is to keep it at a reasonably affordable level for domestic household consumption. The state tries to do justice to the sugarcane growers, sugar mills, and consumers simultaneously while fixing the prices for sugarcane and sugar. However, the problem is most of the sugar is consumed (around 70%) by the sugar-based industries like beverages, chemicals, etc. whereas, only 30 per cent of sugar is consumed by household consumer. There is no differentiation in sugar prices for use of household purpose and commercial purpose. Sugar-consuming industries get more benefits out of low sugar prices than household sugar consumer. The state has not addressed this issue by putting two different prices for the household and commercial uses.

The values of main product and by-products were not taken into consideration while fixing price of sugarcane in India; therefore, the Rangarajan Committee (Rangarajan Committee Report, 2012) has introduced a formula (70:30) to address the issue of sugarcane price fixation, based on revenue sharing. Revenue sharing is an important recommendation for sugarcane farmers, which will help them get a better share of total revenue compared to earlier share, which was only 55–60 per cent of the total revenue earned from sugar and its by-products. Unfortunately, almost majority of state governments in India have not adopted it, except Karnataka. It is interesting to note that, despite adoption of revenue-sharing formula by Karnataka state, the sugarcane growers are facing a crisis now and numbers of farm suicides by sugarcane growers are also high recently.

Consistent rise in FRP of sugarcane and declining sugar prices have resulted in low margins from sugar production and delay in sugarcane payment (see Figure 1). There is a mismatch between sugar prices and sugarcane prices in India, whereas in all the major sugar-producing countries like Brazil, Thailand, and Australia, there is direct linkage between sugarcane and sugar prices. Paying unscientific determined prices for sugarcane is not feasible for the

Figure 1

Trends of Sugarcane and Sugar Prices in India

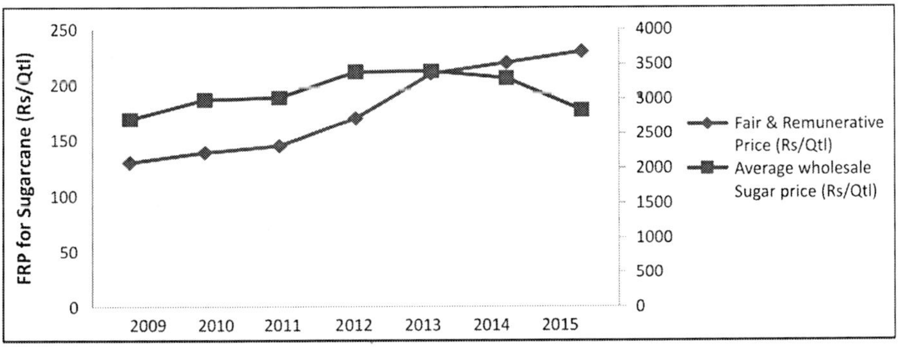

Source: Directorate of Economics and Statistics & Department of Consumer Affairs (Price Monitoring Cell).

sugar mills, which also leads to arrears in payment. It is also causing fluctuations in production and prices of sugar and sugarcane. The way out as recommended by the CACP in 2015–16 report is that the total revenue pot (TRP) should be generated from the sugarcane-sugar value chain and profits should be distributed between the farmers and sugar millers in the ratio of their relative production costs.

Sugarcane Arrears

Among the major sugarcane growing states from tropical and sub-tropical regions, Uttar Pradesh had about ₹ 2.29 thousand crore of total amount of cane arrears till December 2013, followed by Karnataka (₹ 1.53 thousand crore), Maharashtra (₹ 0.47 thousand crore), Andhra Pradesh (₹ 0.24 thousand crore), Tamil Nadu (₹ 0.20 thousand crore), Punjab (₹ 0.11 thousand crore), and Haryana (₹ 0.10 thousand crore). The sugarcane arrears suddenly increased to around ₹ 1.48 and ₹ 0.42 thousand crore in Karnataka and Maharashtra in 2013–14, respectively. Karnataka and Uttar Pradesh also had the highest position in total sugarcane arrears pending till December 2013. In both these states, the sector is dominated by private sugar mills, which may explain the high unpaid arrears in these states. For instance, the total sugarcane arrears to be paid by the private sector mills was ₹ 27,301 lakh (₹ 525.01 lakh per mill) followed by co-operative sugar mills at ₹ 6,091 lakh (₹ 435.07 lakh per mill) and public sector mills at ₹ 539 lakh per mill during the 2012–13 sugar season in Karnataka state. A major reason for increased sugarcane arrears in Uttar Pradesh is the higher percentage share of actual sugarcane price in value of sugar paid to the sugarcane grower. During 2007–08 to 2012–13, the average of share of actual sugarcane price in value of sugar was around 60 per cent in Maharashtra, whereas, it was around 83 per cent in Uttar Pradesh.

The gap between total price payable and total price paid by the sugar mills to the sugarcane grower has been increasing over the years (see Figure 2). It is not a healthy progress from the point of view of sugar mills as well as sugarcane grower. The increasing amount of unpaid sugarcane arrears is not a one-day or one-year phenomenon. This problem started especially after the central government replaced the SMP with FRPs for sugarcane in 2009–10. The pricing of sugarcane is fixed under the Sugarcane (Control) Order, 1966, issued under the Essential Commodities Act (1955). Before 2009–10 sugar season, the central government was fixing the SMP of sugarcane and farmers used to get their share on the criteria of 50:50. The concept of SMP was replaced by the FRP of sugarcane, because the sharing of profits remained practically unimplemented. The main cause of this replacement was the reasonable margins for growers of sugarcane should get on account of risk and this was made effective from the 2009–10 sugar season. The percentage of arrears on price payable to the sugarcane growers was around three per cent in 2008–09, which has gone up to around 50 per cent in 2014–15 (see Figure 2).

Figure 2

Sugarcane Arrears in India

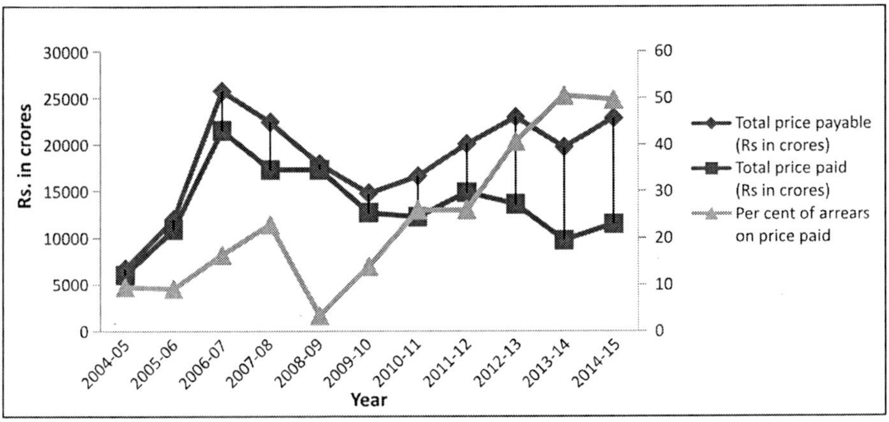

Source: Directorate of Sugar, Department of Food and Public Distribution, GoI.

Do International Sugar Prices Matter?

The sugar mills claimed that they could not pay the arrears due to declining sugar prices at national as well as international markets. However, one could not find logic in their claim as they did not pay the arrears even when the sugar prices were high at domestic as well as international markets. For instance, the price level of sugar was stable at normal level till 2007–08, after that again prices of sugar have increased till 2012–13. If we make a comparison between sugar prices before and after 2012–13, it can be found that before 2012–13, sugar prices were higher at national as well as international levels, compared to post 2012–13. During the same period, sugarcane price was less compared to the latest prices of sugarcane and, mills also could not pay sugarcane arrears to the sugarcane grower.

Out of total sugar availability, about 73 per cent sugar was used for internal consumption and less than one per cent sugar was used for export purpose with a closing stock of sugar about 27 per cent at the end of season in 2004–05. The internal consumption of sugar slightly declined to about 71 per cent and the share in total sugar export was one per cent in 2012–13. In India, the main requirement of sugarcane growing is the domestic sugar consumption. It is a fact that the world sugar prices have declined over the year. However, India's sugar sector depends more on domestic sugar prices. There are other determinants influencing sugar prices such as supply and demand, increasing population and income level, changes in government policies, availability of alternative sweeteners, increase in crude oil prices, diversions of sugarcane for the ethanol production, and adverse climatic conditions. There is no doubt that the falling world sugar prices affects the domestic sugar prices in India, but not as much as claimed by the sugar mills.

Sugarcane Area Reservation and Minimum Distance Criteria

The state has implemented sugarcane area reservation regulation for assured supply of sugarcane to the mills, encourage investment in agriculture, assure buyers for sugarcane growers, especially in surplus year, and avoid unhealthy competition among sugar mills. The government gives permission to the new sugar factory on the basis of distance between two sugar mills' broiler. The states of India have been not done any assessment on the processing capacity of the mills and area under sugarcane. This mismatch leads to a crisis. The government should give permission to new sugar mills on the basis of availability of sugarcane and groundwater.

According to Sugarcane (Control) Order, (1966), the states have the power to allocate sugarcane reserve areas for individual mills. Under this regulation, it is mandatory for every sugar mill to purchase sugarcane from the farmers within the reservation area, and, conversely, the shareholder sugarcane growers also have a compulsion of sugar sale with a particular sugar mill. A minimum distance criterion came into existence to ensure adequate sugarcane supply to the mills. The minimum distance criteria is not uniform for all states. Currently, only Maharashtra, Haryana, and Punjab have 25 kilometre prescribed distance criteria, whereas, other states have 15 kilometre distance criteria (Rangarajan Committee Report, 2012). It is interesting to note that distance criterion is more where the sugarcane production is surplus like Maharashtra state. It creates the problem of delay in harvesting, which eventually affects the recovery. The less recovery is not economically viable for the sugar mills to give payment of sugarcane to the growers, because of the high sugar production cost. Due to sugarcane area reservation system, the sugar mills also lose out on augmented sugarcane supplies, especially when there is a shortage of sugarcane production in the mills' command areas. In addition to this, the sugar mills have to purchase sugarcane as it is, whether it is in good quality or not. This has resulted in inefficiencies, preventing sugar mills from enjoying economies of scale. It can be concluded that the existence of the cane reservation area and minimum distance criteria do not ensure better prices for sugarcane growers and force to existing mills to delay payments.

Regulations Relating to Trade

The state uses the import and export controls as well as temporary bans to achieve stability in domestic sugar prices for consumer. Earlier, the central government regulated the release of non-levy sugar into the markets. Every mill had certain quota of sugar to be release into the market when monthly sugar release system existed. The government partially accepted Tuteja Committee (Tuteja Committee Report, 2004) recommendation and control shifted from monthly to quarterly. The problem with this system was that India's sugar industry was not able to take any advantage of large demand in world market for sugar (Ahmad and Rehman, 2014). In addition to this, the export-import policy of Indian government does not allow mills to have a long-term relation globally (Rangarajan Committee Report, 2012). Though India is the second largest producer of sugar and has 15.8 per cent share in global market, its share in export was only 3.5 per cent in TE 2013–14. On the other hand, Brazil and Thailand, which contributes only 21.4 per cent and 6.1 per cent of the global sugarcane production, respectively, hold 47.5 per cent and 13.4 per cent share in total exports of sugar (CACP, 2014). As per the Rangarajan Committee (Rangarajan Committee Report, 2012) recommendation, the export duty and sugar release mechanism were abolished and import duty fixed at 15 per cent in April 2013. The pressure of sugarcane dues increased due to abolishment of regulated release mechanism and has resulted in declining sugar prices in the short run (CARE, 2013).

Since August 2009, the state had followed 'consumer-oriented sugar policy' with import of sugar from other countries at zero import duty, while export of sugar was highly controlled under the quarterly release mechanism. Jyothi (2014) pointed out the sugar exports and imports vary from time to time due to fluctuations in policies of the government and highly politicised sugar sector. This is creating problems for the sugar mills in formulating marketing strategies, which affects the performance of the sugar mills, which in turn affects large sugarcane cultivation growers of the country. Adverse impacts of these regulations are more on small and medium farmers linked to them are trapped in laws and regulations. One of the major justifications for state regulation was to protect small and marginal farmer. Unfortunately, the state regulations have failed to help them.

Regulations Relating to By-products

Certain restrictions have also been imposed on sugar mills regarding by-products of sugarcane such as ethanol blending, sale of bagasse and molasses. Molasses is a major by-product and is used in the production of alcohol, chemicals, and spirit. It is a very good source of income to sugar mills and sugarcane grower. It will fetch good prices for sugarcane growers if these product prices are attached to sugarcane prices. Though there is a constant watch by State Excise Authority on allocation and distribution of molasses, there are no uniform regulations on molasses across the states. The export of molasses is banned in Tamil Nadu and Karnataka, whereas, inter-state export and import of molasses is free in Maharashtra. Because of this unhealthy regulation on by-products, the sugar industry bears the cost of other industries by providing raw materials at cheaper rates. For example, the liquor industry in Uttar Pradesh receives a large supply of molasses at low prices by the state government, allowing liquor industry to enjoy huge profits at the cost of sugar mills. Moreover, the stock of molasses and bagasse has to finish before new season starts due to insufficient storage facility. Such restrictions reduce the revenue realisation of sugar mills from by-products and economic efficiency (Rangarajan Committee Report, 2012).

Ethanol is an agro-based product, mainly produced from molasses. It helps in reducing pollution, conserve foreign exchange, and increase value addition in the sugar industry. The demand of ethanol has increased after the Cabinet

Committee on Economic Affairs (CCEA) made ethanol blending with petrol compulsory in November 2012 to reduce greenhouse gas emission and reduce dependency on fuel imports. However, there are some restrictions on it. The Ministry of Consumer Affairs, Food and Public Distribution issued an order in December 2007 permitting sugar mills to directly produce ethanol from sugarcane. Even though such kinds of order by the government, there is no single sugar mill ready to produce ethanol directly from sugarcane in India. In addition to this, the government has decided that oil marketing companies shall sell ethanol blended petrol under the Ethanol-Blending Programme. India had a targeted 20 per cent ethanol blending by 2017 year end. The government had given production subsidy at ₹ 4.50 per quintal to sugar mills to achieve the ethanol-blending target. However, the government has imposed a tax on ethanol production from 10 August 2016, withdrawing the earlier tax exemption. As a result of this, ethanol prices have gone down by ₹ 5–6 per litre, which will ultimately affect the profit of ethanol-producing mills. However, the inadequate production of ethanol is a major obstacle to the blending programme. Despite the decision to increase ethanol blending from five per cent to 10 per cent, only 3.5 per cent was achieved due to absence of clear directive, procurement price issue, and delay in settlement of tenders (Directorate of Sugar, 2014–15). The government has dismantled entire bidding process and introduced ex-depot price (₹ 48.50 to ₹ 49.50 per litre) for ethanol to address the ethanol price issue.

Delicensing and Decontrol Policy

Despite the several regulations introduced by the government in sugar sector, the decontrol of sugar sector began in 1998 when licensing requirement for new mills was abolished. Due to delicensing policy, the installed capacity of sugar mills has increased.

There are also a few consequences of delicensing of sugarcane sector. First, the delicensing has led to huge competition among new sugar mills and existing sugar mills. Due to this competition, some sick sugar mills have to pay higher sugarcane prices fixed by the government even though they are not in a position to pay. The result of this unhealthy competition is the increase in the number of non-working sugar mills from 119 in Triennium Ending (TE) 2005 to 162 in TE 2009 (Reddy, 2011). Second, the private sugar mills are totally dependent on farmers' behaviour of selling sugarcane to a particular mill as the private mills have no assured supply of sugarcane. Third, the private sugar mills generally are run for profit; therefore, their contribution in social infrastructure development is not much as compared to contribution of co-operative sugar mills. A problem with private sugar mills is that they will only be ready to purchase sugarcane when it is profitable for them otherwise, they may refuse to purchase sugarcane. Third, an important consequence of delicensing is the problem of capital formation to run the sugar mills. Although the number of sugar mills rose after delicensing, there is not much improvement found in sugarcane productivity, especially in Maharashtra state. Finally, the share of private mills in total arrears is higher compared to the co-operative sugar mills. The total sugarcane arrears to be paid by the private mills is ₹ 15,206 crore, followed by co-operative sugar mills (₹ 6,196 crore) and public sector mills (₹ 434 crore) for the 2014–15 sugar season.

Feasibility of State's Short-Term Patchworks

There is no doubt that state's recent efforts have provided some support to the sugar sector in the short term. However, the long-term impacts of these are doubtful since the state has not addressed the most important issues, that is, the prices of sugar and sugarcane. For long-term sustainability of sugarcane sector, the Rangarajan Committee (Rangarajan Committee Report, 2012) suggested that sugarcane and sugar prices should be inter-linked, but unfortunately this suggestion has not been implemented. Since the linking of sugarcane prices with the actual sugar prices and by-products has worked in several countries like Brazil, Thailand, and Australia, a question arises as to why not in India. Though Thorat Committee (Thorat Committee Report, 2009) recommended that the government should withdraw from fixing the prices of sugarcane, it has been not implemented yet.

The central government on January 2014 has introduced a Scheme for Extending Financial Assistance to Sugar Undertakings (SEFASU). In June 2015, the central government announced ₹ 6,000-crore interest-free loan for the sugar mills, but this still does not address the basic problem of surplus of sugar production, resulting from increased sugarcane-grown area, trade policies, and ample last year's carry forward stock of sugar and suitable mechanism related to the price fixation. Moreover, the state subsidy or financial assistance given directly to the sugar mills, does not reach the sugarcane grower. For instance, the central government is supposed to reimburse a fixed sugar subsidy for public distribution at 18.50 per kilogram limited to the quantity based on existing allocations directly to the state government. The production subsidy was also extended at ₹ 4.50 per quintal to sugar mills to compensate cost of sugarcane and make possible timely payment of cane price dues of farmers for the current sugar season 2015–16. The Maharashtra government recently exempted sugar mills from purchase tax, which means a direct subsidy for the sugar mills. This benefit will not give any support to the sugarcane farmers.

State-wise variations exist in sanction of interest-free loans. The Uttar Pradesh state tops in terms of sugarcane arrears, but the percentage of loan sanctioned to total arrears is only 19.30 per cent during 2014–15. The percentage of loan sanctioned to total arrears is highest at around 72 per cent in Tamil Nadu. Among the states mentioned in Table 3, the percentage of loan sanctioned to total arrears is only 16.07 per cent and 65.94 per cent in Karnataka and Maharashtra respectively. It can be concluded that state-wise allocation of assistance is not based on equity principle. This inequitable distribution of fund from state may create regional inequality. Giving assistance in terms of interest-free loans may not be a proper solution. The state has to solve price fixation and other related problems as a priority.

Table 3

Amount of Loan to Sugar Mills under SEFASU, 2014

State	Arrears 2014-15 (as on 31.03.15)* (₹ in Crore)	Number of Sugar Mills in Operation**	Loan Sanctioned		Loan Disbursed		Percentage of Loan Sanctioned to Total Arrears
			No. of Mills	Amount (₹ in Crore)	No. of Mills	Amount (₹ in Crore)	
Punjab	682.28	18	18	151.30	7	69.22	22.17
Haryana	516.11	14	11	104.10	11	104.10	20.17
Uttar Pradesh	9,715.69	124	74	1,875.27	72	1,764.86	19.30
Maharashtra	2,864.50	170	107	1,889.08	104	1,724.99	65.94
Karnataka	2,402.39	58	37	386.21	31	347.67	16.07
Andhra Pradesh	265.69	37	19	138.79	17	130.04	52.23
Tamil Nadu	842.56	43	37	606.38	37	550.50	71.96

Note: SEFASU, Scheme for Extending Financial Assistance to Sugar Undertakings.

Source: *Ministry of Consumer Affairs, Food and Public Distribution, Lok Sabha Secretariat, New Delhi, 2015 (Starred Questioned No. 385) Annexure. Ministry of Consumer Affairs, Food and Public Distribution, Lok Sabha Secretariat, New Delhi (Un-starred Questioned No. 710) Annexure. ** Directorate of Economics and Statistics, Government of India.

Water management experts have recently made a statement that sugarcane cultivation should be banned in drought prone areas to solve problem of excess sugarcane and water shortage. Farmers would have grown other crops rather than sugarcane, if they get better prices. Despite the fact that Maharashtra was facing water scarcity, the state government provided water to other industries which requires more water than sugar industry which is not a major contributor to the rural economy. Since August 2009, the state has followed zero import duty on sugar, while export of sugar is highly controlled. As a result of zero import duty, India's sugar import was highest in 2009–10. These kinds of state policies may lead to the import of large quantity sugar from other countries. The state pays higher prices for the imported sugar than the domestic sugar when domestic sugar production was less due to low prices. There is a provision of mandatory deduction from sugar mills by the state for a sugar stabilisation fund to solve the problem of mismatch between sugar and sugarcane prices. However, this sugar stabilisation fund tool is not found to be effective since sugarcane arrears and instability in sugar prices have increased. Similarly, there are no proper long-term solutions or mechanisms by the state to solve these problems related to sugarcane prices and water especially in Maharashtra.

Summary and Policy Implications

Overall, it appears that the sugar sector remains highly controlled by the state via various regulations in India today. There is no other agro-based sector, which is heavily controlled by the state as much as sugar sector. The recent issue about announcement of the FRP and SAP is an example of the adverse effects of state intervention in sugarcane price fixation. Although many efforts have been made by the state to promote sugarcane cultivation, the productivity of sugarcane is stagnant in India. Due to the state's unhealthy control on by-products, the sugar industry is bearing the cost of other industries by providing raw materials at cheaper rates. The inequitable distribution of assistance or funds to the sugar mills by the state may also create regional inequality. The introduction of delicensing policy by the state led to some problems like unhealthy competitions, reduced contribution in social infrastructure development, and increased number of sick sugar mills. There is no doubt that the recent state's efforts or measures may provide some support to the sugarcane sector in the short term, but it may not support in the long run. This is because the state has not addressed the most important issues, which are causing the problem. To summarise, the state regulations and controls in sugarcane sector are unviable or unsustainable in India and leads to uncertainty in income of both sugarcane growers and sugar mills.

To address the problems associated with state intervention, this paper suggests the gap between FRP and SAP need to be reduced. The state has to take an initiative to distinguish the prices of sugar for commercial and household uses. In order to reduce the state intervention, the Indian government should follow Brazil's example (minimum role of the state) which will benefit the sugarcane and sugar sector. Like banks, the state should make it compulsory for sugar mills to keep some proportion of fund from profits as reserves. If a sugar mill is unable to pay FRP, then this reserve fund can be used. Finally, the state should be taken into consideration needs and consequences before giving any kind of assistance and putting regulations on the sugarcane sector. In addition, the state also has to look at the larger picture before imposing any tax on sugarcane by-products, which also helps to ensure green development. A subsidy on ethanol could have been a welcome development.

References

Ahmad, M. and Rehman, F., (2014): Changing Paradigms in Regulating and Deregulating the Sugar Pricing Mechanism in India, *RKG Journal of Management*, Vol. 5, No. 2, pp. 77–86.

Baru, S., (1990): *The Political Economy of Indian Sugar: State Intervention and Structural Change*, Oxford University Press, Delhi, pp. 1–225.

Commission for Agricultural Cost and Prices, (2012): *Price Policy for Sugarcane: The 2013–14, Sugar Season*, Department of Agriculture and Co-operation, Ministry of Agriculture (GoI), New Delhi, pp. 1–107.

——, (2013): *Price Policy for Sugarcane: The 2014–15, Sugar Season*, Department of Agriculture and Co-operation, Ministry of Agriculture (GoI), New Delhi, pp. 1–48.

——, (2014): *Price Policy for Sugarcane: The 2015–16 Sugar Season*, Department of Agriculture and Co operation, Ministry of Agriculture (GoI), New Delhi, August 2014, pp. 1–85.

Credit Analysis and Research Limited (CARE), (2013): Sugar Industry Updates, *Care Rating*, New Delhi, pp. 1–8.

Directorate of Economics and Statistics, Department of Agriculture, Co-operation and Farmer Welfare, Ministry of Agriculture and Farmer Welfare, Government of India. http://eands.dacnet.nic.in/APY_Normal_Estimates.htm (accessed on 02.05.2016).

Directorate of Sugar, (2014–15): Department of Food and Public Distribution, Ministry of Consumer Affairs Annual Report, Government of India, New Delhi, pp. 1–35.

——, (2015): Department of Food and Public Distribution, Ministry of Consumer Affairs, Government of India, New Delhi, Report No. 4.

Fertilizer Association of India, (2010–11): Fertilizer Statistics, New Delhi.

Government of India, (2009): The 13th Finance Commission Report, Ministry of Finance, Government of India, New Delhi, pp. 1–476. http://www.prsindia.org/uploads/media/13financecommissionfullreport.pdf (accessed on 12.08.2016).

——, (2015). Ministry of Consumer Affairs, Food and Public Distribution, Lok Sabha Secretariat, New Delhi (Unstarred Questioned No. 710), Annexure.

——, (2015): Lok Sabha Starred Question No. 385, Ministry of Consumer Affairs, Food and Public Distribution, New Delhi. http://164.100.47.132/Annexture_New/lsq16/4/as385.htm (accessed on 10.08.2016).

Government of Maharashtra, (2014): Economic Survey of Maharashtra, 2013–14, *Directorate of Economics and Statistics*, Mumbai, pp. 1–239.

Jugale, V., (2000): *Sugarcane Pricing: Policy, Procedures and Operations*, Atlantic Publication, New Delhi, pp. 1–203.

Jyothi, K., (2014): Impact of Policy of Government on Import and Export of Sugar from India, *IOSR Journal of Economics and Finance*, Vol. 3, No. 2, pp. 40–42.

Mahajan Committee Report, (1998): *Report of the High Powered Committee on Sugar Industry,* Vol. I, Ministry of Food and Consumer Affairs, Government of India, New Delhi, pp. 1–421.

Rangarajan Committee Report, (2012): *Report of the Committee on the Regulation of Sugar Sector in India: The Way Forward,* Government of India, pp. 1–42.

Reddy, A., (2011): Sugar and Cane Pricing and Regulation in India, *International Sugar Journal*, Vol. 113, No. 1352, pp. 548–56.

Sen Committee Report, (1965): *Sugar Enquiry Commission*, Department of Food, Ministry of Food and Agriculture, New Delhi, pp. 1–276.

Thakkar, H., (2013): How Efficient is Maharashtra's Sugarcane Crop?, *South Asia Network on Dams, Rivers and People*, June 2013, pp. 1–3.

Thorat Committee Report, (2009): *Report of the Group of Experts on Sugar*, Department of Food and Public Distribution, Government of India, New Delhi, pp. 1–148.

Tuteja Committee Report, (2004): *Report of the Committee on Revitalization of Sugar Industry*, Department of Food and Public Distribution, Government of India, New Delhi, pp. 1–45.

World Bank, (1997): India's Sugar Industry: Priorities and Reforms, Report No. 15678, IN, South Asia Rural Development Unit, Washington D.C.

World Bank, Government of India, (1998): *Inter-Sectoral Water Allocation, Planning and Management,* Allied Publishers Ltd, New Delhi, pp. 1–165.

Appendix 1

Share of Different States in Total Sugarcane Production in India (in %)

Year	Tropical Region States				Sub-tropical Region States			
	Andhra Pradesh	Tamil Nadu	Karnataka	Maharashtra	Punjab	Uttar Pradesh	Bihar	Haryana
1966–67	8.7	7.4	7.5	10.7	4.7	42.4	4.7	5.5
1967–68	10.4	9.3	7.7	11.0	4.8	39.7	4.2	4.9
1968–69	9.8	6.9	7.8	9.8	4.4	43.4	5.0	5.7
1969–70	8.2	7.6	5.7	10.7	4.6	44.9	4.9	5.9
1970–71	7.2	8.3	6.7	11.7	4.2	43.3	4.9	5.5
1971–72	9.3	8.5	7.7	10.1	3.5	43.5	3.9	4.5
1972–73	7.9	9.7	6.8	9.5	3.8	45.4	3.8	4.8
1973–74	7.7	13.0	6.1	9.2	4.1	43.2	3.7	4.2
1974–75	8.0	10.1	6.0	11.9	4.3	42.6	3.9	4.1
1975–76	7.3	8.5	6.9	13.4	4.4	41.5	3.5	4.9
1986–87	4.7	11.6	8.0	12.9	3.3	45.5	2.0	3.6
1987–88	4.8	10.6	9.0	12.8	3.0	47.5	2.3	2.2
1988–89	5.3	11.7	9.2	12.6	3.0	43.6	2.7	3.2
1989–90	4.9	10.4	9.4	15.1	2.9	43.2	3.0	3.0
1990–91	5.3	9.7	8.7	15.9	2.5	43.0	3.2	3.2
1991–92	5.9	9.8	9.5	14.2	2.7	43.7	2.8	3.5
1992–93	5.3	10.1	9.9	13.5	2.8	45.1	2.6	2.9
1993–94	5.9	11.3	11.6	12.1	2.1	45.3	1.9	2.8
1994–95	5.8	13.2	12.0	16.1	1.9	40.0	2.1	2.5
1995–96	5.4	11.7	8.9	16.6	3.1	42.6	2.0	2.9
1996–97	5.4	9.3	8.4	15.1	4.0	45.2	2.1	3.2
1997–98	5.0	10.8	10.1	13.7	2.6	46.2	1.8	2.7
1998–99	5.7	11.7	12.0	16.3	2.1	40.3	1.8	2.4
1999–00	6.2	11.5	12.6	17.8	2.3	38.6	1.4	2.6
2000–01	6.0	11.2	14.5	16.8	2.6	35.8	1.3	2.8
2001–02	6.1	11.0	11.1	15.2	3.1	39.7	1.8	3.1
2002–03	5.4	8.4	11.3	14.8	3.2	42.1	1.6	3.7
2003–04	6.4	7.5	6.8	11.0	2.8	48.2	1.8	4.0
2004–05	6.6	9.9	6.0	8.6	2.2	50.1	1.7	3.4
2005–06	6.3	12.5	6.5	13.8	1.7	44.6	1.5	2.9
2006–07	6.1	11.6	8.1	22.1	1.7	37.7	1.7	2.7
2007–08	5.8	10.9	7.5	25.4	1.9	35.8	1.1	2.5
2008–09	5.4	11.5	8.2	21.3	1.6	38.3	1.7	1.8
2009–10	4.0	10.2	10.4	21.9	1.3	40.1	1.7	1.8
2010–11	4.4	10.0	11.6	23.9	1.2	35.2	3.7	1.8
2011–12	4.6	10.7	10.7	24.0	1.6	35.7	3.1	1.9

Source: Computed from Directorate of Economics and Statistics, Ministry of Agriculture and Farmer Welfare, GoI.

12 Economic Viability of Marginal Farmers in West Bengal

A District-Level Study

Amit Mandal

Introduction

There has been a significant increase in number of holdings of marginal farmers over the time periods in Indian agriculture. The percentage of marginal farmers were 50.97 per cent in 1970–71 which increased to 59.44 per cent in 1990–91 and further it increased to 62.87 per cent and 67.09 per cent in 2000–01 and 2010–11, respectively, at national level (Government of India). The number of marginal holdings was 80.44 per cent in 2000–01, which increased to 81.17 per cent in 2005–06 and 82.16 per cent in 2010–11 in West Bengal (GOWB). Importantly, it is found that 67.09 per cent of holdings cultivated only 22.50 per cent of area at national level while 82.16 per cent of holding operates 52.47 per cent of land in West Bengal in 2010–11. It is also found that the average size of land-holding of marginal farmers in West Bengal is higher than at the national level although it decreases over time at the national level as well as in West Bengal. Therefore, the distribution of land is relatively more equal in West Bengal, which may be the result of better implementation of land reform measures in West Bengal compared to the rest of the country. We may argue that marginal holdings play a predominant role in Indian agriculture in general and in West Bengal agriculture in particular. In this background, the economic viability of crop production is an essential criterion for the sustainability of the million of marginal farmers. An attempt has been made in the present micro-level field study to capture the economic viability of marginal farmers in the state of West Bengal. The present study is divided into five sections. In second section, we have made a critical review of literature of economic viability

---

The paper is a part of my PhD thesis under the guidance of Professor Apurba Kumar Chattopadhyay, Department of Economics and Politics, Visva-Bharati. Currently, I am working as a Post-Doc Fellow at Indian Institute of Science Education and Research, Bhopal. However, the author takes full responsibility for the errors.

of marginal farmers at all India and West Bengal perspective. We have discussed data sources and methodology in third section followed by the results and discussions in fourth section. Finally, in section five, we have tried to make a concluding observation and future scope of the research.

Review of Literature

In this section, we have made a comprehensive review of literature of economically viable farmers in Indian and West Bengal agriculture.

At All India Perspective

Singh et al. (2009) have found that marginal and small farmers are financially viable in Punjab and the contributing factors for financial viability are farm size, non-farm income, and income from dairy. In a study, Singh (2012) have concluded that the viability of marginal and small farmers in India depends on the creation of job opportunities in rural areas along with suitable policy support for livestock sector especially dairy, goat and sheep farming for the resource-poor farming community. The significant changes were recorded in nominal and real-wage rates of agricultural labour in all major state except few states after implementation of MGNREGS. Haque (1996) has conducted one village-level study in Andhra Pradesh on economic viability of small and marginal farmers. It is revealed that leasing in land, animal husbandry, and poultry had played a positive role in determining above subsistence level of income along with farm income for the marginal and small farmers in the study region. Pasha (1991) has conducted one study in the state of Karnataka on economic viability of small and marginal farmers. He has also found that animal husbandry plays an important role in the farming system of small and marginal farmers. Nithyashree and Pal (2013) have showed the trend of agricultural growth and small farm income taking secondary data from different sources. They revealed that small and marginal farmers are more efficient in terms of yield compared to large farmers. It is also observed that the pattern of input use and access to input in terms of hired labour, machine, and irrigation hours have reduced net returns to marginal and small farmers. Bhalla (2008) have conducted a study based on the National Sample Survey (59th round) data on income, expenditure, and productive assets of farmer households in India. It is revealed that at all India level, farmers got the highest income from cultivation followed by wage income and non-farm income. It is also revealed that farmers with larger holding had substantially higher incomes compared to marginal and small holding. It is revealed that total expenses for cultivation increase with size holding increase. Vyas et al. (1969) conducted one study in two villages (Nadiad and Dehgam villages in Gujarat) to explore the impact of new technology on small holding farmers. The study examines the significance of the new strategy for small farmers in terms of its potential to make non-viable farmers into viable farmers. The study revealed that farm income was insufficient to meet the household consumption requirement of the small farmers irrespective of whether these farms were adopting new agricultural strategy or not and hence these farmers may be treated as non-viable. Bhalla and Chadha (1982) examined the impact of Green Revolution on income distribution in Punjab state. The study revealed that cultivators (marginal and small) have been able to record substantial increase in their output and income through the adoption of new technology. Dingar and Singh (1980) have studied the income viability of the small and marginal farmers who were involved in the various schemes of the SFDA project (Small Farmer Development Agency) under Fourth Five-Year Plan in Fatehpur district of the state of Uttar Pradesh. A viable farmer has been considered as one whose agricultural income is sufficient to maintain his/her family. It is revealed that amount borrowed made and subsidies given to farmers were higher on the small farms than on the marginal farms on per hectare basis because of larger size of farm business. It is also revealed that small farmers make higher consumption expenditure compared to marginal farmers due to larger size of household. In his study, Singh (1986) found that on an average the agricultural labour households earned (₹ 5,817 annually) more than marginal farms (₹ 5,023 annually). The major sources of income of the marginal farmers were found to be farming, supplemented by income from subsidiary activities. Both the categories spent their maximum portion of income in consuming food grains followed by milk and milk products. The study concluded that the economic conditions of the agricultural labourers are relatively better compared to the marginal farmers. Shankar (1990) conducted a study to assess land ownership, asset structure, and income distribution in three villages of eastern Uttar Pradesh. The study revealed that annual income of sub-marginal farmers was from owned land (26%) followed by wage income (15%). Furthermore, the share of income from services and remittances was 30 per cent and 10 per cent, respectively. In the case of marginal farmers, the share of agriculture was substantially higher at 40 per cent followed by services (18%) and remittances income (11%) and wage income (8%). Sharma (2008) has found that contract farming has a positive impact on crop productivity and farm income. The study further revealed that the socio-economic factors like education, age, farm size, access of institutional credit, and off-farm income have a positive role in the creation of corporate-led contract farming for all size classes of farmers. His study was based in three districts of Punjab with a sample size of 127. Jayachandra and Naidu (2006) studied the impact of dairy cooperatives on income, employment, and creation of assets of marginal and small farmers of Andhra Pradesh. Based on their research, they argued that net income of small and marginal farmers have increased due to dairy co-operatives. Dairying also offers an employment opportunity for these sections of farmers. Dev and Rao (2010) have showed that there was a positive impact of agricultural price policy on farm profitability. They examined the effectiveness of price policy in helping farmers to get adequate profits to encourage investment, technology, and productivity. They have argued that price policy can enhance the farm profitability up to 20 per cent, which in turn can be used for future investment (using yield-increasing technology) by the farmers in wheat and rice cultivation, which further can reduce the problem of food security at all India level. Tripathi (2013) has observed similar relationship between price policy and farm profitability in rice and wheat crop at all India level after the reforms period. He argued that after 2004–05, there was a substantial increase in net farm profitability of rice, which registered an annual growth rate of 36 per cent while in case of wheat there was an increased in growth rate of profitability and it registered an annual growth rate of 5.29 per cent up to 2009–10 due to several price policies (minimum support price and subsidy). Joshi et al. (2006) have studied the impact of crop diversification on small holdings and it is revealed that small-scale agriculture has advantages over large farmers in production of high-value crops. Vegetable production is the emerging sector in agricultural diversification would augment income of smallholders and generate employment opportunities. Furthermore, non-availability of improved and good-quality seeds reduces the profitability and increases production risk. Other important factors that restrict expansion of area under vegetables are higher price and yield risks (compared to cereals) and low marketable surplus (that increases transaction costs).

Marginal Farmers in West Bengal

West Bengal is a state in eastern India with 9.13 crore populations and over two-third of which live in rural areas (Census, 2011). West Bengal is the largest rice-producing state in India followed by Uttar Pradesh and Andhra Pradesh (Economic Survey, 2014–15). Cropping pattern in the state is dominated by food crops, which account for about 78 per cent of the area under principal crops. Rice is cultivated in 58.48 lakh hectares (production of 161.48 lakh MT) and total cereals (all combined) in 63.49 lakh hectares and oilseeds in 7.14 lakh hectares, jute in 6.09 lakh hectares, and potato in 3.67 lakh hectares. The state is second largest producer of potato and one of the highest producers of vegetable in the country. The cropping intensity of the state is 180 and Hooghly district stand first in cropping intensity (246). Against the ultimate irrigation potential of 67.43 lakh hectares, the gross irrigation potential created through major, medium, and minor irrigation in the state was 55.01 lakh hectares up to 2011–12. The percentage utilisation of potential created is 81.73 per cent in major and medium irrigation structures and 81.64 per cent in minor irrigation (Statistical Abstract, 2008 and 2012).

West Bengal agricultural economy witnessed stagnation or 'impasse' in agricultural production prior to the 1980s due to structural bottlenecks. Boyce (1987) estimated the growth rate of agriculture to be 1.74 per cent per annum during 1949–1980, which was even less than population growth during the same period. However, the situation reversed in the subsequent period when the structural bottleneck in the form of lack of irrigation eased.

Several studies Saha and Swaminathan (1994); Rawal and Swaminathan (1998); Sanyal et al. (1998); Sen and Sengupta (1995); Datt and Ravallion (1996); Sengupta and Gazdar (1996); Banerjee et al. (2002); Bhattacharyya and Bhattacharyya (2007) have argued that the agricultural growth rate has been increased after the 1980s and they have estimated agricultural growth rate using different statistical measures. Saha and Swaminathan (1994) have estimated the agricultural growth rate during 1980–81 to 1991–92 using different mathematical equations. They have found that the growth of aggregate crop output have been 6.4 per cent per annum and the growth of the food-grain production was the highest in West Bengal compared to other 17 major states in India during 1981–82 to 1990–91. The major factor for the yield improvement was the use of high-yielding variety seeds. It is also found that the growth rate of potato, mustard have been increased while the growth rate of jute, pulses, and wheat have been decreased during this time period. They have also found that after the 1980s the farming practices have been improved and High Yielding Variety (HYV) seeds were used massively than before. They have concluded that newly established panchayat has played an important role in creating improved farming practices. Rawal and Swaminathan (1998); Sengupta and Gazdar (1996); Rogaly et al. (1999); Sen (1992); and Sen and Sengupta (1995) argued that a significant trend break in the growth rate after the 1980s. They have also identified the factors of behind such trend break. They have explained the trend break of agricultural growth in West Bengal in terms of the technological (wider adoption of new technology) and institutional (appropriate implementation of land reforms) ground. These are: belated Green Revolution, better utilisation of fertiliser and rural credit, private and public investment, operation barga, distribution of surplus land, and panchayat raj. They have also argued that this trend break was associated with the diversification of rural activities. Sanyal et al. (1998) have conducted one study based on secondary data on output growth of agricultural sector in West Bengal. The study revealed that West Bengal has registered a rapid rate of growth of output along with the increase in productivity (due to use of high-yielding verities) from 1977 to 1995. It is also revealed that the growth rate of food grains have been very high and cropping patterns have changed in favour of high-value non-food crops in most of the districts of West Bengal during this period. It is also revealed that with the commencement of institutional reforms and huge private investment (which was stagnated before the 1980s), there was an increase in accessibility of institutional credit for small-scale agriculture, which further increased the rate of growth of agricultural sector. Bhattacharyya and Bhattacharyya (2007) have conducted one study to estimate the agricultural growth rate of West Bengal during 1980–81 to 2002–03. They have found that after the 1980s, the agricultural growth rate have been increased up to 1991–92 because of the belated Green Revolution and institutional reforms. On the other hand, the growth rates have been decreased during 1992–93 to 2002–03 due to the different policy initiatives.

We have witnessed that the existing literature has dealt with economic viability and determining factors for viability of marginal and small farmers in the context of Indian agriculture as well as at the state levels. In case of West Bengal, several studies have focused on the growth of the agriculture after Independence during different sub-periods. They have concentrated on the studies of agricultural growth, agrarian stagnation, and suggested probable reasons for that. We were interested to capture the farm income and profit from the cultivation and the objectives may be stated below.

The broad objectives of our study are:

1. To estimate the productivity of paddy and net income from paddy based on primary data and also estimate their variations in different areas under our study. Furthermore, we intend to identify the factor/factors, which influenced the variations.
2. To estimate the annual farm profitability and variations across districts under our study area and to identify the factor/factors which influenced the variations.
3. To estimate the economically viable farmers based on annual farm profitability and identify the factor/factors, which influenced the variations based on marginal effect.

Sample Design and Methodology

We have followed three-stage sampling procedure (selection of districts, blocks, villages, and households) for the selection of households.

Selection of Districts

We have selected old alluvial zone as major portion while some portion allotted to laterite and new alluvial zone which covers the central districts of West Bengal as Murshidabad, Birbhum, Bardhaman, Hooghly, and Nadia. These five central districts are also agriculturally developed among other districts. These five districts occupy 34.23 per cent of area under paddy production, 34.83 per cent of area under total cereals production, 53.86 per cent area under pulses production, 47.78 per cent area under oilseeds production, 55.01 per cent under wheat production, 46.97 per cent under potato production, and 35.35 per cent under total food grains (Statistical Abstract, 2012). The average productivity of paddy of five districts is 2,891 (kg/ha) while the state average is 2,688 kg/ha. The average productivity of the cereals, pulses, and potato are 2,895, 982, and 28,174 kg/ha compared to the state average of 2,706, 890, and 25,641 kg/ha, respectively. It is also seen that except for some crops (like oilseeds) most of the other crops productivity is higher compared to state average. The percentage of gross cropped area of these districts is 32.35. It is observed that except Burdwan and Birbhum the cropping intensity of the other districts are higher than state average. Thus, any fluctuation of the above indicator may lead to a state fluctuation and hence these five central districts may be a good representation of the state and we have concentrated our analysis on these five districts. While the five districts taken together have about 29 per cent of total marginal farms in West Bengal with the highest concentration is in Murshidabad district.

Selection of Blocks and Villages

We have taken compound annual growth rate (CAGR) of paddy production of the all 111 blocks spanning over the five districts for the period of 2001–10. We then ranked all the blocks in terms of CAGR. For the purpose of our study, we have divided the blocks in three categories, viz. higher compound annual growth rate, moderate compound annual growth rate, and lower compound annual growth rate. This implies that we have cluster of blocks into three categories. From each cluster, we have taken one block randomly. These are Bharatpur I block of Murshidabad district, Raina I block of Burdwan, and Chanditola II block of Hooghly district. In each block, two villages have been selected in which one village is agriculturally developed and other village is agriculturally less developed.

Selection of Households

The selection household has been made on the basis of land-holding. The marginal farms in high CAGR block is 93, in moderate CAGR block is 80, in low CAGR block is 94, and the total is 267 marginal farms.

Analysis of Crop

The share of paddy in gross cropped area in three districts is about 55 per cent followed by vegetables (8.94%), total fibres (8.82%), and oilseed (8.27%). For that reason, any variation in paddy production would influence the livelihood of the marginal farms. Therefore, we have taken paddy as the sole agricultural output for the purpose of our analysis.

Model-1A: Net Income from Paddy (Multiple Linear Regression Models)

We have constructed the following model for net income of monsoon paddy in the study area. The multiple regression (model-1A) for monsoon net income of paddy can be written as:

$$Y^{MPNI}_i = \alpha_1 + \alpha_2 D^{LE}_i + \alpha_3 D^{C}_i + \alpha_4 X^{WFA}_i + \alpha_5 X^{TNF}_i + \alpha_6 D^{AS}_i + \alpha_7 D^{SS}_i + \alpha_8 D^{SV}_i + \alpha_9 X^{FC}_i + \alpha_{10} X^{PC}_i + \alpha_{11} X^{HLC}_i + \alpha_{12} X^{IC}_i + \alpha_{13} X^{OC}_i + U_i \quad (1)$$

Where

Y^{PNI} = Dependent variable (net income ₹ per katha),

U = Error term.

α_1 = Intercept term,

$\alpha_2, \alpha_3, \alpha_4, \alpha_5, \alpha_6, \alpha_7, \alpha_8, \alpha_9, \alpha_{10}, \alpha_{11}, \alpha_{12}, \alpha_{13}$ – Slope coefficient of the variable, respectively.

Dummy and Categorical Variables	*Quantitative Variables*
D^{LE} = Level of education (1 = illiterate, 2 = primary, 3 = secondary, 4 = higher secondary, 5 = UG, 6 = PG, 7 = others)	X^{WFA} = Family members engaged in own agriculture.
D^{C} = Caste (1 = ST, 2 = SC, 3 = Gen).	X^{TNF} = Total non-farm income.
D^{AS} = Soil quality (1 = alluvial soil, 0 = otherwise).	X^{FC} = Fertiliser cost (₹ per katha).
D^{SS} = Soil quality (1 = sticky soil, 0 = otherwise).	X^{PC} = Pesticides cost (₹ per katha).
D^{SV} = Seed variety (1 = hyv, 0 = otherwise).	X^{HLC} = Hired labour cost (₹ per katha).
	X^{IC} = Irrigation cost (₹ per katha).
	X^{OC} = Other cost (₹ per katha).

Model-2A: Annual Farm Profitability (Multiple Linear Regression Models)

$$\prod^{AFP}{}_k = \rho_1 + \rho_2 X^{TOL}{}_k + \rho_3 D^{LE}{}_k + \rho_4 X^{TWF} + \rho_5 X^{OL}{}_k + \rho_6 X^{DM}{}_k + \rho_7 X^{TNF}{}_k + \rho_8 X^{CD}{}_k + \rho_9 X^{IC}{}_k + U_k \quad (2)$$

$\prod^{AFP}{}_k$ = Dependent variable (Net annual income (₹ per katha)

The independent variables are:

X^{TOL} = Total operated land.

D^{LE} = Level of education (1 = illiterate, 2 = primary, 3 = secondary, 4 = higher secondary, 5 = UG, 6 = PG, 7 = others).

X^{TWF} = Family members engaged in own agriculture.

X^{OL} = Total outstanding loan.

X^{DM} = Distance from market in kilometre.

X^{NF} = Total non-farm income.

X^{CD} = Crop diversification (Herfindahl index)

X^{IC} = Irrigation cost

ρ_1 = Intercept term

U_k = Error term

$\rho_2, \rho_3, \rho_4, \rho_5, \rho_6, \rho_7, \rho_8, \rho_9$ = Slope coefficient of the variable, respectively.

Model 3A: Economic Viability of Marginal Farmers

Economically viable farms are based on the annual farm profit of the farmer households on that particular reference year. This implies the farms, which have positive income or surplus are called economically viable farms while the farms having negative income are called economically non-viable farms. Here, economic viability is binary in nature, and it has two possible outcomes as 1 (viable farms) and 0 (non-viable farms). To capture the deterministic factors for being economically viable farms; we have applied Probit model. Now, we can write the equation as:

$$\prod^{EV}{}_n = \lambda_1 + \lambda_2 X^{CD}{}_n + \lambda_3 X^{DM}{}_n + \lambda_4 X^{HHS}{}_n + \lambda_5 X^{IC}{}_n + \lambda_6 X^{TOL}{}_n + \lambda_7 X^{TNF}{}_n + \lambda_8 X^{TWF}{}_n + \lambda_9 X^{NREGS}{}_n + \lambda_{10} X^{OL}{}_n + U_n \quad (3)$$

Where $\prod^{EV}$ = Dependent variable (1 = positive income, 0 = otherwise)

Independent variables are:

X^{CD} = Crop diversification (Herfindahl index)

X^{DM} = Distance from market in kilometre.

X^{HHS} = Household size.

X^{TOL} = Total operated land.

X^{IC} = Irrigation cost (₹ per katha).

$\lambda_2, \lambda_3, \lambda_4, \lambda_5, \lambda_6, \lambda_7, \lambda_8, \lambda_9, \lambda_{10}$
= Slope coefficient of the variable, respectively.

X^{TNF} = Total non-farm income.

X^{WFA} = Family members engaged in own agriculture.

X^{NREGS} = Income from NREGS.

X^{OL} = Total outstanding loan.

U = Error term.

λ_1 = Intercept term.

Results and Discussion of the Study Area

As we have discussed, economic viability is important for the farmers for future investment. We have divided this section in two sub-sections viz. characteristic of the selected households followed by economic viability of the farmers.

The Basic Characteristics of the Sample Households

Bhratpur I Block (High CAGR Block)

The basic characteristics of the sample households in the selected villages of high CAGR block of Murshidabad district are shown in Appendix 1. The average family size of marginal farmers of Bharatpur I block of Murshidabad district are 4.49. In Bharatpur-I block, out of 93 marginal farmers, eight farmers (8.60%) are illiterate. We have found that the average number of earning member of marginal farmers is 1.76 in Bharatpur I block. The average land-holding of marginal farmers are 0.39 hectare. The percentage of operated area by marginal famers is 67.52 of total area. The principal occupation of the population in the block is agriculture, but there exists huge non-farm engagement by the household members in our selected households. The farmers are heavily dependent on rain water. In both the villages of Bharatpur I block of Murshidabad district, it is observed that the major source of irrigation (after rain water) is well-irrigation using rented pump set (more than 50%) followed by canal irrigation (28.5%).

Raina I Block (Moderate CAGR Block)

The basic characteristics of the Raina I block of Burdwan district of sample households in the selected villages are shown in Appendix 2. The average family size of the marginal farmer households is 4.44. At the block level, the percentage distribution of Scheduled Caste, Scheduled Tribe, Other Backward Class, and General category are 7.5, 1.2, 11.5, and 80.0 per cents. It is observed that 89.8 per cent marginal farmers are literate. The average size of land holding of marginal farmers is 0.36 hectare. It is found that marginal farmers operate 72.53 per cent of total operated area. Other sources of income are agricultural labour, self-employment, private-salaried employment, own small and big business, etc. for their livelihood. In Burdwan district, it is observed from field that the major source of water for cultivation is well irrigation using rented pump set (more than 60%) followed by canal irrigation (20.1%) and tank irrigation (5.2%).

Chanditola II Block (Less-Developed CAGR Block)

Chanditola II block of Hooghly district fall under the category of low CAGR and it is situated near to Kolkata (30 kilometre) and Dankuni city (20 kilometre) under Serampore sub-division. The basic characteristics of the marginal sample households in the sample villages of Hooghly are shown in Appendix 3. The average family size in developed and less-developed village for marginal is 5.06 and 4.66. The percentage distribution of households belonging to Scheduled Caste, Scheduled Tribe, Other Backward Class, and General category are given in Appendix 3. It is observed from the field data that 2.21 per cent are illiterate for the marginal farmers. The average male earning members for marginal farmers are 1.79. The average land-holding of marginal farmers is 0.35 hectare and it is found that 80.74 per cent of total land is operated by marginal farmers. The important non-farm activities are: agricultural labour, self-employment, own small business, and private employment. We may argue self-employment is higher because of urban centric environment or locational advantages. In low CAGR block of Hooghly district, we have found that the major source of water for cultivation is well-irrigation using rented pump set (more than 81%).

Model 1A: Net Income from Paddy (Multiple Linear Regression Models)

It is found from the secondary as well as primary data that monsoon or *Kharif* paddy is the main crop in our study area. Now, we will look into the variation of monsoon paddy productivity and monsoon paddy net income across the chosen blocks (or the districts) and identify the factors, which are responsible for such variations. Secondary data revealed that high CAGR block (Murshidabad) had the highest productivity of paddy during last decade followed by moderate (Burdwan) and low (Hooghly) CAGR block. We have found from our filed survey data that moderate CAGR block of Burdwan district rank first in terms of monsoon average paddy productivity followed by high CAGR block of Murshidabad district and low CAGR block of Hooghly district. The monsoon paddy productivity is 4,314 kg/ha in moderate CAGR block followed by 4,241 kg/ha in high CAGR block and 4,032 kg/ha in low CAGR block (Appendix 4). This implies the variation in productivity of paddy across the districts. The above Fisher's 't' statistic (Appendix 4) reveals that there exist significant variations in monsoon paddy productivities among the high CAGR block, moderate CAGR block, and low CAGR block. This implies the rejection of our null hypothesis. The calculated 't' value represents the district-wise variation of paddy productivity. It is observed that the value of the calculated 't' between moderate and low CAGR blocks is highest (2.53) compared to high and low CAGR blocks (2.04) and high and moderate CAGR blocks (–0.52). The calculated 't' value is insignificant between high and moderate CAGR blocks, which indicate that there exists variation but not significantly. The calculated 't' value is significant between moderate and low CAGR blocks and between high and low CAGR blocks. Thus, the monsoon paddy productivity is higher in moderate CAGR block followed by high and low CAGR blocks.

The reasons of these variations may be found in the fact that the soil quality of moderate CAGR block (Burdwan) is more suited in the paddy production while the soil quality of low CAGR block (Hooghly) district suits vegetable production. Furthermore, the high CAGR in case of Murshidabad is due to late adoption of new seed technology compared to other districts under our study.

The average net income of monsoon paddy cultivation of marginal farmers in high CAGR block is ₹ 17,443 per hectare while the magnitude for the moderate and low CAGR blocks are ₹ 41,553 per hectare and ₹ 9,356 per hectare, respectively (Appendix 5). Like productivity, average net income from paddy is highest in moderate CAGR block compared to high CAGR block and low CAGR block. Thus, there exists the variation in average net income of monsoon paddy similar to productivity variation of monsoon paddy across the blocks.

It is found that the value of the calculated 't' (Appendix 5) between moderate CAGR block (Burdwan) and low CAGR block (Hooghly) is highest (8.96) compared to high CAGR block (Murshidabad) and moderate CAGR block (Burdwan) (–8.42) and high CAGR block (Murshidabad) and low CAGR block (Hooghly) (0.61). Thus, the monsoon paddy net income is the highest in moderate CAGR block in Burdwan district followed by high CAGR block (Murshidabad) and low CAGR block (Hooghly).

Here, we have also found that the market price (or the selling price) of the high-valued traditional varieties paddy is higher in moderate CAGR block compared to the high and low CAGR blocks. It could be the explanation of higher net income in moderate CAGR block.

Table 1

Coefficient Values of Different Indicators of Linear Multiple Regression Model 1A across Districts for Marginal Farms

S. No.	*Independent or Exogenous Variables*	*Coefficient Value*			
		All Districts	*High CAG (MSD)*	*Moderate CAG (BWN)*	*Low CAGR (HUG)*
1	D^{LE} (level of education)	9.29	1.92	37.74**	0.20
2	D^{C} (caste)	-49.96	-7.93	-84.11*	2.05
3	X^{WFA} (family members engaged in own agriculture)	29.46*	27.09**	32.12	19.76*
4	X^{TNF} (total non-farm income)	0.001	0.004*	0.002**	0.002*
5	D^{AS} (soil quality (1 = alluvial soil, 0 = otherwise))	-55.47**	–	–	–
6	D^{SS} (soil quality (1 = sticky soil, 0 = otherwise))	84.93*	–	–	–
7	D^{SV} (seed varieties (1 = hyv, 0 = otherwise))	117.11*	35.98*	25.17*	15.49
8	X^{FC} (fertiliser cost)	–1.46	–1.03***	–0.22	–1.32*
9	X^{PC} (pesticides cost)	–3.92*	–10.76*	–4.87**	–2.19
10	X^{HLC} (hired labour cost)	–0.21*	–0.32*	–0.07	–0.21**
11	X^{IC} (irrigation cost)	–4.92*	3.13*	–5.56*	–2.38*
12	X^{OC} (other cost)	–1.17*	0.50	–1.37	–0.18
13	Constant	291.32*	257.59*	322.30	225.21*
14	R^2	0.64	0.61	0.61	0.68
15	Adj R^2	0.63	0.57	0.56	0.64
16	F value	39.11*	13.33*	12.54*	17.98*
17	Number of observation	267	93	80	94

Notes: *, **, and *** represent the 1, 5, and 10 per cent level of significance.
Here (-) means no change of the respective value of variable in the respective area.

Source: Field survey.

Now, we have used a multiple regression model (model 1A) where the dependent variable is net income (₹ per katha) from paddy cultivation. We have categorised the explanatory variables into two categories viz. dummy or qualitative or categorical variable and quantitative variable. The qualitative variable are: caste (categorical variable), education level (categorical variable), soil quality (dummy variable), seed varieties (dummy variable) while the quantitative variables are: family workforce participation in own agriculture, total non-farm income, fertiliser cost (₹ per katha), pesticides cost (₹ per katha), hired labour cost (₹ per katha), irrigation cost (₹ per katha), and other cost (₹ per katha). In case of 'other cost', we have merged tractor and bullock cost together.

Education Level (D^{EL})

We have used level of education of the head of the household as a categorical variable. We have found that the coefficients between farm income and education level is positive. Thus, we may argue that level of education have a positive impact (generating awareness regarding the crop pattern, optimal doses of input use, etc. for the cultivation) on the creation of net income of paddy for marginal farmers which also follows the literature.

Caste (X^{C})

We have taken caste (1 = ST, 2 = SC, and 3 = Gen) as a categorical variable. We may argue that Schedule Caste and Schedule Tribes are still engaged in agriculture due to the non-availability of other opportunities in other sectors while general category are moving from traditional agriculture to other sources of income and it may be due to their higher education level.

Family Members Engaged in Own Agriculture (X^{WFA})

Engagement of family members or family labour in own agriculture definitely increases the income of the households as it is more productive. It is observed that in all blocks, the engagement of family labour is positively and significantly (at 1% level of significance) related with the net income of paddy cultivation. We may argue that engagement of family labour has a positive association on net income of paddy in the respective blocks, which also follows the literature.

Total Non-farm Income (X^{TNF})

We may argue that if net income from paddy is below subsistence, then marginal farmers will go for off-farm employment opportunities. The coefficient values for all the districts are positive. In high CAGR block and low CAGR block, non-farm income is positive and significant at one per cent level of significance while moderate block, the association is significant at the five per cent level of significance. We may argue that with the increase in non-farm income, the farm income also increases which may be due to the reinvestment of non-farm income into farm sector.

Soil Quality (D^{SS})

In our study area, we have found three types of soil in three districts. High CAGR block is characterised by alluvial soil while moderate CAGR block and low CAGR block are characterised by sticky soil and loam soil, respectively.

Seed Varieties (D^{SV})

Seed is an important factor in general and high-yielding variety seed is more in particular for production process after Green Revolution in Indian and West Bengal agriculture. The coefficients for all blocks are positively related and associated with one per cent level of significance with the net income for marginal farmers.

Fertiliser Cost (X^{FC})

It is observed from Table 1 that fertiliser cost is negatively associated with net income of paddy from the marginal farms in all three blocks. We have also found in all the blocks that the informal fertiliser markets were working strongly and this also could be a reason for the low return from cultivation. The informal fertiliser agents have given fertiliser to the marginal farmers at a lower cost in the sowing season and they have charged higher price after the harvesting.

Pesticides Cost (X^{PC})

With better soil and good quality of seed, along with proper use of pesticides, the farm productivity can increase. We have also found that pesticides cost is negatively associated and the association is significant with 1 per cent level of significance with net income.

Hired Labour Cost (X^{HLC})

Due to multi-collinearity problem, we have dropped the family labour cost in the model. It is observed that hired labour cost is negatively and significantly associated with net income at one per cent level of significance. We have found that there exists a movement of labour force from the two villages to Maharashtra and Tamil Nadu for different types of works like construction labour, diamond cutting work, etc. We have also found that some labour have migrated from these villages to Kolkata for different non-farm engagement. It is also observed that in low CAGR block, the hired labour is negative and significant (at the 5% level of significance). In low CAGR block, we have also found that migration is taking place but it is from these two villages to near Dankuni and Kolkata (i.e. the migration is rural to urban in nature and daily basis). Due shortage of labour, these two districts are dependent on hired labour. It is observed that the association between hired labour cost and net income is negative in moderate CAGR block due to the advantage of family labour. We have found that occupational diversification is also higher in high and low CAGR blocks compared to moderate CAGR block and it may be the reason for the lower dependence of hired labour.

Irrigation Cost (X^{IC})

Irrigation cost has a negative impact and significant at the level of one per cent for paddy cultivation for marginal farms. In the moderate CAGR block and low CAGR block, the relationship between irrigation cost and net return from paddy cultivation is negative and significant at one per cent level of significance. On the other hand, the relationship between irrigation cost and net return is positive and significant at one per cent level of significance in high CAGR block.

Other Cost (X^{OC})

Other cost has been divided into two categories viz. bullock labour cost and tractor cost. We have found that other cost is negatively and significantly (at 1%

level of significance) related with net income for marginal farms. The negative association implies the squeeze in net return of the farmers.

Taking all districts together, we can say that the following factors have an impact on net income of paddy cultivation: family members engaged in own agriculture, soil quality, seed varieties, pesticides cost, hired labour cost, irrigation cost, and other cost.

Model-2A: Annual Farm Profitability (Multiple Linear Regression Models)

Annual farm profit or annual net return from agriculture is very important for viability and prospective sustainability of the marginal farms in Indian agriculture. Several researchers have argued that annual net return from agriculture helped farmers to reduce the problem of food security and increase the livelihood. It is observed that the highest average return is from low CAGR block in Hooghly district with the net return of ₹ 47,215 per hectare. In moderate CAGR block, average net return from agriculture is ₹ 30,587 per hectare while in high CAGR block the magnitude is ₹ 11,349 per hectare (Appendix 6). We may argue that because of crop diversification, the average net return is highest in low CAGR block, which will be discussed later. There exists significant variation in respect of annual farm profitability in the above districts. The result reveals that marginal farmers in the low CAGR block (Hooghly) earns highest level of yearly net income and which is statistically higher than the other two districts (i.e. Burdwan and Murshidabad).

Table 2

Coefficient Values of Different Indicators Linear Multiple Regression Model 2A across Districts for Marginal Farms

S. No.	*Independent Variables*	*Coefficient Value*			
		Al Districts	*Higher (MSD)*	*Moderate (BWN)*	*Lower (HUG)*
1	X^{TOL} (total operated land)	-1.14*	-2.58*	-1.12*	-1.42*
2	X^{LE} (level of education)	12.25	31.75**	18.77	7.50
3	X^{TWF} (family members engaged in own agriculture)	71.98*	118.88*	21.51	103.89*
4	X^{OL} (total outstanding loan)	-0.0005	0.0002	-0.0004	0.0001
5	X^{DM} (distance from market)	-25.04*	-36.51	-15.97	-66.69*
6	X^{TNF} (total non-farm income)	-0.0001	-0.0003	0.0005	-0.0004
7	X^{CD} (crop diversification)	5.91*	1.55***	2.61**	5.53*
8	X^{IC} (irrigation cost)	-0.12*	0.95	-6.94*	-0.24***
9	Constant	168.55*	-160.85	3.35	305.68
10	R^2	0.43	0.33	0.55	0.51
11	Adj R^2	0.41	0.31	0.49	0.46
12	F value	20.06*	3.47*	9.58*	9.80*
13	Number of observation	267	93	80	94

Note: *, **, and *** imply 1, 5, and 10 per cent level of significance, respectively.

Source: Field survey.

In order to find out the impact of independent variables on annual farm profitability, we have considered the following independent variables: total operated land, level of education, family members engaged in agriculture, total outstanding loan, distance from market, total non-farm income, crop diversification (Herfidhal index), and irrigation cost in our regression model.

Total Operated Land (X^{TOL})

We have found that the net return is decreased with the increase in land size. From Table 2, it is revealed that the total operated land is negatively and significantly associated with annual farm profitability. It is also noted that the relationship between operated area and annual farm profit is negative for all the districts. Thus, we may argue that higher the farm size lower will be the net return even with the marginal category of land. It may be noted that in the survey area cultivation is done mainly using family labour. Average number of parcel per household is about six. Therefore, lower the size of land with the marginal category, higher will be family labour content in the labour force and as a result, productivity will be higher. This is corroborated by our finding that productivity of family labour is higher than that of hired labour in all the districts.

Level of Education (D^{LE})

In our regression result, we have found that the coefficients are positively related with farm profit. Thus, we may argue that level of education have an impact on the annual farm profitability of marginal farmers which also follows the literature.

Family Members Engaged in Own Agriculture (X^{WFA})

We have incorporated family members engaged in agriculture which ultimately increase the net income of the marginal farmers. It is observed that in all the districts, the engagement of family labour is positively and significantly associated with annual farm profitability. Therefore, we may argue that engagement of family labour has a positive impact on net farm profit in the respective blocks, which also follows the literature.

Total Outstanding Loan (X^{OL})

There exists one to one relationship between agricultural production and agricultural credit. Agricultural credit may be institutional or non-institutional. If the amount of outstanding loan is very high then sustainable agriculture would not be possible. Timely and adequate institutional credit has a positive impact on agricultural production and farmers' income. It is revealed from our regression result that outstanding loan is negatively associated with the annual farm profitability. However, the association has not been found to be significant.

Distance from Market (X^{DM})

The variable 'distance from market' is very important in general and for marginal farmers in particular for farm profitability as it may lead to increase the scope of selling of their products. Taking all districts together, our result revealed that distance from market is negatively and significantly associated with farm profitability. In low CAGR block, the value is negative and significant at one per cent level of significance. This is due to the lower distance of market from the villages. From the above, we can argue that with the reduction of distance from local market, average farm profitability increases.

Total Non-farm Income (X^{TNF})

We have found that non-farm income is positively associated in case of net income of paddy but when we consider annual farm it becomes negative. This implies non-farm income cannot give the required money for investment in farm sector in other seasons. The result reveals that higher non-farm income reduces the incentive of the farmers to diversify. In Burdwan district (involving moderate CAGR block), paddy is the main agricultural crop where there is assured irrigation. Higher non-farm income induces the farmers in Burdwan to tide over hurdles before agricultural production and helps to increase net income from agriculture. However, this is not true for other regions under our study. Higher non-farm income, on the other hand, has induced lower crop diversification in areas where non-paddy crops are important. This result in lower net income or profit from overall agriculture. This is clearly corroborated by our field survey data.

Crop Diversification (X^{CD})

Crop diversification as an important indicator for farm profit. It is believed that small farmers can efficiently use their land other inputs and their crop pattern is very much diversified compared to large farmers. We have found that crop diversification is positively and significantly associated with farm profit. In case of low CAGR block, the crop diversification is positive and significant and the coefficient of farm profitability is higher (5.53) as compared to other two blocks. Due to urban connection, low CAGR block are capable to sell their product at regulated market. It is also found that the relationship between crop diversification and annual profit are positive and significant at five per cent and 10 per cent level of significance at moderate CAGR block and high CAGR block, respectively.

Irrigation Cost (X^{IC})

Water is very essential (whether it is surface or ground) for the cultivation. We have found that irrigation cost is negatively associated with annual farm income and the level of significance is one per cent. This implies high informal water charges (or market) have been reducing farm profit. It is found that the relationship between irrigation cost and annual profit is negative and significant at 10 per cent and one per cent level of significance in low and moderate CAGR block, respectively.

Model 3A: Economic Viability of Marginal Farmers based on Annual Farm Profit from Agriculture

The above discussion of farm profitability of marginal farmers in our study area put forward the question that how many farmers' are economically viable across

Figure 1

Percentage of Economically Viable Farmers Across the Districts

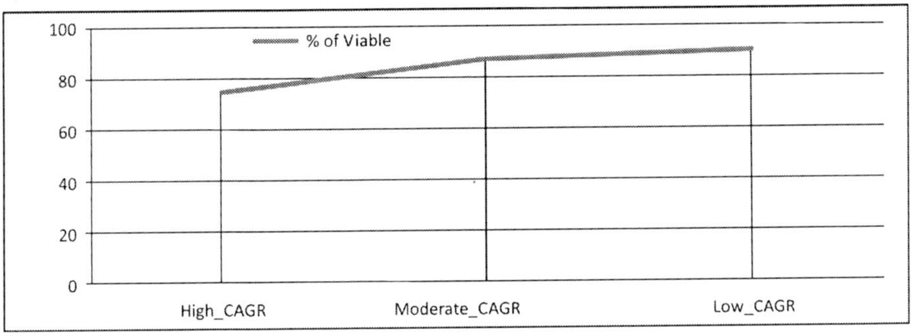

Source: Field survey.

blocks. Economically viable farms measured in terms of positive income left after the payments for inputs. This implies the farms, which have positive income or surplus are called economically viable farms while the farms having negative income are called economically non-viable farms.

Figure 1 shows the percentage of economically viable farmers in the study area. It is found that 89.36 per cent farmers are economically viable in low CAGR block. In moderate CAGR block and high CAGR block, the percentages of economically viable farmers are 86.25 and 74.19, respectively. We may argue that the main reason for that is the better access of regulated market and high crop diversification. It is also found that low CAGR block has the lowest average land size and farmers are using it efficiently compared to other two blocks.

Singh et al. (2009) argued that the farmers having positive surplus are called economically viable while having negative income are called economically non-viable. It is observed that there exists significant (Appendix 7) variation across the districts for economically marginal viable farms. We can reject our null hypothesis at one per cent level of significance stating economically viable farms are more in low CAGR block. It is revealed that the largest proportion of viable farms exist in low CAGR block followed by moderate and high CAGR blocks. The calculated 't' value between high CAGR block and moderate CAGR block suggests that the economically viable farmers are more in moderate CAGR block than high CAGR block. Having identifying the differences in economically viable farms, we would now like to identify the factors for which the variation is taking place. We have applied Probit model to capture the influencing factors. Here, the dependent variable is binary in nature where 1 = the viable farms and 0 = non-viable farms.

In our sample households 223 farmers are economically viable out of 267 farmers. The Probit model indicates that the model is significant at one per cent level of significance (LR-statistic). It is observed that the important factors for economic viability are: crop diversification, distance of market from the village, household size of the family, irrigation cost, and total outstanding loan of the household.

Table 3

Coefficient Values of Different Indicators of Probit Model

Variable	*Coefficient*	*Std. Error*	*z-Statistic*	*Prob.*
Constant	−3.09	0.97	−3.09	0.00*
Crop diversification (X^{CD})	2.17	0.78	2.77	0.01*
Distance from market (X^{DM})	−0.44	0.16	−2.77	0.01*
Size of household (X^{HHS})	−0.12	0.08	−1.69	0.09***
Irrigation cost (X^{IC})	−0.002	0.00	1.65	0.10***
Family members engaged in own agriculture (X^{TWF})	0.43	0.37	1.19	0.23
Total operated land (X^{TOL})	−0.003	0.00	−0.76	0.44
Total non-farm income (X^{TNF})	0.00	0.00	0.88	0.38
Income from NREGS (X^{NREGS})	0.00	0.00	0.87	0.38
Total outstanding loan (X^{OL})	−0.0003	0.00	1.70	0.09***
McFadden R-squared	0.32			
LR statistic	68.46			
Prob (LR statistic)	0.00*			
Observation with Dep = 0	44			
Observation with Dep = 1	223			
Total observation	267			

Notes: * and *** imply 1 per cent and 10 per cent level of significance, respectively.

Source: Field survey.

As we have stated earlier that crop diversification is an important determining factor for income of the marginal farms. It is also seen in our study. The coefficient is positively associated with crop diversification and the significant level is one per cent. We have also observed that low CAGR block (Hooghly district) is highly diversified and highest proportion of economically viable farmer exists in that block.

Agricultural marketing of a commodity always played a pivotal role in creation of income with the help of proper infrastructure and prices of the commodities. The variable, that is, distance of market is negatively associated with viable farms and it is significant at the one per cent level of significance. We may argue that increase in the distance of local regulated market leads to the reduction of viable farms. It may be due to the higher transportation cost and strong role of intermediaries.

Household size is also an important factor for generating the income of the household. We have found that household is negatively and significantly related with the viable farms.

Similarly, irrigation cost is very determining factor for the viability. It is believed that an informal irrigation source, higher irrigation charges, and climate change (irregular rainfall) affect the agriculture in general and marginal farmers in particular. It is observed that irrigation cost reduces the net return of the farmers in the selected districts of West Bengal. The relationship between irrigation cost and economic viability is negative and significant.

One important factor for economic viability is the outstanding loan of the household. We have found that outstanding loan is negatively and significantly associated with economically viable farms. This implies that the increases in loan amount will decrease the number of viable farmers. This also follows the literature.

Some other important factors are: family members engaged in own agriculture, household income apart from agriculture or non-farm income and operated area of the household. We have found that engagement of family labour and household income apart from agriculture is positively associated with economic viability of the marginal farms.

Now, we have constructed marginal effect based on the Probit model. This implies the nature or the direction of the independent variable on dependent variable, which has been selected in the model. The coefficient values of different inputs for the marginal effect are shown in Table 4.

Table 4

Coefficient Values of Different Indicators: Marginal Effect

Variable	*Coefficient (a)*	*Mean (b)*	*Marginal Effect (a × b)*	*P Value*
Crop diversification (X^{CD})	2.17	4.38	9.52	0.01*
Distance from market (X^{DM})	–0.44	2.00	–0.88	0.01*
Size of household (X^{HHS})	–0.12	4.66	–0.59	0.09***
Irrigation cost (X^{IC})	–0.0029	92.98	–0.27	0.10***
Family members engaged in own agriculture (X^{TWF})	0.43	1.292	0.56	0.23
Total operated land (X^{TOL})	–0.00	68.55	–0.23	0.44
Total non-farm income (X^{TNF})	0.00	45,551.3	0.11	0.38
Income from NREGS (X^{NREGS})	0.00	4,652.2	0.11	0.38
Total outstanding loan (X^{OL})	0.00	13,363.2	0.09	0.09***

Notes: * and *** imply 1 per cent and 10 per cent level of significance, respectively.

Source: Field survey.

Now, we will discuss the nature or direction of each independent variable. We can say from Table 4 that one unit increase in crop diversification is likely to have a ninefold increase in the number of viable farms and it is significant at one per cent level of significance in the study area. In case of distance of market, it is observed that one unit decrease in distance from market is likely to have a near one-unit increase in the number of viable farms. We have found that a unit decrease in the household size is likely to have half a unit increase in the club of viable farms and it is significant at 10 per cent level of significance. As we have said earlier that irrigation cost is very important for the cultivation. We have found that a unit decrease in irrigation cost is likely to have a near three units increase in the number of viable farms and it is significant at 10 per cent level of significance. In case of outstanding loan, it has been revealed that a unit's increase in the total outstanding loan has significant positive effect on the probability of existence of viable farms but the extent of the effect is weak and it is significant at 10 per cent level of significance.

Summary and Concluding Observation

In West Bengal, 82.16 per cent of total landholdings are under marginal farmers, which operate 52.47 per cent of total operated land as against 67 per cent of marginal farms operating only 22.5 per cent of total operated area in 2011. Therefore, the distribution of land is relatively more equal in West Bengal compared to that of all India level. The concentration of marginal farms and their possession of more than 50 per cent of the operated land make their role very significant in West Bengal agriculture. We have found that:

1. Overall productivity of land of the marginal farmers is higher than the average productivity of land as per the secondary data (GOWB, 2012). While overall productivity of monsoon paddy at the state level is 2,565 kg/ha in 2011–12, the same has been found to be 4,195 kg/ha in our field survey. The wide difference may be explained in terms of higher productivity of the smaller farm size literature prevalent in the literature.
2. Furthermore, we have found that there exist significant variations in monsoon paddy productivities among the high CAGR block, moderate CAGR block, and low CAGR block. We have found from our filed survey data that moderate CAGR block of Burdwan district rank first in terms of monsoon average paddy productivity followed by high CAGR block of Murshidabad district and low CAGR block of Hooghly district. The reasons of these variations may be found in the fact that the soil quality of moderate CAGR block (Burdwan) is more suited in the paddy production while the soil quality of low CAGR block (Hooghly) district suits vegetable production. Furthermore, the high CAGR in case of Murshidabad is due to late adoption of new seed technology compared to other districts under our study.
3. Like productivity, average net income from monsoon paddy is the highest in moderate CAGR block compared to high CAGR block and low CAGR block. Thus, there exist the variations in average net income of monsoon paddy similar to productivity variation of monsoon paddy across the districts. We have measured the important factors for which the variation is taking place using multiple regression model. The major explanatory factors are: level of education of the head of the household, caste, family member engaged in own agriculture, total non-farm income, quality of soil, seed varieties, fertiliser cost, pesticides cost, irrigation cost, hired labour cost, and other cost.
4. We have calculated annual farm profit or annual net return from agriculture as it is very important for viability and prospective sustainability of the marginal farms. We have found that overall net income from agriculture during the period of our study has been ₹ 29,717 per hectare. There exists significant variation in respect of annual farm profitability in the concerned districts. The result reveals that marginal farmers

in the low CAGR block (Hooghly) earns highest level of annual net income and which is significantly higher than the other two blocks (in Burdwan and Murshidabad districts, respectively). We have also found the important factors for these variations. The important factors are: total operated land, level of education, family labour engaged in agriculture, total outstanding loan, distance from market, total non-farm income, irrigation cost, and crop diversification.

5. Based on the annual farm profit, we have measured the economically viable and non-viable farms. It is revealed that about 83 per cent of the marginal farmers enjoy positive net income from cultivation in our study area. The largest proportion of viable farms exists in low CAGR block (i.e. in Hooghly district) followed by moderate (i.e. in Burdwan district) and high CAGR (i.e. in Murshidabad district) blocks which is statistically significant. The major factors of such variations are: crop diversification, distance from market, household size, irrigation cost, and total outstanding loan. From that, we have also calculated marginal effects of independent variables on dependent variable. It also revealed similar picture.

We have found that there exist variations in monsoon paddy productivity and net income. The variations are taking place due to several important factors, which need to be addressed by the policy makers. It is found that there are more economically viable farms in low CAGR block due to higher level of crop diversification and better market facilities. We may argue that policy makers may initiate some policies for the improvement of crop diversification and structured market facilities.

Irrigation is an important input for the cultivation. It has been found that climate change affects the marginal farms most. Therefore, government should emphasise to channelise irrigation facilities at a cheaper rate beyond monsoon season. Another important factor is the non-farm income. It is revealed that net income from paddy cultivation and non-farm income is positively associated. There should be more and more opportunity for joining non-farm activities in rural area. This will also help to reduce existing structural problem such as over-dependence on agricultural activities of the rural people.

It is revealed that outstanding loan is negatively associated with economically viable farms. We have also found that non-institutional credit markets are strong across the districts. Government has taken several policies to give institutional credit for the marginal farms. However, the ground reality is that marginal farmers are not getting required institutional loans because of lack of education and awareness programme. Policy makers should emphasise on this. It is revealed that hired labour cost occupies highest share among other inputs for the paddy cultivation. Technologies need to be adopted to enhance labour productivity.

Therefore, an integrated approach is needed to increase the farm income, reduce the farmers' dependence on non-institutional sources of credit, enhancement of input facilities including formal irrigation and structured market yards.

One of the important policy requirements for strengthening economic positions of the small farmers may be the strengthening of supportive institutions. In West Bengal, as in India, there are scope for institutional support in research, extension, credit, and marketing, which are of utmost importance for the poor farmers. However, due to poor delivery system, marginal farmers cannot get support from them. Therefore, creation of the supportive institutional framework for the marginal and small farmers is necessary.

Furthermore, there should be suitable instruments to protect this section of the rural population from natural calamities and unforeseen market shock. Governments do undertake certain measures to ameliorate these problems of the poor farmers but these are mostly inadequate.

We have observed that agricultural diversification increases net income and thus reduces vulnerability of the marginal and small farmers. It also helps to reduce environmental degradation. Therefore, government may undertake measures towards integrated rural development. This requires ensuring of markets, creation of rural infrastructure like road connectivity and electricity, irrigation facilities, provisioning of formal credit and insurance and above all, development of non-farm rural sector.

This research has certain limitations. The present micro-level study has focused on five central districts of West Bengal, which may not represent the state properly. Furthermore, the selected samples may not be the actual representation of the concerned districts. Finally, we have also analysed monsoon paddy as a main crop across the districts. Inclusion of more crops and more areas could have yielded better results.

References

Banerjee, A.V., Gertler, P.J. and Ghatak, M., (2002): Empowerment and Efficiency: Tenancy Reform in West Bengal, *Journal of Political Economy*, Vol. 110, No. 2, pp. 239–80.

Bhalla, G.S., (2008): Income, Consumption and Expenditure of Farmers: Stunted Capitalist Development in Indian Agriculture, In Bhaumik, S.K. (ed.). *Reforming Indian Agriculture: Towards Employment Generation and Poverty Reduction Essays in Honour of GK Chadha*, Sage Publications, India.

Bhalla, G.S. and Chadha, G.K., (1982). Green Revolution and the Small Peasant: A Study of Income Distribution in Punjab Agriculture, *Economic & Political Weekly*, Vol. 17, No. 20, pp. 826–33.

Bhattacharyya, M. and Bhattacharyya, S., (2007): Agrarian Impasse in West Bengal in the Liberalisation Era. *Economic & Political Weekly*, Vol. 42, No. 52, pp. 65–71.

Boyce, J.K., (1987): Agrarian Impasse in Bengal: Institutional Constraints to Technological Change. Oxford University Press, Oxford.

Datt, G. and Ravallion, M., (1998): Farm Productivity and Rural Poverty in India, *The Journal of Development Studies*, Vol. 34, No. 4, pp. 62–85.

Dev, S.M. and Rao, N.C., (2010): Agricultural Price Policy, Farm Profitability and Food Security, *Economic & Political Weekly*, Vol. 45, No. 26/27, pp. 174–82.

Dingar, S.M. and Singh, R.B. (1980): Income Viability of Identified Small and Marginal Farmers in SFDA: Project Fatehpur of Uttar Pradesh, *Indian Journal of Agricultural Economic,* Vol. 35, No. 4, pp. 88–89.

Government of India, (2000–01, 2005–06, and 2010–11): All India Reports on Number and Area of Agricultural Holdings. Agricultural Census Division, Directorate of Economics & Statistics, Department of Agriculture, Ministry of Agriculture Co-operation & Farmers Welfare, New Delhi.

——, (2001 and 2011): Provisional Population Census, Census Report.

——, (2013): Agricultural at a Glance 2013. Department of Agriculture and Co-operation, Ministry of Agriculture, New Delhi.

Government of West Bengal, (2000–01, 2005–06, and 2010–11): Agricultural Census, Directorate of Agricultural Census, Ministry of Agriculture.

——, (2000–10, 2013, and 2015): *District Statistical Handbook for Burdwan,* Hooghly, Birbhum, Murshidabad and Nadia, BAE & S, Department of Statistic and Programme Implementation.

——, (2000–2006, 2008, 2010, 2011 and 2012): Economic Review, BAE & S, Department of Statistic and Programme Implementation.

——, (2008 and 2012): Statistical Abstract, BAE & S, Department of Statistic and Programme Implementation.

Haque, T., (1996): *Sustainability of Small Holder Agriculture in India,* Concept Publishing Company, New Delhi.

Jayachandra, K. and Naidu, G., (2006): Impact of Dairy Cooperatives on Income, Employment and Creation of Assets of Marginal and Small Farmers: A Case Study, *Indian Cooperative Review,* Vol. 43, No. 4, pp. 719–24.

Joshi, P.K., Birthal, P.S. and Minot, N., (2006): Sources of Agricultural Growth in India: Role of Diversification Towards High-value Crops (No. 98), International Food Policy Research Institute.

Nithyashree, M.L. and Pal, S., (2013): Regional Pattern of Agricultural Growth and Rural Employment in India: Have Small Farmers Benefitted?, *Agricultural Economics Research Review,* Vol. 26 (conference vol.), pp. 1–11.

Pasha, S.A., (1991): Sustainability and Viability of Small and Marginal Farmers: Animal Husbandry and Common Property Resources, *Economic & Political Weekly,* Vol. 26, No. 13, pp. 27–30.

Rawal, V. and Swaminathan, M., (1998): Changing Trajectories: Agricultural Growth in West Bengal, 1950–96, *Economic & Political Weekly,* Vol. 33, No. 40, pp. 2595–602.

Rogaly, B., Harriss-White, B. and Bose, S., (1999): *Sonar Bangla?: Agricultural Growth and Agrarian Change in West Bengal and Bangladesh,* Sage, Thousand Oaks.

Saha, A. and Swaminathan, M., (1994): Agricultural Growth in West Bengal in the 1980s: A Disaggregation by Districts and Crops, *Economic & Political Weekly,* Vol. 29, No. 13, pp. 2–11.

Sanyal, M.K., Biswas, P.K. and Bardhan, S., (1998): Institutional Change and Output Growth in West Bengal Agriculture: End of Impasse, *Economic & Political Weekly,* Vol. 33, No. 47–48, pp. 2979–86.

Sen, A., (1992): Economic Liberalisation and Agriculture in India. *Social Scientist,* 4–19, November.

Sen, A. and Sengupta, R. (1995): The Recent Growth in Agricultural Output in Eastern India, With Special Reference to the Case of West Bengal, January, quoted from Sen and Gazdar's paper in Ben Rogaly's *Sonar Bangla*, pp. 9–12.

Sengupta, S. and Gazdar, H., (1996): Agrarian Politics and Rural Development in West Bengal, *Indian Development: Selected Regional Perspectives,* Oxford India Paperbacks, Oxford University Press, New Delhi.

Shankar, K., (1990): Land Ownership, Asset Structure, and Income Distribution in Eastern Uttar Pradesh, *Economic & Political Weekly*, Vol. 25, No. 42–43, pp. 2385–87.

Sharma, V.P., (2008): India's Agrarian Crisis and Corporate-Led Contract Farming: Socio-Economic Implications for Smallholder Producers, *International Food and Agribusiness Management Review*, Vol. 11, No. 4, pp. 25–48.

Singh, G., (1986): *Economic Conditions of Agricultural Labourers and Marginal Farmers*, B.R. Publication Corporation, Delhi.

Singh, M., (2012): Challenges and Opportunities for Sustainable Viability of Marginal and Small Farmers in India. *Agriculture Situation India. (3)*, pp. 133–142.

Singh, M., Bhullar, A.S. and Joshi, A.S., (2009): Factors Influencing Economic Viability of Marginal and Small Farmers in Punjab, *Agricultural Economics Research Review*, Vol. 22, No. 2, pp. 269–79.

Tripathi, A.K., (2013): Agricultural Price Policy, Output, and Farm Profitability: Examining Linkages during Post-Reform Period in India, *Asian Journal of Agriculture and Development*, Vol. 10, No. 1, pp. 91–111.

Vyas, V.S., Tyagi, D.S. and Misra, V.N., (1969): New Agricultural Strategy and Small Farmers: A Case Study in Gujarat, *Economic & Political Weekly*, Vol. 4, No. 13, pp. 49–53.

Appendix 1

Basic Characteristics of the Marginal Sample Households in the Sample Villages of High CAGR Block (Murshidabad District)

Indicators		*Developed Village*	*Less-Developed Village*
Average family size		4.85	4.44
Caste	SC (%)	2.12	15.21
	OBC (%)	36.17	32.60
	Gen (%)	61.70	52.17
Education	Illiterate (%)	0.00	17.3
	Primary (%)	53.20	23.9
	HS and above (%)	46.70	58.8
Average land-holding (ha)		0.42	0.36
Average number of parcels per household		6.80	5.58
Average number of earning members		1.90	1.58
Occupational diversification	Agrl + agrl lab (%)	8.50	6.50
	Agrl + own business (%)	10.60	32.50
	Agrl + salary income (%)	12.70	6.40
	Agrl + non-agrl service (%)	53.00	45.50
Nature of irrigation	Rainfed (%)	0.00	6.25
	Surface (%)	41.20	43.40
	Underground (%)	58.80	50.35

Source: Field survey.

Appendix 2

Basic Characteristics of the Marginal Sample Households in the Sample Villages of Moderate CAGR Block (Burdwan District)

Indicators		*Developed Village*	*Less-Developed Village*
Average family size		4.66	4.42
Caste	SC (%)	0	15.8
	OBC (%)	0	23.7
	Gen (%)	100	57.9
Education	Illiterate (%)	4.7	15.8
	Primary (%)	14.0	18.4
	HS and above (%)	80.8	65.8
Average land-holding (ha)		0.43	0.29
Average number of parcels per household		6.7	4.9
Average number of earning members		1.6	1.3
Occupational diversification	Agrl + agrl lab (%)	13.2	23.1
	Agrl + own business (%)	2.6	15.4
	Agrl + salary income (%)	15.8	23.0
	Agrl + non-agrl service (%)	23.6	15.3
Nature of irrigation	Rainfed (%)	0.00	0.00
	Surface (%)	21.1	32.2
	Underground (%)	78.9	67.8

Source: Field survey.

Appendix 3

Basic Characteristics of the Marginal Sample Households in the Sample Villages of Low CAGR Block (Hooghly District)

Indicators		*Developed Village*	*Less-Developed Village*
Average family size		5.06	4.66
Caste	SC (%)	4.5	0.0
	OBC (%)	4.5	26.0
	Gen (%)	88.6	66.0
Education	Illiterate (%)	2.2	2.0
	Primary (%)	13.6	22.0
	HS and above (%)	83.9	76.00
Average land-holding (ha)		0.37	0.33
Average number of parcels per household		6.77	5.50
Average number of earning members		1.88	1.72
Occupational diversification	Agrl + agrl lab (%)	0.0	NA
	Agrl + own business (%)	13.6	16.0
	Agrl + salary income (%)	8.1	2.12
	Agrl + non-agrl service (%)	60.1	58.0
Nature of irrigation	Rainfed (%)	0.0	0.0
	Surface (%)	16.5	18.6
	Underground (%)	83.5	81.4

Source: Field survey.

Appendix 4

Inter-district Variations in the Monsoon Paddy Productivity (MPP)

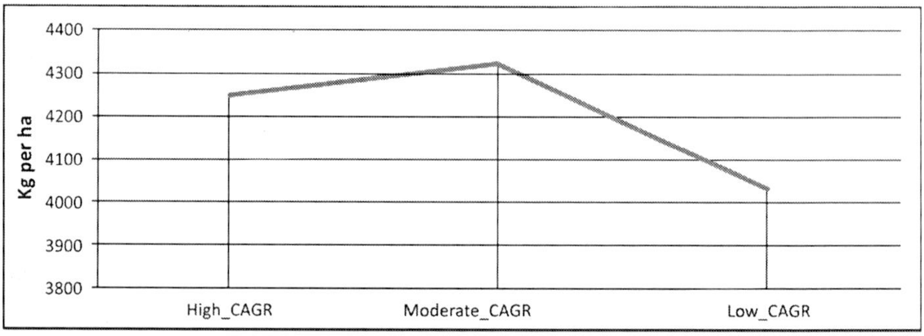

Source: Field survey.

Inter-district Monsoon Paddy Productivity Variation Using Fisher's 't' Test

H_0	H_1	*Obser-vation*	*D.F*	*Cal(t) Value*	*Pr(T < t) L*	*Pr(|T|>|t|) B*	*Pr(T > t) R*
$\mu^{MPP}_{Ai} = \mu^{MPP}_{Aj}$ (MSD = BWN)	$\mu^{MPP}_{Ai} \neq \mu^{MPP}_{Aj}$	173	171	–.52	0.30	0.60	0.69
$\mu^{MPP}_{Ai} = \mu^{MPP}_{Aj}$ (BWN = HUG)	$\mu^{MPP}_{Ai} \neq \mu^{MPP}_{Aj}$	174	172	2.53	0.99	0.01	0.00
$\mu^{MPP}_{Ai} = \mu^{MPP}_{Aj}$ (MSD = HUG)	$\mu^{MPP}_{Ai} \neq \mu^{MPP}_{Aj}$	187	185	2.04	0.97	0.04	0.02

Where *D.F* = degrees of freedom, Cal(t)) = Calculated 't' value, $Pr(T < t)$ L = left tail test, $Pr(|T|?|t|)$, B = both tail test, and $Pr(T > t)$ R = right tail test.

Source: Field survey data.

Appendix 5

Inter-district Variation of Average Net Income of Monsoon Paddy (₹ per Hectare)

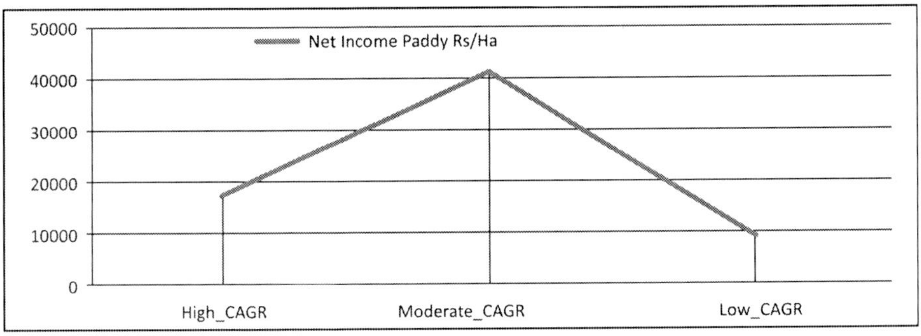

Source: Field survey.

Inter-district Monsoon Paddy Net Income Variation Using Fisher's 't' Test

H_0	H_1	*Obser-vation*	*D.F*	*Cal(t) Value*	*Pr(T < t) L*	*Pr(|T|>|t|) B*	*Pr(T > t) R*
$\mu^{MNI}_{Ai} = \mu^{MNI}_{Aj}$ (MSD = BWN)	$\mu^{MNI}_{Ai} \neq \mu^{MNI}_{Aj}$	173	171	-8.42	0.72	0.54	0.27
$\mu^{MNI}_{Ai} = \mu^{MNI}_{Aj}$ (BWN = HUG)	$\mu^{MNI}_{Ai} \neq \mu^{MNI}_{Aj}$	174	172	8.96	1.00	0.00	0.00
$\mu^{MNI}_{Ai} = \mu^{MNI}_{Aj}$ (MSD = HUG)	$\mu^{MNI}_{Ai} \neq \mu^{MNI}_{Aj}$	187	185	0.61	0.00	0.00	1.00

Where *D.F* = degrees of freedom, Cal(t)) = Calculated 't' value, $Pr(T < t)$ L = left tail test, $Pr(|T|?|t|)$, B = both tail test, and $Pr(T > t)$ R = right tail test.

Source: Field survey data.

Appendix 6

Inter-district Variation in Average Annual Farm Profitability

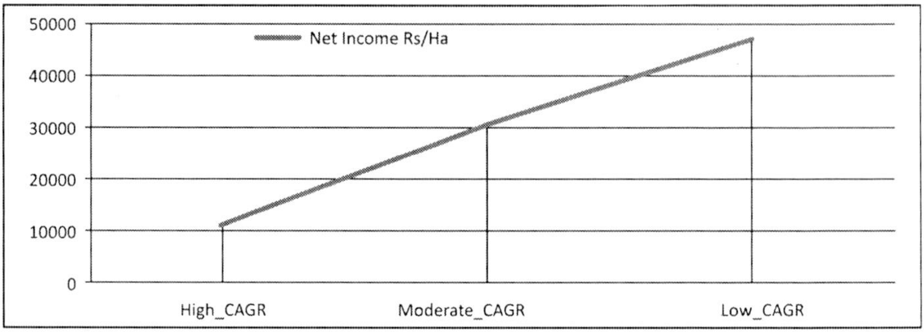

Source: Field survey.

Fisher's 't' Test for the Variation of Annual Farm Profitability across Districts

H0	*H1*	*Observation*	*D.F*	*Cal(t) Value*	*Pr(T < t) L*	*Pr(|T|?|t|) B*	*Pr(T > t) R*
$\mu\prod^{AFP}_{Ai} = \mu\prod^{AFP}_{Aj}$ (MSD = BWN)	$\mu\prod^{AFP}_{Ai} \neq \mu\prod^{AFP}_{Aj}$	173	171	–5.57	0.00	0.00	1.00
$\mu\prod^{AFP}_{Ai} = \mu\prod^{AFP}_{Aj}$ (BWN = HUG)	$\mu\prod^{AFP}_{Ai} \neq \mu\prod^{AFP}_{Aj}$	174	172	–3.56	0.00	0.00	0.99
$\mu\prod^{AFP}_{Ai} = \mu\prod^{AFP}_{Aj}$ (MSD = HUG)	$\mu\prod^{AFP}_{Ai} \neq \mu\prod^{AFP}_{Aj}$	187	185	–9.06	0.00	0.00	1.00

Where *D.F* = degrees of freedom, Cal(t) = calculated 't' value, $Pr(T < t)$ L = left tail test, $Pr(|T|?|t|)$ B = both tail test, and $Pr(T > t)$ R = right tail test.

Source: Field survey.

Appendix 7

Fisher's 't' Test for the Variation of Economic Viability across Districts

H_0	H_1	*Obser-vation*	*D.F*	*Cal(t) Value*	*Pr(T < t) L*	*Pr(|T|>|t|) B*	*Pr(T > t) R*
$\mu€^{EV}_{Ai} = \mu€^{EV}_{Aj}$ (MSD = BWN)	$\mu€^{EV}_{Ai} \neq \mu€^{EV}_{Aj}$	141	139	–5.24	0.00	0.00	1.00
$\mu€^{EV}_{Ai} = \mu€^{EV}_{Aj}$ (BWN = HUG)	$\mu€^{EV}_{Ai} \neq \mu€^{EV}_{Aj}$	156	154	–3.72	0.00	0.00	0.99
$\mu€^{EV}_{Ai} = \mu€^{EV}_{Aj}$ (MSD = HUG)	$\mu€^{EV}_{Ai} \neq \mu€^{EV}_{Aj}$	153	151	–9.00	0.00	0.00	1.00

Where *D.F* = degrees of freedom, Cal(t) = calculated 't' value, $Pr(T < t)$ L = left tail test, $Pr(|T|?|t|)$ B = both tail test, and $Pr(T > t)$ R = right tail test.

Source: Field survey.

13 Addressing Food Security and Government Initiatives

Tarujyoti Buragohain

Introduction

The concept of 'food security' emerged in the 1970s and the public distribution system (PDS) in India was started around this time with an objective to make food grain and other necessary food items available to the economically weaker sections of the society at reasonable prices. Under the system, it is responsibility of the central and state governments to ensure smooth flow of food grain and other commodities to consumers. The Food Corporation of India (FCI), on behalf of the Central Government procures, transports, and stocks the grains in the central godowns (owned or hired).

There were three main features of the concept of food security in India: policy of minimum support price, regular procurement of food crops from the farmers, and building food stocks.

Furthermore, the concept of 'food security' was highlighted during World Food Conference (1974). In the conference, emphasis was essentially on (a) increasing food production in food-deficit countries and (b) on creating a coordinated system of national and international grain reserves. This approach overlooked the demand side of the issue, especially the accessibility to adequate quantity of food at affordable prices at all times and places to vulnerable groups for a normal life.

Currently, World Bank's widely accepted definition of food security (World Bank, 1986) describes food security as 'access to enough food to all people at all times for an active healthy life'.

Food security is thus defined in much broader terms than in terms of self-sufficiency in food, which emphasises increasing domestic food production to meet domestic consumption (Adedeji, 1989).

According to FAO, 'food security' generally implies arrangements whereby people are assured of the minimum but adequate level of food-grain supply in periods of normal as well as poor harvests. Adequate quantity of food may be defined at rural, national, regional, and international levels. The national food security is a function of the ability of the country's production, marketing, trade, and institutional systems to continuously provide an adequate quantity of food to inhabitants even in times of adverse domestic production and international market conditions. It, therefore, depends on such critical factors as domestic food production, income generation and its distribution, foreign exchange earnings' capacity, provision of storage, transportation, and distribution facilities for meeting seasonal and emergency food needs; these are in addition to other factors that may affect the maintenance and improvement of per-capita food consumption (Amiti, 1982).

Food security is said to exist when all people at all times, and physical, social, and economic access to enough, safe and nutritious food that meets their dietary needs and food preferences for an active and health life (FAO, 2009). Climate change adversely impacts on agricultural production, availability, stability, and volatility of food prices. Recently, India experienced bumper crops, due to lack of safe and adequate storage facilities as well as low level of food-processing technology, about one-third of food grains remained unprotected. The uncertainty of adequate domestic production and distribution systems would result in food insecurity, nutrition, and livelihood of vast majority of rural people.

Within this backdrop, in this paper an attempt has been made to discern the following: (a) to understand the government initiatives for food security, (b) to understand the growth performance of important agricultural commodity, and (c) to understand the impact of various initiatives on food security and nutrition.

Government Initiatives for Agricultural Development

Price Policy: Minimum Support Price (MSP) (Rabi)

The price policy for Rabi crops of 2017–18 season to be marketed in 2018–19, the government has fixed the MSP and bonus. The price of common paddy increased by 5.4 per cent in 2017–18 as compared to 4.3 per cent in previous year. Similarly, the price of paddy grade 'A' increased by 5.3 per cent as compared to 4.1 per cent over the previous year. The price of wheat has increased by 6.8 per cent as compared to 6.6 per cent in the previous year. In case of cereals including coarse cereals, FCI and other designated state agencies would continue to provide price support to the farmers by buying their products at MSP.

Minimum Support Price (MSP) (Kharif)

In June 2016, government gave approval for increasing minimum support price (MSP) for all Kharif crops for the season 2016–17. The MSP of paddy increased by 4.3 per cent for common varieties and 4.1 per cent for grade 'A' varieties. The MSP of pulses increased by 9.2 per cent and for oilseeds by 6.7 per cent. Apart from the MSP, the government announced a bonus for the farmers for cultivation of pulses and oilseeds, payable over and above the approved MSP. In order to sell at MSP, FCI was designated central nodal agency for price support operations for cereals, pulses, and oilseeds. The price boost for Kharif MSP is expected to give a strong incentive to farmers to increase area under pulses and invest for increase in productivity of pulses and oilseeds (source: www.cicr.org.in/pdf/press/6-6-2016.pdf).

Opening of Land Customs Station (LCS)

In August 2016, the Central Government opened the eastern and north-eastern border for export of basmati rice to Bangladesh and Nepal through land customs station (LCS). Both the countries are regular importer of basmati rice through sea route to Bangladesh despite large land borders. With the opening transportation through LCS, this export is expeted to get a fillip. (source: www.business-standard.com/.../Commodities/Food & Edible Oils).

Release Pulses from Buffer Stocks

In April 2016, Central Government released 10,000 tonnes of Tur and Urad from the buffer stock and asked state government to use this stock to ensure availability of the pulses in the market at reasonable price (source: https://economictimes.indiatimes.com/topic/buffer-stock/3).

Ban on Import of Milk

The central government extended the prohibition on import of milk and milk products viz.: chocolates, milk products, confectionary/food preparations with milk or milk solids from China till June 2018. India is the largest producer and consumer of milk in the world. India does not import milk products from China and other countries. India imposed the ban for the preventive measure (source: https://www.outlookindia.com/newsscroll/ban-on-import-of-chinese).

Export of Dairy Products to Russia

Russia continues to ban on import of food products from Western countries. Russia has signed the protocol for Indian dairy industry. The dairy plants approved by Russia, however, will have to collect milk from farmers and not from collection centres. This is mandatory (source: blog.frontalrain.com/russia-signs-export-protocol-will-now-import).

Marketing of Agricultural Produce

Indian government has launched a unified trading portal pan India. National Agriculture Market portal is designed to create a unified national market for agricultural commodities. The portal will be run by the Ministry of Agriculture and Farmer's Welfare. The portal has been launched as a part of Digital India Movement and towards doubling the agricultural income. The portal was inaugurated by Prime Minister Shri Narendra Modi in presence of Shri Radha Mohan Singh, Union Minister of Agriculture & Farmer's Welfare in April 2016. A total of 21 *mandis* from eight states have been linked to the e-NAM, the 200 *mandis* will be linked within five months and 585 mandis by March 2018 (source: www.sarkariyojna.co.in/Central Government).

Pradhan Mantri Krishi Sinchayee Yojana (PMKSY)

Pradhan Mantri Krishi Sinchayee Yojana (PMKSY) launched on 1 July 2015 with the motto of 'Har Khet Ko Paani', the PMKSY is being implemented to expand cultivated area with assured irrigation, reduce wastage of water, and improve water use efficiency. PMKSY not only focuses on creating sources for assured irrigation, but also creating protective irrigation by harnessing rain water at micro level through 'Jal Sanchay' and 'Jal Sinchan'. Micro-irrigation is also incentivised through subsidy to ensure 'Per Drop-More Crop' (source: https://www.india.gov.in/.../pradhan-mantri-krishi-sinchayee-yojana).

Pradhan Mantri Fasal Bima Yojana (PMFBY)

Prime Minister Shri Narendra Modi has implemented a new scheme Pradhan Mantri Fasal Bima Yojana (PMFBY) on 13 January 2016. This scheme aims in decreasing the burden of premiums on farmers who take loans for their cultivation and will also safeguard them against the inclement weather.

It has also been decided to make the settlement process of the insurance claim, fast and easy so that the farmers do not face any trouble regarding the crop insurance plan. This scheme will be implemented in every state of India, in association with respective state governments. The scheme will be implemented in every state of India, in association with respective state governments. There will be a uniform premium of only two per cent to be paid by farmers for all Kharif crops and 1.5 per cent for all Rabi crops. In case of annual commercial and horticultural crops, the premium to be paid will be only five per cent.

Paramparagat Krishi Vikas Yojana (PKVY)

It is an organic farming scheme launched by Government of India under National Mission on Sustainable Agriculture (NMSA) during 2015–16 under the participatory guarantee scheme (PGS) certification. The Department of Agriculture and Co-operation has prepared a roadmap of the Paramparagat Krishi Vikas Yojana (PKVY). Under the guidelines, farmers will be organised in a cluster for encouraging them to adopt organic farming. A total of 50 acres will form a cluster and engaged in conversion and adoption of organic farming. The PGS of certification empowers the farmers in the clusters to certify the process of production and have access to the organic market. A separate web portal is also developed for the purpose of PGS certification.

Initially, the scheme is implemented in 10 districts of Assam. The total of 220 clusters have been formed in the selected districts. The total number of farmers is 6,913 with total area of 10,935 acres (4,428.675 hectares) (source: https://diragri.assam.gov.in/.../paramparagat-krishi-vikasyojanapkvy-0).

Functioning of Fertiliser Units

In July 2016, the Union Cabinet has approved for functioning of defunct fertiliser units in Gorakhpur (Uttar Pradesh), Sindri (Jharkhand) of Fertiliser Corporation India Limited (FCIL) and Barauni (Bihar) of Hindustan Fertilisers Corporation Limited (HFCL). These units were lying defunct since their closure during

1990–02. Therefore, the units and other associated facilities were lying unutilised. It is important to mention here that there is no functional urea unit in the eastern part of the country except two small units at Namrup (Assam). Earlier in 2015, government had approved revival of these three units (source: pib.nic.in/newsite/mbErel.aspx?relid=147036).

Imports of Various Food Commodity

Government has been continuously importing important food commodities to ensure smooth flow of food grain at reasonable price. The import of pulses has increased from 34,96,000 tonnes in 2011–12 to 66,61,000 tonnes in 2016–17. The import of other cereals has also increased from 11,000 tonnes in 2011–12 to 2,28,000 tonnes in 2016–17. The import of wheat has been increased unbelievably – from 22 tonnes to 6 million tonnes during the same period. The import of non-basmati rice is more stable, whereas despite bumper harvest of onion, government has to import a sizeable amount of onion to prevent shortage of onion as well as price volatility (Table 1).

Table 1

Extent of Import of Various Food Commodities

	Pulses (000 MT)	*Other Cereals (000 MT)*	*Fresh Onion (MT)*	*Non-Basmati Rice (MT)*	*Wheat (MT)*
2011–12	3,496	11	13	598	22
2012–13	4,020	40	450	718	2,944
2013–14	3,655	8	17,844	1,442	11,271
2014–15	4,634	19	387	1,903	27,973
2015–16	5,862	24	34,362	1,020	5,16,167
2016–17	6,661	228	87	1,141	57,49,431

Source: DGCIS.

Government Procurement of Rice and Wheat

Table 2 provides pattern of government procurement of rice and wheat for allotment of these two commodities for PDS. The allotment of both rice and wheat is for mostly PDS stable; whereas in case of rice, offtake for distribution through retail shops from the allotment has increased from 48 per cent in 2004–05 to 96.5 per cent in 2016–17. In case of wheat, the per cent of offtake from allotment has also increased from 35 per cent to 95 per cent during the same period.

Performance of Agriculture

Farmers' Households

Over the years, the agricultural households have been declining and a large majority of farmers are not willing to continue agriculture as the return on investment has been declining.

Table 2

Extent of Procurement of Rice and Wheat

	Rice (Million Tonnes)					Wheat (Million Tonnes)				
	Production	Procurement	Allotment for TPDS	Offtake for TPDS	Offtake % of Allotment	Production	Procurement	Allotment for TPDS	Offtake for TPDS	Offtake % of Allotment
2004–05	83.1	24.7	34.5	16.5	47.8	68.6	16.8	37.2	12.9	34.6
2005–06	91.8	27.6	40.0	19.1	47.7	69.4	14.8	31.6	12.0	38.1
2006–07	93.4	25.1	43.2	21.1	48.8	75.8	9.2	14.4	10.3	71.1
2007–08	96.7	28.7	27.3	22.4	82.2	78.6	11.1	12.0	10.6	90.6
2008–09	99.2	34.1	20.0	18.5	92.3	80.7	22.7	11.5	10.2	89.0
2009–10	89.1	32.0	24.8	23.4	94.3	80.8	25.4	22.8	19.0	83.4
2010–11	96.0	34.2	26.1	24.8	95.2	86.9	22.5	21.4	18.9	88.0
2011–12	105.3	35.0	26.1	24.3	93.1	94.9	28.3	22.7	18.8	82.5
2012–13	105.2	34.0	27.1	25.2	93.0	93.5	38.1	23.3	19.6	84.2
2013–14	106.7	31.8	26.9	24.5	91.3	95.9	25.1	23.3	20.0	86.1
2014–15	105.5	32.0	30.4	25.6	84.1	86.5	28.0	21.6	19.0	88.0
2015–16	104.3	33.5	28.4	27.3	96.2	93.5	28.1	23.9	22.3	93.0
2016–17	110.2	33.0	30.4	29.3	96.5	98.4	22.9	24.0	22.9	95.4

Source: Ministry of Consumer Affairs.

Figure 1

Per cent of Agricultural HHs

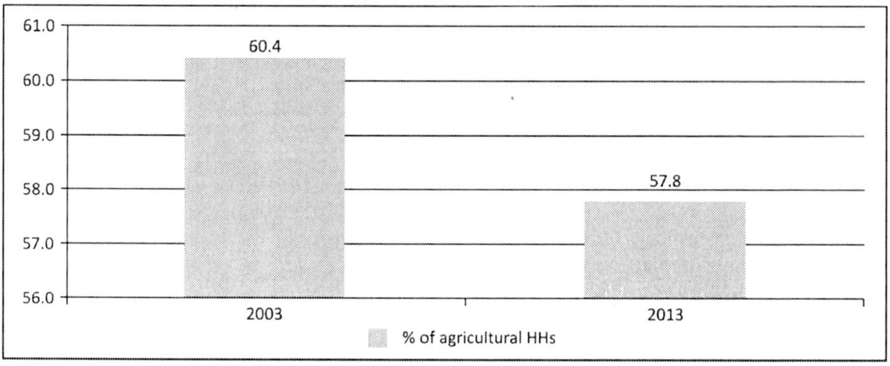

Source: NCAER estimation from Situation of Agricultural Households in India, NSSO 70th round (2014) and Situation Assessment Survey of Farmers, NSSO 59th round, Report No. 497 (2005).

According to NSSO 70th round July 2012–June 2013, India has 90.2 million agricultural households, which is about 57.8 per cent. Agricultural households have been declining from 60.4 per cent in 2003 to 57.8 per cent in 2013 (Figure 1).

Operational Holdings

One-third of the economically active population obtains its livelihood from agriculture, of which the vast majority of the world's farms are small or very small in size. Globally, farms of less than one hectare account for 72 per cent of all, but control only eight per cent of all agricultural land.

In India, 67 per cent of marginal farmers operate only 22 per cent of agricultural land. *Farmers' income is closely linked with the land size of cultivation.* Various studies also found that unequal distribution of land size is the major cause of poverty among agricultural households. Higher the land size under operation, higher the incomes derived from cultivation. In India, the total number of rural operational holdings increased from 88.9 million in 1980–81 to 137.76 million in 2010–11. The operational holdings increased among marginal holdings (who cultivate less than 1 hectare of land) from 56.37 per cent in 1980–81 to 67.04 per cent in 2010–11, while the shares of small, semi-medium, medium, and large holding groups decreased from 18.11 to 17.94 per cent, 14.01 to 10.05 per cent, 9.08 to 4.25 per cent, and 2.44 to 0.73 per cent, respectively, during the same period. On an average, these farmers cultivate 0.39, 1.42, 2.21, 5.73, and 17.38 hectares, respectively. The average land size operated by the farmers was 1.15 hectares in 2010–11, which saw a decline from 1.84 hectares in 1980–81 (Figure 2).

Table 3 presents the growth of various crops during 10th- and 11th-plan periods and latest years. During 10th-plan period, there was a huge gap between the target and achievements in food grains, coarse cereals, pulses, oil seeds, sugarcane, and cotton.

Figure 2

Average Size of Holding (Hectare)

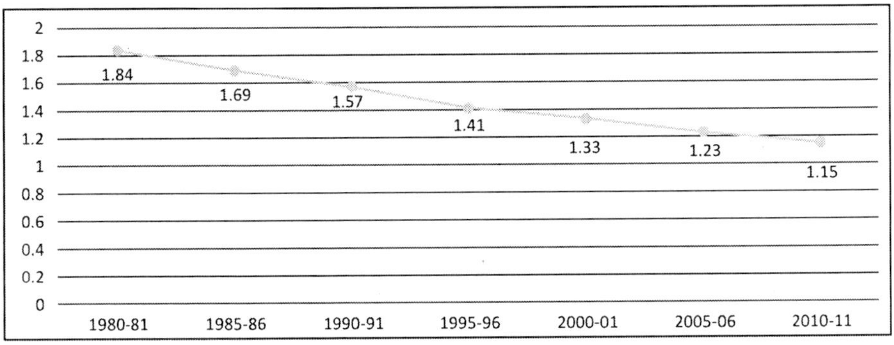

Sources: Several rounds of agricultural census, Department of Agriculture and Cooperation, Government of India, Ministry of Agriculture.

Table 3

Target and Achievement of Production (Million Tonnes)

Productions	*10th Plan (2002–07)*		*Gap*	*11th Plan (2007–12)*		*Gap*
	Target	*Achievement*		*Target*	*Achievement*	
Food grains	1100.10	1012.20	-87.9	1183.10	1187.43	+4.33*
Coarse cereals	176.84	165.11	-11.73	208.60	200.03	-8.57
Pulses	76.60	66.76	-9.84	81.00	79.32	-1.68
Oil seeds	133.88	116.65	-17.23	160.15	144.85	-15.3
Sugar cane	1417.50	1395.02	-22.48	1655.00	1628.94	-26.06
Cotton	80.00	79.91	-0.09	134.00	140.38	+6.38

*High contribution of wheat production target was 399.00 million tonnes achievement 421.80 million tonnes.

Products	*2013–14*		*Gap*	*2015–16*		*Gap*
	Target	*Achievement*		*Target*	*Achievement*	
Food grains	259.0	265.04	-6.04	264.10	251.5	-12.6
Coarse cereals	42.50	43.29	-0.79	43.20	38.52	-4.68
Pulses	19.00	19.25	-0.25	20.05	16.35	-3.7
Oil seeds	31.00	32.75	-1.75	33.00	25.30	-7.7
Sugarcane	340.00	325.14	14.86	355.00	352.16	2.84
Cotton	35	35.9	-0.9	35.15	30.14	5.01

During 11th-plan period, growth is more visible in the production of these crops. Production of food grains and cotton has crossed the targeted amount and generated surplus by 4.33 and 6.38 million tonnes, respectively. Growth in wheat production has contributed significantly in the growth of food gains production. In the beginning of 12th-plan period, the gap between targeted production and achievement has further declined and the production of sugarcane crossed the targeted production by 14.86 million tonnes in the year 2013–14. However, in the year 2015–16, the gap has increased again. The Table 4 presents the food balance sheet of various important food commodities in India.

Table 4

Food Balance Sheet (Million Tonnes)

	Supply and Demand Status of Various Food Commodities (Million Tonnes)									
	Rice		Wheat		Maize		Pulses		Edible Oils	
	2015–16	2016–17	2015–16	2016–17	2015–16	2016–17	2015–16	2016–17	2015–16	2016–17
	October–September	October–September	October–September	October–September	October–September	October–September	October–September	October–September	October–September	October–September
Beginning stocks	14.2	15.9	15.3	6.5	1.0	0.5	0.0	0.2	1.5	1.4
Production	103.5	107.0	88.5	96.0	22.5	25.3	16.5	21.8	4.6	6.8
Imports	0	0.0	0.0	5.0	0.1	0.2	5.5	6.5	15.8	16.0
Total supply	117.7	122.9	103.8	107.5	23.6	26.0	22.0	28.5	21.9	24.2
Consumption	98.5	92.4	87.8	94.0	2.6	4.2	21.9	27.5	19.6	21.6
Exports	9.0	10.5	0.5	0.5	0.8	0.1	0.1	0.50	0.1	0.003
Total utilisation	100.5	94.4	89.3	100.0	22.3	24.9	22.0	27.8	20.3	22.7
Closing stocks (%)	8.2	18.0	14.0	7.0	0.5	1.0	0.0	0.5	1.5	1.5
Total distribution	117.7	122.9	191.6	107.5	26.2	30.2	22.0	56.3	41.5	45.8

Source: Agricultural Outlook and Situation Analysis reports NCAER.

Impact Assessment

Food Security and Nutrition

Food security and improved nutrition is one of the major challenges confronting the entire world. Out of 17 intertwined sustainable development goals with 169 associated targets set by UN Open Working Groups to be achieved by 2030, goal 2 is 'End hunger, food security and improved nutrition and promote sustainable agricultural'. These goals and targets came into effect on 1 January 2016 to be achieved within 15 years. In India, the estimated production of food grains is 275.7 million tonnes for 2016–17, an increase from 198.36 million tonnes in 2004–05. The production of rice and wheat has also increased from 151.73 million tonnes in 2004–05 to 208.55 million tonnes in 2016–17. The country has been producing enough for its population. The government procurement of rice and wheat too increased from 41 million tonnes in 2004–05 to 62 million tonnes in 2015–16. However, the distribution of food to its population continues to be problematic and erroneous. As per NSSO's various rounds, the percentage of population who accessed PDS cereals in 2011–12 (latest round) was much higher than in 2004–05 and 2009–10. In 2004–05, only 23.3 per cent of all households accessed the PDS purchased of cereals increased to 44.8 per cent in 2011–12. In 1997, government implemented targeted public distribution system (TPDS) to supply grains, especially rice and wheat supply to its below poverty lines population. In 2004–05, the allotment of rice and wheat for TPDS was 71.7 million tonnes of which only 29.4 million (41%) were offtake for distribution. Therefore, the allotment of rice and wheat for TPDS declined for next subsequent years. However, from 2009 to 2010, there is continuous increase of allotment of rice and wheat for TPDS from 47.6 million tonnes in 2009–10 to 52.4 million tonnes in 2015–16. As a consequence, offtake of rice and wheat for TPDS has also increased from 42.4 million tonnes (89% of allotment) in 2009–10 to 50.2 million tonnes (96% of allotment) in 2015–16

Figure 3

Extent of Procurement, Allotment under TPDS and Offtake for TDPS of Wheat and Rice

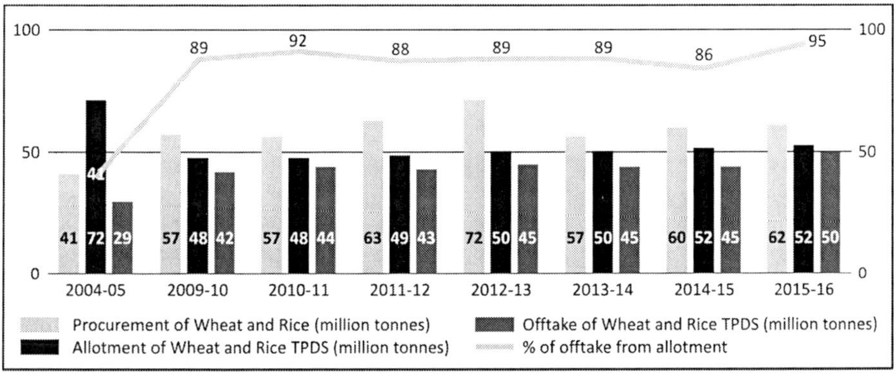

Source: Ministry of Finance, Government of India.

Various studies have documented the extent of PDS leakage by estimating the difference between 'offtake' and 'purchased' from PDS. These studies find that there has been a considerable decline of PDS leakage over the years. Despite all, as per 'The State of Food Security and Nutrition in the World 2017' report prepared by Food and Agricultural Organization (FAO), International Fund for Agricultural Development (IFAD), United Nations Children's Fund (UNICEF), World Food Programme (WFP), and World Health Organisation (WHO) estimate that in India, 182.8 million people are severely food insecure for the year 2014–16. About one-third – 27.43 per cent – of world's food insecure people live in India.

As per the report, the proportion of under-nourished people worldwide declined from 14.1 per cent in 2004–06 to 10.7 per cent in 2014–16. Globally, 789.1 million people are under-nourished down from 919.6 million during the same period. In India, the under-nourished people declined from 234.9 million in 2004–06 to 190.7 million in 2014–16. Still, India is the home of about one-fourth – 24.17 per cent – of world's undernourished people. Undernourishment is defined as the condition in which an individual's habitual food consumption is insufficient to provide the amount of dietary energy required to maintain a normal, active, and healthy life.

In case of childhood-stunted children, which is a condition defined as height for age under five years of age on a reference growth curve. This is an important indicator of the prevalence of malnutrition or nutrition-related disorder among an identified population. India's economy as well as food-grain production and distribution have been growing at impressive rates, but the country still has highest stunted children, about 31 per cent of world's stunted children live in India as per the world report 2017. Even though, there is a decline of stunted children from 62.2 million in 2004–05 to 47.5 million in

Figure 4

Undernourished People, Severely Food Insecure, Anaemia among Women and Stunted Children in India

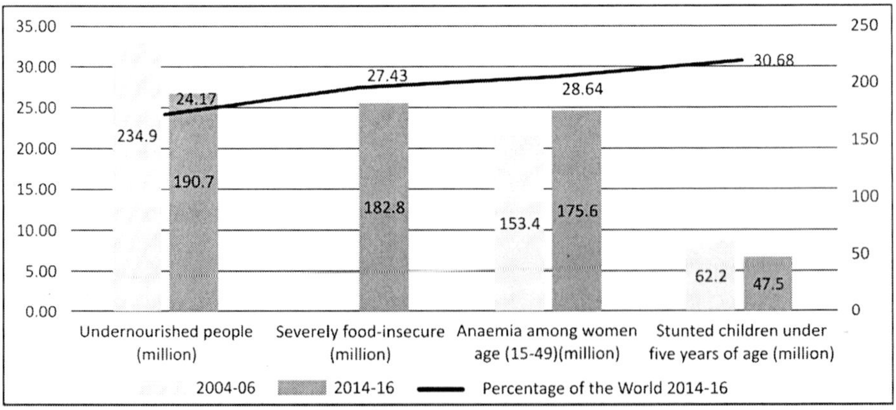

Source: FAO, IFAD, UNICEF, WFP, and WHO 2017. The State of Food Security and Nutrition in the World 2017, building, resilience for peace and food security.

2014–16. Stunting among children reflects chronic under-nutrition, which affects brain development, diminished mental ability and learning capacity, poor school performance, and increased risks of nutrition-related diseases.

Most importantly, anaemia among women in age group 15–49 is worsening in India. In 2004–05, anaemia among women in reproductive age groups was 153.4 million increased to 175.6 million in 2014–16. About 28.64 per cent of world's anaemia among reproductive age group women live in India. The anaemia among women reproductive age group is defined as percentage of women in such age group with haemoglobin concentration below 110 g/l for pregnant women and below 120 g/l for non-pregnant women. Anaemia is an indicator of both poor nutrition and poor health due to lack of adequate dietary energy for women in reproductive age.

Despite bumper food-grain production in India, there has been a gap between production and distribution of grains and adequate nutrition requirement for health. The sustainable development goal 2, ending hunger, and all forms of malnutrition and ensuring food security through promotion of agricultural productivity may not be achieved if the current trend continues in India.

Conclusion and Policy Implication

India has been producing enough for its population and maintaining a decent balance sheet of demand and supply of various food commodities. In India, the estimated production of food grains is 275.7 million tonnes for 2016–17, an increase from 198.36 million tonnes in 2004–05. The production of rice and wheat has also increased from 151.73 million tonnes in 2004–05 to 208.55 million tonnes in 2016–17. The government procurement of rice and wheat too increased from 41 million tonnes in 2004–05 to 62 million tonnes in 2015–16. However, the distribution of food to its population continues to be problematic and erroneous. In India, 182.8 million people are severely food insecure for the year 2014–16. About one-third – 27.43 per cent – of world's food insecure people live in India. India is the home of about one-fourth – 24.17 per cent – of world's under-nourished people. Most importantly, anaemia among women in age group 15–49 is worsening in India. In 2004–05, anaemia among women in reproductive age groups was 153.4 million increased to 175.6 million in 2014–16. About 28.64 per cent of world's anaemia among reproductive age group women live in India.

Various studies find that there has been a considerable decline of PDS leakage over the years. Still, there is a gap of timely and adequate distribution of supply of food grain to the large number of poor households who mostly depend on PDS.

References

Adedeji, A., (1989): Interaction between Structuralism, Structural Adjustment and Food Security Policies in Development Policy Management, European Centre for Development Policy Management (ECDPM) Occasional Paper, Maastricht, p. 13.

Amiti, M., (1982): Food Security and Shortage Policies, *Proceedings of the Workshop on Food Policy Research Priorities*, Nairobi, 14–17 June, p. 154.

FAO, (2009): The State of Food Insecurity in the World. Food and Agriculture Organisation of the United Nations, Rome, 2009.

World Bank, (1986): *Poverty and Hunger: Issues and Options for Food Security in Developing Countries*, World Bank Policy Study, Washington D.C., p. 99.

World Food Conference, (1974): Rome, 5–16 November 1974. Communication from the Commission to the Council. SEC (74) 4955 final, 9 December 1974.

14 Analysis of Growth and Instability in Area, Production, Yield, and Price of Rice in India

Ankur Jain

Introduction

Agricultural growth with stability is considered important for development of agriculture, especially when it is the case of developing country. There is considerable literature on growth and instability of yield and production of crops both from theoretical and empirical perspectives. Instability is one of the important deciding parameters in development dynamics and more so in the context of agricultural production. An analysis of instability in crop output, apart from growth, is of importance for understanding the nature of food security and income stability. The variations in crop output not only affect prices and bring about sharp fluctuation in them but also result in wide variations in disposable income of the farmers. The magnitude of fluctuations depends on the nature of crop production technology, its sensitivity to weather, economic environment, availability of material inputs, and many other factors. The estimates of Dev and Pandey (2012) showed that there is a continuous decline in trend growth rate in the value of output of all cereals. The growth rate in value of the output of cereals declined from 2.76 per cent in the 1980s to 2.02 per cent in the 1990s and it further declined to 1.25 per cent the during 2000s. In the case of paddy, the trend growth rate in the value of output declined from 3.31 per cent during the 1980s to 1.80 per cent in the 1990s and it declined further to 1.13 per cent.

A large number of studies have been conducted on growth and instability in agricultural production in general and food-grain production in particular. Almost all the studies observed a substantial gain in area, production, and productivity of wheat in all the Indian states during post-Green Revolution period. Rice also recorded an increase in area, production, and productivity, particularly in states that adopted rice cultivation during post-Green Revolution period. It is difficult to identify and even more difficult to quantify the causes of fluctuation in food-grain production. However, Hazell (1982) assigned much importance to the growth for increasing instability, but Dev (1987), identified rainfall, irrigation, and agro-physical situations as important factors influencing instability in food-grain production during post-Green Revolution period. The application of new technology (seed fertiliser) has also been found responsible for variability in food-grain production during post-Green Revolution period (Mehra, 1981). While some studies in India and Pakistan (Mehra, 1981; Hazell, 1982; Ray, 1983) indicate that new technology has added to instability in production. Most of the previous studies have done research on instability in food-grain production (Hazell, 1982; Dev, 1987). The drawbacks in these studies are included that they calculated instability at aggregate level not at disaggregated level, that is, state-wise analysis.

Although there is improvement in technology and due to increasing subsidies on inputs related to agriculture, the input access to farmers has also improved. Still, there are large fluctuations and variation in prices and farm income across states. These year-to-year fluctuations in prices and farmers income affect farmer's decision for investment in agriculture. While the need for increasing agricultural production or growth is obvious, the increase in instability in agricultural production is considered adverse for several reasons. It raises the risk involved in farm production and affects farmers' income and decisions to adopt high-paying technologies and make investments in farming. Instability in production affects price stability and the consumers, and it increases vulnerability of low-income households to market. Instability in agricultural and food production is also important for food management and macroeconomic stability (Chand and Raju, 2008).

Instability affects both production and productivity per hectare. There are studies which emphasise that instability is a consequence of growth which means growth and instability are positively related. The present chapter analyses growth and instability in area, production, yield, and price of paddy across states.

Data and Methodology

Data on important variables like area, production, and yield of rice for the period 1970–71 to 2011–12 and cost of cultivation data were compiled from Directorate of Economics and Statistics, Ministry of Agriculture, Government of India, New Delhi. Other relevant data used in this analysis were compiled from secondary data taken from various published sources such as Agricultural Statistics at a Glance, Land Use Statistics, Agriculture Prices in India, state-wise value of Output of Agriculture and allied activities by Ministry of Statistics and Programme Implementation (MOSPI), and Agmarknet Portal maintained by Directorate of Marketing and Inspection (Ministry of Agriculture).

The compound annual growth rate of area, production, and yield of paddy is calculated using semi-log model. For calculating instability, this study use the methodology used by Chand and Raju (2008) to calculate instability using the following instability index:

Instability Index = Standard deviation of the natural logarithm (X_{t+1}/X_t)

Here X_t refers to area (A), production (P), yield (Y), and farm harvest price (FHP) in the year 't'; and X_{t+1} denote these for the next year. This index is unit free and robust and measures deviations from underlying trend (log linear in this case). When there are no deviations from the trend, the ratio of X_{t+1} and X_t remains the same and their standard deviation is zero.

The main objective of this paper is to analyse the compound annual growth rates of area, production, and yield of paddy and to measure the instability in area, production, and yield of paddy across states. This study also analyses the instability in farm harvest prices and wholesale prices of paddy across states. The time period used under the study is 1970–71 to 2011–12 and it is divided into four decades, that is, period I starts from 1970–71 to 1979–80; period II starts from 1980–81 to 1989–90; period III starts from 1990–91 to 1999–00; and period IV starts from 2000–01 to 2011–12.

Results and Discussion

Figure 1 shows the upward trend in area, production, and yield of rice. In this graph, 1970–71 is used as the base year by taking value 100 for all area, production, and yield. There are fluctuations in the trend lines but before the 1990s there was continuous rise and fall of all three key variables, namely, area, production, and yield. There is not much increase in area under rice as area line is almost stable. While there is significant increase in production which shows that India has become self-sufficient in rice and also has the potential to export

Figure 1

Variation in All India Area, Production, and Yield of Rice from 1970–71 to 2011–12

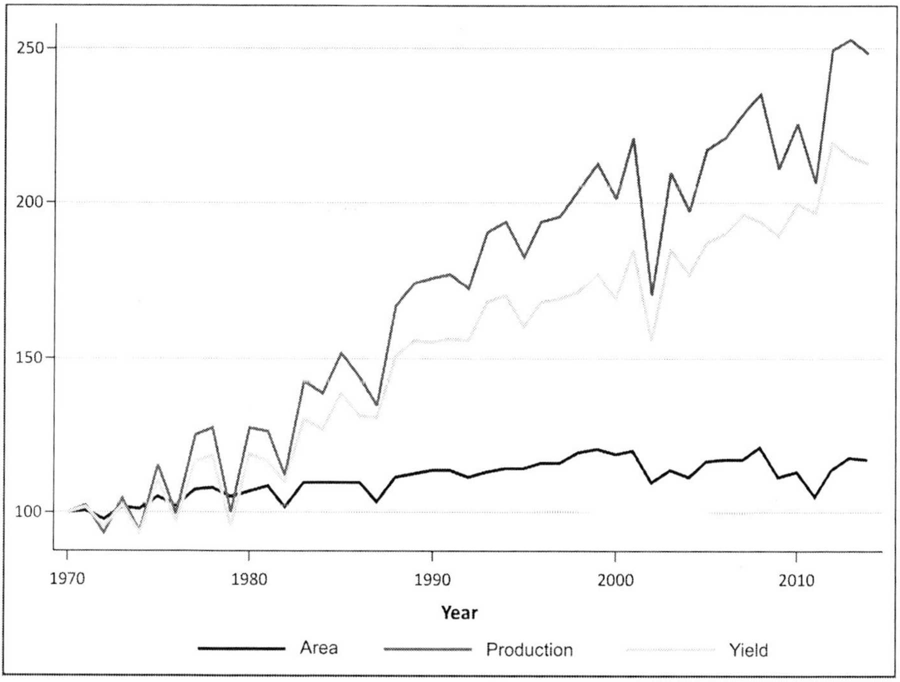

Source: Computed from Government of India various issues.

rice to other countries. The yield of rice has also increased over the period but it is still below if we compare it with other major rice-producing countries such as Thailand and China.

Table 1

Share in State-wise Value of Output of Paddy at 2004–05 Prices (%)

States	*TE 1992–93*	*TE 2002–03*	*TE 2010–11*	*TE 2013–14*
Andhra Pradesh	13.97	13.56	14.3	6.57
Assam	4.35	4.77	4.49	3.76
Bihar	6.42	6.04	4.05	5.88
Gujarat	1.69	1.38	1.56	1.52
Haryana	4.66	5.33	4.98	4.94
Himachal Pradesh	0.16	0.16	0.16	0.17
Jammu & Kashmir	0.95	0.67	0.73	0.74
Karnataka	2.82	2.85	4.6	3.65
Kerala	1.67	1.03	0.64	0.53
Madhya Pradesh	7.7	1.61	1.74	2.71
Maharashtra	3.31	2.79	2.7	3.47
Manipur	0.49	0.54	0.53	0.37
Odisha	7.1	5.51	6.54	6.45
Punjab	9.13	10.62	11.4	10.79
Rajasthan	0.26	0.21	0.42	0.32
Tamil Nadu	7.58	6.18	5.17	5.08
Tripura	0.95	1.03	0.95	0.62
Uttar Pradesh	13.48	14.08	12.59	13.77
West Bengal	14.2	15.82	13.82	13.13

Source: Author's calculation.

Note: Value for TE 2013–14 are in 2011–12 prices.

Table 1 shows the share of state-wise value of output of paddy during different time periods. There is large variation in value of output of paddy across states. Uttar Pradesh, West Bengal, and Punjab hold the top three positions in percentage share of state-wise value of output of paddy during TE 2013–14 at 2011–12 prices. Andhra Pradesh also had higher share before Telangana was formed. During TE 2010–11, Andhra Pradesh, West Bengal, Uttar Pradesh, and Punjab hold the first four positions in percentage share in state-wise value of output of paddy at 2004–05 prices, respectively. Punjab is the state where there is continuous increase in the percentage share in the state-wise value of output of paddy from 1992–93 to 2010–11. In states such as Andhra Pradesh, Bihar, Jammu & Kashmir, Madhya Pradesh, Maharashtra, Odisha, Rajasthan, and Tamil Nadu, there is decline share of value of output of paddy from TE 1992–93 to TE 2002–03. In states such as Assam, Bihar, Haryana, Kerala, Maharashtra, Tamil

Nadu, Tripura, Uttar Pradesh, and West Bengal, there is decline in the percentage share in value of output of paddy from 2002–03 to 2010–11 at 2004–05 prices. There is increase in percentage share in value of output of paddy in states such as Andhra Pradesh, Gujarat, Jammu & Kashmir, Karnataka, Madhya Pradesh, Odisha, Punjab, and Rajasthan during the same period.

Growth Rate at All India Level of Rice

Table 2 shows the all India compound annual growth rate (CAGR) of area, production, and yield of rice from 1950–51 to 2010–11. All the growth rates are positive except area during 2000–01 to 2011–12. There is decline in growth rate in area from 1.26 per cent in 1950–51 to -0.003 per cent during 2000–01 to 2011–12. There is also decline in compound annual growth rate of production and yield during the same period. The CAGR of production was 4.46 per cent per annum during 1950–51 to 1959–60, which declined to 1.82 per cent per annum, which is not significant during 2000–01 to 2011–12. In addition, CAGR of yield was 3.15 per cent during 1950–51 to 1959–60, which declined to 1.82 per cent during 2011–12. This implies that growth rate over the period under study are positive but gradually declining. The growth rate (CAGR) of production of rice was 3.62 per cent during the 1980s and 2.2 per cent during the 1990s, which are significant at 1 per cent level. In case of yield, CAGR of yield was highest during the 1980s at 3.19 per cent which declined to 1.34 per cent during the 1990s and again there is improvement in CAGR of yield to 1.82 per cent during the 2000s.

Table 2

Compound Annual Growth Rate in Area, Production, and Yield of Rice (%)

Period	*Area*	*Production*	*Yield*
1950–51 to 1959–60	1.26***	4.46***	3.15***
1960–61 to 1969–70	0.83	1.19	0.36
1970–71 to 1979–80	0.88***	1.9	1.01
1980–81 to 1989–90	0.41	3.62***	3.19***
1990–91 to 1999–00	0.67***	2.02***	1.34***
2000–01 to 2011–12	-0.003	1.82	1.82***

Source: Author's calculation.

Notes: *** means significant at 1 per cent level, ** means significant at 5 per cent level, and * means significant at 10 per cent level.

Growth Rate at State Level

Table 3 shows the growth in area of rice at state level from 1970–71 to 2011–12 across various states. There is large variation in the growth rates of area of rice across states. During period I, Punjab, Rajasthan, and Haryana were the top three states with high CAGR in area. During period II, except West Bengal there was decline in CAGR in area of rice as compared to period I. There is also decline in all India CAGR of rice from 0.89 per cent in period I to 0.41 per cent in period II. During period III, there is improvement in all India CAGR of area of rice from 0.41 per cent to 0.67 per cent, which is also significant at 1 per cent level. However, at state level there are mixed results as in some states there is a fall in CAGR of rice while in many other states there is increase in CAGR of rice. There is much improvement in Haryana during period III as CAGR of area of rice improved from 2.40 per cent in period II to 6.10 per cent in period III. However, in case of Punjab there is continuous decline in CAGR of area of paddy. During period IV, there is decline in CAGR of area of rice in many states except Andhra Pradesh, Gujarat, and Manipur. At all India level also, there is decline in CAGR of rice from 0.67 per cent in period III to 0.003 per cent during period IV. Therefore, the CAGR of area of rice is declining continuously at all India level and at the state level growth rates are positive in many states but declining.

Table 3

State-wise Compound Annual Growth Rate in Area of Rice from 1970–71 to 2011–12

States	*Period I 1970–71 to 1979–80*	*Period II 1980–81 to 1989–90*	*Period III 1990–91 to 1999–2000*	*Period IV 2000–01 to 2011–12*
Andhra Pradesh	1.91*	0.54	0.55	2
Assam	1.49***	0.51	0.1	-0.25
Bihar	0.51	0.25	0.11	-0.79
Gujarat	0.26	0.41	0.5	2.37**
Haryana	6.64***	2.40*	6.10***	2.29***
Himachal Pradesh	-1.08*	-1.45**	-0.23	-0.66***
Jammu & Kashmir	2.54***	-0.03	-0.46	0.68***
Karnataka	-0.09	0.38	1.72***	1.37
Kerala	-1.07**	-4.13***	-5.58***	-4.48***
Madhya Pradesh	0.88***	0.36**	0.74***	-0.40**
Maharashtra	1.69***	-0.09	-0.69***	0.03
Manipur	1.94*	-0.67	0.35	2.68***
Odisha	-0.91**	0.41	0.16	-0.56**
Punjab	12.46***	5.39***	2.48***	1.02***
Rajasthan	5.87***	-3.15	4.07***	1.07
Tamil Nadu	0.23	-2.02*	1.06	0.39
Tripura	0.29	-1.42***	-0.78	0.52
Uttar Pradesh	1.53**	0.03	0.95**	0.06
West Bengal	-0.05	1.12**	0.55**	-0.73
All India	0.89	0.41	0.67***	0.003

Source: Author's calculation.

Notes: *** means significant at 1 per cent level, ** means significant at 5 per cent level, and * means significant at 10 per cent level.

Table 4

State-wise Compound Annual Growth Rate in Production of Rice from 1970–71 to 2011–12

States	*Period I 1970–71 to 1979–80*	*Period II 1980–81 to 1989–90*	*Period III 1990–91 to 1999–00*	*Period IV 2000–01 to 2011–12*
Andhra Pradesh	4.2**	2.5	1.7	3.0*
Assam	0.6	1.1	1.1*	1.4
Bihar	0.3	4.1	3.1	0.3
Gujarat	4.2	-0.2	3.7***	9.0***
Haryana	11.3***	2.2	4.4***	9.0***
Himachal Pradesh	-0.9	-1.8	1.6***	0.5
Jammu & Kashmir	3.5**	-0.7	-1.8	2.4***
Karnataka	1.4	0.2	3.6***	2.6
Kerala	-0.5	-2.9***	-7.1	-2.5***
Madhya Pradesh	-3.1	2	-0.1	4.9**
Maharashtra	6.9*	-0.7	1.4**	1.9
Manipur	6.4**	0.3	2.8	2.6*
Odisha	-1.4	4	-1.3	2.8
Punjab	18.5***	6.7***	2.5***	2.8***
Rajasthan	5	-1.9	6.0**	7.6**
Tamil Nadu	0.5	3.9**	-0.1	1.7
Tripura	4.3*	2.2**	-0.2	2.6***
Uttar Pradesh	1.6	5.7***	3.2***	1
West Bengal	0.8	6.8***	2.5***	0.2
All India	1.9	3.6***	2.0***	1.82**

Source: Author's calculation.

Notes: *** means significant at 1 per cent level, ** means significant at 5 per cent level, and * means significant at 10 per cent level.

Table 4 shows the growth in production of rice at state level from 1970–71 to 2011–12 across various states. There is large variation in the growth rates of production of rice across states. During period I, Punjab, Haryana, Maharashtra, Andhra Pradesh, Manipur, Rajasthan, and Tripura are states with high growth rates in production of rice. During period I, Punjab showed the highest growth rate of 18.3 per cent and it is significant at 1 per cent level followed by Haryana with 11.3 per cent growth rate and is significant at 1 per cent level. States such as Himachal Pradesh, Kerala, Madhya Pradesh, and Odisha show negative growth rate during period I. There is improvement in growth rate in period II in states such as Assam, Madhya Pradesh, Odisha, Tamil Nadu, Uttar Pradesh, and West Bengal. In West Bengal, CAGR of production of rice increased from 0.8 per cent in period I to 6.8 per cent in period II. The all India CAGR of production of rice also increased from 1.9 per cent in period I to 3.6 per cent in period II.

During period III, the all India level of CAGR of production of rice declined from 3.6 per cent in period II to 2 per cent in period III. At state level, there is improvement in growth rates in some states such as Gujarat, Haryana, Himachal Pradesh, Karnataka, Maharashtra, Manipur, and Rajasthan. However, in major states there is steep decline in CAGR of production of rice such as in Andhra Pradesh growth rate declined from 2.5 per cent during period II to 1.7 per cent in period III, in case of Punjab growth rate declined from 6.7 per cent in period II to 2.5 per cent in period III, in case of Uttar Pradesh growth rate declined from 5.7 per cent in period II to 3.2 per cent in period III, and in case of West Bengal growth rate declined from 6.8 per cent in period II to 2.5 per cent in period III. During period IV, at all India level there is further decline in CAGR of production of rice to 1.82 per cent. However, at state level there is much improvement in many states except Uttar Pradesh, Bihar, and West Bengal. In Uttar Pradesh, there is decline in CAGR from 3.2 per cent in period III to 1 per cent in period IV and in West Bengal growth rate declined from 2.5 per cent in period III to 0.2 per cent in period IV.

Table 5

State-wise Compound Annual Growth Rate in Yield of Rice from 1970–71 to 2011–12

States	*Period (I) 1970–71 to 1979–80*	*Period (II) 1980–81 to 1989–90*	*Period (III) 1990–91 to 1999–00*	*Period (IV) 2000–01 to 2011–12*
Andhra Pradesh	2.2**	2.0**	1.1*	1.0*
Assam	-0.9	0.6	1.0***	1.7**
Bihar	-0.2	3.9*	2.9	1.1
Gujarat	3.9	-0.6	2	0.7
Haryana	4.4*	-0.1	-1.6	1.2*
Himachal Pradesh	0.1	-0.4	1.9***	1.2
Jammu & Kashmir	1	-0.7	-1.3	1.7**
Karnataka	1.5	-0.1	1.9***	1.2
Kerala	0.6	1.2*	10.2**	-7.1***
Madhya Pradesh	-3.9	1.7	-0.8	5.3**
Maharashtra	5.2	-0.6	2.1***	1.9
Manipur	4.4*	1	2.4	-0.1
Odisha	-0.5	3.6	-1.4	3.4*
Punjab	5.4*	1.3	5.6	1.0**
Rajasthan	-0.8	1.3	-5.4	6.5***
Tamil Nadu	0.2	6.0***	-1.2	1.3
Tripura	4.0*	5.1	0.5	2.0***
Uttar Pradesh	0.1	5.6***	2.2***	0.9
West Bengal	0.8	5.6***	1.9***	0.9***
All India	1	3.2***	1.3***	1.82***

Source: Author's calculation.

Notes: *** means significant at 1 per cent level, ** means significant at 5 per cent level, and * means significant at 10 per cent level.

Table 5 shows the growth in yield of rice at state level from 1970–71 to 2011–12 across various states. There is large variation in the growth rates of yield of rice across states. During period I, the CAGR in yield of rice is positive in most of the states. During period I, Punjab, Maharashtra, Haryana, Manipur, Tripura, and Gujarat are the states with higher CAGR in yield of rice. During period II, there is increase in CAGR in yield of rice at all India level from 1 per cent in period I to 3.2 per cent in period II. However, at state level there is decline in growth rate in yield of rice in many states and improvement in some major rice-producing states such as Tamil Nadu, Uttar Pradesh, and West Bengal. During period III, there is decline in all India CAGR in yield of rice to 1.3 per cent. However, at state level there is decline in CAGR of yield of rice in some major states such as Andhra Pradesh, Uttar Pradesh, Haryana, Odisha, and West Bengal, while some states show improvement in CAGR during period III such as Kerala, Maharashtra, and Punjab. During period IV, there is some improvement in CAGR in yield of rice to 1.82 per cent. The CAGR in yield of rice during period IV is positive in all the states except Kerala and Manipur. However, in some important states such as Punjab, Uttar Pradesh, and West Bengal there is decline in CAGR in yield of rice.

Instability at National Level

Table 6 shows the instability in area, production, and yield of rice at all India level. Instability in area of rice increased from 3.1 to 4.8 from period I to period II, then it declined to 1.4 in period III and finally in the latest decade there is rise in instability in area of rice as it reached to five in period IV which is the highest value in all four decades. The instability in production of rice showed declining trend till period III. However, in the latest decade there is rise in instability from 4.7 in period III to 12.2 during period IV. The instability in yield of rice also showed declining trend till period III but during period IV there is rise in instability in yield of rice. The instability in production of rice increased from 4.7 in period III to 12.2 in period IV and instability in yield of paddy increased from 3.8 in period III to 8.2 in period IV. Analysis revealed that there was continuous decline in instability in first three periods in area, production, and yield while in the latest decade there was rise in instability in all three variables.

Table 6

Instability in Area, Production, and Yield of Rice in Different Periods at All India Level

Variables	*Period I 1970–71 to 1979–80*	*Period II 1980–81 to 1989–90*	*Period III 1990–91 to 1999–00*	*Period IV 2000–01 to 2011–12*
Area	3.1	4.8	1.4	5
Production	16.2	12.6	4.7	12.2
Yield	13.3	8.5	3.8	8.2

Source: Author's calculation.

Instability at State Level

Table 7 shows the instability in area of rice at state level from 1970–71 to 2011–12. There is large variation in area instability across states. During period I, Andhra Pradesh, Gujarat, Karnataka, Rajasthan, and Tamil Nadu were the states with higher instability. During period II, area instability was higher in states such as Andhra Pradesh Gujarat, Haryana, Rajasthan, and Tamil Nadu (Anoopkumar, 2014; Das, 1978; Deshpande, 1982). During period III, instability was high in states such as Andhra Pradesh, Rajasthan, and Tamil Nadu. During period IV, Andhra Pradesh, Bihar, Karnataka, Rajasthan, Tamil Nadu, and Uttar Pradesh were the states with high value of instability. There was overall decline in instability in states such as Gujarat, Haryana, Maharashtra, Odisha, Punjab, and Tripura when compared to period I and period IV. While at all India level there is rise in area instability from period I to period II, decline in area instability from period II to period III and there is rise area instability from period III to period IV. Similarly, at state level there is increase in instability from period I to period II in most of the states, decline in area instability from period II to period III and rise in instability from period III to period IV.

Table 7

State-wise Instability in Area of Rice from 1970–71 to 2011–12

States	*Period (I) 1970–71 to 1979–80*	*Period (II) 1980–81 to 1989–90*	*Period (III) 1990–91 to 1999–00*	*Period (IV) 2000–01 to 2011–12*
Andhra Pradesh	10.5	12.9	10.9	19.1
Assam	3.9	4	3.5	5
Bihar	7	7.7	5.2	13.6
Gujarat	12.6	22.1	7.3	8.1
Haryana	7.9	14.9	6.2	6.6
Himachal Pradesh	6.3	7.1	2.8	1.5
Jammu & Kashmir	3.5	2.2	3.6	4.2
Karnataka	11	8.8	4.5	11
Kerala	2	3.4	3.9	4.9
Madhya Pradesh	1.4	1.6	1.3	2.8
Maharashtra	4.2	5.9	1.5	2.2
Manipur	7.3	4.6	5.8	9
Odisha	5	4.5	2.3	3
Punjab	7.6	4.9	4.3	2.5
Rajasthan	9.9	25.4	9.5	20.2
Tamil Nadu	12	14.6	8.2	14.6
Tripura	6.2	5.9	7.1	4.1
Uttar Pradesh	5.3	7.4	2.7	9.6
West Bengal	5.4	5	2.5	6.6
All India	3.1	4.8	1.4	5

Source: Author's calculation.

Table 8

State-wise Instability in Production of Rice from 1970–71 to 2011–12

States	*Period (I) 1970–71 to 1979–80*	*Period (II) 1980–81 to 1989–90*	*Period (III) 1990–91 to 1999–00*	*Period (IV) 2000–01 to 2011–12*
Andhra Pradesh	18.9	18.7	16.4	22.5
Assam	10	13.1	6.2	11.1
Bihar	19.4	27.3	43.5	42.9
Gujarat	81.6	53.7	11.6	41.3
Haryana	26.4	18.5	12.7	7.6
Himachal Pradesh	25.2	24.6	6.3	20.4
Jammu & Kashmir	19.8	16.8	19.1	7.9
Karnataka	24.2	16.6	6.6	27.5
Kerala	5.4	5.8	70.8	11.4
Madhya Pradesh	38.7	22.1	14.9	39.7
Maharashtra	40.5	23.3	7	25.8
Manipur	18.2	17.5	22.8	19
Odisha	28.4	30.9	22.1	37
Punjab	13.2	12.4	6.9	4.4
Rajasthan	50.6	73.4	26.8	44.4
Tamil Nadu	24.5	22.2	60.1	28.3
Tripura	29.4	9.5	33.2	7.6
Uttar Pradesh	32.7	15.6	7.8	19.1
West Bengal	13.2	20.2	5.3	8.3
All India	16.2	12.6	4.7	12.2

Source: Author's calculation.

Table 8 shows the instability in production of rice from 1970–71 to 2011–12 across various states. There is considerable variation in production instability of rice at state level. It can be seen from the table that instability in production of rice is higher in most of the states as compared to instability in area of paddy during all the four periods under study. During period I, all India instability in production of paddy was 16.2. Most of the states have instability in production higher than all India level. States such as Gujarat, Rajasthan, Maharashtra, Madhya Pradesh, and Uttar Pradesh are most instable states during period I. During period II, there is decline in all India instability in production of rice from 16.2 in period I to 12.6 in period II. During period II, states such as Rajasthan, Gujarat, Odisha, Bihar, and Himachal Pradesh are the most instable states. There is decline in value of instability at state level during period II as compared to period I in most of the states. However, in Assam, Bihar, Kerala, Odisha, Rajasthan, and West Bengal there is rise in instability in period II as compared to period I. During period III, there is fall in instability at all India level from 12.6 in period II to 4.7 in period III. Similarly, at state level also there is decline in instability during period III as compared to period II in most of the states. However, in some states such as Bihar, Jammu & Kashmir, Kerala, Manipur, Tamil Nadu, and Tripura there is rise in instability in period III as compared to period II. During period III, most instable states were Kerala, Bihar, Tamil Nadu, and Tripura. During period IV, instability in production rose from 4.7 in period III to 12.2 at all India level. There is also rise in instability at state level as most of the states show higher instability in period IV as compared to period III. The states with higher instability in production during period IV are Rajasthan, Bihar, Gujarat, Madhya Pradesh, and Odisha.

Table 9 shows the instability in yield of rice from 1970–71 to 2011–12. There is a large variation in instability of rice across states. During period I, instability is higher in states such as Gujarat, Rajasthan, Madhya Pradesh, Maharashtra, Tripura, Odisha, and Haryana. During period II, there is decline in instability in yield at all India level from 13.3 in period I to 8.5 in period II. At state level also, there is decline in instability in period II as compared to period I in most of the states, for example, in Gujarat instability has declined from 69.8 in period I to 35.9 in period II. The most instable states in yield during period II are

Table 9

State-wise Instability in Yield of Rice from 1970–71 to 2011–12

States	*Period I 1970–71 to 1979–80*	*Period II 1980–81 to 1989–90*	*Period III 1990–91 to 1999–00*	*Period IV 2000–01 to 2011–12*
Andhra Pradesh	11.9	10	7.1	8
Assam	7.4	9.8	3.4	6.5
Bihar	15.9	21.2	41.5	36.7
Gujarat	69.8	35.9	17.9	8.3
Haryana	23.1	8.9	15.6	8.8
Himachal Pradesh	20.9	21.6	5.6	21.5
Jammu & Kashmir	19.9	16.6	17.6	6.2
Karnataka	14.9	8.4	3.9	20.1
Kerala	4.9	3	43.4	25.1
Madhya Pradesh	38	21.5	15.2	38.1
Maharashtra	37.3	20	7.3	25
Manipur	12.8	15.8	19.9	11.6
Odisha	25	26.7	20.8	34.4
Punjab	11.9	10.2	60.7	3.4
Rajasthan	44.4	50.3	73.1	30.9
Tamil Nadu	13.6	11.4	60.6	18.5
Tripura	27.1	41.9	36.1	5.3
Uttar Pradesh	29.2	9.8	7.6	11.2
West Bengal	11.4	16.7	6.4	3.4
All India	13.3	8.5	3.8	8.9

Source: Author's calculation.

Rajasthan, Tripura, Gujarat, Odisha, and Madhya Pradesh. During period III, there is further decline in instability at all India level from 8.5 in period II to 3.8 in period III. At state level also, there is fall in instability in most of the states but in some states there is rise in instability. During period III, states such as Bihar, Haryana, Jammu & Kashmir, Kerala, Manipur, Rajasthan, and Tamil Nadu show rise in instability. During period IV, there is rise in instability in yield at all India level from 3.8 in period III to 8.9 in period IV.

States such as Madhya Pradesh, Bihar, Odisha, Rajasthan, Maharashtra, and Kerala are most in stile states in yield during period IV. However, at state level there is rise in stability in 8 states out of 19 states under study. It is found that in some major rice-producing states, such as Andhra Pradesh, Haryana, Punjab, Uttar Pradesh, and West Bengal, the value of instability is low as compared to other states during period IV.

State-wise Cropped Area and Input Use in Rice Cultivation

Table 10 shows the percentage of gross cropped area across states. There is large variation in gross cropped area across states. In some states, there is increase in

Table 10

State-wise Percentage of Gross Cropped Area of Rice (in Thousand Hectares)

States	*TE 1992–93*	*TE 2004–05*	*TE 2011–12*
Andhra Pradesh	29.58	24.38	30.09
Assam	65.52	63.01	61.15
Bihar	50.04	41.08	42.33
Gujarat	5.31	4.09	6.38
Haryana	11.56	15.65	19.05
Himachal Pradesh	8.51	8.61	8.19
Jammu & Kashmir	25.51	22.73	22.74
Karnataka	10.28	9.88	11.69
Kerala	18.03	9.95	8.21
Madhya Pradesh	21.77	8.65	7.14
Maharashtra	7.44	6.83	6.68
Manipur	80.54	71.66	63.95
Odisha	46.47	52.55	79.2
Punjab	27.3	32.92	35.71
Rajasthan	0.7	0.51	0.58
Tamil Nadu	29.78	29.19	32.85
Tripura	57.11	80.42	78.6
Uttar Pradesh	21.6	21.93	21.81
West Bengal	66.59	61.04	57.76
All India	–	22.59	22.12

Source: Computed from Government of India various issues.

percentage of gross cropped area while in others there is decline in gross cropped area of rice. There is slight decline in gross cropped area under rice at all India level. In states such as Bihar, Kerala, Madhya Pradesh, Manipur, and West Bengal, there is decline in percentage of gross cropped area of rice from TE 1992–93 to TE 2011–12. On the other hand, states, such as Andhra Pradesh, Haryana, Odisha, Punjab, Tamil Nadu, and Tripura, show that there is increase in percentage of gross cropped area of rice. In Tripura, Assam, and Manipur, the percentage of gross cropped area is high during 2011–12, which proves the effort of the government towards shifting rice cultivation in eastern states. The other states in which gross cropped area of rice is high during 2011–12 are Odisha, West Bengal, Bihar, Punjab, Tamil Nadu, and Andhra Pradesh.

Table 11

State-wise Percentage of Irrigated Area to Total Cropped Area of Rice

States	*2003–04*	*2004–05*	*2005–06*	*2006–07*	*2007–08*	*2008–09*	*2009–10*	*2010–11*	*2011–12*	*2012–13*
Andhra Pradesh	38.66	39.83	44.88	47.38	46.32	48.74	45.89	49.29	49.31	45.92
Assam	4.38	4.39	3.59	3.77	3.7	7.29	5.49	4.09	3.91	3.82
Bihar	57.94	56.72	58.47	60.19	60.85	61.16	60.76	61.83	67.45	68.49
Chhattisgarh	20.66	22.96	23.94	25.92	26.48	27.05	26.74	28.29	29.09	30.31
Goa	23.74	23.73	22.23	21.9	23.19	21.99	23.47	22.75	24.99	22.37
Gujarat	36	38.02	41.45	44.71	45.95	45.57	44.37	45.82	48.18	46.93
Haryana	83.64	84.58	83.74	85.4	85.99	85.25	87.31	85.22	87.53	88.96
Himachal Pradesh	18.84	19.21	19.67	19.78	20.19	20.29	19.76	20.56	20.59	20.62
Jammu & Kashmir	40.46	41.11	41.62	40.73	40.85	41.45	41.91	42.02	41.34	41.95
Jharkhand	10.28	9.93	9.37	8.71	9.39	9.69	11.07	12	11.33	14.16
Karnataka	23.6	25.98	27.88	28.96	29.39	31.87	31.82	32.76	34.3	34.11
Kerala	14.38	15.2	15.41	16.8	16.49	17	17.06	17.65	20.49	17.67
Madhya Pradesh	29.19	30.65	29.98	32.53	32.17	32.5	33.45	33.66	36.54	38.76
Maharashtra	18.42	17.84	17.93	18.77	19.26	19.27	19.25	19.4	18.92	18.48
Manipur	18.39	22.73	22.72	22.72	21.7	21.9	22.3	20.98	18.83	15.7
Meghalaya	30.26	27.93	24.93	29.23	25.75	21.5	21.94	21.98	23.59	36.75
Mizoram	18.36	19.23	19.28	12.47	9.99	11.79	8.43	10.05	13.52	12.62
Nagaland	28.06	27.48	27.44	26.2	29.11	20.46	17.57	20.24	19.4	18.92
Odisha	29.16	30.86	33.56	35.77	36.7	35.03	29.29	28.35	28.95	29.51
Punjab	97.66	97.12	97.61	97.52	97.71	97.63	97.95	97.99	98.31	98.39
Rajasthan	29.51	33.68	36.03	36.96	36.42	34.74	33.61	32	36.33	39.47
Sikkim	9.41	9.24	15.12	15.12	14.64	15.4	13.66	13.22	13.7	13.55
Tamil Nadu	46.62	52.42	56.3	56.64	55.92	58.26	58.12	58.19	59.75	58.2
Tripura	38.18	38.22	36.03	36.22	36.47	36.64	36.62	35.02	34.9	34.88
Uttarakhand	44.76	44.5	45.32	45.79	46.7	47.75	48.58	48.02	49.02	49.26
Uttar Pradesh	72.86	74.2	74.96	75.62	75.6	77	76.08	76.62	76.72	78.2
West Bengal	55.76	56.06	57.7	57.93	58.14	57.66	57.97	58.81	58.13	63.08
All India	41.15	42.43	43.73	45.09	45.11	45.51	45.02	44.99	46.89	47.62

Source: Computed from Government of India various issues.

In Andhra Pradesh, the share of irrigated area to total cropped area of rice has showed by and large increasing trend. Punjab, Haryana, Uttar Pradesh, and West Bengal are the top most states with highest percentage of irrigated area to total cropped area during 2012–13 (Table 11). There is much increase in percentage of irrigated area to total cropped area in states such as Bihar and Tamil Nadu. In case of Bihar, it increased from 57.94 per cent in 2003–04 to 68.94 per cent in 2012–13; and in Tamil Nadu, it increased from 46.62 per cent in 2003–04 to 58.20 per cent in 2012–13. In case of Maharashtra, share of irrigated area to total cropped area was just 18.48 per cent in 2012–13, which was much below the national average of 47.62 per cent. In north-eastern states, the percentage of irrigated area to total cropped area was very low and there was a decline in states such as Manipur, Mizoram, Nagaland, and Tripura. At all India level, proportion of irrigated area to total cropped area increased from 41.15 per cent in 2003–04 to 47.62 per cent in 2012–13. At state level except north-eastern states, there was increase in percentage of irrigated area to total cropped area but still there are many states which are lacking in providing adequate irrigation facilities to farmers.

Table 12

State-wise Input Use in Paddy Cultivation in India

State/Year	*Seeds (Kg)*			*Fertiliser (Kg Nutrients)*			*Manure (Qtls.)*		
	2000–01	*2005–06*	*2013–14*	*2000–01*	*2005–06*	*2013–14*	*2000–01*	*2005–06*	*2013–14*
Andhra Pradesh	86.1	77.2	73.9	189.46	201.35	239.24	35.58	16.69	15.77
Assam	64.81	65.05	58.02	12.03	9.78	16.66	4.5	3.77	5.17
Bihar	63.22	53.47	46.31	75.36	84.84	98.92	1.29	1.22	0
Chhattisgarh	–	103.6	84.46	–	85.39	122.5	–	7.78	8.46
Gujarat	–	14.94	10.55	–	143.4	153.6	–	19.22	16.83
Haryana	0	0	0	197.7	229.4	207.8	3.07	3.62	0.07
Himachal Pradesh	–	98.4	91.6	–	43.0	19.7	–	25.7	6.0
Jharkhand	–	55.29	50.84	–	39.51	50	–	0.95	6.07
Karnataka	88.8	74.8	65.5	222.1	263.6	260.6	20.37	13.53	12.3
Kerala	0	0	0	106.5	127.2	176.2	28.33	17.76	10.16
Madhya Pradesh	98.4	91.95	66.84	50.71	50.2	105.6	20.24	17.04	7.54
Maharashtra	–	88.45	57.64	–	117.6	143.4	–	22.86	10.19
Odisha	104.9	91.86	89.13	81.18	83.88	78.59	25.2	25.41	21.13
Punjab	0	0	0	171.3	191.6	209.1	19.62	35.26	24.08
Tamil Nadu	–	0	0	220.2	224.2	240.1	32.76	30.24	37.15
Uttar Pradesh	0	0	0	110.0	129.6	156.8	9.46	8.42	0.91
Uttarakhand	–	0	0	–	79.35	115.6	–	67.03	10.86
West Bengal	71.59	71.27	63.36	95.81	94.03	132.3	30.91	23.36	25.1

Source: Computed from Government of India (cost of cultivation data various issues).

Table 12 shows that there is continuous decline in seeds (kg) and manure (quintals) in most of the states and there is continuous increase in fertiliser (kg nutrients) use in most of the states. However, there is large variation in input use across states. In Haryana, Kerala, Punjab, Tamil Nadu, Uttar Pradesh, and Uttarakhand seeds are not used in paddy cultivation. During 2013–14, there was high use of seeds in states such as Himachal Pradesh, Odisha, Chhattisgarh, and Andhra Pradesh. There is also large variation in fertiliser use across states. In Assam, Himachal Pradesh, and Jharkhand, the use of fertiliser is below 50 kg nutrients during 2013–14. The use of manure is below 20 kg in most of the states during 2013–14. In states such as Assam, Bihar, Chhattisgarh, Haryana, Himachal Pradesh, Jharkhand, and Uttar Pradesh, the use of manure is less than 10 kg during 2013–14.

Instability in Prices

Table 13

Instability in Wholesale Prices of Paddy from 1990–91 to 2016–17

States	*1990–91 to 1999–00*	*2000–01 to 2016–17*
Andhra Pradesh	7.9	33.4
Assam	13.7	10.3
Bihar	9.3	8.6
Gujarat	19	25
Haryana	42.1	31.8
Himachal Pradesh	13.2	24.8
Karnataka	13	19
Kerala	20.6	28.1
Madhya Pradesh	21.2	31.2
Maharashtra	8.1	22.1
Manipur	5.1	22.8
Odisha	6.8	14.2
Punjab	24	46.6
Tamil Nadu	9.3	22.8
Tripura	21.4	24.8
Uttar Pradesh	6.9	16.9
West Bengal	7.5	19.2

Source: Author's calculation.

Table 13 shows the instability in wholesale prices of paddy from 1990–91 to 2016–17 across various states. There are large fluctuations in wholesale price of paddy across states. During the 1990s, instability in wholesale prices is higher in states such as Haryana, Punjab, Tripura, Madhya Pradesh, and Kerala. There is rise in instability in wholesale prices in latest period, that is, the 2000s as compared to the 1990s in most of the states except few states such as Assam,

Bihar, and Haryana. During the 2000s, in states such as Punjab, Andhra Pradesh, Haryana, Madhya Pradesh, Kerala, Gujarat, Himachal Pradesh, and Tripura instability in wholesale prices was considerably high.

Table 14

State-wise Instability in Farm Harvest Prices of Paddy from 1990–91 to 2011–12

States	*1990–91 to 1999–00*	*2000–01 to 2011–12*
Andhra Pradesh	7.6	11.3
Assam	12.3	5.2
Bihar	9.6	7.4
Gujarat	17.8	7.7
Haryana	51.9	39.7
Himachal Pradesh	14.5	9.1
Jammu & Kashmir	13.3	3.9
Karnataka	8.9	50.6
Kerala	10.3	10.7
Madhya Pradesh	19.9	18.4
Maharashtra	10.7	10.9
Manipur	11.2	14.2
Odisha	11	9.9
Punjab	14.6	27.5
Rajasthan	21.4	24.5
Tamil Nadu	11.4	11.7
Tripura	21.6	11.3
Uttar Pradesh	11.4	10.6
West Bengal	18.4	14.6

Source: Author's calculation.

Table 14 shows the instability in farm harvest prices of paddy from 1990–91 to 2011–12 across various states. It can be seen that there are large fluctuations in farm harvest prices of paddy at state level. The most instable states in farm harvest during the 1990s are Haryana, Tripura, Rajasthan, Madhya Pradesh, and West Bengal. There is fall in instability in farm harvest prices during the 2000s in most of the states as compare to the 1990s. The states which are most instable in farm harvest prices during the 2000s are Karnataka, Haryana, Punjab, Rajasthan, and Madhya Pradesh.

Figure 2 shows the farm harvest prices and wholesale prices of paddy at all India level from 1990 to 2012. It is clear that in most of the years, wholesale prices are above the farm harvest price, which shows that farmers are not getting remunerative prices for paddy and they were selling at distress. From the early 1990s to the 2000s, the gap between whole prices and farm harvest prices increased but in the recent decade this gap has declined. After 2010, both farm harvest price and wholesale prices become nearly equal.

Figure 2

Farm Harvest Price and Wholesale Prices of Paddy at All India Level (Current Price)

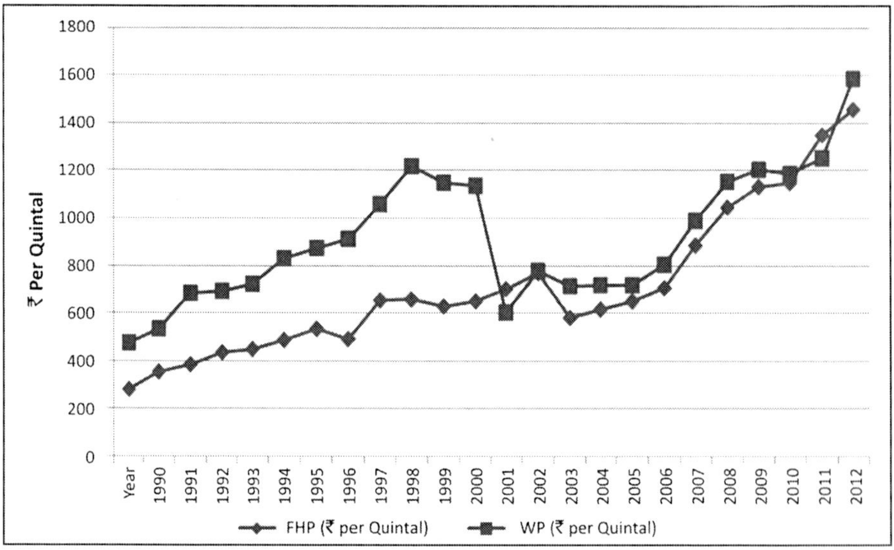

Source: Computed from Government of India various issues.

Table 15 shows the ratio of farm harvest prices to wholesale prices of paddy across states. When the value of this ratio is less than 1, it means there is distress sale by the farmers as farm harvest prices are the prices received by the farmer at the village site and when this ratio attains the value greater than 1 it means the cultivation of paddy is profitable to the farmers. From the analysis of this table, it can be concluded that during the 1990s in all the states except Haryana and Tripura the ratio of farm harvest prices to wholesale prices is less than 1 and many times the value of this ratio lies between 0.5 and 0.7. In case of Punjab, the value of this ratio is 0.1 and 0.2 during the 1990s, which is very low. This shows the pathetic condition of the farmers in Punjab during the 1990s as there was distress sale during the 1990s. In Andhra Pradesh, Uttar Pradesh, and West Bengal the ratio lies between 0.5 and 0.6, which is also very low and demonstrates the distress sale by the farmers in these states during the 1990s.

During the 2000s, the situation of the farmers has improved in many states as the ratio of farm harvest price to wholesale price has improved. In Andhra Pradesh, there was distress sale till 2005–06 but after 2005–06 the ratio lies between 0.9 and 1.2. In states such as Assam, Bihar, Karnataka, and Manipur, there is improvement in ratio but paddy cultivation is still not profitable as in most of the years the ratio attains the value between 0.7 and 0.9. In case of Punjab, there is improvement in the ratio of farm harvest price to wholesale price as compared to the 1990s but still farmers are selling in distress in many years. It is only during 2003–04, 2005–06, 2006–07, and 2009–10, the ratio attains the value greater than 1 in Punjab when cultivation of paddy was profitable for the farmers. In Uttar Pradesh and West Bengal, there is much

Table 15

Ratio of Farm Harvest Prices to Wholesale Prices of Paddy in Different Years

State	1990-91	1991-92	1992-93	1993-94	1994-95	1995-96	1996-97	1997-98	1998-99	1999-00	2000-01	2001-02	2002-03	2003-04	2004-05	2005-06	2006-07	2007-08	2008-09	2009-10	2010-11	2011-12	2012-13	2013-14
Andhra Pradesh	0.6	0.6	0.5	0.5	0.5	0.5	0.5	0.5	0.6	0.5	0.5	0.5	–	0.9	0.4	0.9	0.9	1.1	1.2	1.2	1	1	1.2	1.1
Assam	0.7	0.9	0.6	0.6	0.7	0.7	0.6	0.6	0.7	0.6	0.5	0.5	–	0.9	1.1	0.9	–	0.9	0.9	0.9	0.9	1	1	0.8
Bihar	0.5	0.6	0.5	0.5	0.6	0.5	0.5	0.5	0.6	0.5	0.4	0.5	–	0.8	0.9	0.8	0.9	0.9	0.9	–	–	–	0.8	0.8
Gujarat	0.6	0.9	0.7	0.6	0.6	0.7	0.7	0.8	0.7	0.5	0.5	0.5	1.2	1.1	1	0.9	1	1.1	1	1	1	1	1.1	1
Haryana	1.4	1.6	1.8	2.6	1.5	0.7	1	1.2	3	0.9	0.9	1.5	1.6	0.8	0.9	0.9	–	–	–	–	1.2	0.8	1.5	1.3
Himachal Pradesh	0.6	0.7	0.6	0.8	0.7	0.6	0.6	0.6	0.6	0.6	0.7	0.5	–	–	–	–	–	–	–	–	–	–	–	–
Karnataka	0.5	0.6	0.5	0.5	0.6	0.6	0.5	0.5	0.5	0.4	0.4	0.5	1	2.6	0.7	0.7	0.8	0.9	0.9	0.8	0.9	0.9	1	0.7
Kerala	0.7	0.8	0.8	0.6	1	0.8	0.9	0.8	0.7	0.6	0.5	0.5	–	0.4	0.5	–	0.9	0.6	1.1	1.1	1	1	1.1	0.9
Madhya Pradesh	0.5	0.6	0.4	0.5	0.4	0.4	0.7	0.5	0.6	0.5	0.6	0.5	1.5	1.2	0.9	0.9	0.9	1.1	0.9	1.1	0.9	1.1	1.2	0.9
Maharashtra	0.6	0.8	0.6	0.6	0.6	0.6	0.6	0.5	0.6	0.5	0.6	0.6	0.9	0.7	0.9	–	–	–	0.8	0.8	0.9	1.3	1	0.8
Manipur	0.5	0.5	–	–	0.5	0.5	0.5	0.4	0.6	0.6	0.4	0.4	0.9	0.7	0.9	0.8	0.7	0.8	–	–	0.7	0.6	0.7	0.9
Odisha	–	–	–	–	–	–	–	–	0.5	0.5	0.4	0.5	0.8	0.8	0.9	0.9	0.8	1.1	1	1	1	1	1	1
Punjab	0.2	0.2	0.1	0.2	0.2	0.2	0.2	0.1	0.1	0.1	0.2	0.3	1.6	1.4	–	1.3	1.3	0.7	0.8	1.1	0.7	0.7	0.8	0.5
Tamil Nadu	0.6	0.5	0.6	0.7	0.6	0.5	0.5	0.5	0.5	0.4	0.4	0.4	0.9	0.8	0.8	0.7	0.8	1	1	0.9	0.9	1	1.1	1
Tripura	1.3	1.1	1	1.1	1.1	1	1.1	0.9	0.5	0.9	–	1.1	–	1.4	–	0.7	0.7	1	–	–	0.8	1	1.3	1.1
Uttar Pradesh	0.5	0.6	0.5	0.6	0.5	0.5	0.5	0.5	0.6	0.5	0.5	0.5	0.9	0.9	0.9	1	1	0.9	1	1.1	0.8	1	1	0.8
West Bengal	0.6	0.6	0.5	0.6	0.5	0.6	0.6	0.5	0.7	0.5	0.5	0.5	0.8	0.9	0.9	0.9	0.9	0.7	0.9	1.1	0.9	0.9	1.1	1.1

Source: Computed from Government of India various issues.

improvement in the situation of the farmers after 2002–03 as the ratio attains the value between 0.8 and 1.1 after 2002–03. Therefore, it can be inferred that there is much improvement in reduction of distress sale by the farmers during last five years in most of the states.

Conclusions and Policy Implications

At all India level compound annual growth rate of area, production, and yield of rice were positive but it had been declining gradually over the periods. There is further decline in compound annual growth rate of area, production, and yield of rice after economic reforms took place. The instability in area at all India level increased from period I to period II, decreased from period II to period III and then again increased from period III to period IV. The instability in case of production and yield at all India level decreased from period I to period II, decreased from period II to period III, and then increased from period III to period IV. This shows that there is no positive association between growth rate and instability as after reform period growth rate of area, production, and yield declined while instability in area, production, and yield increased. The rise in instability can be due to various factors such as low percentage of irrigated area to total cropped area, decline in use of seeds and manure, and other inputs necessary for agriculture. There is increase in instability in wholesale prices of paddy across various states from 1990–91 to 2016–17. The most unstable states in wholesale prices during the 2000s were Punjab, Andhra Pradesh, Haryana, Madhya Pradesh, Kerala, Gujarat, Himachal, and Tripura. However, in case of farm harvest prices there is decline in instability in most of the states after reforms took place. The states that are most instable in farm harvest prices during the 2000s were Karnataka, Haryana, Punjab, Rajasthan, and Madhya Pradesh. Therefore, there are differences in instability in wholesale prices and farm harvest prices as instability in the latest period, that is, after the 2000s increased in case of wholesale prices and declined in case of farm harvest prices. The ratio of farm harvest price to wholesale price has improved in many states after 2005 onwards, which shows that during last five years the distress sale by farmers has reduced in many states. The instability in area, production, and yield of rice can be reduced by providing adequate agricultural inputs to all the farmers including marginal and small farmers. Therefore, there should be more emphasis on certified and High Yielding Variety (HYV) seeds, expansion on expansion of area under irrigation by using watershed development and promoting water saving practices. In addition, there should be emphasis on development of crop varieties resistant to insects and pests and there is need to fight climate change with the adoption of climate resilient crops.

References

Anoopkumar, M., (2014.): Intra Year Price Instability of Commercial Crops in India: Exploring the Underlying Dynamism, *International Journal of Food and Agricultural Economics*, Vol. 2, No. 1, pp. 145–156.

Chand, Ramesh and Raju, S.S., (2008): Instability in Indian Agriculture, NPP Discussion Paper 01/2008, National Centre for Agricultural Economics and Policy (NCAP) Research Pusa, New Delhi.

——, (2009): Instability in Indian Agriculture During Different Phases of Technology and Policy, *Indian Journal of Agricultural Economics*, Vol. 64, No. 2, pp. 189–207.

Das, P.S., (1978): Growth and Instability in Crop Output in Eastern India, *Economic & Political Weekly*, Vol. 13, No. 41, pp. 1741–1748.

Deshpande, M.V., (1982): Agricultural Growth, Instability in Productivity and Rainfall: Case of Karnataka, *Economic & Political Weekly*, Vol. 17, No. 52, pp. A127–A134.

Dev, S. Mahendra, (1987): Growth and Instability in Foodgrains Production: An Inter-State Analysis, *Economic & Political Weekly*, Vol. 22, No. 39, pp. A82–A92.

Dev, S. Mahendra and Pandey, Vijay Lakshmi, (2012): Performance and Key Policy Issues of Indian Agriculture, in S. Mahendra Dev (eds), *India Development Report 2012–13*, Oxford University Press, New Delhi, pp. 107–122.

Hazell, P.B., (1982): *Instability in Indian Foodgrain Production.* IFPRI.

Mehra, S., (1981): *Instability in Indian Agriculture in the Coontext of New Technology.* IFPRI.

Ray, S.K., (1983): An Empirical Investigation of the Nature and Causes for Growth and Instability in Indian Agriculture: 1950–80, *Indian Journal of Agricultural Economics*, Vol. 38 , No. 4, October–December, pp. 459–474.

15 Two-Tier Approach to Prioritise Climate Smart Agriculture in Madhya Pradesh

Barun Deb Pal, Parmod Kumar and P.K. Joshi

Introduction

The agriculture sector in India is heterogeneous in terms of its bio-physical characteristics, natural resource supply, and socio-economic conditions of the farmers across various states. Therefore, climate smart technologies and their feasibility will vary across regions. Hence, identifying feasible climate smart technologies for different regions and region-specific prioritisation will be a logical step to achieve climate smart agriculture (CSA) in India (FAO, 2010). The main aim of this paper is to assess farmers' preference on feasible climate smart technologies for the state of Madhya Pradesh. This study first explores the technical and economic feasibility of various climate smart technologies across selected four districts of the state of Madhya Pradesh. Farmers' preferences about various climate smart technologies are assessed using stated preference method after providing detail training to the selected farmers within the selected districts. Results of this assessment reveal that the highly preferred technologies by the farmers are not necessarily highly feasible. Rather farmers prefer the technology which is input saving even if productivity does not increase much as compared to their current practises. Such behaviour of farmers is corroborated by the fact that farmland in Madhya Pradesh is by and large rainfed and availability of agricultural machinery is concentrated among large farmers. Nevertheless, the adoption of highly feasible technologies requires assured supply of inputs like water, energy, and machines, which are poor in supply in the state. Despite the above fact, it is to be noted that farmers are interested to replace their traditional cultivation practises with climate smart practises although less feasible with the priority of input cost saving. Summing up, this study fills the gap between scientific knowledge about the agricultural smart technologies, their technical feasibility across various regions, and farmers' preference in adoption of those technologies (Taneja et al, 2014).

Causes of Low Productivity: Climate Dependency and Climate Change Impacts

Almost half of the agriculture land in Madhya Pradesh is still rainfed as only 39 per cent of gross cropped areas are irrigated (GoMP, 2015). Therefore, crop cultivation in this state is highly dependent on climatic condition and hence climate change is one of the key factors behind the low productivity of this state. Rise in minimum temperature, variability in rainfall, frost and frequent drought events are major climate-related factors directly affecting productivity of crops irrespective of the season. Analysis in the literature shows that an increase in surface temperature by three per cent will reduce yield of soybean and wheat by 20–30 per cent. It is also observed from the fact that, due to excess rainfall the yield of soybean has been fallen by 10 per cent in the year 2013 as compared to 2012. On the other hand, the vulnerability atlas prepared by CRIDA, Government of India, has identified almost 26 districts (i.e. 50%) as vulnerable (high and very high) due to climate change impact (GoI, 2014, 2015).

Government's Strategies to Cope with Climate Change Impact

Table 1 shows that the Government of MP has taken several policies to conserve necessary resources like water, soil, and fertiliser to cope with the climate change impact and achieve sustainable agricultural development for the state. However, these initiatives are still at nascent stage and focus is given on strategic planning at the regional level. As a part of this strategic planning, the state action plan on climate change has been drafted and district contingency plans have also been prepared with the objective of capacity building among the stake holders to develop feasible policies for climate change adaptation and prioritise them at the regional level to achieve climate resilient agriculture at this state.

Table 1

Important Strategies Adopted by the Government in Madhya Pradesh

Strategies	*Policies/Programmes/Projects*	*Key Objectives*
Adoption of improved cultivation techniques and resource conservation	District contingency plan prepared under NICRA project	Suggest farmers about change in sowing dates, crop establishment method, resource management, seed replacement and treatment, and choice of crops and variety of seeds
Capacity building of policy makers	State action plan for climate change (SAPCC)	Understand long-term impact of climate change, capacity building of the stakeholders to design policies
	Vulnerability Assessment (MoEF) and Vulnerability Atlas (CRIDA)	Understand climate change exposure at district level and their adaptive capacity

Cont'd...

Strategies	*Policies/Programmes/Projects*	*Key Objectives*
Irrigation intensification	Irrigation development projects	Lining canal to bring rainfed area under irrigated
	Micro and minor irrigation	Subsidy on sprinkler and drip irrigation to increase water use efficiency
	Installation of tube well	Subsidy on cost of installation to increase irrigation facilities
	Balaram Tank Yojana	Rain water harvesting for better irrigation facility and groundwater recharge
Soil conservation	Integrated nutrient and pest management	Balancing fertiliser use to improve productivity and soil fertility
	Soil-testing laboratories	To fulfil nutrient deficiencies in the soil
Weather advisories	Information and communication technologies for weather forecasting and farm management	Prior information about rainfall and required management practises through mobile SMS
Extension	Field level demonstration of modern agriculture implements	Broad bed furrow for moister conservation and rain-water management
		Ridge and furrow method for rain-water management and moister conservation
		Zero tillage for moister and nutrient management
		Systems of root intensification to increase input use efficiencies

Understanding the Steps to Identify the Gaps in Implementing CSA

Steps involved in achieving CSA as described in Figure 1 start from innovation and end at implementation. However, these steps are not unique for CSA alone but they are general process of transforming agriculture enabling farmers for adjustment from one situation to another. As described in the figure, innovation is the primary stage in the process, which includes any innovative idea or technology or practise to reach to the final destination. However, in agriculture sector all innovative ideas or technologies may not be feasible for every location and hence, one has to identify the most feasible technology, idea, or practise. The identification mentioned in this process possesses two relevant questions – First, whether the innovative technologies are technically feasible? Second, even if they are feasible technically will there be economic benefit to the beneficiaries?

To answer first question, one has to understand regional heterogeneity in terms of bio-physical characteristics and map them with the bio-physical characteristics necessary in adoption of any new technology. On the other hand, there

Figure 1

Gap in Steps to Achieve Climate Smart Agriculture

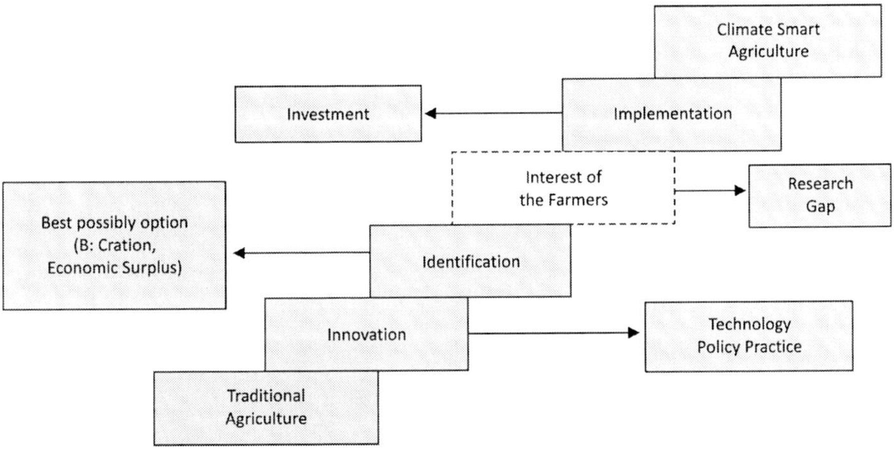

are several studies available to answer the second question. These studies have described various methods like assess benefit cost ratio and estimate economic surplus for each innovative intervention and describe their implication to the society as a whole. Therefore, if a new technology is technically feasible and will have positive impact to the society it can be identified for implementation. So far, majority of the government policies and projects were conceived and implemented by considering their feasibility and implication to the society. However, less number of attempts are made to understand interest of the beneficiaries to adopt any new technology or policy for their development. Hence, there is a major gap in the process of transformation. Hence, to achieve climate smart agriculture by increasing adoption of climate smart practises, interest of farmers must be included in the process of implementation and transformation. In this context, aim of this study is not only to understand technical and economic feasibility of the climate smart agriculture, instead it focuses on assessing farmers' interest in adoption of climate smart agriculture practises and upscale them at the regional level. Therefore, incorporation of farmers' interest in the steps to achieve CSA is a unique contribution of this study.

Approach and Methodology

As most technologies are at demonstration level and only a few are being adopted, we have followed an ex-ante assessment approach to assess preference about the climate smart practises among the randomly selected farmers in various regions of Madhya Pradesh. Again, according to the vulnerability atlas of Madhya Pradesh, rising minimum temperature is common climate change phenomena across districts and selected districts are not exception to this. Keeping this issue in mind, we have categorised the selected four districts as described in Figure 2.

Figure 2

Heterogeneous Profile of the Districts Under Common Climate Change Exposure

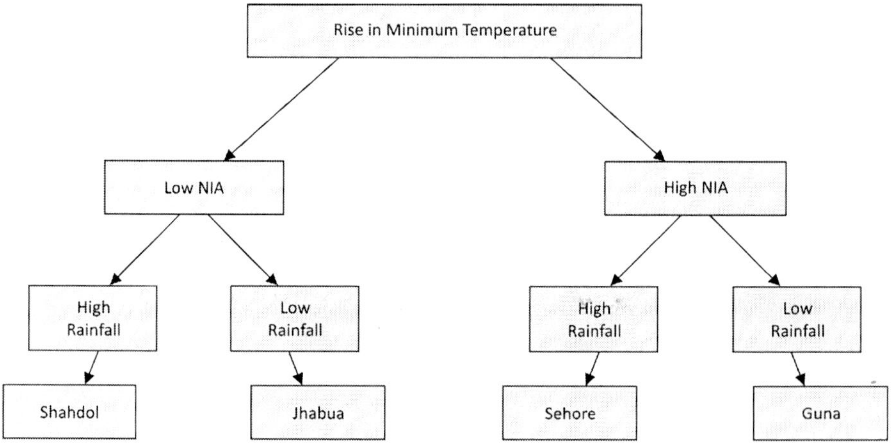

Selected Crops

Table 2

Selected Crops from Each Districts

Districts	*Cropping System*	*Selected Crops*	*Per cent in GCA*
Sehore	Kharif soybean and rabi wheat zone	Soybean	52.1
		Wheat	36.5
		Gram	9.3
Jhabua	Kharif soybean and rabi wheat zone	Soybean	43.7
		Wheat	37.9
		Gram	5.6
Guna	Rabi wheat and kharif soybean and rice zone	Rice	18
		Soybean	33.4
		Wheat	38.8
		Gram	5.5
Shahdol	Kharif rice and rabi wheat zone	Rice	56.2
		Wheat	25.3

Assessment of Farmers' Preference

While accessing the farmers' preference about the climate smart technology, we have followed the above-stated criteria. The sample size of our training was 180 farmers from four districts namely Sehore, Guna, Jhabua, and Shahdol. We have selected three developmental blocks from each districts and one village form each block with taking the criteria of highest number of agricultural household existing block/village and from each village we have randomly selected 15 farmers

Figure 3

Assessment of Farmers Preference

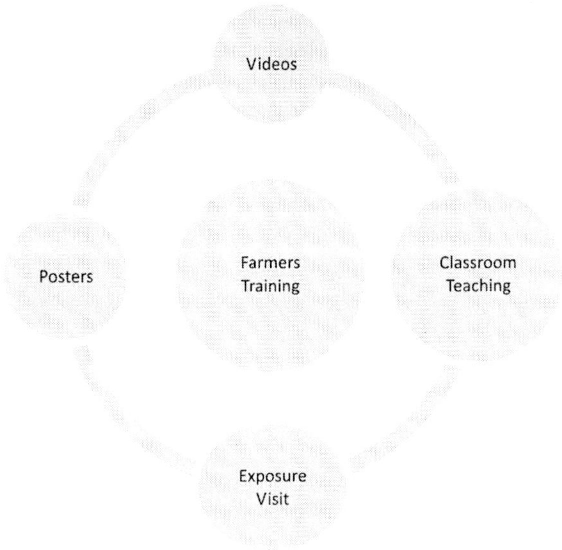

Figure 4

Location Map of Vulnerable Districts in Madhya Pradesh

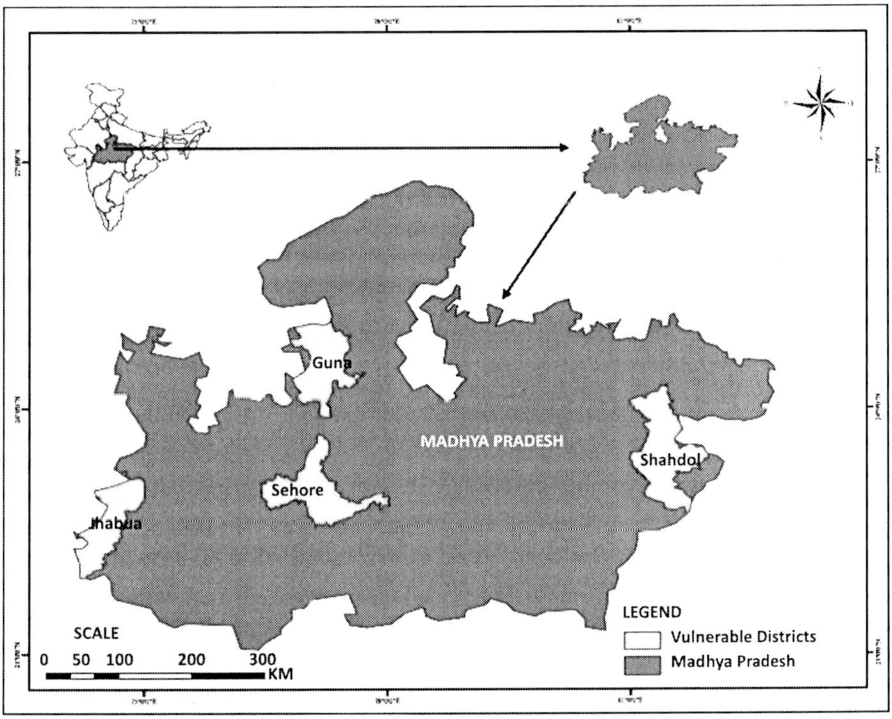

household for the training purpose. Through the farmers' training, we have tried to improve farmers' understanding and the awareness level about the economic and technology feasibility of climate smart technologies.

The farmers' training has been done in four phases: First, we have shown poster presentation to the farmers to give a basic idea of the feasible climate smart technologies in the region and also explained the basic characteristics of the technology. Second, we tried to apply the Information and Communication Technology (ICT) method where we have shown the videos of different technologies to the farmers where learning through video communication method has been adopted. Third, the two ways learning process has been applied through classroom teaching method, where the KVK's scientists have been involved and a rigorous discussion has been made with the farmers to understand their problems. Last, an exposure visit was conducted to the KVK's cafeteria crop zone to rigorously understand farmers' preferences for different crop options.

Through the above-stated criteria, we have tried to access the farmer's preference of technologies for different crops in different regions. The observed farmers' preferences of different crops in the selected districts are discussed in the following section.

Farmers' Preference and Scientific Feasibility of Climate Smart Technologies

Table 3 presented the comparative analysis of technologies between their scientific feasibility and level of farmers' preference. Using input-output data for technologies from the demonstration field, research stations, and KVKs, we have prepared a climate smart feasibility index for each technology corresponding to each crop. The climate smart feasibility index for technologies has been estimated in terms of their impact on water use efficiency, energy use efficiency, nitrogen use efficiency, and productivity. Higher the feasibility implies, higher is the level of climate smart agricultural transformation for the selected crops and selected region. On the other hand, farmers' preference has been assessed among the technologies irrespective of their level of feasibilities. Thus, the above-mentioned two methods are independent to each other to avoid the preference bias. Thus, it is clearly observed from Table 3 that the highly feasible technologies are not highly preferred by the farmers, rather farmers prefer technologies based on their farming experience and constraints associated with the adoption of technologies. However, it is observed from Table 3 that farmers are willing to transform their farming practise to move towards CSA even at low-level CSA in the beginning.

Conclusion and Policy Recommendations

It is observed during this study that farmers are interested to adopt modern technologies to increase their profitability. However, identifying technologies to

Table 3

Scientific Feasibility and Farmers' Preference

CSFI: Degree of Feasible	*Degree of Farmers Preference*
Wheat Crop	
Very high feasible	*Sehore District*: (Highly preferred technology) SPNK + SWI + SDV
Moderately feasible	*Guna District*: (Highly preferred technology) BBF+SDV
Moderately feasible	*Jhabua District*: (Highly preferred technology) BBF + INM + IPM + SDV
Moderately feasible	*Shahdol District*: (Highly preferred technology) ZT + SDV + ST
Soybean Crop	
Moderately feasible	*Sehore District*: (Highly preferred technology) BBF + INM + IPM + SDV
Highly feasible	*Guna District*: (Highly preferred technology) BBF + INM + IPM + SDV
Highly feasible	*Jhbua District*: (Highly preferred technology) BBF + INM + IPM + SDV
Gram Crop	
Moderately feasible	*Sehore District*: (Highly preferred technology) BBF+INM+IPM+SPNK
Low feasible	*Guna District*: (Highly preferred technology) SPNK + SDV + FP
Low feasible	*Jhabua District*: (Highly preferred technology) BBF + INM + IPM + SDV + SPNK
Rice Crop	
Infeasible	*Guna District*: (Highly preferred technology) DSR + LLL
Highly Feasible	*Guna District*: (Moderately preferred) SRI + ST
Low Feasible	*Shahdol District*: (Highly preferred technology) LLL + INM + IPM + ST + FP

link their profitability with sustainability is crucial. On the other hand, due to regional heterogeneity identifying feasible technology and understanding farmers' willingness is required to achieve CSA in Madhya Pradesh. In this context, this study makes a unique contribution by prioritising climate smart practises across various regions to achieve the goal of CSA in this state. Key policy recommendation can be derived from this study as follows:

1. Link farm mechanisation with regional priority and need. Hence, zero tillage and Laser Land Leveling (LLL) can be focused in rice-wheat zone for better productivity and resource conservation. Broad Bed Furrow (BBF) can be promoted in soybean-wheat zone for better water management and productivity.
2. Irrigation intensification through tank irrigation in the low irrigated but high rainfall area will be helpful to achieve irrigation intensification without much threat into the groundwater availability.
3. It is observed that, farmers apply more fertiliser and seed in the rainfed region with the perception of higher yield. On the other hand, most of the farmers (around 75% out of 180 selected farmer household in the selected regions) are not aware and trained with the Integrated Nutrient Management (INM) and Integrated Pest Management (IPM) methods. Therefore, training on nutrient and pest management to the rainfed region and distribution of information about the existing policies and support by the government would help to increase adoption of INM and IPM practises at the farmers' field.

Acknowledgements

We acknowledge the CGIAR Fund Council, Australia (ACIAR), Irish Aid, European Union, International Fund for Agricultural Development (IFAD), the Netherlands, New Zealand, Switzerland, UK, USAID, and Thailand for funding to the CGIAR Research Programme on Climate Change, Agriculture and Food Security (CCAFS).

References

FAO, (2010): *Climate-Smart Agriculture: Policies, Practices and Financing for Food Security, Adaptation and Mitigation.* Rome: FAO. www.fao.org/docrep/013/i1881e/i1881e00.pdf.

GoI, (2014): Economic Survey of Madhya Pradesh, https://data.gov.in/dataset-group-name/economic-survey-madhya-pradesh-2013-and-2014 last accessed August 2015.

——, (2015): Directorate of Economics and Statistics, Department of Agriculture, http://eands.dacnet.nic.in/last accessed on September 2015.

GoMP, (2015): Department of Agriculture, Government of Madhya Pradesh, http://www.mpkrishi.org/krishinet/Compendium/Basic_agroclimatic.asp last accessed on April 2015.

Taneja, G., Pal, B.D., Joshi, P.K., Aggarwal, P.K. and Tyagi, N.K., (2014): Farmers Preference on Climate Smart Agriculture: An Assessment in Indo-Gangetic Plain in India, IFPRI Discussion Paper, 01337, Washington DC, USA.

16 Agricultural Crops Land Operation

Irrigation Illustration in Mandya District of Karnataka

Srikantha Nayaka

Introduction

Agriculture is the art of raising plant life. From the soil for the use of mankind agriculture provides a free fare and fresh environment, abundant food for diving out famine, favour's friendship by eliminating fights. Satisfactory agriculture production brings peace, prosperity, harmony, health and wealth. Agriculture in narrow sense means the cultivation of soil for the production of agriculture crops. However, in a broad sense, agriculture covers not only the cultivation of agriculture crops but also allied actives such as maintenance of livestock on farms and poultry farming. Agriculture is the oldest profession of the people of India. It provides employment opportunities to more than 65 per cent of the total work force and provides raw materials for many industries.

Karnataka is India's eighth largest state in geographical area covering 1.92 lakh square kilometre and accounting for 6.3 per cent of the geographical area of the country. The state is delineated into 30 districts and 176 taluks spread over 27,481 villages. The state receives normal annual rainfall of 1,139 mm, mainly through south-west monsoon (June–September – 806 mm) and north-east monsoon (October–December – 195 mm). The rainfall during post-monsoon period, that is, January–March is about 14 mm and in pre-monsoon period (April–May) it is 124 mm. Karnataka has a typical composition of having regions with most of the agro-climatic condition in the country, except the snow-clad mountainous region. A large portion of the land falls under semi-arid conditions facing severe agro-climatic and resource constraints. Interestingly, coexisting with this are a few patches of high value high-tech agriculture. Consequently, Karnataka's agriculture is at the same time diversified and segmented in many ways.

Karnataka is one of the few states with the lowest proportion of their area under irrigation. Majority of farmers here have no other option but to grow low-value crops. Under such speckled situation, agricultural sector of the state is growing moderately despite severe climatic and strong resource constraints. Accordingly, the state has three agricultural seasons – Kharif (April–September), Rabi (October–December), and Summer (January–March). Agricultural crops are cultivated in an area of about 107 lakh hectares annually. Out of this, in Kharif season it is about 69 lakh hectares (64%), in Rabi season it is about 32 lakh hectares (30%), and the rest 6 lakh hectares (6%) come in summer season. Out of gross cultivated area of agricultural crops, an area of about 22 lakh hectares (20.5%) comes under irrigation.

Table 1

Share of Different Soil Types in Karnataka

Soil Type	*Area (Lakh Ha)*	*%*
Red soil	71.08	37
Black soil	52.93	28
Alluvio-colluvial soil	29.98	16
Lateritic soil	11.65	6
Forest soil	11.47	6
Coastal soil	7.44	4
Rock lands, water bodies, and urban areas	5.96	3
Total	190.50	100

Source: Mandya district at a glance 2012–13.

Figure 1

Share of Different Soil Types in Karnataka (%)

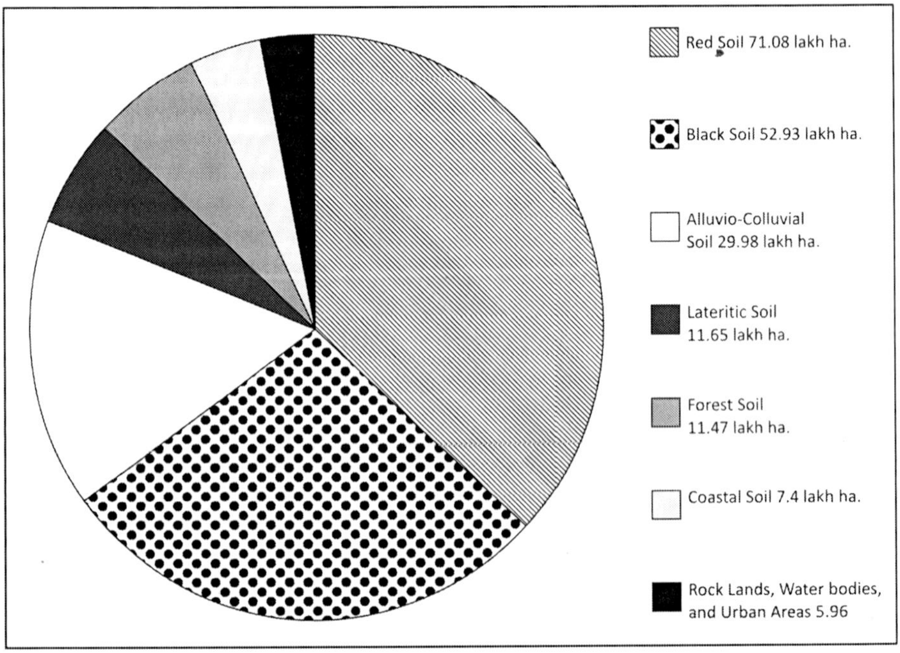

In Karnataka, agriculture is the major occupation for a majority of the rural population. As per the population Census 2011, agriculture supports 13.74 million workers, of which 23.61 per cent are cultivators and 25.67 per cent agricultural workers. A total of 1,23,100 square kilometre of land is cultivated in Karnataka constituting 64.6 per cent of the total geographical area of the state. The agricultural sector of Karnataka is characterised by vast steppes of drought prone region and sporadic patches of irrigated area. Thus, a large portion of agricultural land in the state is exposed to the vagaries of monsoon with severe agro-climatic and resource constraints. Agriculture employs more than 60 per cent of Karnataka's workforce. Agriculture in Karnataka is heavily dependent on the south-west monsoon. While only 26.5 per cent of the sown area (30,900 square kilometre) is under irrigation, 64.60 per cent of the total geographical area is under cultivation. It is the third largest producer of sugar and ranks fourth in sugarcane production. Out of the total cultivable area of 123.07 lakh hectares, as per the statistics of 2001–01, the net cultivated area was 100.31 lakh hectares and the gross cultivated area was 116.70 lakh hectares, indicating a cropping intensity of 116 per cent. Out of the gross cultivated area, the area under irrigation was 30.89 lakh hectares (26.5%). As per the 2010–11 agricultural census, Karnataka's cultivable area is 12.2 millihectares of which nearly 10 millihectares was cultivated and 3.4 millihectares was irrigated in 2011–12 (GoK, 2015).

Agriculture with almost 50 per cent of its area getting assured irrigation water, Mandya district naturally was the focus of agricultural development programmes in the state during the post-independence period especially the Green Revolution era. The prosperity of the district is tied to the irrigated agriculture in general and two irrigated crops namely paddy and sugarcane in particular. However, there are dry land taluks in the district, which still continue to depend on rainfall, with the major crop being ragi. For the development of these areas in particular, the thrust programmes in the agricultural sector of the district are: expansion of area under vegetables, composite orchards/dry land horticulture, micro and conjunctive irrigation, crop intensification in coconut gardens, and organic farming.

Objectives

1. To analyse the important source of irrigation and cropping systems, land in boundary area has been identified.
2. To analyse the impact of irrigation on crop patterns in the district of Mandya.

Discussion

Mandya district is known as one of the sugar and paddy bowls of India. Administratively, the district can be divided into seven taluks viz., Krishnarajpet (KR Pet), Maddur, Malavalli, Mandya, Nagamangala, Srirangapatna (SR Patna), and Pandavapura. The district comes under the group of districts known as the *maidan* (plains) districts, and is situated in the southern part of Karnataka state and lies to the north of Mysuru district of which it was once a part. The district lies between 76°19' and 77°20' east longitude and 12°13' and 13°04' north latitude.

The district has 89,357 hectares under paddy cultivation, 79.670 hectares under ragi, 5,938 hectares under maize, 1,74,965 hectares under cereals and minor millets, 22,257 hectares under sugarcane, and 34,691 hectares under horticulture crops. Mandya district ranks third place in Karnataka state for its sericulture produce. Sugar factories, milk-processing units, paper mills, rice mills, oil extraction, and jaggery making are the district's chief industrial-sector activities. Mandya has the oldest sugar factory in Karnataka with a crushing capacity of 5,000 tonnes of sugarcane per day.

Physiography

Most of the land is flat, interspersed with hilly regions and sparsely vegetated by thorns and boshes. The district is situated at a height of 762–914 metres from the sea level. The district has fertile land with red soil mixed with sand, red clay soil, and red soil mixed with stones. Mandya, Maddur and Nagamangala blocks have red soil mixed stone and iron content which has less water-holding capacity. Malavalli, Shrirangapattanna and Pandavapura blocks have clay-soil mixed red soil. Mandya district is popularly known as the belt of sugar.

Rainfall

The average rainfall in the district is 691.2 mm. The rainfall is generally uniform in the district except in the western border where the rainfall is a little higher. The rainfall varies from 742 mm at KR Pet to 670.6 mm at SR Patna. The rainy season is mostly confined to the period from April to November. The district receives rainfall both in the south-west monsoon and in the retreating monsoon seasons. The heaviest rainfall is in the post-monsoon month of October. The rainfall in the summer, south-west monsoon, and the retreating monsoon seasons constitutes 25 per cent, 40 per cent, and 33 per cent, respectively, of the annual rainfall. On an average, there are 45 rainy days (i.e. day with rainfall of 2.5 mm or more) in a year.

Land, Soil, and Natural Resource

Land is certainly a crucial element in the group of all natural resources. Land-use trends can impact the economy and ecology simultaneously and at times with serious effects (Government of Karnataka, 2006).

Endowments

The total geographical area of Mandya district is 4,962 square kilometre (4.98 lakh hectares), which is 2.62 per cent of geographical area of the state. Out of the total geographical area of the district, Nagamangala taluk ranks first with 20.85 per cent. SR Patna taluk occupies 7.18 per cent of the total geographical area of the district. The district's forest area is just 4.77 per cent of the district's total geographical area and 0.78 per cent of the state's total area under forests. Malavalli and KR Pet taluks possess 71 per cent of the total area under forests in the district. The net sown area of the district is about 2.47 lakh hectares and the gross sown area is about 2.85 lakh hectares.

Soil Types

The soil of Mandya district is derived from granites and gneisses interpreted with occasional patches of schist in SR Patna, Mandya, and Pandavapura *taluks*. The soils range from red sandy loams to red clay loam very thin in ridges and higher elevations and comparatively thick in valley portions. The soils in Mandya, Malavalli, Maddur, and Nagamangala taluks are thin gravelly and underlain with a murrum zone containing weathered rock. The soils are highly leached and poor in bases. The water-holding capacity is low. On the other hand, the soil under the old channel areas of Malavalli, Pandavapura, and SR Patna is high in clay. The infiltration rates of red loamy and red soils are 2–12 cm/h and 1–3 cm/h.

Water Resources along with Irrigation

Water resources irrigation is an important source of raising productivity in agricultural sector. Expansion of both the groundwater and surface water resources has helped to increase the cultivated area under irrigation in the state over time. There are three major catchment areas in the district: (a) Cauvery (b) Shimsha and (c) Lokapavani. Many streams join these rivers. Cauvery, Hemavathi, Lokapavani, Shimsha, and Veera Vaishnavi are the important rivers of the district. Bindenahalli Tore, Amruthuru Tore, Nidasale Tore, Handihalla, Hebballa, and Bhima are some of the important streams. A total of 1.43 lakh hectares of cultivated land have been brought under irrigation by making use of these sources. The district has a total of 14,735 hectares water-spread area, out of which 12,924 hectares are covered by Krishna Raja Sagara (KRS) (submerged area). There are 224 large tanks with water-spread area of 9,779 hectares. There are 596 small tanks with a water-spread area of 1,733 hectares. The topography of the area shows gradual slope towards east and the stream flowing in this area mainly join the Bay of Bengal.

Irrigation water is an essential ingredient for food production. Initially, natural rains provided water supply to agriculture in forest areas. There was no conscious effort to tap water resources. As the population increased, civilisations came up on the banks of rivers. Rain water is available only on the day of rain, but river water is available for a longer duration. Hence, dependability increases with river water. In the case of perennial rivers, one can say that production is assured. Further increase in population led to the growth of communities away from riverside also. Then we have the situation of one set of communities depending on rain water only for its agriculture and another on rivers. The first one had an unpredictable situation – if rains were delayed or rainfall was poor in a particular year, the resultant droughts caused major short falls in production and occasional famines.

Rainfed agriculture occupies a prominent place in Indian economy, food security, and rural livelihoods. At present, about 55 per cent of the total net sown area is rainfed, contributing 40 per cent of the total food-grain production and supporting 60 per cent of livestock population. Before the irrigation water was made available, the farmers in Mandya district used to grow crops only under rainfed conditions. During those days, the major crops being grown were ragi, paddy, and horse gram. The district started glowing with greenery only after the KRS dam's water was made available to farmers for irrigation purpose. The district comes under the river Cauvery basin. The gross irrigated area from various sources is 1,67,002 hectares. Of the total, net irrigated area from varies sources is 1,35,290 hectares.

Mandya is predominantly an agriculture district and vast majority of its population derive its livelihood from agriculture. The seasonal rainfall begins with the pre-monsoon showers from end March to middle of May and June. The south-west monsoon season covers the period from June to August with high winds thus causing a lowering of the temperature. With almost 50 per cent of its area getting assured irrigation water, Mandya district naturally was the focus of agricultural development programmes in the state during the post-independence period especially the Green Revolution era. The prosperity of the district is tied to the irrigated agriculture in general and two irrigated crops namely paddy and sugarcane in particular. However, there are dry land *taluks* in the district, which still continue to depend on rainfall, with the major crop being ragi. For the development of these areas in particular, the thrust programmes in the agricultural sector of the district are: expansion of area under vegetables, composite orchards/dry land horticulture, micro and conjunctive irrigation, crop intensification in coconut gardens, and organic farming. The agricultural development plan of Mandya district is formulated by and large in accordance with the panchasutra[1] laid out in the New Agriculture Policy (2006) of the Government of Karnataka, of course, keeping in view the situation obtaining at the end of the 10th-plan period. The district intends to accord priority to the following aspects, which have direct or indirect bearing on the development of agriculture:

1. Protection and improvement of soil health.
2. Water management and micro irrigation.
3. Supply of quality seeds.
4. Integrated approach to production, processing, and value addition.
5. Reducing the gap between lab and land.

The land-use pattern of the district indicates very small percentage of the geographical area under forest. The district has about half of the cultivated land under irrigation, thanks to the Cauvery and Hemavathi rivers as also their tributaries, which provide year-long assured irrigation for crops. Paddy and sugarcane are dominant crops grown in almost the entire canal-irrigated area, while *ragi* and horse gram are the major crops in dry-land agriculture. Sericulture is an important commercial crop in virtually every *taluk* of the district.

The total geographical area of the district is 4,98,244 hectares, out of which 2,53,067 hectares form the sown area. More than half of the total land area in the district is put to agricultural use. A total of 94,779 hectares of land is irrigated. Mandya district is basically dependent on agriculture and a few agro-based industries such as sugar for income and employment of the people.

With a total population of 19.25 lakhs, around five lakh people are employed in the agriculture sector.

The land of sugar and rice, Mandya is a prominent agricultural district, formed in the year 1939. Blessed with the irrigation waters of river Cauvery and Hemavathi, half of the district countryside is lush in various hues of green throughout the year. About half of the agricultural land in the district receives assured irrigation from the KRS and the Hemavathi reservoirs. The other half is dependent on the south-west monsoons. Paddy and sugarcane are the main crops of the irrigated region. Ragi and horse-gram are the major crops. Agriculture is the main occupation of people in the district.

Table 2

Agriculture Land Utilisation 2012–13 (Hectares)

Taluks	*Geographical Area*	*Area Sown*		*Total*	*%*
		Net	*More than Once*		
KR Pet	91,551	34,936	4,865	39,801	43.47
Maddur	61,846	27,639	2,918	30,557	49.40
Malavalli	80,949	25,556	4,710	30,266	37.38
Mandya	71,512	27,279	9,645	36,924	51.63
Nagamangala	1,03,850	9,694	3,402	33,096	31.86
Pandavapura	52,743	29287	3,532	32,819	62.22
Srirangapatna	35,758	13,919	6,848	20,767	58.07
Total	4,04,744	1,88,310	35,920	2,24,230	55.40

Source: Mandya district at a glance 2012–13.

According to Table 2, 55 per cent of land is utilised for agricultural activities. In the entire district, the highest agriculture is noticed in Pandavapura and lowest was recorded in Nagamangala *taluk*.

Land and Irrigated Area

The land of sugar and rice, Mandya is a prominent agricultural district blessed with the irrigation waters of rivers Cauvery and Hemavathi. About half of the agricultural land in the district receives assured irrigation from the KRS and the Hemavathi reservoirs. The other half is dependent on the south-west monsoons. Paddy and sugarcane are the main crops of the irrigated region. Ragi and horse gram are the major crops of dry-land agriculture. Agriculture is the main occupation of people in the district. Most of the industries in the district agro-processing depending on agriculture produce as their raw material. Sugar mills, jaggery-making units, and rice mills are the prominent industries of this district. In Mandya district, before irrigation rainfed was the only source of water for cultivation. The construction of KRS dam, the importance of the area now comprising the Mandya district grew and in order to facilitate the acquisition of land in connection with the Irwin canal now known as Vivesvaraya canal (VC). The major source of irrigation to the district is the construction of KRS dam across the river Cauvery designed by Sir M. Visvesvaraya.

Land management on farms has a major impact on water availability and quality. Soil from eroded areas, for example, flows into rivers, changing their flow, and reducing the storage capacity of dams (Amy Goldblatt, 2008). Agriculture being the main occupation of the either state and also district, irrigation plays a significant role in increasing the yields from the land.

Table 3 shows canal-dependent irrigation is predominant and followed by tank- and groundwater-dependent irrigation in the district. The highest canal-dependent net area irrigated is observed in Maddur taluk and lowest irrigation was found in Nagamangala taluk. The highest net tank irrigated area is noticed in Maddur and lowest is observed in SR Patna. The groundwater-dependent net irrigation is found in Pandavapura and lowest was observed in SR Patna.

Cropping Pattern in the District

The cropping pattern of the district as a whole is dominated by food-grain crops, especially paddy and ragi. Cereals and minor millets occupy over half of the total crop area. Commercial crops occupy a quarter of the total cropped area and sugarcane accounts for bulk of the commercial crops. Fruits and vegetables and oil seeds together account for hardly 8.32 per cent of the cropped area. Mandya district is known as one of the sugars and paddy bowls of India. The district has 89,357 hectares under paddy cultivation, 79.670 hectares under ragi, 5,938 hectares under maize, 1,74,965 hectares under cereals and minor millets, 22,257 hectares under sugarcane, and 34,691 hectares under horticulture crops.

Figure 2

Agriculture Land Utilisation 2012–13 (Hectares)

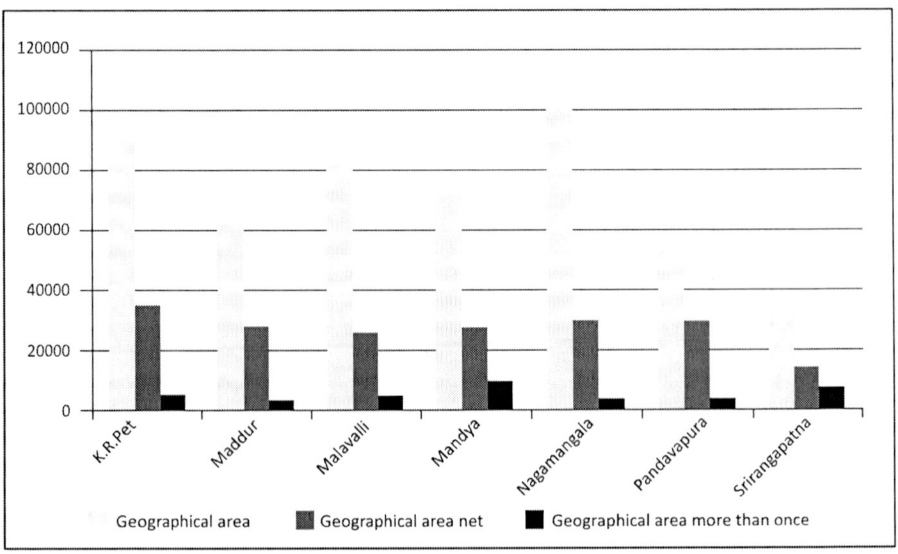

Mandya district ranks third place in Karnataka state for its sericulture produce. Sugar factories, milk-processing units, paper mills, rice mills, oil extraction, and jaggery making are the district's chief industrial-sector activities. Mandya has the oldest sugar factory in Karnataka with a crushing capacity of 5,000 tons of sugarcane per day. All the taluks of the districts are covered by the Command Area Development Authority, Cauvery Basin. Sericulture being a profitable occupation has resulted in wide-spread mulberry cultivation throughout this district (Government of Karnataka, 2014).

Crops

The main crops grown in the district are paddy, sugarcane, jowar, maize, cotton, banana, vegetable, mulberry, gram, ragi, groundnut, horse gram, coconut, etc. During those days, the major crops were ragi, paddy, and horse gram. The district started glowing with greenery only after the KRS water was made available to farmers for irrigation purpose. Land is one of the most important natural resources on which all mankind activities are depended on, and a thorough knowledge of its utilisation is very much essential for a number of planning activities. As per our study, the total geographical area of Mandya district is 4,98,246 hectares. A total of 24,765 (4.97%) hectares land is a forest area, 1,89,090 (37.95%) hectares land is area available for cultivation, and 3,428 (0.69%) hectares land has trees and groves. Remaining 2,80,963 hectares (56.39%) land is uncultivated by considering as non-agricultural land, barren, pastured land, fallow land, and so on. We can notice that more than 56 per cent of the land is not used for cultivation.

Water Resources

Access to water and irrigation is a major determinant of land productivity and the stability of yields. Irrigated land productivity is more than double that of rainfed land (World Development Report, 2008). A total of 1.43 lakh hectares of cultivated land have been brought under irrigation by making use of these sources. The district has a total of 14,735 hectares water-spread area, out of which 12,924 hectares is occupied by KRS (submerged area). There are 224 large tanks with water-spread area of 9,779 hectares. Similarly, there are 596 small tanks with water-spread area of 1,733 hectares. The topography of the area shows gradual slope towards east and the stream flowing in this area mainly join the Bay of Bengal.

The previous to the irrigation water was made available, the farmers in Mandya district used to grow crops only under rainfed conditions. During those days, the major crops being grown were ragi, paddy, and horse gram. The district started glowing with greenery only after the KRS dam's water was made available to farmers for irrigation purpose. The district comes under the river Cauvery basin.

The gross irrigated area from various sources is 1,67,002 hectares. Of the total, net irrigated area from various sources is 1,35,290 hectares. Now,

Table 3

Different Sources in Irrigated Area Mandya District

Taluks	*Canals*			*Tanks*			*Wells*		
	Length in Km	*Grass Irrigated Area*	*Net Area Irrigated*	*Length in Km*	*Grass Irrigated Area*	*Net Area Irrigated*	*NOs*	*Grass Irrigated Area*	*Net Area Irrigated*
KR Pet	386.25	17,065	15,034	142	5,534	984	1,145	2,138	984
Maddur	92.80	20,874	18,670	143	3,114	1,121	1,910	1,200	1,121
Malavalli	84.80	17,360	16,970	47	1,257	854	2,006	951	854
Mandya	44.80	20,710	1,984	95	2,841	1,357	2,024	1,942	1,357
Nagamangala	7.00	4,989	4,314	136	2,534	594	2,590	640	594
Pandavapura	84.00	14,570	13,341	48	3,669	1,534	1,478	1,800	1,534
Srirangapatna	80.20	9,252	8,561	19	287	407	697	434	407
Total	779.85	1,04,820.00	96,731.00	630.00	19,236.00	6,851.00	11,850.0	9,105.00	6,851.00

Source: Mandya district at a glance: (2012–13).

Table 4

Irrigation in Mandya District 2011–12: Net Area Irrigated by Different Sources (Area in Hectares)

Taluks	*Canal*	*Tanks*	*Well*	*Tube well*	*Lift Irrigation*	*Total*	*Rank*
KR Pet	12,034	5,314	984	1,234	138	19,704	4
(%)	61.07	26.97	4.99	6.26	0.70	100	
Maddur	18,670	3,215	1,121	380	84	23,470	2
(%)	79.55	13.70	4.78	1.62	0.36	100	
Malavalli	18,970	1,748	1,248	720	53	22,739	3
(%)	83.42	7.69	5.49	3.17	0.23	100	
Mandya	21,421	4,150	1,357	564	-	27,492	1
(%)	77.92	15.10	4.94	2.05	-	100	
Nagamangala	4,314	2,894	894	1,120	-	9,222	7
(%)	46.78	31.38	9.69	12.14	-	100	
Pandavapura	12,341	3,669	1,534	270	154	17,968	5
(%)	68.68	20.42	8.54	1.50	0.86	100	
Srirangapatna	12,800	438	497	960	-	14,695	6
(%)	87.10	2.98	3.38	6.53	-	100	
Total	88,209	17,759	6,101	4,978	275	11,7322	
(%)	75.18	15.13	5.20	4.24	0.23	100	
Rank	1	2	3	4	5		

Note: Figures in parentheses are percentages to the row-wise totals.

Source: District at a glance: Mandya (2012–13).

Mandya has many sources of irrigation for cultivation. Major contribution for this source is from canals by quantifying for around 1,04,820 hectares. Tanks, well, and tube well supplies for 19,236, 9,105, and 6,257 hectares, respectively. KR Pete, Maddur, Malavalli, and Pandavapura have opted for lift irrigation for around 429 hectares. Apart from all these in KR Pete, Nagamangala, and Pandavapura, there are also other sources of irrigation. Since KR Pete is sourced with all kind of irrigation, it stands in the first position for irrigation. Mandya stands next successively and Nagamangala is at the last position, making it a very dry land (Table 5).

Cropping Pattern

Cropping systems of a region are decided by and large, by a number of soil and climatic parameters, which determine overall agro-ecological setting for nourishment and appropriateness of a crop or set of crops for cultivation. Nevertheless, at farmers' level, potential productivity and monetary benefits act as guiding principles while opting for a particular crop/cropping system. These decisions with respect to choose of crops and cropping systems are further narrowed down under influence of several other forces related to infrastructure facilities, socio-economic factors and technological developments, all operating interactively at micro level. These are: infrastructure facilities: irrigation, transport, storage, trade and marketing, post-harvest handling and processing, etc. Socio-economic factors: financial resource base, land ownership, size and type of land holding, household needs of food, fodder, fuel, fibre and finance, labour availability, etc. (Das, 2008). Cropping pattern means the proportion of various crops in an area of land at a specific time period. The cropping system is an important component of any farming system. It is the proportion of area with various crops at a specific period of time.

Figure 3

Taluk-wise Sources of Irrigation 2013–14 in Mandya District

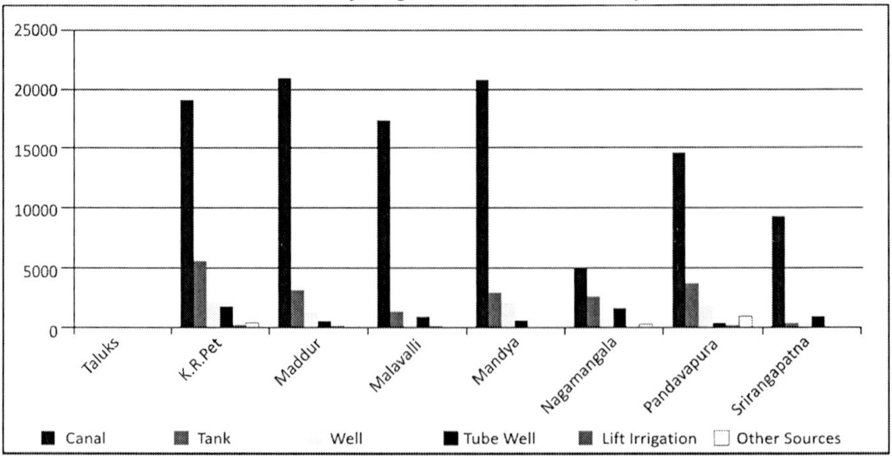

Table 5

Taluk-wise Sources of Irrigation 2013–14 in Mandya District (in Hectares)

Taluks	*Canal*	*Tank*	*Well*	*Tube Well*	*Lift Irrigation*	*Other Sources*	*Total*	*Rank*
KR Pet	17,065	5,534	2,138	1,651	138	328	26,854	I
(%)	63.54	20.60	7.96	6.14	0.51	1.22	100	
Maddur	20,874	3,114	1,200	450	84	0	25,722	III
(%)	81.15	12.10	4.66	1.74	0.32	0	100	
Malavalli	17,360	1,257	951	890	53	0	20,511	V
(%)	84.63	6.12	4.63	4.33	0.25	0	100	
Mandya	20,710	2,841	1,942	540	0	0	26,033	II
(%)	79.55	10.91	7.45	2.07	0	0	100	
Nagamangala	4,989	2,534	640	1,508	0	216	9,887	VII
(%)	50.46	25.62	6.47	15.25	0	2.18	100	
Pandavapura	14,570	3,669	1,800	350	154	856	21,399	IV
(%)	68.08	17.14	8.41	1.63	0.71	4.00	100	
Srirangapatna	9,252	287	434	868	0	0	10,841	VI
(%)	85.34	2.64	4.00	8.00	0	0	100	
Total	1,04,820	19,236	9,105	6,257	429	1,400	1,41,247	
(%)	74.21	13.61	6.44	4.42	0.30	0.99	100	
Rank	I	II	III	IV	VI	V		

Source: Mandya district at a glance – 2013–14..

Table 6

Taluk-wise Cropping Pattern 2013–14 in Mandya District in Per cent

Taluks	*Paddy*	*Ragi*	*Jowar*	*Maize*	*Sugar-cane*	*Pulses*	*Oil Seeds*	*Fruits*	*Vege-tables*
KR Pet	33.85	25.21	0.02	0.23	8.02	17.58	4.45	3.97	6.68
Maddur	32.43	21.98	0.01	0.00	33.38	8.66	1.40	2.03	0.10
Malavalli	27.36	21.06	0.68	10.12	13.68	13.86	6.86	2.96	3.43
Mandya	39.73	13.48	1.32	0.00	30.85	6.78	4.02	0.88	2.94
Nagamangala	2.37	54.37	0.01	0.00	0.23	31.41	5.99	0.55	5.07
Pandavapura	20.66	22.21	0.00	0.00	25.12	21.52	0.92	1.37	8.20
Srirangapatna	51.72	6.01	0.80	0.25	24.70	9.00	2.00	1.45	4.07
District Total	29.73	23.47	0.40	1.51	19.42	15.54	3.66	1.88	4.35
Rank	I	II	IX	VIII	III	IV	VI	VII	V

Source: Mandya district at a glance – 2013–14.

As per our data in Table 6, paddy is the major crop in Mandya district, which covers 29.73 per cent of the cultivated area in SR Patna, Mandya, and Maddur. Second most cultivated crop is ragi with covers 23.47 per cent of the area and sugarcane covers 19.42 per cent of the area in the district. These three crops are the major crops accounting to 72.62 per cent of the cultivated area and other crops like jowar, maize, oil seeds, fruits, vegetables, and pulses are also grown with very minimal focus.

Figure 4

Taluk-wise Cropping Pattern 2013–14 in Mandya District in Per cent

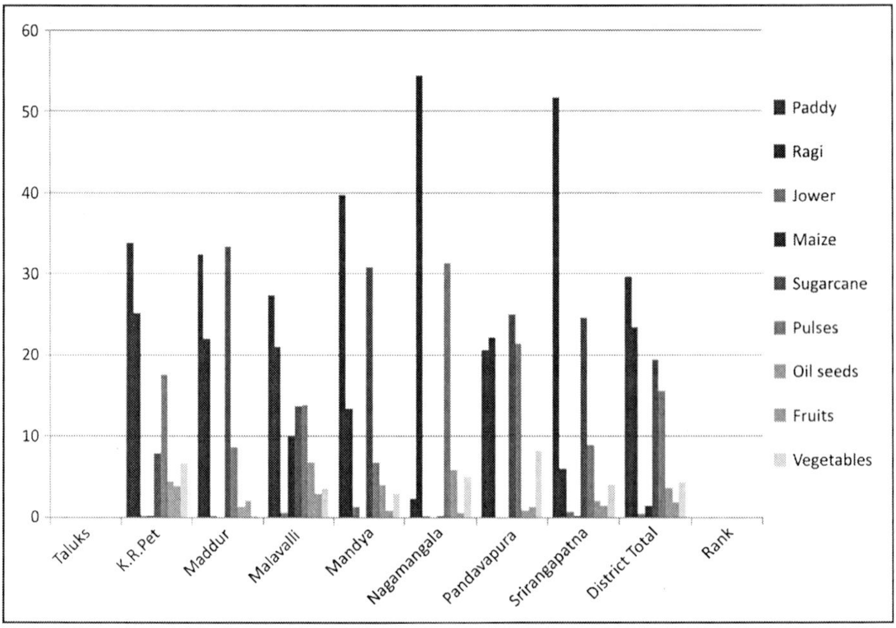

Conclusions

Based on the above study, irrigated area in Mandya district is increased from year 2012–13 to 2013–14. Paddy and sugarcane are the main crops of the irrigated region. It covers nearly 50 per cent of cropping pattern of the district. These crops are mainly depending upon the canal irrigation ragi and horse gram are the major crops of dry-land agriculture. The irrigation facilities in the district are dominated by canals, tanks, and borewells. Mandya district is irrigated to the extent of 52 per cent of the total sown area. The district is blessed with irrigation from two major reservoirs, KRS and Hemavathi. Besides these, there are number of anecut channels. Hemavathi left bank canal is irrigating parts of KR Pet, Nagamangala, Pandavapura, and Mandya taluks. In all, about 48 per cent of the total area in the district is irrigated from all sources of irrigation. The major vegetables grown are tomato, gourd varieties, brinjal, lady finger, leaf vegetables, and others. Mandya district is one of the most agriculturally prosperous districts in Karnataka. With the advent of irrigation from the KRS reservoir, there was substantially marked transformation in cropping pattern, composition of crops, better grown yield level, ultimately leading to better economic conditions of the people.

Note

1. Karnataka State Agricultural Policy 2006 is based on five principles known as "Panchsutra" announced in 2006–07 budget. All these five principles provide integrated support to agricultural sector in accelerating the growth rate.

   Panchasutra for Agriculture Development

   (1) Protect and improve the soil health

   (2) Conservation of natural resources, with special emphasis on water and Micro irrigation.

   (3) Timely availability of credit and other inputs to the farmers.

   (4) Integrate post-harvest processing with the production process.

   (5) Reduce the distance between lab and land in transfer of technology.

   The policy document identified the strategies to operationalize these principles into action. For each of these five principles the following strategies are proposed.

   - To protect and improve soil health it is proposed to provide micro nutrients, bio fertilizers, bio pesticides organic fertilizers etc, to farmers at discount price.
   - For the conservation of natural resources with giving special attention to water and micro irrigation the policy envisaged on proper utilization of water under micro irrigation program bringing in more and more area under irrigation.
   - To improve the timely availability of credit and other inputs to the farmers- it is proposed to provide sowing seed and other inputs and plant protection chemicals and other modern agriculture equipments to farmers at discount price to take up agricultural activities in time.
   - To integrate post-harvest processing with the production process the policy proposes to provide processing units and tarpaulins to farmers at discount price.

- In order to reduce the distance between lab and land in transfer of technology the policy proposes to encourage departmental training, demonstrations, agriculture fairs, study tours and other extension programs and also by using mass media to educate the farmers about technology. Several initiatives are introduced implement to the strategies proposed in the policy.

(*Source:* https://shodhganga.inflibnet.ac.in/bitstream/10603/97247/12/12_ chapter %203.pdf, accessed on 31/08/2020.

References

Das, P. (2008): Status of Farm Mechanisation in India, Indian Council of Agricultural Research, New Delhi.

Goldblatt, A. (2008): Agriculture: Facts & Trends South Africa.

Government of Karnataka (2006): Karnataka Agricultural Policy, Bangalore.

——, (2014–15): Mandya District Human Development Report, Directorate of Statistical Bangalore.

——, (2015–16): Karnataka Economic Survey, Bangalore.

——, Mandya District at a Glance (2013–14). Bangalore.

——, (2015–16): Mandya District Human Development Report, Directorate of Statistical Bangalore

World Development Report, (2008): Agriculture for Development, The World Bank Washington, DC.

17 Migration and Changing Livelihood Profile for Ensuring Food Security Among Tribal Female Youth

Emerging Issues and Challenges in Chhattisgarh

Vikram Singh and Suman Lakra

Introduction

From last six years, author has been working in Department of Social Work Guru Ghasidas Central University at Bilaspur, Chhattisgarh. The subjects that author taught at the institute (i.e. Social Work/Sociology) have field practicum and minor research as core of the pedagogy. Hence through field practicum and minor researches (done/conducted by UG/PG students), from last four years, author also have conducted various preliminary surveys among 300 people with the help of students placed under his supervision in the nearby region of Bilaspur, Chhattisgarh.

These surveys have conducted deliberately to know about the pattern of migration, changing livelihood pattern, and gender profile among tribes as Chhattisgarh is a tribal belt state of India.

One essential component of study on tribal population is the study of migration emerging out of diverse, social, cultural, economic, and political reasons. For a large country like India, a complexity of a movement of population in different parts of the country helps in understanding the dynamics of the society. At this crucial juncture in the social and economic development in our country, study on migration assumes special significance.

Historically, the 'Indian society had been stratified on the caste, class and creed lines; which were later termed in tribes and were initially developed based on the occupation'. This inequality is a key component of human mobility and it has a huge potential for growth of human development. Today, we see that occupations and positions are fixed and set at birth, and are transmitted from father to child through rigid schemes have little room for innovation and fulfilment at either the individual or collective level (Azam, 2013) and appropriately has attracted considerable attention across many countries.

The tribal population of the country, as per 2011 Census, is 10.43 crore, constituting 8.6 per cent of the total population. A total of 89.97 per cent of them live in rural areas and 10.03 per cent in urban areas. The decadal population growth of the tribal's from Census 2001–11 has been 23.66 per cent against the 17.69 per cent of the entire population. A total of 91.7 per cent of these tribal people live in rural areas, mostly in and around forests. India is home to tribal people, that is, 8.6 per cent of India's total population; there are about 700 state-specific tribes and 75 primitive tribe groups (PTGs). Since the tribal communities reside in the remote interiors, which are not easily accessible, and therefore these people are underdeveloped.

Structural Changes among Tribal Community and Migration

The best-known world novelist Albert Camus's famous book 'Outsider' illustrates the story of the pathetic alienation of the man who becomes the outsider of the society. In case of Chhattisgarh, the state has a major share of tribal population and they often been migrate under developmental projects. As a result, there is a devastating blow on social capital – which is the base of their survival and identity and ultimately leads to the disintegration of their rich culture.

The government polices (specifically forest laws and developmental policies) have enforced tribes to move, they have to move in the direction of the larger population. This is how shift is happening because they are migrating from their clans where there is larger extinct taking place in the culture, dialects, rituals, etc. Hence, in contemporary situation tribal community has different connotations.

- Tribal: a cultivator in a self-contained society (before migration)
- Peasant: a producer as a part of larger society (after migration)

This happening due to the changes in Chhattisgarh over the past 10–15 years after separation from Madhya Pradesh, there is now a new dynamic logic that ties the operations of 'tribal society' (comprising the peasantry, artisans, and petty producers in the informal sectors; including youth) with the hegemonic role of the bourgeoisie in 'civil society' in terms of corporate social responsibility (e.g. MNCs, PSUs, etc.).

'This logic is provided by the requirement of reversing the effects of primitive accumulation of capital with activities like anti-poverty programmes. This is a necessary political condition for the continued rapid growth of corporate capital. The state, with its mechanisms of electoral democracy, becomes the field for the political negotiation of demands for the transfer of resources, through fiscal and other means, from the accumulation economy to programmes aimed at providing the livelihood needs of the tribes' (Chatterjee, 2008). The growth of industries has created a paradigm shift among tribal societies changing dynamic shift towards rural–urban area and agriculture-non-agricultural occupations.

Hence, voluntary by choice they separated from their place and occupation, which is shaped by the perception of new opportunities and new desires among tribal youth (both male and female).

Citizenship and Social Citizenship

Citizenship refers to the relationship between the 'citizens' and the state within the context of rights and obligations and is based on the civil, political, and social rights and entitlements enable all citizens to be a member of a nation, to participate equally and meaningfully in matters that govern their lives. At its core, citizenship refers to the relationship between the 'citizens' and the state within the context of rights and obligations and is based on the principles of 'inclusion' and 'exclusion' of members.

It has become clear, however, that many social groups feel excluded from the 'common culture' despite possessing the common rights of citizenship. Thus, political inequality operating through these structures limits the possibility of actors engaging actively in the public sphere, for accessing their rights. Furthermore, they act not in isolation but in overlapping which hinders their ability to claim their rights. 'In reference to the rights and duties of members of a nation state, citizenship is a politico-juridical status that confers an identity, and determines the distribution of resources within society' (Marshall, 1950). 'Citizenship is an important element in social justice, because it includes responsibilities of state (i.e. welfare, development, education, security, etc.). Citizenship as rights signifies the rights necessary to achieve full and equal membership in society' (Volpp, 2007). Marshall defines this as efforts to gain the enjoyment of civil, political, and social rights in societies. Welfare states achieved the conciliation of class with less focused towards the inequalities in social and political class.

In Rural Set-Up: The Tribal Community (Lenin and Mao)

- Landlords
- Rich peasants
  - Rich landowners
  - Rich tenants
- Middle peasants
  - Landowners of medium size
  - Tenants with substantial holdings
- Poor peasants
  - Land not sufficient for the subsistence of the family, rent other's land
  - Tenants with some tenurial security
  - Share croppers
- Landless labourers

These sets are based on two points:

1. Ownership and non-ownership of means of production which is rooted in the concept of exploitation.
2. Class situation as a market situation which is rooted in the concept of 'life chances'.

These imbibed inequalities are also not addresserd properly beacause the class-caste interface is not properly addressed in the stratification existing in the society in contemporary era which is as follows in Indian context.

- The Indian big bourgeoisie
  Absentee landlords, big business operations – industry, trade banking, transport, etc.
- Medium bourgeoisie
  Business families, bureaucrats, doctors lawyers, state- and national-level politicians, landowners with more than 20 acres of land.
- Independent entrepreneurs
  Petty commodity producers and traders.
  Middle peasants, carpenters, builders, blacksmiths, etc.
- Semi-proletariat
  Poor peasants or the tenants at will.
  Village servants – weavers, washermen, and barbers.
- Agricultural labourers

Bismarck defined the modern welfare state, and social citizenship that it was developed without significant civil and political rights, and this authoritarian welfare system developed as legitmised process. This process strategised the conservetive modernisation and promoted citizenship as an exclusionary practice of hierarchy in globlised world. This absence of elementary rights, agrarian backwardness, rapid industrialisation led towards violent social process and change. These authortative systems did not developed the concept of citizenship, in totality though civil rights were obliterated by state power.

Migration

'Migration is generally defined as a permanent change in place of residence by the crossing of specified administrative or political boundaries. The persons who fulfil these two criteria are regarded as migrants' (Singh, 2012). In migration, it can look that it is a process in which people move from one place to another which is separated by their wants, needs, aspirations, and in search of better livelihood to overcome massive likelihood posed by geography or any other situation hindering their daily bread earning and creating the position of disequilibrium in their life. The last few centuries of modern and transitional development are the evidence that now and in which circumstances people either voluntarily or through force tried to put down new roots, this can also seen as a search of freedom in terms class, caste, and oppression as a minor to seek opportunity, or to make one's destiny (Singh, 2012). For this perfect example, all over the globe is India where the concept of citizenship based on equality and inequality, based on social order, which include exclusion and oppression followed by a rigid caste system, which divides people into a hierarchy that governs the distribution of power, status, and identity in society. Migration is a process where people move from one place to another which is divided by their wants, needs, aspirations, and in search of better livelihood to overcome massive likelihood posed by geography or any other situation which hindering their two times daily bread earning and creating the position of disequilibrium in their life.

'Indeed the long history of rural in-migration in some of the source areas in India combined with agricultural and rural stagnation seems to corroborate the stabilising role of out-migration' (Sasikumar, 2003). 'Saora, Munda, and Santhal tribes have a long history of migration, with male only migration among the Saora (plantation cultivation in Assam and Arunachal Pradesh), whereas Mundas and Santhals migrate as household units, mainly to NALCO site in Denkanal district of Orissa' Oraon, Gond, and Abuj Madiya migrate as household units to NTPC/SECL side in Bilaspur district, Chhattisgarh' (Menon, 1995).

Livelihood

In tribal community, people live very close to the physical environment, which supports them in living and determines their economic activity. Their main economic activities were hunting and food gathering from forest. In later days, the traditional way of livelihood of tribal people has been based on shifting cultivation and collection of forest products. Such types of stuff were rendered sustainable by a level and a pattern of utilisation of land and forest resources, which ensured the tribal's self-generating capacity for their livelihood. When shifting cultivation began to decline near about 20th century, the tribal people weighed down for agriculture as a main occupation for their livelihood. They actively adopted by growing a large variety of crops. Slowly, they have been utilising information and technology for better production. Thus, it needs lots of technical knowledge and skill to acquire more products, which was also known as an 'extensive' system of production that we could understand the role and effectiveness of education on development of occupational mobility for their better livelihood. Over the course of time, people choose how much education to obtain, which occupation to work in, and when to move in between for livelihood. These decisions are inherently interrelated, yet existing research has generally examined educational attainment, occupational choices, and on-the-job human capital accumulation separately from decisions about job search. As a result of this separation in the literature, there is currently no way to assess the importance of interactions between these decisions, or to determine the importance of human capital relative to the importance of educational and occupational mobility for livelihood. From extensive learning and practice, various definitions have emerged that attempt to represent the complex nature of a livelihood. This document embraces the definition suggested by Chambers and Conway: A livelihood comprises the capabilities, assets (including both material and social resources), and activities required for a means of living. A livelihood is sustainable when it can cope with and recover from stress and shocks and maintain or enhance its capabilities and assets both now and in the future, while not undermining the natural resource base (Chambers and Conway, 1991). The livelihoods capabilities include mental, intellectual, social (e.g. traditional knowledge, technology, information, skills and expertise), educational, and political (e.g. information) capabilities the household members possess, which are essential to perform livelihood activities. People use means (resources) and capabilities to construct/contrive a living. This means that the available and accessible resources and the capabilities together make it possible to perform various livelihood activities, which further result into creating or obtaining (gaining) outputs.

Migration and Food Security

Migration and food insecurity can feed into each other, creating a circle for tribal populations. The State of Food Security and Nutrition in the World 2017 highlights that, because of migration in tribal areas and target productive agricultural assets such as infrastructure, land, and livestock, the economic impacts often hit agricultural sectors disproportionately hard. Those living under poverty often face a difficult choice: risk becoming victims of the hunger and starvation hence they migrate for highly certain future to ensure the food security. Available evidence suggests that food security is a main reason why people abandon their livelihoods and migrate in search of new place. Food security, strong social networks, and better livelihood opportunities, in contrast, are key reasons people opt to stay where they are.

The Disequilibrium Syndrome of Migration

Migration as a field of demographic study has often been viewed differently by economists and political scientists although both subscribe to the disequilibrium theory. Migration can be of various types on the basis of motivation, distance, and time.

Based on motivation of movement, migration can be economic and social. Based on distance, migration can be classified as long distance and short distance. Likewise, migration can be short term and long term depending on the period of stay (Chandna, 2007).

On the basis of location, migration can be classified as in-migration and out-migration. In-migration refers to movement into a particular area while out-migration is movement out of a particular area. For example, migrants coming from rural area of Chhattisgarh to urban area of Chhattisgarh are 'in-migrants' for urban area of Chhattisgarh and 'out-migrants' for rural area of Chhattisgarh. The place from which a move is made is called the place of origin or departure. The place of arrival or the place of destination is the place where the movement ends. In-migration and out-migration together constitute internal migration, that is, migration inside a country. Net migration is the difference between the number of in-migrants and the number of out-migrants in a place. It can be positive or negative. If the number of in-migrants exceeds the out-migrants, the net migration is positive and the region has net in-migration.

However, if the number of out-migrants exceeds that of the in-migrants, then net migration is negative and the region has net out-migration. The volume of migration or gross migration is the total of the arrivals of immigrants/ in-migrants and departures of emigrants/out-migrants.

On the basis of number, migration may be individual or mass migration. It can also be forced or voluntary. Figure 1 shows the fundamental distinction between forced and voluntary migration and also between national and

Figure 1

Classification of Mobility

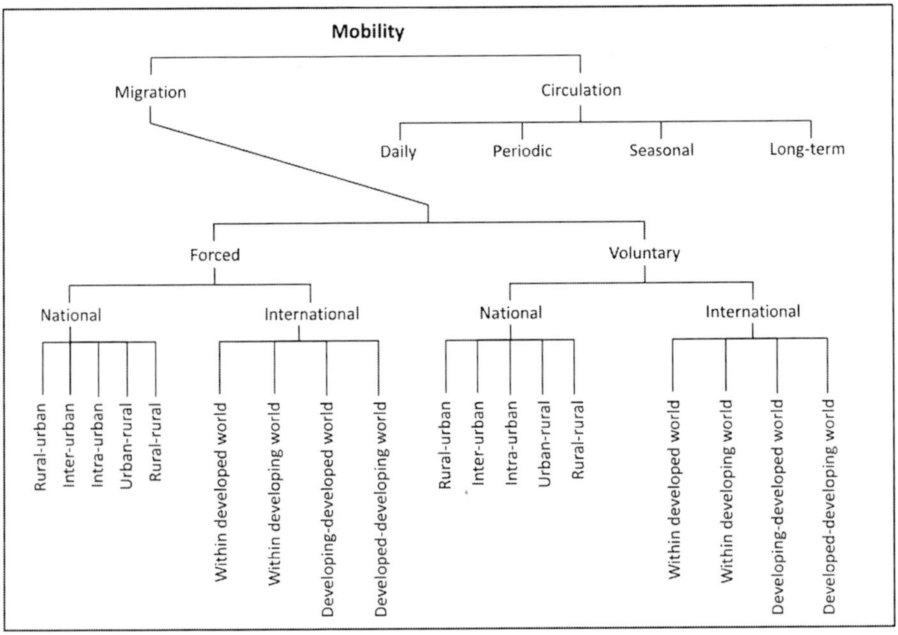

Source: Witherick 1990 cited in Singh, 2012.

international migration. Forced migration occurs due to persecution, military and ethnic conflict, war, etc. which leads to the displacement of a large number of people as refugees. The third aspect in the figure highlights the directional distinction of urban and rural in internal migration, and between developed world and developing world in the context of international migration. Internal migration can be studied in terms of migration streams, depicted in the figure. 'When people are involved in migration, they form a migration stream which can be of four types: rural to urban, urban to urban, rural to rural, and urban to rural' (Singh, 2012).

'Therefore, the so called push factor is in operation resulting in out-migration from the sending countries. There is another factor that is called pull factor, which is in the form of brain drain also. Push factors function in areas of out-migration, causing people to move out of their present places of residence. Pull factors operate in areas of in-migration attracting people to migrate. It is often not easy to differentiate between push and pull factors since both operate in an area and their perception varies from individual to individual' (Singh, 2012).

Rapid transformation of Indian Economy, improvement in level of education, transport, and communication facilities, shift of workforce from primary (agriculture) to secondary (industry and construction) and other tertiary activities has accelerated mobility among tribes in the recent times.

Human migrations may be explained as a natural function of social development. It has taken place at all the times and in the greatest multiplicity of circumstances. Development is usually perceived as a multidimensional process, reflected in a broader context like improvement in the quality of life, achieving demographic transition, population stabilisation, creating economic infrastructure and much needed investment.

Linking Migration Theories with Livelihood Promotion

While livelihood strategies are varied and multiple, for many poor people, migration represents a central component. Thus, understanding migration as primarily economic survival strategies for those immediately involved does allowed for a detailed analysis of migration and the chronically poor. The complexities and multifarious ways in which the relationship between migration and poverty is conceived and analysed, reflect both the diversity of definitions and understanding of migrants and migration, as well as of poverty and poverty analysis. Despite dominant representation of 'the poor' in development theory, policy and practice as a homogenous group, the poor are heterogeneous group reflecting differential access to resources power and control. Their lives are variously formed by the particular set of vulnerabilities that they experience and thus, the range of decision, choices, and options that they can pursue are similarly varied. Although migration remains central to many households' strategies, it represents one response to conditions of poverty to some.

Consequently, it cannot be assumed that all amongst the poor always have the option to migrate. Individuals and groups may remain chronically poor by adopting migration as a livelihood strategy (Kothari, 2002).

Interaction between migration and poverty – both at migrants' origins and destinations – is among the least research and understood topics in the economics of sociology. The vast majority of world's migration originates in rural areas, where most of the worlds' poverty also intensifies. How the migration of humans out of rural area affects those left behind is important from a social welfare point of view. In the light of increasing integration of markets, it also may have ramifications for economic growth outside of tribal area (e.g. by affecting food productions, agricultural exports, the rural demand for manufactured goods, and future economic surplus in agriculture available for investment anywhere in the economy). Moreover, the socio-economic welfare of non-migrants positively persuades future migration demands. At migrants' destinations, immigrants labour enters into local production activities harmonising some factors while possibly competing with others (including some types of non-immigrants labour). It influences both the level and distribution of income in migrants-host economies. The positive features of migration are that it reduces poverty in source areas by shifting population from low-income rural sector to the relatively high-income urban economy.

Distress migration of male-members inter-alia, results in increase in female-headed households; feminisation of poverty, impact on reproduction and population growth in sending areas; no formal entitlements to land and ownership; depended on irregular and insufficient remittances; loss of social and other support networks; not enough labour to work on the land and limited political participation. The elderly are likely to be more dependent on family and 'community' networks, which may decline through the out-migration of others. Increased dependent on government services and social welfare mechanism; loss of young people and subsequent decline in the agricultural sector, consequences of an ageing population; social security systems are undermined (Tripathy, 2005).

The economic theory of migration has its historical roots in models of development (Lewis, 1954). According to this theory, rural–urban migration is caused by geographic differences in the supply and demand for labour. Migration is possible due to assumptions of wage differentials between rural and urban areas, reserve army of 'underemployed' labour in agriculture, full unemployment, zero transfer costs, and reinvestment of urban enterprise profits into production. Lewis model, especially the assumption of full employment the Harris-Todaro model (1970) and its extension has been crucial in modelling rural-to-urban migration in less-developed countries. The underlying micro-foundations of these models are that expected wage in urban areas is the driving force of rural migrants. Soon after the Harris-Todaro model, many other researchers have extended the model by incorporating new factors that have increased the choices of individuals to migrate (Todaro, 1970).

In the Harris-Todaro model, labour migration is modelled in the context of inter-sectoral (rural–urban) wage inequality. Migration decisions are made by rational self-interested individuals looking for higher paid work in urban areas.

Migration occurs if the economic benefits in terms of expected wages at urban destination – accounting for risk of initial spell of unemployment – exceed economic cost of moving and of foregone wages at rural origins (Lucas, 1997).

Tribal Youth Migration and Profile of Chhattisgarh

'Chhattisgarh state was carved out of the erstwhile Madhya Pradesh state on 1 November 2000 and has a total area of 1,35,194 square kilometres comprising of 16 districts, 146 blocks, and 19,744 inhabited villages. According to the 2001 Census, the total population of Chhattisgarh is 2.08 crore out of which 79.9 per cent is rural in nature. The density of population in the state is 130 persons per square kilometre. The state has a predominant ST population accounting for 31.8 per cent, SCs 11.6 per cent, and the rest other communities including backward classes. The sex ratio of the state is 989 females per 1,000 males. About 33 per cent of the state's population is estimated to be living below poverty line (BPL) and the majority of it is STs. As per the 1997 BPL survey, 5.89 lakh tribal families are below the poverty line. The primitive tribe population is 1.11 lakh and their entire population is under BPL category' (SRRA, 2010).

'The central belt covers more than one-third area, consisting of 11 districts of the state and partial sub-plan area belongs to this region. The northern and southern belts comprise major tribal-populated districts of Bastar, Dantewada

Figure 2

Number of Districts in Chhattisgarh

Source: Census of India 2011, Chhattisgarh, District Census Handbook, Part XII-B.

Figure 3

Distribution of Tribal Population District-wise in Chhattisgarh

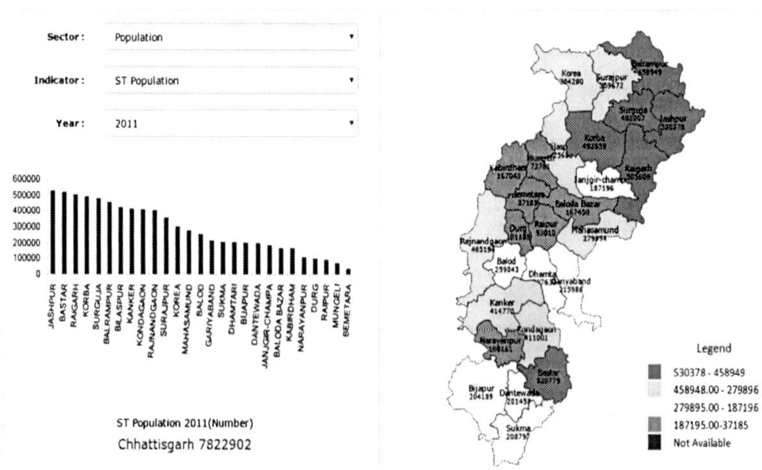

Source: Census of India 2011, Chhattisgarh, District Census Handbook Part XII-B.

Figure 4

Distribution of Female Tribal Population District-wise in Chhattisgarh

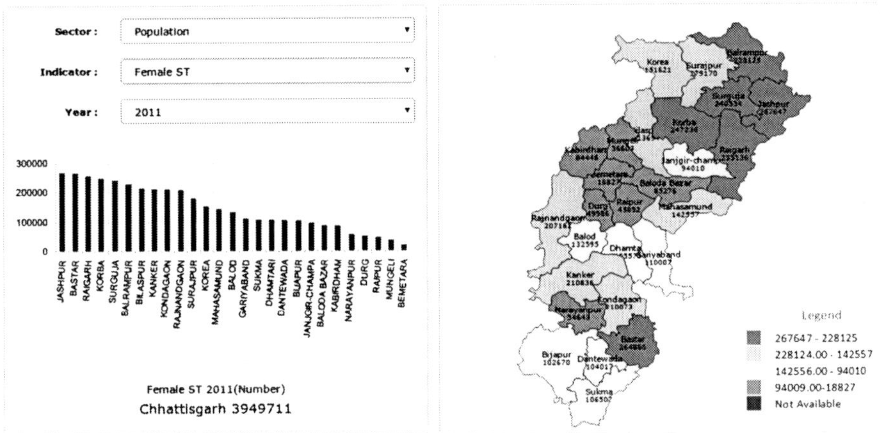

Source: Census of India 2011, Chhattisgarh, District Census Handbook Part XII-B.

in the south, and Koriya, Surguja, and Jashpur in the north. Work participation rate in the state is around 46.5 per cent and 44.5 per cent have returned as cultivators, 31.9 per cent as agricultural labourers, and 2.1 per cent as household industry workers. The state is endowed with rich mineral resources like iron, coal, bauxite, tin, and dolomite. The decadal growth rate of the state is 18.6 per cent against the national average of 21.01 per cent and the literacy rate is 64.7 per cent which is equivalent to the national average' (SRRA, 2010).

'The work participation rate (WPR) of the Chhattisgarh scheduled tribe population is 53.40 per cent that is slightly lower than the national average of 49.10 per cent. The WPR for male and female tribal population is 56.70 and 50.20 per cent, respectively. The majority of the scheduled tribe population in the state, that is, 56.60 per cent, is categorised as "cultivators" while "agricultural labourers" category constitutes 32.70 per cent. The national average for "cultivators" and "agricultural labourers" 44.7 per cent and 32.7 per cent, respectively. "Other workers" are about 9.70 per cent while the "house hold industry (HHI)" category constitutes about 1.20 per cent of the WPR of the state' (SRRA, 2010).

Christian missionaries played a vital role in the lives of tribal youth specifically among females in India. Initially, Christian missionaries came to India and began to spread their religious messages. They started their work with the goal of spreading the messages of Christ; but they soon realised that other complementary activities, such as spread of education and helping the people in other small ways, were necessary to reach their main goal. Though, the spread of school education and widespread exposure to modern communications media by Christian missionaries among them, moreover widespread desires among younger members, both male and female, of tribes do not want to live their life at the margins and the outskirts of the society. This pulls tribal female youth to

Table 1

Sex-wise Tribal Population (in each district) of Chhattisgarh

S. No.	District	Male	Female	Total	Percentage of Females to Total Population
1	Koriya	1,31,957	1,28,083	2,60,040	49.26
2	Surguja	5,41,949	5,34,720	10,76,669	49.66
3	Jashpur	2,33,166	2,36,787	4,69,953	50.39
4	Raigarh	2,22,470	2,25,233	4,47,703	50.31
5	Korba	2,10,373	2,09,516	4,19,889	49.90
6	Janjgir-Champa	75,454	77,615	1,53,069	50.71
7	Biiaspur	1,97,984	1,99,120	3,97,104	50.14
8	Kawardha	60,510	61,447	1,21,957	50.38
9	Rajnandgaon	1,66,587	1,75,101	3,41,688	51.25
10	Durg	1,72,038	1,76,763	3,48,801	50.68
11	Raipur	1,81,409	1,83,864	3,65,273	50.34
12	Mahasamund	1,14,221	1,18,264	2,32,485	50.87
13	Dhamtari	91,748	93,767	1,85,515	50.54
14	Kanker	1,80,825	1,84,206	3,65,031	50.46
15	Bastar	4,28,973	4,37,515	8,66,488	50.49
16	Dantewada	2,77,670	2,87,261	5,64,931	50.85
	Chhattisgarh	32,87,334	33,29,262	66,16,596	50.32

Source: Census 2001.

migrate to the town or the city because of entice and upward mobility among them instead of anticipating fear of all hardships and uncertainties they may face in future.

This is mainly significant for Chhattisgarh where the life of poor tribes in tribal society is marked not only by the disadvantage of class but also by the discriminations of caste, compared to which the complete inscrutability of life in the urban area is often seen as liberating them from past condition based on gender and caste.

'Migrants do not constitute a homogenous category, and migrants are differentiated according to gender, class, ethnicity, language, and religion. Women constitute an overwhelming majority of migrants, 70.7 per cent of internal migrants as per Census 2001 and 80 per cent of total internal migrants as per NSSO'. Marriage is given by women respondents as the most prominent reason for migrating: cited by 91.3 per cent of women in rural areas and 60.8 per cent of women in urban areas (NSSO 2007–08). However, several researchers are working to uncover the more complex reality lying behind statistics and consider that women migrate for a number of other reasons that are not captured by census and macro-data surveys. 'About 30 per cent of internal migrants in India belong to the youth category in the 15–29 years age group' (Unicef, 2013).

Table 2

Percentage of Employment Among STs Women in Overall Employment in Rural Area

S. No.	Characteristics	No. of Persons Usually Working								
		Agricultural			Non Agricultural			All		
		All	Female	Percentage of Female Employment to All	OAE	Female	Child-F	All	Female	Percentage of Female Employment to All
1	Non Perennial	1,34,105	60,088	44.81	24,738	6,827	310	1,58,843	66,915	42.13
2	Without Premises	1,44,569	63,530	43.94	59,986	14,016	276	2,04,555	77,546	37.91
3	Social Group									
	(A) SC	8,451	3,688	43.64	24,129	4,295	88	32,580	7,983	24.50
	(B) ST	96,680	42,813	44.28	38,486	12,311	279	1,35,166	55,124	40.78
	(C) OBC	35,060	13,508	38.53	1,59,869	27,651	665	1,94,429	4,159	2.14
4	No Power	1,51,561	64,848	42.79	2,06,227	37,337	869	3,57,788	1,02,185	28.56

Source: Economic Census 2005.

Data Representation and Interpretation

Data representation used in this paper is result of various preliminary surveys conducted by author among 300 people with the help of students placed under his supervision in the nearby region of Bilaspur, Chhattisgarh.

Figure 5

Migrants from Outside of Bilaspur

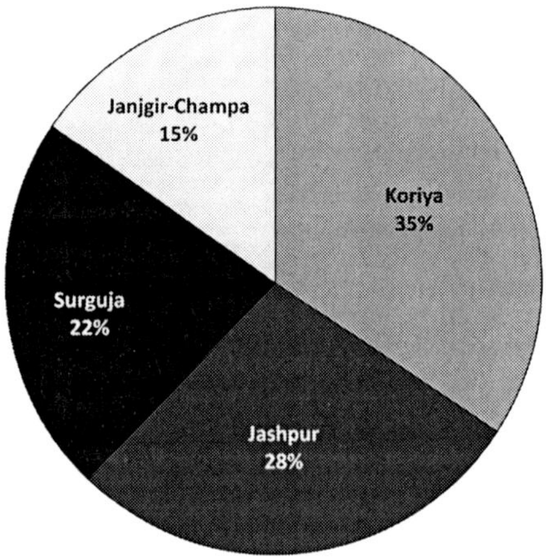

In survey conducted among 300 tribal migrants, it has been found that almost all the migrants came from four districts of Chhattisgarh in descending order (i.e. Koriya, Jashpur, Surguja, and Champa). Most of the migrants identify themselves as converted Christians and very few as Hindus.

Figure 6

Age Distribution

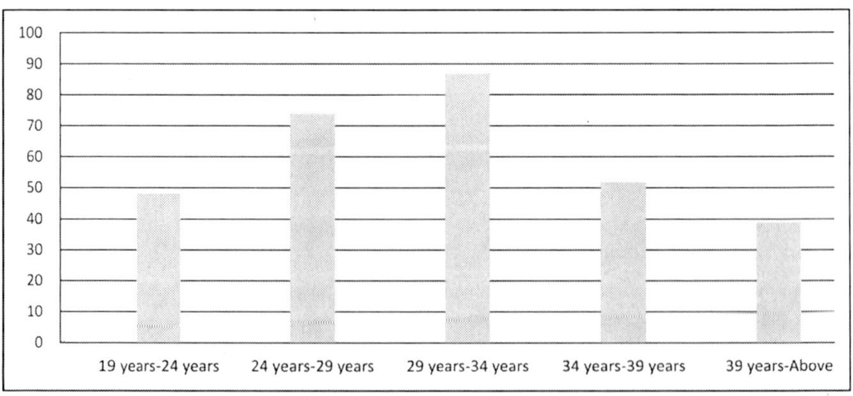

Figure 6 depicts that the age group of the migrants is ascending in nature, hence it increased from 19 years age group to 34 years age group, and afterwards it has decreased. It shows that migration among tribal youth is very rampant.

Figure 7

Male-Female Distribution Age-wise

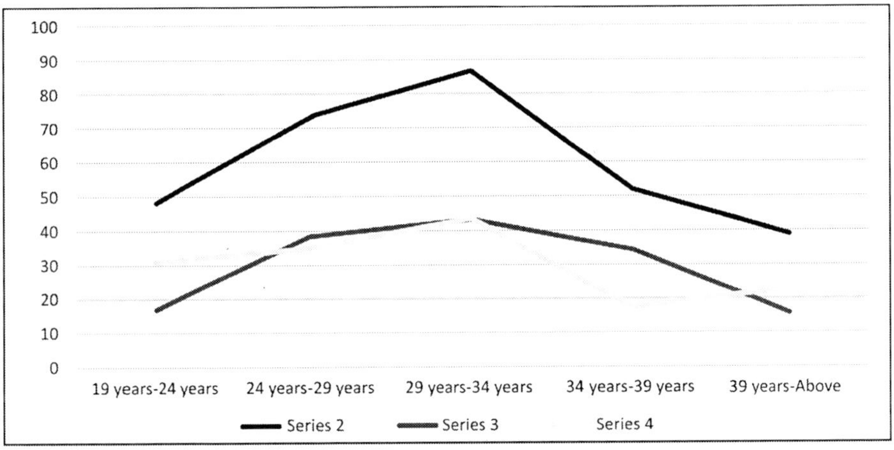

This Figure 7 shows the male-female distribution among migrants age-wise. Data reveal that among 300 migrant workers, 149 are female members (series 03) and 151 are male members (series 04). These data also depict that there is positive correlation between age and migration among male and females. However, it is stronger among females.

Figure 8

Reasons to Migrate

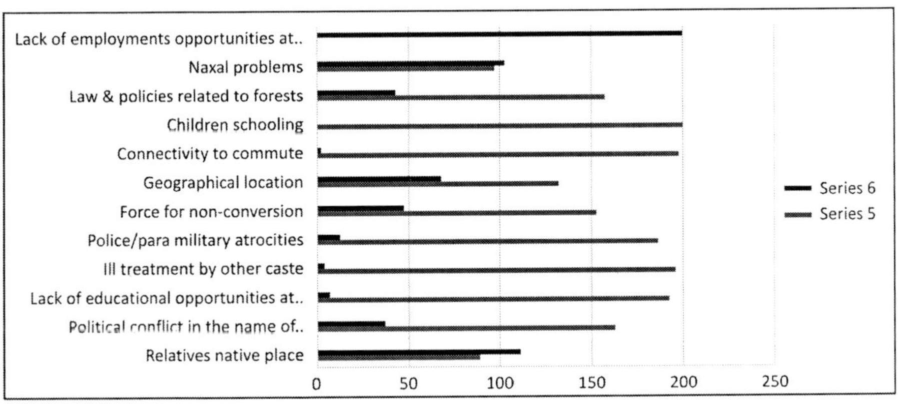

Figure 8 shows the responses given by migrants in reply to 12 variations in reasons to migrate; hence series 05 shows their response in Yes and series 06 in No among all of 300 migrants individually.

Figure 9 shows the responses given by female migrants in reply to seven variations in reasons to migrate; hence series 05 shows their response in Yes and series 06 in No among all of 149 migrants individually. They stated about first reason that among tribal community there a period of prohibition before

Figure 9

Reason of Female Members to Migrate

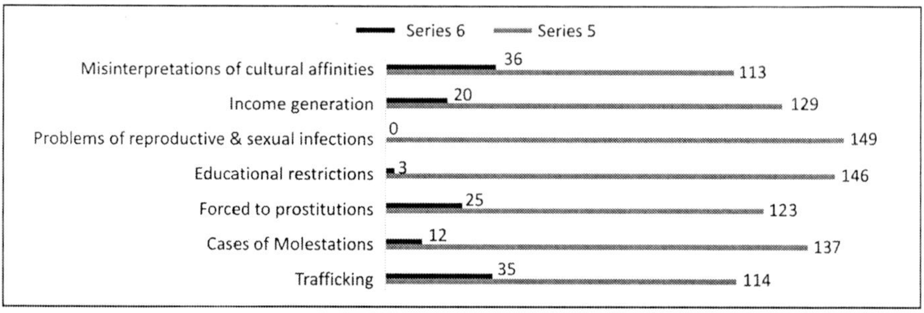

marriage among couples they select from their own community/clan, if they find themselves suitable for each other than they will marriage. During this period, couple can intimate as it is allowed in their cultural affinities, but almost male members left the female after prohibition. It shows how the manifestation of gender discrimination has woven through misinterpretations of cultural affinities. In addition, they all stated that among women problem of cancer (cervical) is very high.

Analysis and Conclusion

In a tribal dominated area, poverty-stricken state like Chhattisgarh, landlessness and marginalisation of the poor people turns-out to be the main cause of them moving to other more-developed regions of the country in the hope of better livelihood. With regard to the history of youth out-migration in Chhattisgarh, it dates back to the period of droughts, other natural calamities, and various anti-governance movements in Chhattisgarh. The agriculture labour and landless labour were migrating from rural areas to urban area in search of employable livelihood.

In the context of tribal community in Chhattisgarh, youth coupled with external influences has brought remarkable changes in the traditional socio-economic, cultural, and livelihood for ensuring food security. This has furthered dynamic changes in lifestyle with rapid and constant needs and wants as well as redefines the citizenship rights among tribes.

Hence, it can be analysed that migration among tribal youth has expanded opportunities of employment, ensured food security, and developed new horizons of social development among them especially females who faced double dose of exploitation (i.e. being female and being female of tribal community). Youth female migration also comes across with the declination in multiple risks factors (i.e. exclusion, marginalisation, gender-based violation, health care services, and job opportunities).

The tribal youth who migrate presently are poorly employed. They are engaged in unskilled work earning low income. The works include stone breaking, hand pump digging, tube well digging, and works at construction sites as unskilled labour. The working conditions of the migrated population continue to be poor receiving low wages, temporary employment, lack of employment welfare benefits, etc. The rural economy in tribal belts of Chhattisgarh has been almost entirely confined to agriculture and non-timber-forest-products. Livelihood opportunities allied to agriculture or in non-farming sector offer substantial potential for growth. These include horticulture, forestry, poultry, piggery, etc.

Older generation member of the tribal community opined that the fast pace change process that has seeped into the tribal youth is irreversible and unstoppable. Lifestyles of tribal community people are changing rapidly and demand of the younger generation for quick returns for anything they engage in is starting to have repercussions on society at large. There are also stark dimensional changes of tribal female youth needs and wants, which have led to fundamental varying conceptions of tribal community life and living with entry of new ideas through modern education and ever-imposing system of governance in the form of state. All these processes put together have stimulated changes among female tribal youth's way of life, which has led to an increased demand for migration among them to satisfy their needs. While in the midst of all these humongous changes, the demand for migration have picked up by female tribal youth's in the region.

Among tribal females who were contributing in subsistence production because existence of gender relation, where subsistence means the condition of only just having enough food (or money) to stay alive, hence the expressions are subsistence farming/subsistence agriculture and subsistence production. For them the desired future is to move out of the traditional servitude of rural labour into other urban occupations for their own worth, self-respect, and dignity.

Currently, changes taking place in tribal-belts of Chhattisgarh are stimulated with both external and internal factors. There are external socio-political pressures exerted by the government, which hopes to bring tribal population within its manoeuvre by politico-economic pressure, *hinduvata* forces (forcing tribal population towards non-conversion into Christianity), the massive presence of para-military along with increased market interest to enter these belts/areas of Chhattisgarh (because of richness in natural resources), ill treatment by dominant castes, naxal problems, and women suppression in patriarchy which bring with it in flow of migration.

Within the in-migration process (qualified as those from outside moving into the Bilaspur tribal female youth population). There are temporary migrants who come for a specific time period only (i.e. education, pre-job coaching, etc.). Contract and casual migrants who could stay longer depending on the contract period and finally those migrants who are in search of some degree of permanency in residence in Bilaspur.

Female tribal youth who have migrated from tribal belts of Chhattisgarh – developed areas of Chhattisgarh are engaged in many activities and are employed by governments, contractors, individual contractors, homeowners, large-scale agricultural land owners, self-employment, etc.

In case of female youth migration, who has been interviewed as respondent group, it can be conceptualised on the basis of data interpretation that migration has empowered them in both progression.

Individual empowerment: In which the attainment of individuality and ability for self-determination, as well as means to allow individuals to widen their prospects.

Collective empowerment: Through this process of empowerment capability of a group to effect social change is increased and it moves towards a just and equivalent society, specifically in terms of men and women. In addition, it is very significant in promoting well-being because well-being of an individual is hampered when they have limited access to other assets, income, health, shelter, education, nutrition, and entitlement over constitutional rights (World Bank, 2000–01). When these risk profiles hinder them to realise their capability, which directly as well as indirectly affect well-being among tribal women, 50 per cent of the population continue to be tribal in Chhattisgarh among which 80 per cent lives in rural area and 40 per cent representation of female, and among them majority lives BPL. Even though there is increase in rural income, still a large number of populations lagging behind (Jodhka, 2014, p. 29). It is well known that rural poverty is far behind in many dimensions as encompassing not only low income but also landlessness, low achievement of education, poor health, no housing, and lack of other facilities (Moodie, 2008, p. 455). It is no coincidence that these broad ranges of risk profile directly affect social and economic well-being of their rural household. It means that tribal women people struggle daily to survive for their livelihood (Drèze and Sen, 2002; Moodie, 2008). Apart from this, when these risk profiles combined together, they drag poor into a downward spiral of misery (Kapoor and Ojha, 2006, pp. 67–68). On this ground, migration is emerging as hope for the tribal women that brought deprived, marginalised upward to get rid of poverty. The discourse on quality life and well-being of an individual in society depend on various aspects. Indian well-being index in a broader way covers all aspects of wellness. That includes home amenities, kitchen facilities, education, health, entertainment, communication, transportation, and hygiene.

References

Azam, Mehtabul, (2013): Intergenerational Occupational Mobility in India, IZA Discussion Papers, No. 7608, Institute for the Study of Labor (IZA), Bonn.

Chambers, Robert and Conway, Gordan R., (1991): Sustainable Rural Livelihoods: Practical Concepts for the 21st Century, IDS Discussion Paper 296, December, https://www.ids.ac.uk/files/Dp296.pdf

Chandna, R., (2007): *Geography of Population: Concepts, Determinants and Patterns,* Kalyani Publishers, New Delhi.

Chatterjee, P., (2008): Democracy and Economic Transformation in India. *Economic & Political Weekly*, Vol. 43, No. 16, pp. 53–62.

Drèze, J. and Sen, A., (2002): Democratic Practice and Social Inequality in India, *Journal of Asian and African Studies*, Vol. 37, No. 2, pp. 6–37.

Jodhka, S.S., (2014): Changing Face of Rural India. *Economic & Political Weekely*, Vol. XLIX, No. 14, pp. 28–31.

Kabeer, Naila, (2001): Reflections on the Measurement of Women's Empowerment, in Sisask, Anne, (ed.) *Discussing Women's Empowerment: Theory and Practice*. SIDA Studies (3). Swedish International Development Cooperation Agency, Stockholm, Sweden, pp. 17–57.

Kapoor, S. and Ojha, R.K., (2006): Vulnerability in Rural Areas Potential Demand for Microinsurance, *International Journal of Rural Management*, Vol. 2, No. 1, pp. 67–83.

Kothari, U., (2002): Migration & Chronic Poverty, Working Paper No. 16, Institute for Development Policy and Management, University of Manchester.

Lewis, W.A., (1954): Economic Development with Unlimited Supplies of Labour, *The Manchester School of Economic and Social Studies*, Vol. 22, pp. 139–91.

Lucas, R., (1997): Internal Migration in Developing Countries, In M.R. Stark (ed.), *Handbook of Population and Family Economics*, Elsevier Science Publishing, Amsterdam.

Marshall, T.H., (1950): *Citizenship and Social Class and Other Essays*. Cambridge University Press, Cambridge.

Menon, G., (1995): The Impact of Migration on the Work and Status of Tribal Women in Orissa, In *Women and Seasonal Labour Migration*. Indo-Dutch Series on Development Alternatives 16, by L. Schenk-Sandbergen. Sage, New Delhi.

Moodie, M., (2008): Enter Microcredit. *American Ethnologist*, Vol. 35, No. 3, pp. 454–65.

Sasikumar, R.S., (2003): An Overview of Migration in India, Its Impacts and Key Issues. *Regional Conference on Migration, Development and Pro-Poor Policy Choices in Asia*, Refugee and Migratory Movements Research Unit, Dhaka, Bangladesh and the Department for International Development, UK.

Singh, V., (2012): Citizenship, Migration and Livelihood in Era of Globalisation, *Jharkhand Journal of Development and Management Studies (JJDMS)*, Vol. 10, No. 3, pp. 5017–31.

SRRA, (2010): *Migration of Tribal Women: Its Socio-economic Effects–An In-Depth Study of Chhattisgarh, Jharkhand, M.P. and Orissa*, Society for Regional Research and Analysis, Gurgaon.

Todaro, J.H., (1970): Migration, Unemployement and Development: A Two Sector Analysis, *American Economic Review*, Vol. 60, pp. 126–42.

Tripathy, S., (2005): *Female Headed Households in India*. Sonali Publications, New Delhi.

Unicef, (2013): *Social Inclusion of Internal Migrants in India*, UNESCO New Delhi

Volpp, Leti, (2007): The Culture of Citizenship. *Theoretical Inquiries in Law*, Vol. 8, No. 2, pp. 571-601.

World Bank, (2000–01): Oxford University Press, New York.

18 The Question of Development

Land Acquisition, Land Marginalisation, and Proletarianisation of Peasants

Animesh Roy

> 'Land is limited. Land is precious. Land holds a special value to farmers and their families. It's not an impersonal, dematerialised share certificate that you buy and sell with every swing of the Sensex.'
>
> — Gopalkrishna Gandhi, Former Governor, West Bengal (2008)

Introduction

In India, the fact that has become a cliché in the context of post-economic reform development is that the present form of land-based development largely driven by the private capital under the aegis of the government is against the welfare and benefit of the farming communities. The issues of insufficient compensation and loss of livelihood of farmers caused by the acquisition of agricultural land for urbanisation, industrialisation, infrastructure development projects, and setting up special economic zones (SEZs) have raised a key debate under the neoliberal land-based development in the country in recent years. Studies across the world, especially in developing countries, reflect the fact that land acquisition for development projects results in deprivation of property rights, marginalisation (Asif, 1999; Amirthalingam and Lakshman, 2009; Cernea, 1997, 1999, 2000; Fernandes, 1998, 2005, 2009; Penz et al., 2011; Ge, 2012; Tang et al., 2012; Hui and Bao, 2013) and social exclusion of the dispossessed people (De Wet, 2001; Council for Social Development, 2008; Mahapatra, 1999; Advani, 2009; Sharma, 2010; World Bank, 2004).

In the last few decades, particularly after the economic reforms in 1991, vast tracts of agricultural land have been acquired by various state governments including the incumbent Biju Janata Dal (BJD), Government of Odisha in the name of development under the disguise of larger public interests. Latest data from the Ministry of Agriculture, Government of India, show that the country has registered a decline of 4.06 lac hectares of cultivable land due to various development activities over a short span of only four years between 2007–08 and

2010–11 (Mohan, 2013). The phenomenal rise in the incidences of acquisition of agricultural land for development activities across the country has pushed the traditional farming communities in a cumbersome insecurity to earn their livelihoods (Chandra, 2008; Khan, 2011a, 2011b; Nath et al., 2013). Agricultural land holds a special value to the farmers. It generates employment for their family members; renders income from the crops in the form of a rent and profit; and provide a sense of security and social esteem to them (Sau, 2008). However, acquisition of these limited resources has become an engine of oppression (Venkatesan, 2011) and is altering the socio-economic scenario of the dispossessed who established their foothold on such land to earn their living. The benefits of the development activities are enjoyed by the capitalist, not by the under privileged people for whom they were actually destined (Banerjee and Roy, 2007; Bhattachariya, 2007; Bapat, 2009). This paper examines two of such development ventures taken off on acquired land from the farmers in Kujanga C.D. Block near Paradeep Port in Odisha.

Contextual Backdrop

India followed the socialist inspired policies for its economic development immediately after the independence (Patra, 2012). Many sectors added on state ownership and its extensive regulations virtually isolated India from rest of the world economy. Consequently, the Indian economy (Net Domestic Product) grew only at around one per cent per annum for the next three decades after independence. This could be one of the many reasons for which India remained a poor nation even after 60 years of independence. In the 1980s, India slowly started opening up. The major turnaround, however, came in 1991–92 with the liberalisation and globalisation of the Indian Economy that provided leverages to private capital and invited foreign direct investment (FDI) and technologies resulting in, as claimed by the proponents of the neoliberal model, a slowly declining poverty (Banerjee et al., 2007).

The socio-economic progress of India in the post-independence period has not at all been uniform across the region/state. Some states have experienced a substantial economic development compared to others. Interestingly, the states that have encouraged industrialisation, infrastructure development, and the enhancement of the quality of human resources along with agriculture performed better than the remaining states that were predominantly agriculture based. Odisha has always been considered one of the most socially and economically backward states in the country due to frequent onslaught of natural calamities like flood, cyclones, etc. unequal distribution of agricultural land-holdings and the unskilled labours. The poverty in Odisha is even more than some of the African countries, *such as Malawi* (Patra, 2012). The population of Odisha is largely dependent on agriculture and poor. Despite a long coastline and rich mineral resources endowment, until the end of the last century, Odisha had barely been taken into consideration for setting up large manufacturing enterprises by the giant industrialists and infrastructure developers. This was due to insufficiency in formulation of enthralling industrial policies. However, the precept of the neoliberal economic policy adopted by the Government of India at the centre started reflecting in Odisha's development paradigm since the beginning of current century when the BJD Government brought about the Industrial Policy Resolution of 2001 for bringing in a large-scale domestic and foreign capital through industrialisation and infrastructure development by facilitating lower cost of incorporation, easy credit, and tax benefits, etc. to the large private capital giants. Shockingly, most of these capitalist establishments have come up on acquired agricultural or forest land, on which a large rural mass was dependent for livelihoods.

Land acquisition is not a recent phenomenon in Odisha. In pre-economic reform stage between 1960 and 1990, the state government mostly acquired land on a large scale for the construction of major dams, such as Hirakud, Kolab, Balimela, Rengali, Indrawati, etc. under the purview of public purposes laid down in the Land Acquisition Act (LAA) of 1894. However, there has been a substantial change in this pattern in post-economic reform stage, particularly in the 2000s and thereafter. In the neoliberal regime, especially after the enactment of Special Economic Zone (SEZ) Act of 2005, the role of state has undergone a substantial change (Bedi, 2013) and begun to acquire vast tracts of agricultural and forest land for industrialisation, urbanisation, and infrastructure development in different parts of the state (e.g. Sundergarh, Sambalpur, Jharsuguda, Angul, Cuttack, Dhenkanal, Jagatsinghpur, Angul, Gopalpur, Kalinganagar, etc.) under the aegis of the same 'public purpose clause' for private capital-led development ventures (steel, sponge iron, and power plant projects). In most of the cases until now, acquisition of land has been accomplished without the consent of a large volume of stakeholders of such land, as it has been noticed in our undertaken field area (Bhutamundai village in Kujanga block) where the incumbent BJD Government had acquired about 2,000 acres of land in the second half of the 2000s, mostly fertile agricultural land for setting up two large industries, namely Indian Farmers Fertiliser Cooperative Limited (IFFCO) and ESSAR Steel Plant. The protagonists of the ruling party in the state postulate that the present government is engaged in eradicating backwardness tag of Odisha by bringing large-scale domestic and foreign direct investment, which would provide new openings and increase the net state domestic product. The land grab on a large-scale across the state for private capital has not only led the project affected people to rage against the government and land-acquiring bodies for not to be parted with their lands and livelihoods but also ignited them to get into clashes with authorities on several occasions. Conversion of agricultural land into non-agricultural land through acquisition has developed a process of social and economic transformation leading to changes in economic activities, housing structures, and utilisation durable luxury goods. Both the development ventures have been, as we mostly see in other cases across the country, more of capital intensive, less of labour absorptive. Consequently, a significant proportion of farmers have established their footholds in menial works such as casual workers and wage labourers. The loss of land has not only made them marginalised but also forced them to lose their social dignity, resulting in a feeling of selflessness. Hence, this paper has sought to examine these issues in the context of IFFCO and ESSAR Steel Plant affected households keeping the concept of Marxian 'primitive accumulation' in focus. The analytical discourse of the paper proceeds further, keeping the following research questions in view: (a) How far do the land-based private capital-led development ventures that dispossessed the peasants from their means of subsistence (land) provide alternative livelihoods? (b) Are they capable of establishing a foothold for a decent livelihood activity outside the farm economy? (c) To what extent do the existing socio-economic attributes get affected by such a land loss for development projects?

Data, Sampling, and Methodology

The data for this study had been obtained through the structured questionnaire-based household survey carried out in 2015 and from a few secondary sources. Given the underlying socio-economic consequences briefed above, the ESSAR and IFFCO project-affected people were purposively chosen for drawing samples; and an acquisition torn revenue village Bhutamundai was chosen for conducting the household survey. With the help of the concerned *Sarpanch*, local NGO workers and a group of dispossessed farmers, a census/list of total dispossessed households in the village was prepared. The listing was ended with a number of 243 dispossessed households, of which 80 households (about one-third) were randomly[1] drawn for the survey. The secondary data had been collected from the Department of Agriculture, Government of Odisha, Bhutamundai Panchayat Office, and Primary Census Abstract of 2001 and 2011.

The sample dispossessed households have been grouped into four categories of agrarian status (large, medium, small, and marginal households) considering the mean (average) size of operational land-holding at the pre-acquisition stage among them. They have also been divided into four income groups (high, medium, low, and very low) on the basis of the quartile values (Q_1, Q_2, and Q_3) of income ₹ distribution and the level of inequality among them has been assessed with the help of coefficient of variation (CV). The methods for determining income groups/classes are as follows:

Income Groups	*Method of Determining Class*
High	Above Q_3 value
Medium	Q_2 to Q_3 value
Low	Q_1 to Q_2 value
Very low	Below Q_1 value

The two most important indicators by which the economic status of a family or society is measured are: (a) Per capita income and (b) Per capita consumption expenditure at household level. Since getting actual data on total income or per capita income generated by a farming household in any rural area in India is very difficult and is also prone to be under-reported, the second indicator (per capita consumption expenditure of some selected food items, education, transportation, and other necessary stuffs[2] for last 30 days from the day of survey in a particular sample household) had been chosen for the present study to analyse the economic status of the dispossessed households. The quantity of each and every food and other item consumed by a household for the above-mentioned period was multiplied by the per unit local market price prevailing at the time of survey (rupees per kg or rupees per piece). Thus, the total monthly consumption expenditure (in rupees) per sample household as well as monthly per capita consumption expenditure (MPCE) at a sample household had been estimated. On the basis of estimated monthly per capita consumption expenditure, all the sample households have been grouped into three categories of economic status (low, medium, and high) with the methods as follows:

Category of Economic Status	*Method of Determining Class*
High	Above (M + MD)
Medium	(M – 0.5 MD) to (M + 0.5 MD)
Low	Below (M – 0.5 MD)

Note: (i) 'M' and 'MD' stand for mean and mean deviation, respectively.

The graphical and mathematical assessment of the degree of inequality among the sample households in post-acquisition stage has been done with the help of Lorenz curve and CV (Coefficient of Variation), respectively.

Study Area: A Contextual Glimpse

Kujang block/tehsil is located successively 43 kilometres and 83 kilometres away from district headquarters Jagatsinghpur and the state capital Bhubneswar towards the east. It is surrounded by the Bay of Bengal in the East, Ersama block in the south, and Raghunathpur and Tirtol block in the west. It has been bounded by the Mahanadi River in the north. Paradeep port is situated in the eastern part of Kujanga block. Since the liberalisation in India in 1991–92, Kujanga as a geographical space has gained a great importance from the industrialists for its adjacent location to the Paradeep port. During the time between 2006 and 2011, the Government of Odisha had acquired 1,966.67 acres of land in Kujanga, mostly agricultural land, from a large number of farmers of eight revenue villages for setting up two giant industries: the ESSAR Steel Plant and the IFFCO Private Ltd by dispossessing them from their land (Table 1).

Village at a Glance

Bhutamundai is a Village Panchayat and a revenue village. According to the *Primary Census Abstract 2011*, 850 households with a population size of 3,933 persons inhabit in Bhutamundai village. It is located only six kilometres away from the *Tehsil* towards the east along the Cuttack-Paradeep Highway. Despite having witnessed a rapid structural change in the economic activities, agriculture is still considered the mainstay among the rural households. In 2006–07, the Government of Odisha through Odisha Industrial Infrastructure

Table 1

Revenue Village-wise Scenario of Acquired Land in Kujanga Block

Phase	*Industrial Project*	*S. No.*	*Type Acquired Land*	*Panchayat(s)*	*Revenue Village(s) Where from Land has been Acquired*	*Area Acquired (Acre)*	*Dwelling Revenue Villages of Dispossessed Households*
(2006–07) Phase-I	ESSAR	1	Agricultural Land	Nuagarh	Nuagarh and Udaychandrapur	335.76	Nuagarh and Udaychandrapur
		2	Agricultural Land	Paradeepgarh	Udaybata and Bijaychandrapur	932.34	Paradeepgarh, Udaybata and Bijaychandrapur
	IFFCO	1	Agricultural Land	Bhutamundai	Bhutamundai	209.23	Bhutamundai and Biswali
		2	Paradeepgarh	Paradeepgarh	Paradeepgarh	91.79	Paradeepgarh and Balidia
(2009–10) Phase-II	ESSAR	1	Agricultural Land	Bhutamundai	Chakradharpur and Pipal	139.41	Bhutamundai, Jagati, Chakradharpur and Pipal
		2	Agricultural Land	Nuagarh	Nuagarh	121.17	Nuagarh
		3	Forest Land	Bhutamundai Panchayat and Paradeepgarh Panchayat	Chakradharpur, Udaybata, Paradeepgarh and Bijaychandrapur	136.97	CPRs-Government owned
Total Acquired Land (Agricultural + Forest) in two phases						1966.67 acres	

Source: Bhutamundai Panchayat, 2015.

Development Corporation Limited acquired 209.23 acres of fertile agricultural land from the farmers of this village for industrialisation, and a large proportion of which was, as claimed by the Sarpanch and dispossessed households, a fertile multi-cropped land.

Sectoral Land Utilisation: A Changing Scenario

Change in land use has been a phenomenon ever since the beginning of human civilisation. However, this phenomenon has attained a momentum in last two decades, especially in those states, which have followed an escalating path of land-based capitalist development. Consequently, cultivable land is incessantly going out of agriculture for non-agricultural purposes, mainly industrialisation, infrastructure development, and creation of housing complexes. This phenomenon has been soaring in many coastal blocks in the state, such as Kujanga, Ersama, etc. altering the traditional and normal distribution of land put under different uses.

The data on land put under different uses over a period of 16 years from 1995–96 to 2011–12 in Kujanga block obtained from the Land Use Hand Book of Jagatsingpur district shows that the agricultural land has shrunk noticeably while the area under non-agricultural uses has expanded steadily and phenomenally (Figure 1). The increase in share of land under non-agricultural uses has, however, been faster in the second half of the last decade (Table 2). The area under non-agricultural uses has increased at the rate of 3.23 per cent per annum. The reverse scenario has been noticed in case of forest, cultivable land,

Figure 1

Changes in Share (%) of Different Categories of Land in Kujanga Block

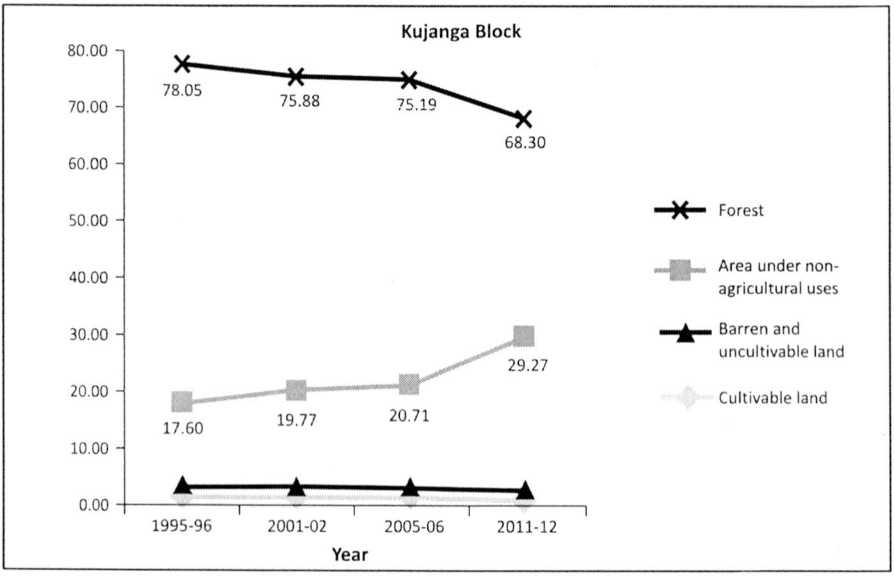

Source: Land Use Handbook of Jagatsinghpur District, 1998, 2008, and 2014.

barren and uncultivable waste land, and land under miscellaneous tree crops. The share of cultivable land has declined by 10 per cent in last 16 years. Acquisition of agricultural land for private capital is playing a substantial role to it and promoting urbanisation and real-estate boom. We will focus on this issue in the latter part of the paper.

Table 2

Changes in Share of Different Categories of Land in Kujanga Block

Category of Land	*Land (in Hectares)*				*Percentage to Total Land*			
	1995–96	*2001–02*	*2005–06*	*2011–12*	*1995–96*	*2001–02*	*2005–06*	*2011–12*
Forest	196	183	171	59	0.87	0.81	0.76	0.26
Area under non-agricultural uses	3,978	4,470	4,681	6,616	17.60	19.77	20.71	29.27
Barren and uncultivable land	576	539	523	397	2.55	2.38	2.31	1.76
Permanent pastures and grazing land	27	23	23	14	0.12	0.10	0.10	0.06
Land under miscellaneous trees	186	237	211	79	0.82	1.05	0.93	0.35
Cultivable land	17,643	17,154	16,997	15,441	78.05	75.88	75.19	68.30
Total land	22,606	22,606	22,606	22,606	100.00	100.00	100.00	100.00

Source: Land Use Handbook of Jagatsinghpur District, 1998, 2008, and 2014.

Land Acquisition and Change in Agrarian Status of Dispossessed Households

Agricultural land is a 'preeminent' resource to farming households. It generates employment for the family members, provides a sense of security in hard time, and brings social esteem. It is the symbol of a status in an agrarian society. Hence, the size of land-holdings had been considered as an important indicator to measure agrarian status of the dispossessed households at Bhutamundai. The study shows that the IFFCO and ESSAR project-affected farming households have witnessed a dramatic alteration in their agrarian status. In pre-acquisition stage, more than one-fifth of total sample households belonged to the status of large and medium farming households. However, in the post-acquisition stage, none of them has reported as a large or a medium farming household (Table 3). There has been a sharp decline in the average size of land-holdings from 3.40 acres in the pre-acquisition stage to only 0.65 acres in the post-acquisition stage. No sample household was cultivable landless before acquisition, whereas a considerable proportion (17.50%) of sample households have been agricultural landless.

Table 3

Change in Agrarian Status of the Dispossessed Households at Bhutamundai

Agrarian Status (Based on Size of Land-Holding before Acquisition)	*Before Acquisition*		*After Acquisition*	
	Count	*%*	*Count*	*%*
Large (above 6.00 acres)	10	12.50	–	–
Medium (4.00–5.99 acres)	8	10.00	–	–
Small (2.00–3.99 acres)	42	52.50	6	7.50
Marginal (below 2.00 acres)	20	25.00	60	75.00
Cultivable landless	–	–	14	17.50
Total sample households	80	100.00	80	100.00

Source: Household Survey, 2015.

Note: Mean size of land-holding before and after acquisition are 3.40 and 0.65 acres, respectively.

Patterns of Livelihood Before and After Dispossession

The most sensitive issue that the contemporary development policy of India is facing today is the alienation of farmers from their land and traditional livelihood through expropriation of land for capital. Destruction of livelihood by taking away farmers' land in various guises in the name of public interests is showing everyday how development ventures initiated by the private capital giants under the aegis of the state power can alter the socio-economic structure of the dispossessed farming communities. The culpability of this act has been evidenced in several places across the country, as in Nandigram in West Bengal and more recently in the POSCO project site at Jagatsinghpur district in Odisha.

Acquisition of agricultural land and its conversion into non-agricultural land in Bhutamundai has not only trimmed down the agrarian status of the dispossessed households in the post-acquisition stage but also brought about a striking change in the livelihood structure of the existing workforce of the land loser households. This structural change has mostly happened towards non-farm casual activities that include non-farm workers, waged construction labourers, tailors, tutors, and petty businessmen. A majority (71.21%) of the workforce of dispossessed households were cultivators before acquisition (Table 4). Acquisition of their agricultural land has, however, brought down this share to only 31.82 per cent in the post-acquisition stage. On the contrary, there has been a substantial increase of labourers – agricultural labourers, and construction and waged labourers – in the post-acquisition stage. In other words, a large section has become proletariats who have nothing but to sell their labour force. Despite having taken off both the industries on the land forcefully expropriated from the peasants, they failed to absorb the dispossessed workforce, set even a small section (6.06%) unemployed. The non-capitalistic mode of production (land) has turned into a capitalistic one under the aegis of the state patronage. This phenomenon corroborates the Marxian 'primitive accumulation' and 'proletarianisation'.

Figure 2

Share (%) Different Categories of Workers in Bhutamundai

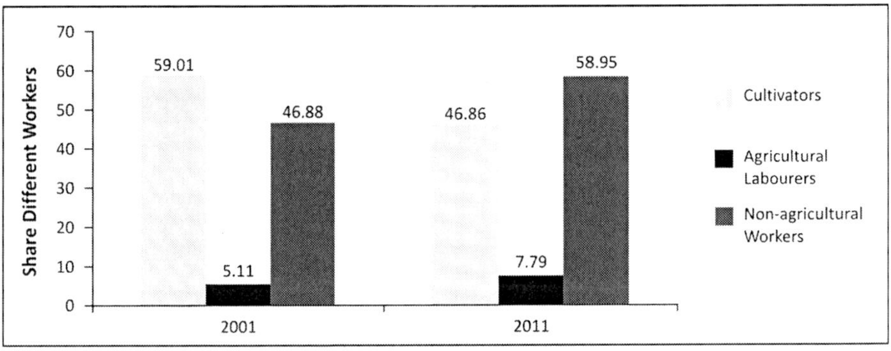

Source: Primary Census Abstract, 2001 and 2011.

Inter-sectoral change in occupational structure appears to be a resonating phenomenon. Although majority of the workforce in Bhutamundai still consider cultivation their main economic activity, a substantial change in occupational structure has been observed in the last census decade between 2001 and 2011. The share of cultivators to total workers has declined significantly from 59.01 per cent to 48.86 per cent during this time (Figure 2). On the contrary, share of non-agricultural workers has increased substantially over the same time from 38.55 per cent to 45.35 per cent. This changing pattern in economic activities from cultivation to non-firm activities signifies a transitional stage of socio-economic transformation.

Table 4

Change in Livelihood/Occupation of the Working Population of Dispossessed Households at Bhutamundai

Occupation/Livelihood of Workers of Dispossessed Households	*Before Acquisition*		*After Acquisition*	
	Count	*%*	*Count*	*%*
Cultivators	94	71.21	42	31.82
Agricultural labourers	10	7.58	14	10.61
Non-agricultural workers and waged labourers	4	3.03	37	28.03
Dairy and fishing	–	–	2	1.52
Business	12	9.09	15	11.36
Regular salaried government/private firm employees	12	9.09	12	9.09
Others (anganwadi workers, tailors, tutors, etc.)	–	–	2	1.52
Jobless	–	–	8	6.06
Total count of workers	132	100.00	132	100.00

Source: Household Survey, 2015.

Note: The table has included those members/workers who were above 15 years and below 60 years at the time of acquisition and were engaged in economic activities.

Income of the Dispossessed Households and Its Distribution

Estimation of actual income generated by a rural farming household is very difficult and is prone to be under-reported. However, given the underlying purpose of this study, monthly income at the dispossessed household has been taken into consideration to analyse the pattern of income distribution and level of inequality among the different income groups (high, medium, low, and very low).

Figure 3

Distribution of Monthly Income of Dispossessed Households at Bhutamundai

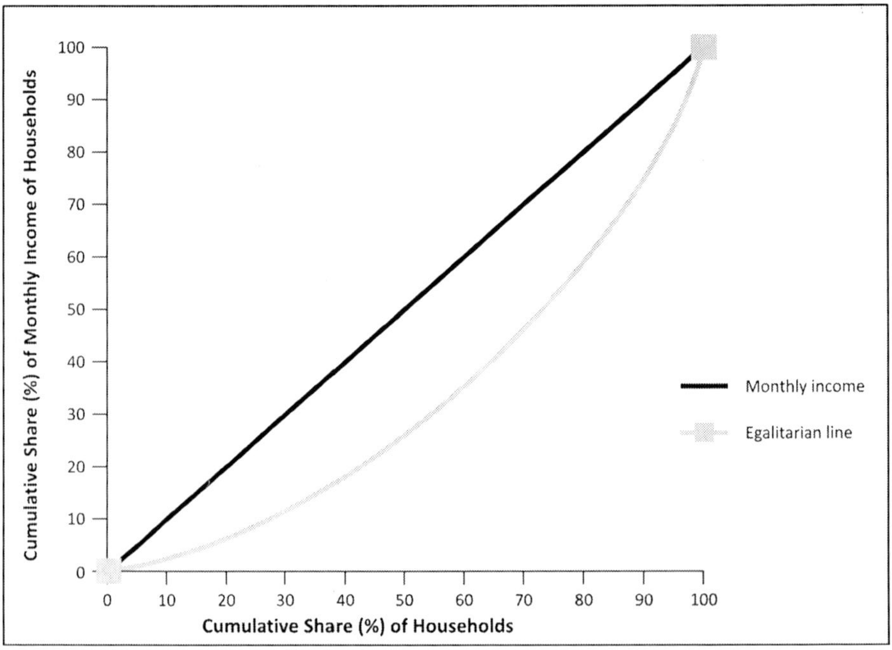

Source: Household Survey, 2015.

The Lorenz curve (Figure 3) shows a clear deviation of the monthly income curve from the egalitarian line (or line of equal distribution), which, in turn, signifies the inequality in terms of monthly household income.

Now, it would be a meaningful attempt to identify the level of inequality among different income groups, and furthermore, which income group(s) is (are) relatively playing greater role in creating overall inequality. The estimation of CV for above mentioned four income groups (Table 5) reflects that the very low-income groups has the highest CV value (36.02%) meaning thereby highest inequality followed by high-income group (25.01%). The average monthly income among the households of high-income group has substantially been higher than the rest, particularly very low-income group. This variation in income distribution between the two extreme groups would further increase the value of CV for the entire range of income distribution.

Table 5

Level of Inequality of Income among the Different Income Groups of the Dispossessed Households at Bhutamundai

Income Group	Income Class (₹)	Dispossessed Households	Range of Income Class (₹)	Average Income (₹)	Standard Deviation	Coefficient of Variation (%)
High	Above 10125	20	3,000	16,800.00	4,203.38	25.01
Medium	7,550–10,125	20	2,500	8,850.00	874.64	9.88
Low	4,875–7,550	20	2,400	6,037.50	851.76	14.11
Very low	Below 4,875	20	14,500	2,950.00	1,062.52	36.02

Source: Household Survey, 2015.

Note: Income groups have been determined on the basis of quartiles (Q_1 = ₹ 4,875, Q_2 = ₹ 7,550, and Q_3 = ₹ 10,125) of income of all dispossessed household.

Lifestyle and the Use of Luxury Goods

'Lifestyle' can simply be defined as the way of living of individuals, families or/and societies, which they manifest in coping with their physical, psychological, social, and economic environment on day-to-day basis.

With the dramatic alteration in the occupational or livelihood structure of the working populations of dispossessed households, acquisition of agricultural land in Bhutamundai has subsequently developed a process of social transformation leading to substantial change in housing structure, utilisation of durable luxury goods like motor bikes, cars, washing machines, etc. which they have mostly purchased with the compensation money received for their acquired land. Motorbike, television, and refrigerator have been considered as the most prioritised luxury goods (Figure 4). The share of dispossessed households using television and motorbike has gone up rapidly in post-acquisition stage. In pre acquisition stage, only 13.75 per cent of sample households had motorcycles, which went up to 31.25 per cent. Similar trend has been found in case of television. However, the highest absolute change in percentage share of households using a single luxury item between pre- and post-acquisition stage (till the day of household survey) has been both motorbike and television (17.50%) followed by refrigerator (Table 6).

Development project always brings forth some conspicuous positive changes in the concerned society or locality. So has been the case with Bhutamundai wherefrom a tract of 209.23 acres of fertile cultivable land was acquired for IFFCO. Shortly after the completion of acquisition, IFFCO adopted the two project affected revenue villages (Bhutamundai and Pipal) of Bhutamundai Panchayat as model villages for five years following their proposed 'Rehabilitation, Resettlement and Project Affected Area Development Plan'. As a model village, the villagers of Bhutamundai experienced several community development plans like electrification, street light, metal road construction, providing drinking water for the villagers, school renovation, infrastructure development, etc.

Figure 4

Scenario of Using Luxury Goods by the Dispossessed Households Before and After Acquisition at Bhutamundai

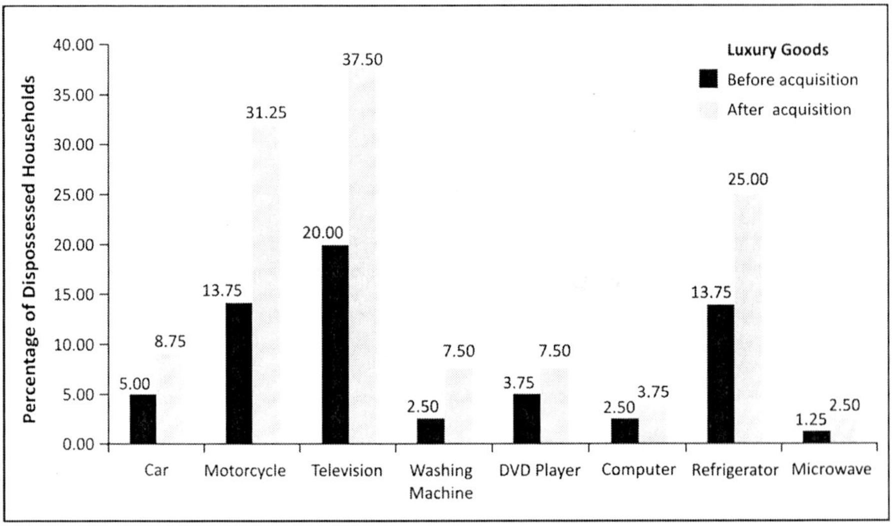

Source: Household Survey, 2015.

Table 6

Scenario of Using of Luxury Goods by the Dispossessed Households in the Post-acquisition Stage at Bhutamundai

Luxury Goods	*Before Acquisition*		*After Acquisition*		*Absolute Percentage Change (a–b)*
	Households	*% (a)*	*Households*	*% (b)*	
Car	4	5.00	7	8.75	3.75
Motorcycle	11	13.75	25	31.25	17.50
Television	16	20.00	30	37.50	17.50
Washing machine	2	2.50	6	7.50	5.00
DVD Player	3	3.75	6	7.50	3.75
Computer	2	2.50	3	3.75	1.25
Refrigerator	11	13.75	20	25.00	11.25
Microwave	1	1.25	2	2.50	1.25
Total sample	80	100.00	80	100.00	

Source: Household Survey, 2015.

Note: Luxury goods-wise sum of total sample households might not be equal to or more than the total sample size because one household might use more than one luxury good.

Consumption Expenditure and Determination of Economic Status

Considering the underlying limitation associated with the estimation of monthly household income in rural areas (as discussed earlier in the methodology section), monthly per capita consumption expenditure has been taken on for determining the economic status of the dispossessed households at Bhutamundai. Despite several development measures adopted by the IFFCO Private Ltd for the community development at Bhutamundai, our estimation shows that almost half (47.50%) of the dispossessed households belong to the category of low economic status (Table 7), which is certainly an outcome of the proletarianisation of labour in the post-acquisition stage. Only a little more than one-fifth of the sample households have come under high economic status.

Table 7

Economic Status of the Dispossessed Households at Bhutamundai

Method	*Category based on Monthly per Capita Consumption Expenditure (₹) at Household*	*Economic Status*	*Dispossessed Households*	
			Count	*%*
Above (M + 0.5 MD)	Above 2,550	High	18	22.50
(M – 0.5 MD) to (M + 0.5 MD)	1,450–2,550	Medium	24	30.00
Below (M – 0.5 MD)	Below 1,450	Low	38	47.50
Total sample households			80	100.00

Source: Household Survey, 2014.

Note: (i) Mean (M) = ₹ 2,002.01, which has been approximated to ₹ 2,000.
(ii) Mean deviation (MD) = ₹ 1,099.87, which has been approximated to ₹ 1,100.

Conclusion

The Government of India has always attempted to uphold a commitment to the higher industrial growth and accelerated infrastructure development after the end of colonial rule. This commitment has even become stronger in recent years with liberalisation and globalisation of Indian economy, which has given birth to emerging growth opportunities to private investors, especially large capital giants. The neoliberal economy of India has led its many constituent states to compete with each other for pulling in industries and infrastructure developers by providing lucrative incentives. Consequently, the demand of land for non-agricultural sector (industrial and service sector) has increased phenomenally and the incidence of government-driven land acquisition has become far more numerous than ever before. These phenomena have brought tremendous social and economic impact on the dispossessed farming community and compelled them to sacrifice their mainstream sources of livelihoods for the sake of so-called public interests.

The study, however, broadly uncovers that the area under non-agricultural uses is incrementing rapidly at the cost of cultivable and forest land. The acquisition of agricultural land has trimmed down the average land-holding size of the dispossessed households from 6.40 acres in the pre-acquisition stage to only 0.65 acres in the post-acquisition stage. Acquisition of land for capital has not only reduced the land-holding size at greater extent but also developed a process of social and economic transformation leading dramatic change in occupational structure of the working population of dispossessed households. Given the conditions, this transformation has been associated with two characteristic: first, the major shift in livelihood from cultivation has happened towards non-farm activities that includes casual workers, waged labourers, businessmen, tailors, and so on; and second, a small share of workers has become jobless. The transformation of social means of subsistence and production (land) into capital for the ESSAR Steel Plant and IFFCO, and setting a large section of dispossessed farmers unemployed or waged labourers corroborate the Marxian 'primitive accumulation' and proletarianisation. The income inequality happens to be higher among the bottom and upper quartiles of the dispossessed households.

Notes

1. The sample households were randomly drawn because every dispossessed farmer was not ready to provide required information. Many dispossessed farmers were even suspicious about the political affiliation and association of strangers with the government.
2. The foods, other consumable items, education, and transport expenses which have been selected for the estimation of consumption expenditure at household level are: (i) cereals – rice, wheat, suji/sewai, bread, muri, and other rice product; (ii) pulses – *arhar*, *moong*, *masur*, soyabean, and *besan*; (iii) milk and milk products – milk, milk powder, curd, and butter; (iv) egg, fish, and meat; (v) vegetables – potato, onion, carrot, pumpkin, papaya, cauliflower, cabbage, leafy vegetables, tomato, capsicum, lemon, garlic, and ginger; (vi) fruits – banana, coconut, guava, orange fruits, litchi, apple, grapes, and other citrus; (vii) education – books, journals, newspaper, stationery, tuition, and institution fees; (viii) telephone/ mobile, transport, and domestic servants; (ix) others – sugar, salt, chillies, tea and coffee, cold beverages, smoking, kerosene and dung cake, LPG and coal, cloths and footwear.

References

Advani, M., (2009): *Urbanisation, Displacement and Rehabilitation*, Rawat Publications, Jaipur.

Amirthalingam, K. and Lakshman, R.W.D., (2009): Displaced Livelihoods in Sri Lanka: An Economic Analysis, *Journal of Refugee Studies*, Vol. 22, No. 4, pp. 502–24.

Asif, M., (1999): Land Acquisition Act: Need for an Alternative Paradigm, *Economic & Political Weekly*, Vol. 34, No. 38, pp. 1564–66.

Banerjee, A. et al., (2007): Beyond Nandigram: Industrialization in West Bengal, *Economic & Political Weekly*, Vol. 42, No. 17, pp. 1487–89.

Banerjee, P.S. and Roy, D., (2007): Behind the Present Peasant Unrest in West Bengal, *Economic & Political Weekly*, Vol. 42, No. 22, pp. 2048–51.

Bapat, J., (2009): Resettlement Entitlements Moral Economy of Land Rights and Beyond, In Mohanty, N., Sarker, R., and Pandey, A. (eds), *India Infrastructure Report 2009: Land-A Critical Resource for Infrastructure*, Oxford University, New Delhi, pp. 97–102.

Bedi, H.P., (2013): Special Economic Zones: National Land Challenges, Localised Protest, *Contemporary South Asia*, Vol. 21, No. 1, pp. 38–51.

Bhattachariya, M., (2007): Nandigram and the Question of Development, *Economic & Political Weekly*, Vol. 42, pp. 1895–99.

Cernea, M.M., (1997): The Risk and Reconstruction Model for Resettling Displaced Populations, *World Development*, Vol. 25, No. 10, pp. 1569–87.

——, (1999): Why Economic Analysis is Essential to Resettlement: A Sociologist's View, In Cernea, M.M. (ed.), *The Economics of Involuntary Resettlement: Questions and Challenges*, World Bank, Washington D.C.

——, (2000): Risks, Safeguards and Reconstruction: A Model for Population Displacement and Resettlement, *Economic & Political Weekly*, Vol. 35, No. 41, pp. 3659–78.

Chandra, N.K., (2008): Tata Motors in Singur: A Step Towards Industrialisation and Pauperisation, *Economic & Political Weekly*, Vol. 43, No. 50, pp. 36, 41–51.

Council for Social Development, (2008): *Indian Social Development Report, 2008: Development and Displacement*, Oxford University Press, New Delhi.

De Wet, C., (2001): Economic Development and Population Displacement: Can Everybody Win?, *Economic & Political Weekly*, Vol. 36, No. 50, pp. 4637–46.

Fernandes, W., (1998): Land Acquisition (Amendment) Bill, 1998 Rights of Project Affected People Ignored, *Economic & Political Weekly*, Vol. 33, No. 42 & 43, pp. 2703–06.

——, (2005): Rehabilitation as a Right: Where is the Policy?, *Social Action*, Vol. 55, No. 2, pp. 123–37.

——, (2009): India's Half Century Search for a Resettlement Policy and the Right to Livelihood, In Modi, R. (ed.), *Beyond Relocation: The Imperative of Sustainable Resettlement*, SAGE Publications, New Delhi, pp. 102–26.

Ge, H.E., (2012): Farmland Acquisition System in China: Problems and Responses, *Canadian Social Science*, Vol. 8, No. 4, pp. 258–63.

Hui, E.C.M. and Bao, H., (2013): The Logic behind Conflicts in Land Acquisition in Contemporary China: A Framework based upon Game Theory, *Land Use Policy*, Vol. 30, pp. 373–80.

Khan, A., (2011): Two Policemen, Farmer Killed as U.P. Hostage Drama Turns Violent, *The Hindu*, Vol. 134, No. 18, p. 2.

——, (2011): Farmers Agitation Spreads to Agra, Aligarh, *The Hindu*, Vol. 134, No. 110, p. 1.

Mahapatra, L.K., (1999): *Resettlement, Impoverishment and Reconstruction in India: Development for the Deprived*, Vikas Publishing House, New Delhi.

Mohan, V., (16 August 2013): Cultivable Land Continues to Shrink, *Times of India*, p. 7.

Nath, Anusha et al., (2013): Land Acquisition and Compensation: What Really Happened in Singur?, *Economic & Political Weekly*, Vol. 48, No. 21, pp. 32–44.

Patra, D., (2012): The Marketing Strategy of Economic Development in Kalahandi, *Odisha Review*, Vol. 69, No. 2, pp. 80–91.

Penz, P., Drydyk, J. and Bose, P.S., (2011): *Displacement by Development: Ethics, Rights and Responsibilities*, Cambridge University Press, New York.

Sau, R., (2008): A Ballad of Singur: Progress with Human Dignity, *Economic & Political Weekly*, Vol. 43, No. 43, pp. 10–13.

Sharma, R.N. (2010): Changing Facets of Involuntary Displacement and Resettlement in India, *Social Change*, Vol. 40, No. 1, pp. 503-24.

Tang, Y., Mason, R.J. and Sun, P., (2012): Interest Distribution in the Process of Coordination of Urban and Rural Construction Land in China, *Habitat International*, Vol. 36, pp. 388–95.

Venkatesan, J., (2011): Land Acquisition Act as an Engine of Oppression: Supreme Court, *The Hindu*, Vol. 134, No. 161, p. 2.

World Bank, (2004): *Involuntary Resettlement Sourcebook: Planning and Implementation of Development Projects*, World Bank, Washington D.C.

Editor and Contributors

Abnave Vikas Bajrang, Doctoral Fellow, Institute for Social and Economic Change, Bengaluru. E-mail: vksabnave@gmail.com

Ajit Kumar, independent scholar researcher, based in Nagpur. E-mail: ajitokumar@gmail.com

Amarnath Tripathi, Associate Professor, Economics and International Business, Sharda University, Noida, Uttar Pradesh. E-mail: amarnath.tripathi@sharda.ac.in

Amit Mandal, Assistant Professor, Head in Charge, Department of Economics, Mankar College, University of Burdwan, Mankar, West Bengal. E-mail: amit1987m@gmail.com

Animesh Roy, Assistant Professor, Giri Institute of Development Studies, Lucknow. E-mail: animeshroy4@gmail.com

Ankur Jain, PhD Research Scholar, Centre for Studies in Regional Development, JNU, New Delhi. E-mail: ankurjain869@gmail.com

Barun Deb Pal, Project Manager, International Food Policy Research Institute, New Delhi.

Bijoy Kumar Swain, Chief Executive Officer, Orissa State Association for Financial Inclusion Institution, Bhubaneswar, Orissa. E-mail: bk.swain2@gmail.com

D.M. Diwakar, Professor of Economics and Former Director, A.N. Sinha Institute of Social Studies, Patna, Bihar. E-mail: dmdiwakar@yahoo.co.in

Dinesh Kumar Nayak, Economist, National Institute of Public Finance and Policy, New Delhi. E-mail: dineshcsrd@gmail.com

M. Devendra Babu, Honorary Professor, Karnataka State Rural Development and Panchayat Raj University, Gadag, Karnataka.
E-mail: devendrababu@yahoo.com

M. Sabarisakthi, ICSSR Institutional Doctoral Fellow, Institute for Studies in Industrial Development (ISID), New Delhi.
E-mail: ssidappadi@gmail.com

Manu Gautam (Editor), Associate Professor, M.P. Institute of Social Science Research, Ujjain, M.P. E-mail: gautam.ujjain@gmail.com

Minaketan Behera, Associate Professor of Economics, Centre for Informal Sector and Labour Studies (CISLS), School of Social Sciences, Jawaharlal Nehru University, New Delhi.

P.K. Joshi, Director, International Food Policy Research Institute – South Asia Chapter, New Delhi.

Parmod Kumar, Professor, Institute for Social and Economic Change, Bangalore.

S. Rajendran, Professor and Head, Department of Economics, Gandhigram Rural Institute – Deemed University, Gandhigram, District-Dindigul, Tamil Nadu. E-mail: myrajendran@gmail.com

Sanatan Nayak, Professor, Department of Economics, Babasaheb Bhimrao Ambedkar University, Lucknow.

Srikantha Nayaka, Guest Faculty PG in Economics, Field Marshal KM Cariappa College, Madikeri, Mangalore University, Karnataka.
E-mail: gsnayaka@gmail.com

Suman Lakra, Research Scholar, Department of Social Work, Guru Ghasidas Vishwavidyalaya (A Central University), Koni, Bilaspur (C.G.).

Sunita Sangar, Senior Consultant, National Mission for Empowerment of Women, Ministry of Women and Child Development, Government of India, New Delhi. E-mail: sunitasangar@yahoo.com

Surendra Singh, Senior Research Fellow, Department of Economics, Babasaheb Bhimrao Ambedkar University, Lucknow.
E-mail: surendra.singh735@gmail.com

Tarujyoti Buragohain, Associate Fellow, National Council of Applied Economic Research (NCAER), New Delhi. E-mail: taru@ncaer.org.

Udita Mehta, Postgraduate Scholar, Punjab University, Chandigarh.
E-mail: uditamehta1404@gmail.com

Vikram Singh, Assistant Professor and Head, Department of Social Work, Guru Ghasidas Vishwavidyalaya (A Central University), Koni, Bilaspur (C.G.).
E-mail: vsvikkysingh@gmail.com